**Keep this book. You will need it and use it throughout your career.**

## About the American Hotel & Lodging Association (AH&LA)

Founded in 1910, AH&LA is the trade association representing the lodging industry in the United States. AH&LA is a federation of state lodging associations throughout the United States with 11,000 lodging properties worldwide as members. The association offers its members assistance with governmental affairs representation, communications, marketing, hospitality operations, training and education, technology issues, and more. For information, call 202-289-3100.

*LODGING*, the management magazine of AH&LA, is a "living textbook" for hospitality students that provides timely features, industry news, and vital lodging information.

## About the American Hotel & Lodging Educational Institute (EI)

An affiliate of AH&LA, the Educational Institute is the world's largest source of quality training and educational materials for the lodging industry. EI develops textbooks and courses that are used in more than 1,200 colleges and universities worldwide, and also offers courses to individuals through its Distance Learning program. Hotels worldwide rely on EI for training resources that focus on every aspect of lodging operations. Industry-tested videos, CD-ROMs, seminars, and skills guides prepare employees at every skill level. EI also offers professional certification for the industry's top performers. For information about EI's products and services, call 800-349-0299 or 407-999-8100.

## About the American Hotel & Lodging Educational Foundation (AH&LEF)

An affiliate of AH&LA, the American Hotel & Lodging Educational Foundation provides financial support that enhances the stability, prosperity, and growth of the lodging industry through educational and research programs. AH&LEF has awarded millions of dollars in scholarship funds for students pursuing higher education in hospitality management. AH&LEF has also funded research projects on topics important to the industry, including occupational safety and health, turnover and diversity, and best practices in the U.S. lodging industry. For more information, go to www.ahlef.org.

# SUPERVISION in the HOSPITALITY INDUSTRY

# Educational Institute Books

# SUPERVISION in the HOSPITALITY INDUSTRY

## Fifth Edition

Jack D. Ninemeier, Ph.D., CHA
Raphael R. Kavanaugh, Ed.D., CHA

American
Hotel & Lodging
Educational Institute

# Disclaimer

This publication is designed to provide accurate and authoritative information in regard to the subject matter covered. It is sold with the understanding that the publisher is not engaged in rendering legal, accounting, or other professional service. If legal advice or other expert assistance is required, the services of a competent professional person should be sought.

*— From the Declaration of Principles jointly adopted by the American Bar Association and a Committee of Publishers and Associations*

The authors are solely responsible for the contents of this publication. All views expressed herein are solely those of the authors and do not necessarily reflect the views of the American Hotel & Lodging Educational Institute (the Institute), the American Hotel & Lodging Association (AH&LA), or the Club Managers Association of America (CMAA).

Nothing contained in this publication shall constitute a standard, an endorsement, or a recommendation of the Institute, AH&LA, or CMAA. AH&LA, the Institute, and CMAA disclaim any liability with respect to the use of any information, procedure, or product, or reliance thereon by any member of the hospitality industry.

**Printed in the United States of America**
1 2 3 4 5 6 7 8 9 10 17 16 15 14 13 12

ISBN 978-0-86612-405-8
ISBN 978-0-86612-406-5 (with online component)

**Editor:** Tonya Schafer

# Contents

# Dedication In Memoriam

Raphael (Ray) Kavanaugh

Educator, colleague, and mentor

Thank you, Ray, for your friendship, help, and encouragement over so many years.

# Chapter 1 Outline

Definition of Management
    Levels of Management
    Basic Management Principles
The Components of Management
    Planning
    Organizing
    Coordinating
    Staffing
    Directing
    Controlling
    Evaluating
Skills for Effective Supervision
    Technical Skills
    Human Relations Skills
    Conceptual Skills
    Why Supervisors Fail
Supervisory Responsibilities
    Your Boss
    Employees
    Guests
    The Profession
    Yourself
Keys to Supervisory Success

# Competencies

1.  Define management and describe different management levels and the numerous demands placed on supervisors. (pp. 3–6)

2.  Identify basic management principles. (p. 6)

3.  Explain the management functions of authority, delegation, and responsibility. (pp. 6–7)

4.  Describe the traditional components of management (planning, organizing, coordinating, staffing, directing, controlling, and evaluating). (pp. 7–16)

5.  Distinguish among technical, human relations, and conceptual skills and their importance to supervisory success. (pp. 16–19)

6.  Identify fundamental supervisory responsibilities. (pp. 19–21)

# The Supervisor and the Management Process

$I$N THE HOSPITALITY INDUSTRY, the term **supervisor** generally refers to someone who manages entry-level or other employees who do not have supervisory responsibilities. For example, a head cook supervises entry-level cooks; housekeeping supervisors are responsible for room attendants. The supervisor's work, in turn, is directed by a **manager,** who often has been promoted from a supervisor role.

In the **labor-intensive** hospitality industry, supervisors are the linking pins that facilitate communication between entry-level staff members and those at higher organizational levels. Many supervisors have been promoted from the ranks of those whom they now supervise, so they have the knowledge and skills needed to perform the work of their **subordinates**. However, they also require a vastly different set of **competencies** to be successful in their supervisory role.

For example, hospitality supervisors must know and understand basic principles of management and apply them while managing the resources of a lodging or food service operation. The management process is essentially the same in any type of business and at all management levels in an organization, even if the goals and the work environments of businesses differ. While supervision generally focuses on directing the work of employees, directing is only one of the management tasks supervisors perform.

Much of a supervisor's time and effort involves managing the work of others, effectively dealing with employees on a personal and professional level, and making decisions. This chapter will review the important role of supervisors and explain the context within which they work. It will also define management, outline basic management principles, and discuss the components of management. Technical, human relations, and conceptual aspects of the job and supervisory responsibilities will be discussed. Finally, reasons that supervisors fail and some keys for success are presented so you will have a benchmark for supervisory excellence.

## Definition of Management

**Management** is the process of using what you have to do what you want to do. What you have are resources; what you want to do is meet organizational goals.

Resources are the **assets** of lodging and food service operations. There are seven basic types of resources:

- People (employees at all organizational levels)
- Money
- Time
- Work procedures and methods
- Energy
- Materials (e.g., food and beverage products, guestroom linens)
- Equipment and tools

All resources are in limited supply. No supervisor has all the resources he or she needs. Therefore, your job becomes one of determining the best way to use your limited resources to reach organizational goals.

Organizational goals ("what you want to do") outline what the hospitality operation wishes to accomplish and indicate why the business exists. Goals vary at different organizations, but they typically include:

- Increasing profits (for commercial operations) or lowering costs (for non-commercial operations)
- Defining and attaining quality and quantity standards for products and services
- Maintaining or creating a good public (corporate) image
- Providing professional development opportunities for staff members

Supervisors have pressures placed on them by many groups, as well as by characteristics of the organization (see Exhibit 1). They are confronted with demands not only from employees, but also from governmental agencies, higher management levels (especially their own manager), guests, internal departments (such as human resources, accounting, and purchasing), and, if the property is unionized, union representatives. In addition, the organization itself, through its culture, informal work groups, and changing goals and strategies, exerts pressure on the supervisor. "Demanding" can certainly be added to the description of a supervisor's job!

## Levels of Management

There are four levels of management at most hospitality properties (see Exhibit 2). The level of a specific management position varies among properties. For example, in a privately owned hotel, the general manager and perhaps the assistant or resident manager might be considered top managers. Department heads might be viewed as middle managers. Other staff members whose duties, in part, involve directing supervisors would be classified as managers. Those who direct the work of entry-level employees would be considered supervisors. But in a large company with many properties, there may be a board of directors, a chief executive officer (CEO), and national and regional managers who would be considered top managers. In large companies such as these, general managers as well as department heads in individual properties might then be considered middle managers from the perspective of the total organization.

**Exhibit 1    Demands on the Supervisor**

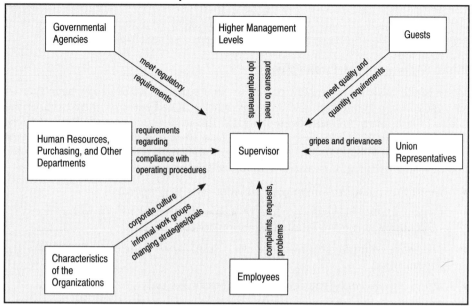

**Exhibit 2    Management Levels in Hospitality Properties**

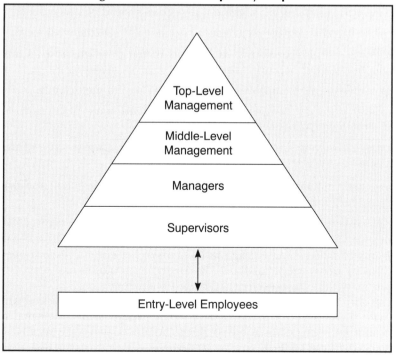

For our purposes we will consider management levels at the property level. The general manager and assistant general manager are considered top managers. Department heads are classified as middle managers. Managers direct the work of supervisors, who, in turn, are responsible for entry-level employees.

## Basic Management Principles

Many of the basic management principles that supervisors use have been known for many years. While some of these principles have been modified to meet the needs of changing business organizations, the underlying foundations of these principles have held steady over time. One of the pioneers of management research, Henri Fayol, studied management more than 60 years ago.[1] Among his management principles are many that are still relevant today:

- *Concept of authority*—managers must be able to give orders.
- *Organizational hierarchy*—a line of authority should run from top management down to the lowest organizational levels.
- *Discipline*—employees must respect rules and policies that govern the organization.
- *Unity of command*—each employee should have only one boss.
- *Common good*—the interests of the organization are more important than the interests of individual employees or employee groups.
- *Compensation*—fair wage and salary administration plans must be used.
- *Centralization*—many management processes should be centralized.
- *Division of labor*—employees should specialize in specific work tasks.
- *Matching*—employees should be placed in the positions most suitable for them.
- *Staff stability*—high employee turnover rates lead to inefficiency.
- *Employee initiative*—employees should be given some freedom to develop and implement plans.
- *Team spirit*—when employees work together as a team, a sense of unity can develop that will benefit the organization.

Three basic management concepts require special discussion: authority, delegation, and responsibility.

**Authority.** Authority is the power an organization gives to a supervisor to do something or to get something done. For example, a front desk supervisor has the authority to schedule and assign tasks to his or her employees; a supervisor in the purchasing department has the authority to buy products and services for the organization, within limits established by top managers.

There are two types of authority: formal and informal. **Formal authority** comes with the position a person holds in the organization. **Informal authority**, also referred to as personal authority, is the power you have because of your abilities and personal traits. If you are a supervisor with excellent technical skills, charisma (the ability to inspire employees), lots of excellent ideas, or other unusually special traits, then you may have personal authority to go along with your formal authority.

**Delegation.** Delegation is the act of assigning a task to another person. Sometimes authority is also delegated if it is necessary to get the work done. Since you can't personally perform all of the tasks that are assigned to your department or work area, delegating is obviously an important part of your job. Usually, tasks should be assigned to the lowest level at which employees have the ability and information necessary to complete them.

**Responsibility.** Those with formal authority are held accountable for the use of that authority. When you accepted your promotion to supervisor, you also accepted the responsibility that goes with the new position. Supervisors are evaluated on how well they accomplish the tasks assigned to them. You can accomplish some tasks alone; you need the help of your employees to accomplish others. You can delegate a task or parts of a task to your employees. However, even when you delegate a task, you are ultimately responsible for your employees' performance. If they fail to accomplish a task that you delegate to them, it will be your failure as well. Being responsible or held accountable for the actions of their employees is one of the hard facts of organizational life for supervisors.

## The Components of Management

The management process can be separated into components: planning, organizing, coordinating, staffing, directing, controlling, and evaluating. Each element (sometimes called a function or activity) defines what a manager must be able to do. Exhibit 3 illustrates the sequential nature of these components. In practice, the components are interrelated, and supervisors are likely to be addressing different resources with different management activities at the same time. When you look at Exhibit 3, note the following:

**Exhibit 3   The Management Process**

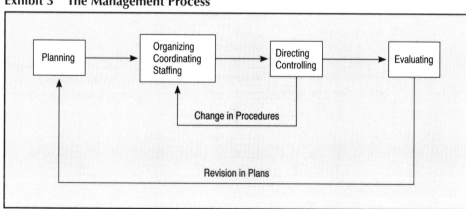

- Planning is done before organizing, coordinating, and staffing activities are implemented.

- When planning, organizing, coordinating, and staffing tasks are completed, directing and controlling activities become important. Sometimes changes in organizing, coordinating, and staffing procedures come about because of discoveries you make during the directing and controlling processes.

- The last task, evaluating, assesses how well objectives developed during the planning stage of the management have been met. After evaluation, you can make new plans to achieve new objectives or map out a different plan of attack if you did not achieve the first objective.

## Planning

The **planning** activities of most hospitality organizations can be categorized as either strategic or operational. **Strategic planning** activities are general and futuristic in nature, while **operational planning** activities are more specific and usually cover a planning horizon of no more than one year. Exhibit 4 outlines one possible sequence of common organizational planning activities.

There are many possible sequences to strategic planning activities. Some organizations prefer to develop a mission statement before a values statement; others prefer to start with creating a vision statement. Regardless of the sequence of specific strategic planning activities, operational planning activities always come after strategic planning activities because they are driven and supported by strategic plans. The number and level of participants in these planning activities varies tremendously from organization to organization. Some organizations may

**Exhibit 4   One Sequence for Strategic and Operational Planning**

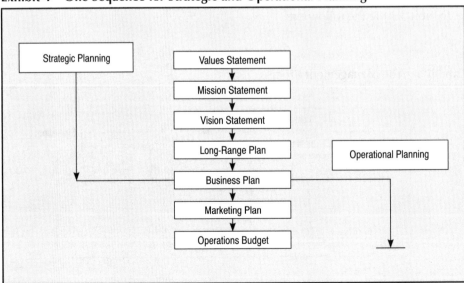

limit strategic planning functions to only its highest level managers; others may include all levels of management and even line-level employees.

Strategic planning sometimes begins with the creation of a values statement for the organization. A **values statement** identifies the core values that should shape the culture of the organization and guide the behavior of individuals. These core values are shared values, common convictions, and acknowledged principles that unite an organization's management and staff as they create the organization's future. A long list of values does not create a shared foundation upon which to build a future. Too many values can complicate what should be simple and confuse what should be clear. An organization's value statement could be as short and to the point as:

*At the Downtowner Hotel, we believe in and are committed to:*

- *Guest satisfaction*

- *Employee satisfaction*

- *Ethical business practices*

- *Service to our community*

- *Environmentally safe practices*

A **mission statement** is a broad description of an organization's reason to exist. It outlines the fundamental purpose of the organization and focuses managers, supervisors, and employees in a single direction. In times of fast change and potential confusion, everyone within the organization can turn back to the organization's mission for clarity and stability. Depending on the needs of the organization, a mission statement can be short and simple or long and complex. Consider the following mission statement for the fictional Downtowner Hotel:

*The mission of the Downtowner Hotel is to be the convention hotel of choice for meeting planners and business travelers by meeting all their away-from-home needs for lodging, food service, and conference facilities.*

This brief statement presents the nature of the organization (a convention hotel) and why it exists (to provide lodging, food service, and conference facilities). It also identifies its major markets (meeting planners and business travelers) and projects its desired public image (to be the hotel of choice). This brief mission statement helps to provide a clear focus for everyone working in the organization.

While a mission statement describes the fundamental purpose of an organization, its **vision statement** projects the organization's future—where it wants to be and what it wants to look like at a specific point in time. Building on the mission statement, the vision statement projects a standard of future success:

*Our vision of the Downtowner Hotel is to be the premier convention hotel in the upper Midwest within five years.*

By contrasting where the organization is today with where it wants to be in five years, managers are able to focus their efforts on a long-range plan to move the hotel to where it wants to be. A **long-range plan,** generally covering a time period of three to five years, outlines how the organization intends to close the gap between where it is today and where it wants to be in the future. A long-range plan for the Downtowner Hotel would indicate the actions that individual hotel departments plan to implement over the next five years to help drive the organization toward achieving its vision of becoming the premier convention hotel in the upper Midwest. Long-range plans are routinely reviewed, at least once a year, and are revised, as necessary, to adapt to unanticipated changes in the economy, the competition, and markets, as well as to other concerns. Each year, the long-range plan can be extended so that it will, for example, always project a five-year planning horizon.

A **business plan** bridges strategic and operational planning activities by specifying how the organization will move forward in the upcoming year toward attaining long-range goals. Departmental **action plans** are prepared that list the step-by-step activities specifying the who, what, where, when, and how of implementing a strategy. Operational planning then continues with the development of a **marketing plan** that indicates how the goals set by the business plan will be achieved in the upcoming year. For example, the marketing plan of the Downtowner Hotel would present a calendar of promotional and sales activities designed to attract business travelers and reach meeting planners that would affect business in the upcoming year. Supporting the goals set in the business plan and in the marketing plan, the **operations budget** details management's plan for generating revenue and incurring expenses for each department within the organization. Annual operating budgets are typically subdivided into monthly periods, providing managers with a monthly revenue and expense plan. In some properties, monthly budgets are broken down into weekly segments for even tighter analysis and control.

The business plan, the marketing plan, and the operations budget are only the beginning of operational planning, which also includes establishing routine operating procedures and all day-to-day planning activities. Routine operating procedures are established for such recurring situations as cleaning rooms or serving food and beverage products. These situations require standard plans that can be used frequently. These plans are often made by department heads, for example, in working with managers and supervisors. Daily planning includes planning for special events, new training programs, and other activities. Supervisors are responsible for developing many of these plans.

Regardless of the planning activity or the level of planning involved, effective planning incorporates the following principles:

- Goals must be established before plans can be developed.

- You must regularly set aside time to plan. It should be done as an important part of your job, not only when time permits.

- All necessary information should be gathered before plans are developed.

- Planning should be done at the appropriate organizational level. It's not good use of a top manager's time to write employee schedules, for example.

- You should be allowed to contribute to plans that affect your work. In turn, you should allow your employees to contribute to plans that affect their jobs.

- You should be flexible when planning and recognize that situations change, and that plans may need revision.

- Plans must be implemented. At the appropriate time, you must act with the best plan available.

## Organizing

**Organizing** involves establishing the flow of authority and communication between people and organizational levels. Further, it specifies relationships between positions in the property. Exhibits 5, 6, and 7 present sample organization charts for a full-service hotel, a large restaurant, and a small country club.

General organizing principles and responsibilities include the following:

- Authority should flow in an unbroken line from the top to the bottom of the organization.

- Each employee should have only one supervisor.

- Relationships between departments in the organization must be considered when managers organize. Events in one department often have an impact on other departments.

- Similar activities should be grouped together to structure departments within the property. For example, activities relating to rooms can be separated into front desk and housekeeping departments.

- Similar tasks should be grouped together to create a position within a department. A position or job is a group of tasks to be performed by one person.

- **Line managers** such as the general manager, department heads, and supervisors are in the chain of command, and they have decision-making authority. In contrast, **staff managers** are technical specialists and do not have decision-making authority. They provide advice to line managers. Examples of staff managers include those in the accounting, human resources, and purchasing departments.

- A business's structure changes continually. Organization charts and related documents must be revised to reflect these changes.

## Coordinating

The management skill of **coordinating** involves the ability to efficiently use resources to attain the organization's objectives. You must be able to coordinate the efforts of your employees through good planning and effective organization. A well-coordinated department or work crew performs its tasks correctly and on time.

Principles of coordinating include the following:

- Supervisors must have the authority to enforce assignments, commands, and decisions.

- Not only must you coordinate your resources and employees to complete your assigned tasks, you must also do your part to help coordinate the efforts of the organization as a whole. This means communicating and cooperating

**Exhibit 5   Organization Chart: Management Positions in a Full-Service Hotel**

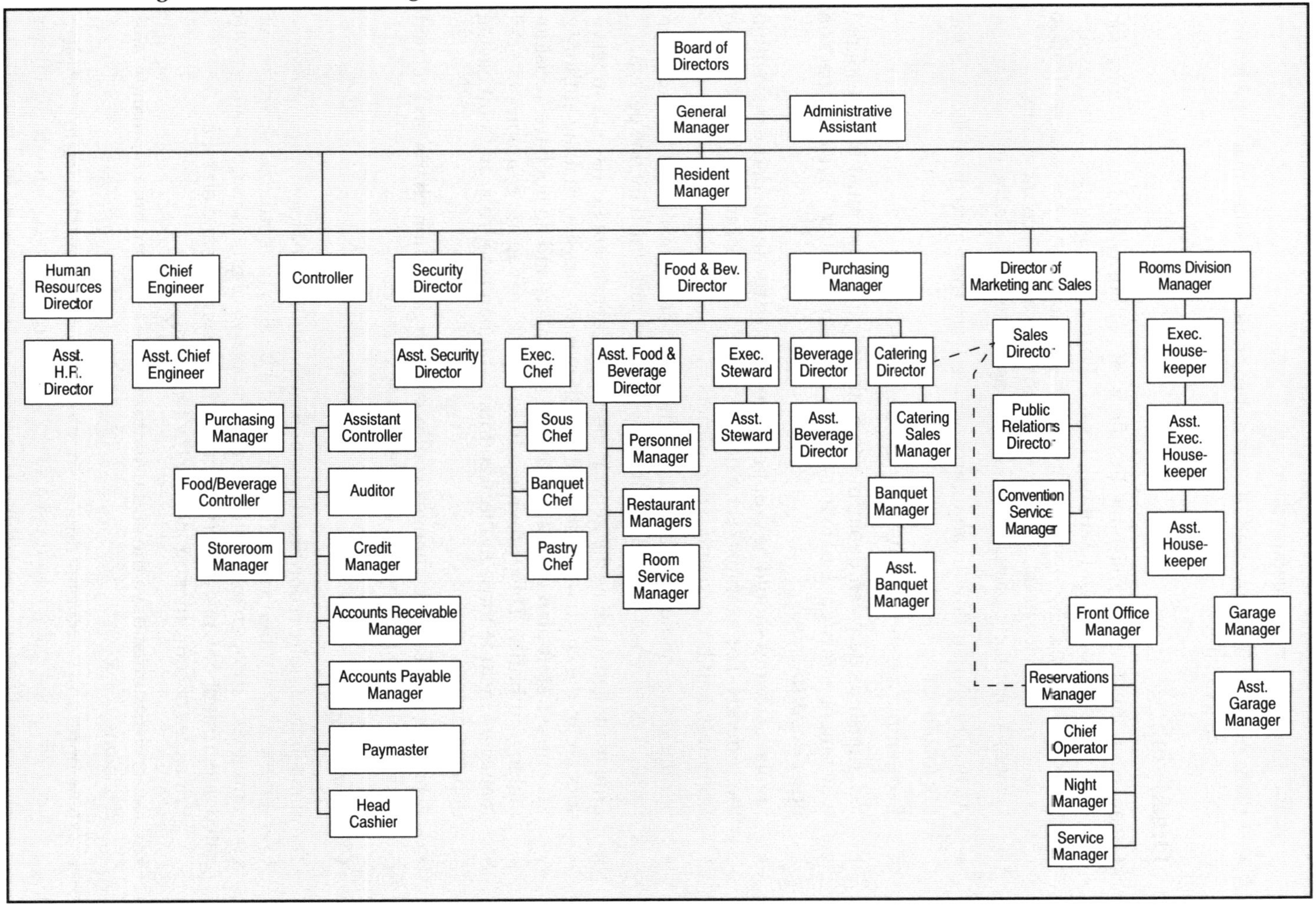

Board of Directors

General Manager — Administrative Assistant

Resident Manager

- Human Resources Director — Asst. H.R. Director
- Chief Engineer — Asst. Chief Engineer
- Controller
  - Assistant Controller
    - Auditor
    - Credit Manager
    - Accounts Receivable Manager
    - Accounts Payable Manager
    - Paymaster
    - Head Cashier
  - Purchasing Manager
  - Food/Beverage Controller
  - Storeroom Manager
- Security Director — Asst. Security Director
- Food & Bev. Director
  - Asst. Food & Beverage Director
    - Personnel Manager
    - Restaurant Managers
    - Room Service Manager
  - Exec. Chef
    - Sous Chef
    - Banquet Chef
    - Pastry Chef
  - Exec. Steward — Asst. Steward
  - Beverage Director — Asst. Beverage Director
  - Catering Director
    - Catering Sales Manager
    - Banquet Manager — Asst. Banquet Manager
- Purchasing Manager
- Director of Marketing and Sales
  - Sales Director
  - Public Relations Director
  - Convention Service Manager
- Rooms Division Manager
  - Exec. Housekeeper
    - Asst. Exec. Housekeeper
    - Asst. Housekeeper
  - Front Office Manager
    - Reservations Manager
    - Chief Operator
    - Night Manager
    - Service Manager
  - Garage Manager — Asst. Garage Manager

**Exhibit 6   Organization Chart for a Large Restaurant**

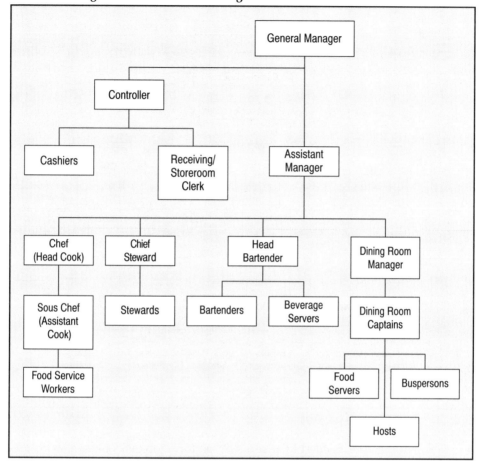

with other areas and departments in your property. Many hospitality organizations have **executive committees** comprising top-level managers and department heads that meet regularly to discuss organization-wide concerns.

## Staffing

**Staffing** involves recruiting applicants and hiring those best qualified. In small operations, a manager or supervisor might recruit and hire applicants. In large properties, recruiting is frequently performed by a human resources department, although line managers should still be involved in interviewing and make the hiring decisions. All properties should use basic principles of staffing such as the following:

- Jobs must be defined according to the specific tasks to be performed. Job tasks are listed in **job descriptions**.

**Exhibit 7   Organization Chart for a Small Country Club**

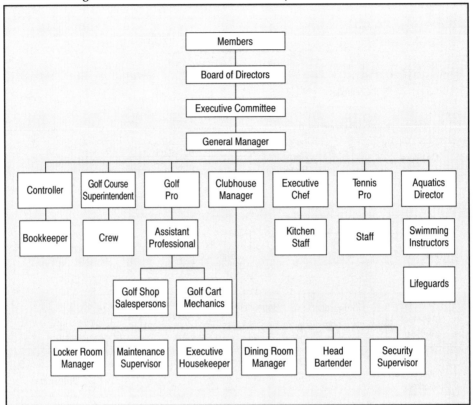

- Personal qualities needed to adequately perform job tasks must also be considered. These are recorded in **job specifications**.

- All possible sources of job applicants should be considered.

- Job application forms should be used to collect information about applicants.

- Applicants should be screened. Tests can be used to assess the abilities of applicants. Preliminary interviews and reference checks may also help eliminate unqualified applicants.

- Employee orientation, training, and evaluation programs should be developed and implemented.

- Decisions about transfers, promotions, and other personnel-related actions are part of the staffing process.

## Directing

**Directing** includes all the activities necessary to oversee, motivate, train, evaluate, and discipline employees. Many of the functions supervisors perform focus on some aspect of directing employees. Directing incorporates the following principles:

- The number of employees each supervisor directs should be carefully determined. There is no formula for calculating the optimum number of employees for each supervisor. The right number depends on many variables, including the supervisor's experience, complexity of the work, and frequency with which problems are likely to occur. No supervisor should facilitate the work of more people than he or she can handle.

- Employees must know what they are expected to do. They should be properly oriented and trained. Further, assignments must be clear and supervisors must follow up as needed to determine if additional direction or resource allocation is required.

- Organizational goals are easier to attain when they mesh with some of the personal goals of employees.

- Delegation—the act of giving formal organizational authority to an employee—is a directing technique.

- Directing includes motivating your employees. Keep in mind that your own attitude affects employee attitudes and performances.

- Procedures for employee discipline should include positive reinforcement as well as a variety of actions that you can use to help employees correct improper behavior. These actions range from informal counseling to termination.

- Don't relate to all employees the same way. Your leadership style should vary according to each employee's needs.

- It's important to gain employee cooperation, and to treat employees fairly and honestly.

- Solicit employee ideas and, whenever possible, use them.

- Show your appreciation to employees who perform their jobs well.

## Controlling

**Controlling** helps to ensure that you are attaining your objectives. The control process begins with establishing performance standards, continues with assessing actual performance, and then involves making a comparison between performance standards and actual performance to determine whether—and to what extent—corrective action is necessary. Control is based on several principles:

- Operating budgets are the most important control tools because they indicate revenue and expense expectations.

- Preventive controls are more effective than controls imposed after problems arise.

- Control cannot be accomplished until budget estimates or performance standards have been set.

- Control depends on setting intermediate deadlines or goals to help you know whether you are on track. If you miss an intermediate deadline or goal, identify and resolve whatever problem or situation is hindering you.

- Corrective action is necessary when an employee's performance does not meet the organization's standards.

- The most significant problems or obstacles should be addressed first.

## Evaluating

**Evaluating** means considering how well you and your employees achieved your objectives. Many supervisors evaluate haphazardly or overlook this management task entirely. Evaluating principles include the following:

- Time to evaluate must be set aside regularly.

- Evaluation helps to establish new objectives.

- Input from guests and others outside the property is useful in the evaluation process.

- Evaluation helps in the assignment of organizational resources.

## Skills for Effective Supervision

A supervisor needs three basic types of skills: technical, human relations, and conceptual. Exhibit 8 illustrates the amount of technical, human relations, and conceptual skills necessary for all levels of management. Note that, while supervisors need more technical skills and fewer conceptual skills than do other managers,

**Exhibit 8    Relative Importance of Technical, Human Relations, and Conceptual Skills**

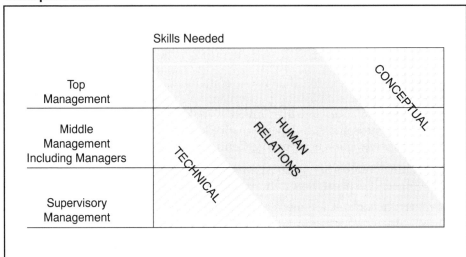

they need the same amount of human relations skills. That's because all levels of managers typically must meet their objectives by working effectively through others.

## Technical Skills

**Technical skills** are the skills you need to perform your job and effectively supervise the work of your employees. While technical skills are not the major factor in determining supervisory success, they are necessary. To train employees and direct them in their work, you must know how to do the work and be able to recognize when it's being done correctly, and when to provide further assistance.

Supervisors, however, may not be required to have the ability to perform employee jobs as fast or efficiently as their employees. It can be argued that supervisors must know only the basic components of their employees' jobs, understand job performance standards, and be able to recognize the extent to which their employees are meeting those standards. However, it is often easier to command the employees' respect if you are good at most of their jobs, if not all of them. This knowledge can add to your personal authority.

## Human Relations Skills

When one considers the list of **human relations skills** that a supervisor must possess, it's easy to understand why it's difficult to be a good supervisor. The art of dealing with employees begins with understanding your responsibility as a supervisor and continues with mastering human relations skills. It's no wonder that many supervisors in the hospitality industry have more difficulty acquiring and applying human relations skills than they do technical skills. Human relations skills include communication, leadership, and understanding how people work in groups, among many others. Other important human relations skills will be covered later in the book.

## Conceptual Skills

You must be able to understand the components of management and how they relate to and affect your work. Effective supervisors can conceptualize problems as well as possible ways to solve them. They gather and study a great deal of information, relate one situation to another, and draw on personal experiences and those of others. Much of the supervisor's work, then, involves intellectual or **conceptual skills.**

The ability to make a decision is one of a supervisor's most important conceptual skills. Some decisions are relatively easy to make. For example, if you have a staffing guide that tells you how many room attendants to schedule for a given occupancy rate, it's easy to decide how many attendants to schedule when, for example, an 80 percent occupancy rate is forecast. Other decisions are more difficult to make. For example, how can labor costs in your work section be reduced to meet a tough new operating budget? To comply with the budget, a great deal of research and thought, including a re-evaluation of standard operating procedures, performance standards, scheduling practices, training programs, and other concerns, will likely be necessary. When you are facing a decision, ask yourself several questions:

- *Is it my decision to make?* Generally, the closer to its origin that a problem is resolved, the better the decision is likely to be. A general rule is to pass as few decisions as possible up the organization and to pass as many decisions as possible down the organization.

- *Is this an easy decision to make?* Wise supervisors save time for more important matters by delegating the authority to make easy decisions to someone else. If you can't delegate, you should at least make the easy decisions quickly and move on.

- *What are the consequences of the decision?* Generally, the more important the consequences, the more time and other resources should be committed to investigating the situation and making a decision.

- *Have I allowed a reasonable amount of time for making the decision?* Hasty decisions can lead to trouble. Taking time for careful study and analysis can often yield better alternatives.

- *Am I looking for the perfect solution?* Often, there are only satisfactory solutions to problems in the real world, not perfect solutions. Supervisors often waste a lot of time trying to find the elusive "perfect" solution when a satisfactory solution will do.

## Why Supervisors Fail

You may be surprised to learn that an inability to perform technical aspects of the job is not likely to be a primary reason that supervisors fail. Instead, more supervisors are unable to effectively manage and relate to their employees. When supervisors don't get along with their employees, low productivity, low morale, and high employee turnover are among the likely results. In these circumstances, work probably is not completed on time, nor does it meet quality or quantity standards. This affects the supervisor's professional reputation and the relationship between the supervisor and his or her boss. If you are not performing to expectations, you will probably not be considered for promotion and eventually you may find yourself looking for another job.

Supervisors sometimes fail because of character and personality shortcomings. Supervisors who are prejudiced, have low self-esteem, or have other personality problems may not be able to handle the responsibilities and pressures associated with the job.

The inability to perform the basic management tasks—planning, organizing, coordinating, staffing, directing, controlling, and evaluating—can cause serious problems for supervisors. Again, the story is the same. If you fall short in any or all of these management tasks, your job performance will suffer, your relationship with your employees and boss will suffer, and the quantity and quality of your work and the work of your employees will suffer.

All supervisors can improve their skills. Supervisors are made, not born. You can learn how to manage employees and perform other management activities more effectively and efficiently by applying the basic principles of supervision and management. In addition, you can learn a great deal by copying the behavior of successful managers and leaders in your organization. As your competence grows, so will your ability to help the organization meet its goals.

## Supervisory Responsibilities

Supervisors do not work alone. You are responsible to various individuals inside and outside the organization. The most important of these include your boss, employees, guests, the profession, and yourself.

### Your Boss

Everyone has a boss. Your boss reports to someone. Even the owner(s) of your property must answer to a number of government agencies and, possibly, stockholders as well.

You are responsible to your boss for performing assigned work tasks. You help your boss and the organization fulfill objectives by meeting deadlines, performance standards, and other expectations; operating within budget limitations; following company policies; maintaining records; and writing reports in a timely fashion.

You should be respectful to your boss and accept reasonable assignments without complaint. Think about how you would like your employees to treat you. You should treat your boss in much the same way.

Since you must implement the plans and procedures as assigned by your boss and other managers, you must be cooperative. The saying, "If you are not part of the solution, you are part of the problem," is one supervisors would do well to recall. If you constantly argue with your boss about his/her plans, resist necessary changes, or are otherwise uncooperative, you are not meeting your responsibility as a team player to get the job done. As well, you are not setting the proper example for those whom you supervise.

### Employees

You have responsibilities to your employees as well as to your boss. First, you should recognize employees as individual human beings with differing backgrounds, interests, and needs. To the extent you do this, you help the organization, the employees, and yourself. Employees who are treated as individuals with genuine dignity and respect and not just "warm bodies" usually have higher morale and productivity. Other responsibilities to employees include:

- Providing a safe working environment.

- Adequately representing employees to higher managers.

- Disciplining all staff members in a positive and fair manner.

- Being consistent and fair in all decisions that affect your employees.

- Providing opportunities for career development. This includes whatever assistance is necessary to help a deserving employee get ahead.

## Guests

You have an obligation to look at the organization as a whole, your work, and the work of your employees from your guests' perspectives. You should ask questions such as, "If I were a guest, what kind of products and services would I want? At what quality level?" To the extent that you can answer these questions and improve your own and your employees' performances, you will be fulfilling your responsibility to guests.

## The Profession

Often, as supervisors work their way up the organizational ladder, they benefit from the experiences and assistance of others. There comes a time in the career of every supervisor when some of this assistance can be returned. When appropriate, you can assist others by **coaching** them or serving as a **mentor**. You can also become involved in professional associations and continuing education activities. Supervisors may also positively represent their profession by becoming active in community groups involving local schools, service/volunteer work, organizations with religious affiliations, and so on.

## Yourself

Finally, you have a responsibility to yourself. Being a good supervisor not only helps the organization but helps you as well. Most of us feel good about ourselves when we know we are doing the best possible job. When you do your job well, you also are more likely to be promoted. To be fair to yourself, you should have a career plan, including short- and long-range career goals, and you should work with your boss to develop strategies to reach them.

# Keys to Supervisory Success ─────────────────

For many years management experts searched for common traits found among good supervisors. It was thought that, through research, success factors in such areas as education, experience, intelligence, and personality could be identified. But, just as supervisors are different, so are the work environments within which they supervise. With so many variables, it is not possible to come up with any concrete conclusions. Each situation calls for certain skills and abilities. Skilled leaders adjust their approach to the unique needs of each situation and the available resources.

Can any keys to supervisory success be identified? Yes. The master key is to keep focused on the core duties and responsibilities of a supervisor. Exhibit 9 lists some special fundamental supervisory skills. Mastery of these skills is an important step toward success as a supervisor and toward a management career in hospitality.

There are also general traits to consider that many effective supervisors possess. First and foremost, the successful supervisor is a good communicator. The importance of speaking, listening, and writing well cannot be overstated. Successful supervisors accept the duties and responsibilities of their jobs and put the

**Exhibit 9   Fundamental Supervisory Skills**

- Understanding the role of the supervisor
- Providing leadership
- Improving communications
- Conducting effective orientation and training progress
- Successfully handling problems and conflict
- Motivation and team building
- Staffing and scheduling
- Improving employee performance
- Managing time (one's own and that of employees)
- Recruiting and selection procedures
- Managing productivity and controlling labor costs
- Evaluating and coaching employees
- Disciplining procedures
- Managing change
- Decision-making and problem-solving tactics

good of the organization first. They withstand day-to-day pressures, using them as motivators to do the job better. Successful supervisors also have a good self-image and positive personality that helps them shape the work environment. They are enthusiastic and they like to lead. These qualities help keep employee morale and motivation high and help transform a work crew from a group of individuals into a team. Successful supervisors always seek to improve themselves, and they set career goals and plan action steps to achieve them.

## Endnote ——————————————————————

1. Henri Fayol, *General and Industrial Management* (London: Sir Isaac Pitman & Sons, 1949).

## Key Terms ——————————————————————

**action plans**—Step-by-step activities defining the who, what, where, when, and how of implementing a strategy.

**assets**—Things that are of significant value to the hospitality organization.

**business plan**—Bridges strategic and operational planning activities by specifying how the organization will move forward in the upcoming year toward attaining long-range goals.

**coaching**—A supervisory procedure that involves complimenting an employee for desired behaviors and correcting performance problems at the time they are observed.

**competencies**—Knowledge and/or skills required for successful job performance.

**conceptual skills**—One of three critical supervisory skills. Conceptual skills are the intellectual skills supervisors need to perform their jobs well, including the ability to visualize problems, develop solutions, and make decisions.

**controlling**—The supervisory task of measuring actual results against expected results. Controlling also refers to safeguarding the operation's property and revenue.

**coordinating**—The supervisory task of assigning work and organizing people and resources to achieve the operation's objectives.

**directing**—The supervisory task of managing, scheduling, and disciplining employees. Directing includes such things as training and motivating employees.

**evaluating**—The supervisory task of: (1) reviewing the operation's progress toward organizational goals, and (2) measuring employee performance against the organization's standards.

**executive committee**—A group consisting of top-level managers and department heads that meets regularly to discuss organization-wide concerns.

**formal authority**—The authority that comes with the position a person holds in the organization.

**human relations skills**—One of the three critical supervisory skills. Human relations skills include all those abilities necessary to deal effectively with employees on a personal level including communication, leadership, and team building.

**informal authority**—The power someone has because of his or her abilities, charisma, or other personal traits. Also referred to as personal authority.

**labor-intensive**—The concept that many tasks required in the hospitality industry must be performed by people, and these persons cannot be replaced by technology (machines).

**line managers**—A manager with decision-making authority in the chain of command.

**long-range plan**—Generally covers a time period of three to five years and outlines how the organization intends to close the gap between where it is today and where it wants to be in the future.

**management**—The process of using available resources to achieve organizational goals.

**manager**—A person who directs the work of supervisors.

**marketing plan**—Indicates how the goals set by an organization's business plan will be achieved in the upcoming year through marketing and sales efforts.

**mentor**—An experienced employee who advises less experienced staff members about issues related to the job, the organization, and their professional careers.

**mission statement**—A broad description of an organization's reason to exist, forming a basis for developing goals and objectives and guiding the allocation of resources within the organization.

**operational planning**—Specific activities usually cover a planning horizon of no more than one year. Activities include developing a business plan, a marketing plan, and an operations budget.

**operations budget**—Management's detailed plans for generating revenue and incurring expenses for each department within the operation; also referred to as the revenue and expense budget.

**organizing**—The supervisory activity that attempts to best assemble and use limited human and other resources to attain organizational goals. It involves establishing the flow of authority and communication among people.

**planning**—The supervisory task of creating objectives and action plans to reach them.

**staff managers**—Technical specialists without decision-making authority.

**staffing**—The supervisory activity of recruiting and hiring employees.

**strategic planning**—General activities that guide an organization toward a desired future state. Activities include developing a vision statement, mission statement, and values statement that culminate in a three- to five-year long-range plan.

**subordinates**—Persons who are at a lower organization level.

**supervisor**—Someone who manages entry-level or other employees who do not have supervisory responsibilities.

**technical skills**—One of the three critical supervisory skills. These skills form the basic work behaviors of any job. For example, technical skills required of a food server are basic math, good eye-hand coordination, balance, strong communication, and so on.

**values statement**—Embodies the shared beliefs, common convictions, and acknowledged principles that unite managers, supervisors, and staff members as they create the organization's future.

**vision statement**—A projection of an organization's future: where it wants to be and what it wants to look like at a specific point in time.

 # Review Questions

1. What is management?
2. What are the seven basic categories of resources?
3. What are the basic types of demands that confront supervisors?
4. What are the four management levels in a hospitality property?
5. What are some of Henri Fayol's basic management principles?
6. What are common planning activities?

7.  What are some basic principles applicable to the management functions of organizing, coordinating, staffing, directing, controlling, and evaluating?

8.  What three basic skills must supervisors possess?

9.  Why do supervisors often fail?

10. What responsibilities do supervisors have to their boss, their employees, their guests, other professionals, and themselves?

11. What are some keys to supervisory success?

## Case Study

### "I Never Wanted to Be a Supervisor Anyway"

John is a food server at the Lakeside Inn, a 200-room hotel with a coffee shop and a full-service restaurant called Hummingbirds. Two years ago, John started out as a busperson in the coffee shop, but because of his outstanding performance he was quickly transferred to Hummingbirds and made a food server.

John's excellent record continued in his new position. John was always on time, was great with the guests, and was a real team player. When the buspersons fell behind, he helped them catch up without being asked. When another server needed help, John was always willing to take on tables in addition to his own. He also got along well with the cooks. Within weeks at his new position, he knew everyone's name and was usually the center of attention in the employee break-room. As time went by, he won employee of the month so many times it became somewhat embarrassing.

Phil Brown, the dining room supervisor at Hummingbirds, was John's boss. Because John got along with the staff so well, Phil asked John to fill in for him every Wednesday—one of Phil's days off and the slowest day of the week for the restaurant. John seemed to do a good job in this role. Serious problems seldom came up on Wednesdays, and if one did, John would tell Phil about it on Thursday morning so Phil could take care of it.

When Phil was made restaurant manager of another hotel in the chain, he encouraged John to apply for his position. "I think you'd make a great supervisor. The job will be posted internally for three days, and I'm not sure who's going to apply, but you can count on me for a glowing recommendation." Phil not only thought this would be good for John, but also knew that the company encouraged promotion from within; additionally, it would be a feather in Phil's cap if one of his employees took over his position and succeeded in it.

At first, John was not enthusiastic about the supervisor job—"I really enjoy what I'm doing," he told Phil—but, bolstered by Phil's confidence in him, he finally decided to apply. His interview was with three people: Phil; Phil's boss, Alan, the restaurant manager; and Susan, the hotel's human resources director. John was outgoing and personable during the interview, and after John left the room, Phil cited John's initiative, high energy level, leadership skills, and high quantity and quality of work as reasons John should get the job. Although Alan and Susan were concerned about John's lack of formal supervisory training, they decided, given John's excellent record, to give him a chance.

The next day, John went with Phil to Phil's new restaurant and spent a week in training. At the beginning of the week, Phil went over a checklist of supervisory skills John needed to acquire and gave him some training materials to study. Throughout the week, Phil helped John fill out the paperwork a dining room supervisor must deal with. At the end of the week, Phil wished John good luck, gave him a pep talk, and told him to call anytime he had a problem.

John reported for work at Hummingbirds the next morning, uncomfortable in his new suit and tie but feeling confident and determined to do a good job. It didn't take him long to discover that the biggest adjustment he faced was in relating to his former co-workers. When he was a food server, everyone was his friend and he had enjoyed all the during-work and after-hours socializing the employees did together. But now he was left out. In this and many other ways, his former co-workers made him feel that he wasn't "one of the gang" anymore. That was bad enough, but he began to suspect that his friends, now his employees, were taking advantage of him. For one thing, they didn't really treat him as a manager. When Alan walked through the kitchen, all the servers and cooks snapped to attention; when John walked through, they just looked around—"Oh, hi John"—or didn't acknowledge him at all and continued casually chatting. Because they knew John so well, they constantly asked him for favors: "Can I trade nights with Lisa?" "Can I have tomorrow off?" "Can Sam and I switch table assignments?" "You remember I'm a bowler, right? Could you please not schedule me Thursday nights? The league's starting up next week." The requests went on and on. John soon learned that, try as he might, he couldn't write a schedule that pleased everybody or didn't have to be changed constantly. The few times he couldn't give employees the day off they wanted, some of them called in sick. John wondered if they were lying, of course, but he couldn't prove anything and he didn't want to think they would treat him so badly. All he knew for certain was that he felt abused and taken advantage of by the very people he used to be so close to.

Despite these feelings, John wanted to preserve his relationships with his staff, and he wanted to please his new boss, too. So he didn't let Alan know about the pressures he was feeling, and he granted almost every employee request. This often meant that John found himself doing his old job of serving customers, busing tables, even filling in for dishwashers, while his employees either called in with an excuse and didn't show up, or didn't put forth the effort John thought they should. Too many times John found himself waiting tables, fretting about the mountain of paperwork on his desk, and watching other servers working at what he considered half speed.

As the first few weeks went by, he also became disappointed in Martha's performance. Martha was the senior server on the staff, and she had inherited John's old role as the "head server," the person John counted on to be a team leader and fill in for him when he had time off. But Martha never did the little things that would have really helped him out, and never went the extra mile for anyone. Why couldn't she just volunteer and pitch in like he used to do?

That Monday morning started out like most Monday mornings at Hummingbirds—extremely busy. The normally big breakfast crowd was swelled even larger by several busloads of sales executives who had just arrived at the hotel for a four-day meeting. John was at his desk, hurrying through some reports he had promised Alan would be finished yesterday. He knew it was only a matter of time before he'd be called into the dining room. His three six o'clock servers were trying to take care of the rapidly increasing crowd, and Janice, one of his three seven o'clock servers, had called him the night before to tell him she wouldn't be in till eleven—her basement had flooded and she had to meet with a cleaning crew and an insurance adjuster in the morning. So today of all days he would be one server short for the breakfast crowd.

When John's telephone rang right at 7:00, his heart sank. Sure enough, Sally, another of his seven o'clock servers, was calling to say she was sick and wouldn't be coming in. She was a good employee who had never called in sick before, so he fought back his feeling of panic and told her to take care of herself and not worry about a thing. He no sooner thanked her for calling and hung up when the phone rang again. It was Rich, the third seven o'clock server, calling in sick, too. This was the fourth time Rich had called in sick in the two months John had been supervisor, and John knew that Rich had a habit of drinking too much on the weekend—in fact, John used to help Rich think of excuses to tell Phil back when Phil was the supervisor. But he really did sound sick this time, so John put aside his suspicions and told Rich to come in later if he felt better.

John gave up all thoughts of catching up on his reports and grabbed the schedule. The only people he might be able to call in were Wendy and Maria. No answer at Wendy's house. Maria was home, but she couldn't come in because she was a chaperon that morning for her daughter's sixth-grade field trip. She was very sorry.

"That's okay," John said wearily, and with exaggerated carefulness placed the receiver back in its cradle. It was all he could do to keep from throwing the phone across the room. Instead of six servers for the morning, he was down to three, with a bigger crowd than usual and no one he could turn to for help. Even Alan was unavailable—he was in a staff meeting with the hotel's general manager. John grimly straightened his tie and headed for the dining room.

Hurrying through the kitchen, he was assaulted by the sounds of a staff under pressure: cooks yelling orders, dishes clattering violently, oven doors slamming. He charged through the double swinging doors into the dining room just in time to see Steve, one of his buspersons, heading for the restaurant's entrance, holding a towel tightly wrapped around his right hand.

"What happened to him?" John asked Martha.

"He was hurrying too much, broke a coffee cup and cut himself. I sent him to the doctor—looks like he'll need stitches."

Great, John thought as he surveyed the situation. Every table was packed, and the roar of a hundred conversations made it almost as noisy in the dining room as it had been in the kitchen. John couldn't remember the restaurant ever being so crowded, and there was a line of guests extending from the restaurant's entrance into the hotel lobby, waiting for a table.

Taking a deep breath, John threw himself into the fray. He tried to be everywhere at once, waiting tables, pouring coffee, seating guests, running the cash register, all the while trying not to notice the frowns from guests angry at the inevitable delays in service. Each guest complaint muttered within earshot—"What kind of a place is this?" "Great service around here"—hit him like a lash. John fought down the waves of helplessness and frustration he felt and threw encouraging words at harried staff members whenever he rushed past one of them. He was in the middle of yet another long apology to an irritated guest when, out of the corner of his eye, he saw Martha at the cash register, standing on tiptoe and waving to him furiously above a long line of guests waiting to pay their bills.

He excused himself with a strained smile and hurried over to Martha. "What's the problem?"

"I don't know," Martha said breathlessly, "the register just stopped working."

John stared in frustration at the silent machine; he didn't have a clue about how to get it working again. "What did you do?" he barked at Martha.

"I didn't do anything!" Martha wailed. "It's not *my* fault."

"It's not *my* fault either," John snapped. "Damn it, think! Did you do something just before it quit?"

"Hey!" one of the guests back in the middle of the line called up to John, "I had to wait for my food, wait for my check, and now I have to wait to give you my money? Come on, do something!"

"I'm trying to do something, sir," John said through clenched teeth.

"Well, do it now, 'cause I'm tired of this crap." There was a murmur of agreement from the other guests in line.

John grabbed Martha by the arm much harder than he intended and half shoved her toward the kitchen. "Go to my office and get my calculator."

Martha pulled her arm away. "I don't know where it is."

John slammed his fist down on the counter. "Damn it, do I have to do everything myself?!" he shrieked.

A hush fell over the restaurant. Everyone froze; all eyes turned toward John. Martha blinked back tears and was starting to say something when her gaze shifted past John's shoulder and her eyes widened. John turned around to see his boss, Alan, looking around the restaurant incredulously. "What in hell is going on here?" he demanded.

Later that day…

Alan looked across his desk at John and sighed. What could have gone so wrong? This morning's incident was just the latest in a series of problems he'd had with John ever since John took the dining room supervisor's job. John didn't seem to understand budgets and was not keeping up with the administrative part of the job—late reports, botched purchase orders, unsigned invoices—the list was rather lengthy. John didn't even seem to be handling the people-skills part of his job very well. Several employees had come to Alan with complaints that John was playing favorites when it came to scheduling. And grabbing Martha this morning—Alan just hoped she didn't cause the hotel any headaches over that.

It had taken a while, but Alan had gotten Hummingbirds under control again with the help of George, the coffee shop manager. After the crisis was past, Alan had left George in charge of the restaurant and had taken John up to his office for a long-overdue counseling session. But now he wasn't sure where to begin.

"John," he said finally, "what happened? I couldn't believe my eyes when I saw you ranting and raving in front of a room full of guests."

"Look," John said defensively, "I had my hands full. You weren't around, we were working short-handed, the register went dead—I didn't know what to do. I was doing the best I could. I was never trained for that kind of situation."

"But John, you had training. You spent a week with Phil; he said you were ready. You worked in the restaurant for two years. I don't know what else we could have done for you."

"You never prepared me for an emergency like that."

"But no one could have foreseen what happened this morning!" Alan exclaimed. "Besides, managers are supposed to be able to cope with all the crazy things that go wrong. That's why we put you in that position; we thought you could handle it."

"Well, maybe you were wrong," John blurted out, "maybe you shouldn't have promoted me in the first place." John looked down at his feet and mumbled, "I never wanted to be a supervisor anyway."

## Discussion Questions

1. Did Phil and Alan make a mistake in promoting John? Why or why not?

2. What should Alan do about John?

3. Assuming Alan decides to keep John on as supervisor, what are the immediate steps Alan should take with John?

4. If John stays on as supervisor, what are the immediate steps Alan and John must take with other people affected by John's outburst?

---

Case Number 3566CA

The following industry experts helped generate and develop this case: Philip J. Bresson, Director of Human Resources, Renaissance New York Hotel, New York, New York; and Jerry Fay, Human Resources Director, Aramark Corporation, Atlanta, Georgia.

This case also appears in *Managing Hospitality Human Resources*, Fifth Edition (Lansing, Mich.: American Hotel & Lodging Educational Institute, 2012), ISBN 978-0-86612-396-9.

# Chapter 2 Outline

Overview of Communication
    Types of Business Communication
    How Communication Works
Communication Challenges
    Communication Myths
    Communication Barriers
    Personal Biases and Communication
Speaking Skills
    Think About the Details
    Speaking on the Job
    Formal Presentations
Listening Skills
    Obstacles to Listening
    A Listening Model
    Active Listening Skills
Nonverbal Communication: Body
    Language
    Facial Expressions
    Posture and Body Movement
    Gestures
    Body Language on the Job
Writing Skills
    Clear Writing Is Important
    Business Writing Techniques
    Plain English and Short Sentences
    Memos
    E-Mail
Important Workplace Communication
    Issues
    Relationships Between Employees
    Relationships Between Departments
    Negotiations

# Competencies

1. Identify three types of business communication and provide an overview of a basic model for communication. (pp. 31–32)

2. Explain how communication myths, communication barriers, and personal biases can affect communication. (pp. 32–38)

3. Review basic speaking skills useful when communicating on the job and when making formal presentations. (pp. 38–41)

4. Discuss obstacles to listening, a four-stage listening model, and procedures for effective listening. (pp. 41–47)

5. Describe how nonverbal communication impacts the understanding of messages. (pp. 47–50)

6. Explain the basics of effective business writing. (pp. 50–58)

7. Describe how technology is affecting communication procedures and explain how effective communication procedures improve relationships between employees and between departments and promote better negotiation. (pp. 58–64)

# 2

# Effective Communication for Supervisors

SUPERVISORS MUST COMMUNICATE EFFECTIVELY as they interact with their own and other managers, their peers (i.e., other supervisors), employees, guests, vendors, and numerous other persons. They must have excellent speaking, listening, and writing skills, because almost all aspects of their work involve communication. The more effectively they communicate, the better they can perform their jobs.

Supervisors, like other hospitality industry leaders, must be good "people persons," which means they must have good interpersonal skills for dealing with a wide variety of people. The increasing diversity of the workforce creates new communication challenges for managers almost everywhere. Excellent **nonverbal communication** skills are important for those who orient, train, and coach employees with limited English-language skills. Getting to know one's employees and communicating with them is crucial to retaining them. In contrast, poor communication can contribute to high staff turnover.

Many managers believe that one of the best ways to be a good communicator is to be a good listener. Being a good listener is not a passive activity. Managers who want to be good listeners must listen not only to *what* is being said but also to *how* it is being said and *why* it is being said, staying alert for the feelings behind the words.

Supervisors must effectively address the needs of their guests. They do so as they discover what their guests want, as they deliver products and services that meet these needs, and as they evaluate the effectiveness of their efforts. Each of these activities, whether undertaken by conversation, survey, group or committee discussion, "managing by walking around," or other methods, involves communication.

## Overview of Communication

Supervisors should understand that there are different types of business communication. This section will present a basic communication model that describes how the communication process works.

### Types of Business Communication

In terms of business communication, supervisors must communicate well not only with employees, but with their bosses and other supervisors. There are three different types of business communication:

- **Downward communication**—the passing of information from an organization's higher levels to its lower levels.

- **Upward communication**—the passing of information from an organization's lower levels to its higher levels.

- **Lateral communication**—the passing of information between persons at the same level in an organization.

Think of the various levels of management and employees, and how they are joined together in a network of communication "linking pins." In a large hospitality organization, for example, line employees are linked to department managers through supervisors; the department heads serve as linking pins between department managers and the division head.

Peers across the organization are linked to each other. As a supervisor, you play an important role that links line employees and upper-level managers, and you are also linked to the organization's other supervisors. These links are strengthened through good communication, but they are weakened if communication is poor.

Exhibit 1 offers tips to help you increase your effectiveness in communicating throughout your organization. Note that whether communication is upward or downward depends on your point of focus. A conversation between a supervisor and an employee is downward for the supervisor and upward for the employee.

## How Communication Works

How does the basic communication process work? Exhibit 2 answers this question. As you review Exhibit 2, note that, when two people communicate, the message sender has a thought or feeling, puts it into words and/or actions, and then sends the message to the other person. The receiver decodes/interprets the message, develops a response, puts the response into words or actions, and sends a new message, thus providing feedback.

Successful communication occurs when a speaker or writer sends a message, the listener or reader receives it, the message is understood, and it is acted upon by both parties. The basic communication process seems simple. However, the difficulty lies in carrying out the process.

# Communication Challenges

Let's explore some common myths, barriers, and personal biases that can detract from effective communication.

## Communication Myths

Several myths create misunderstandings about communication and can become obstacles to effective communication:

- *"We communicate only when we want to."* In fact, managers communicate every day and all day, often without realizing it. For example, suppose a manager is listening to an employee present a report. The manager travelled for

**Exhibit 1   Communication Tips for Supervisors**

**Downward Communication**

Developing effective downward communication skills helps supervisors identify potential problems, gain staff commitment, and gather information for making decisions. Some tips to help you develop better downward communication skills include the following:

- Maintain an open-door policy, and let employees know they can come to you with problems.
- Listen attentively and objectively to your employees' concerns and contributions.
- Don't react emotionally or critically when someone brings you bad news. Becoming angry at the message bearer will cut off your communication in the future.
- Use active listening skills.
- Be sure that employees know that you care about their opinions and suggestions.

**Upward Communication**

A successful supervisor knows that communicating with his or her manager is very important. Upward communication takes care and planning. Some tips to help you communicate with your manager include the following:

- Be sure your message is important; your manager's time is limited.
- Be sure the information is accurate and complete.
- Be brief.
- Communicate both the good news and the bad news.
- Communicate regularly.
- When you present a problem, suggest potential solutions.
- Make an agenda; some managers appreciate receiving a list of topics you will discuss in advance so that they, too, can be prepared.
- Be sure your timing is right; presenting information to your manager at the wrong time can derail the communication process.
- Establish clear objectives; know in advance what you want to accomplish during your talk with your manager.
- Don't go over your manager's head unless it is absolutely necessary.

**Lateral Communication**

Lateral communication skills enable you to communicate effectively with other supervisors. This helps ensure that information will continue to flow your way and enhances your career opportunities. Tips that can help you develop better lateral communication skills include the following:

- Get to know as many supervisors in the organization as you can.
- View peer communication as a chance to establish relationships that work for both parties.
- Share information; nobody wants to talk to someone who doesn't share in return.
- Constantly look for overlapping areas of responsibility or interests that might help improve your interaction with other supervisors.

*(continued)*

**Exhibit 1**    *(continued)*

- Take a "big picture" perspective and communicate about issues that might help the whole organization, not just your part of it.
- Give sincere and positive feedback when asked.
- When appropriate, offer your help.
- Use positive body language when communicating.
- Work a day or two in another department to help you understand some of the problems and issues your peers are discussing.

**Exhibit 2    Sender-Receiver Model**

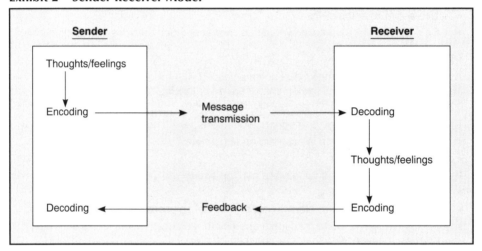

many hours the night before, returning from a managers' meeting, is very tired, and so yawns almost continually. The employee doesn't know about the sleepless night and concludes the manager is uninterested in the report. An incorrect message has just been sent.

- *"Words mean the same to everyone."* Words have different meanings to different people, based on their backgrounds and viewpoints. Suppose a manager tells an employee that his or her work is "above average" because the manager thinks the employee is a good worker and has great potential. The manager assumes the employee will respond in a positive way. Instead, the employee is a high achiever and, to him or her, "above average" means barely acceptable—the employee was hoping to hear that his or her work was "great" or "excellent." Now the employee's morale and work quality may suffer because of concern that success is not likely.

- *"We communicate chiefly with words."* In reality, supervisors communicate many of their messages nonverbally. They may say one thing but reveal their real feelings by their tone of voice, facial expressions, eye contact, gestures, or how they sit or walk. For example, assume that a manager sees an employee in his office and asks how he feels. The employee responds, "Fine, thanks," but slumps in the chair, stares at the floor, and sounds and looks distressed. The manager observes these nonverbal cues and knows that the employee is not "fine"—something is wrong!

- *"Nonverbal communication is silent communication."* Nonverbal communication is done without words. However, nonverbal communication such as laughter, crying, and tone of voice does involve sounds. When a manager hears an employee whistling a happy tune, he or she usually assumes that the employee is having a good day and typically that assumption is correct.

- *"The best communication is a one-way message from me to you."* This myth suggests that speakers talk *at* listeners rather than *with* them. Effective communication is best when both parties participate actively. They do this when the listener gives the speaker feedback. **Feedback** is a listener's reaction to the speaker's verbal and nonverbal message. When managers give instructions to employees, they probably want feedback to ensure the employees understand the message. Examples of nonverbal feedback include shaking one's head or frowning. An employee may provide verbal feedback by saying "I see" or "I don't understand."

- *"The message communicated is the message received."* Sometimes managers assume that listeners receive their messages exactly as intended. These assumptions can lead to trouble. Suppose a supervisor asks an employee on Monday morning to write a report and states that she needs it "soon." The employee plans to work on it Wednesday and give it to her on Thursday. But the next day (Tuesday), the manager asks the employee for the report. In this instance the communication failed, because "soon" meant "tomorrow" to the manager and "this week" to the employee.

- *"There is no such thing as too much information."* Too little information is not good, but neither is too much information. Problems can occur when employees are overwhelmed with information. Supervisors waste time if they tell employees about matters that neither affect nor interest them. Focus on the quality of communication rather than its quantity. More is not necessarily better.

## Communication Barriers

Barriers exist that can decrease the effectiveness of communication. Knowing about them is the first step toward overcoming them.

**Distractions.** Workplace distractions can include too much noise, excessive heat or cold, interruptions, and physical discomfort. Spoken communication is enhanced when it occurs in settings that are as distraction-free as possible. Suppose an employee wants to talk to her manager about a problem with a co-worker because the manager has always emphasized an "open door" policy. However, the manager leaves the office door open during the meeting and there is a lot of noise outside. The manager also accepts two telephone calls and shuffles papers on the desk. Because of all these distractions, this employee is not likely to confide in the manager in the future.

**Differences in Background.** Message senders and receivers have different—sometimes very different—educational, experience, and knowledge backgrounds. This can create communication barriers. A new dishwasher may try to make friends with the executive chef but be rejected. A recent hospitality management school graduate may be ignored when he tries to tell a much older manager how to improve performance. A speaker may send a message based on personal knowledge, but the message may not be understood if the listener does not have similar knowledge. Persons with different backgrounds can have difficulty in sharing ideas and working together, and supervisors must address these challenges.

**Poor Timing.** Poor timing may cause both parties to say things they do not mean. Someone may say something in anger and later regret it, or a person who should be listening may be distracted or simply unwilling to listen at the moment. The best communication occurs when both parties are ready and want to participate in it.

Assume a supervisor wants to discuss an upcoming meeting with an employee who appears distracted. Usually an attentive listener, the employee on this occasion seems lost in thought, doesn't provide the active feedback expected, and quickly "forgets" things that were discussed just a few minutes ago. Upon questioning the employee, the manager learns that the employee has a serious family problem on her mind, so the manager reschedules the discussion to enable her to work through the problem.

**Personality Differences.** The personalities of those who are communicating can pose communication obstacles. For example, assume that a manager is conducting an employee meeting with two employees: one attendee is a favorite employee, and the second is someone with whom the manager has previously had serious disagreements. During the meeting the manager may pay close attention to the first employee and disregard whatever the second employee has to say.

**Prejudice.** A supervisor may want a report completed in a specific way because "that's the way we've always done it" and she is positively prejudiced toward that process. Another manager has had poor experiences with a product vendor and, even after the business changes ownership, he is still reluctant to buy from the company. In both examples, the manager should keep an open mind and not be closed off to new processes or new personnel.

**Differences in Knowledge and Assumptions.** Communication may be hampered if the receiver lacks the knowledge or experience required to understand the message but the sender assumes that she does. Only a partial message is sent when the sender assumes the receiver has the same knowledge and so communicates without conveying needed background information. To minimize this problem, senders should determine and consider what is already known by receivers before sending their messages.

**Stress.** Everyone reacts differently to stressful situations. Stress can be positive, such as the sense of concentration managers may feel when they are confronted with new and challenging situations. Positive stress can help a person to concentrate, focus, and perform at peak efficiency. Stress becomes negative when a manager doesn't (or can't) relax after facing a challenge.

Stress can also relate to the vague sense of anxiety a person feels after having "one of those days." In difficult situations, stress must be controlled and managed to provide the best possible results.

Given the nature of the hospitality industry, the need to communicate under stress occurs frequently. One of the best ways to minimize the impact of stress on communications is to plan ahead. Being well-organized and having a clear sense of priorities should help provide managers with a clear direction when tension builds. As the pressure grows, supervisors can keep calm by thinking positive thoughts about the situation ("This will all work out") as they use the resources available to tackle the difficulties.

## Personal Biases and Communication

Supervisors should consider how their own personal biases may interfere with their ability to effectively communicate. The best managers make every effort to become more aware of their biases and take actions to minimize their impacts when carrying out responsibilities. There are many types of personal biases that affect the communication process on the job.

**First Impressions.** When managers first meet someone, they sometimes make immediate judgments about that person based on external factors such as appearance, accent, and age. However, first impressions may later prove incorrect. It is important to obtain more information, especially when interviewing job applicants and orienting newly hired employees.

**Stereotypes.** Managers may form general opinions about certain groups and then apply predetermined beliefs to individuals in those groups. If an employee acts in a different way than other members of the group, the manager may overlook the differences or assign positive or negative values to them. The best approach: try to think of each employee as an individual, not as a member of a specific group.

**Just-Like-Me.** Many supervisors tend to like those who behave or think as they do or who have similar backgrounds and characteristics. They then may favor those who are like them and disregard those who differ from them. Supervisors should be especially careful to avoid this type of thinking when interviewing job applicants or conducting performance evaluations.

**Halo or Pitchfork Effects.** Sometimes managers favor someone for one positive characteristic and overlook the person's other traits (the halo effect). Conversely, they may dislike someone only because of a single characteristic that they see as negative (the pitchfork effect). In both cases, these positive or negative views based on one trait color the manager's perceptions of the whole person. Managers must avoid this all-or-nothing thinking, particularly when selecting and training employees or evaluating their performance.

**Contrast Effect.** Managers sometimes compare employees with others and rank them according to their perceptions of "best performance." Instead of comparing employees with other employees, it is always best to evaluate them based on job performance standards. This is especially important when coaching employees and evaluating their performance.

**Leniency/Severity Effect.** Some managers view the world positively, while others are clouded by negativity. When employees are seen too positively, the problems they create may be excused. If employees are viewed too negatively, the manager's judgments may be too severe. When managers are having a good day, they may react less sternly to an employee's policy violation or failure to complete a task according to standards. Managers must evaluate performance consistently and try to see their employees' strengths and weaknesses without bias. This is especially important when coaching, evaluating, and disciplining employees.

# Speaking Skills

Effective speaking, whether in front of a group or in a personal conversation, generally involves introductory remarks, the main body (points to be made), and a conclusion. The introduction portion of an informal talk or speech should get the attention of listeners and communicate the purpose for speaking. Speakers should think about what they want to say before saying it. They should identify the main points they want to make and then address them, sticking to the topic.

An effective communicator gets a listener's attention by announcing his or her intentions. Effective communicators explain what they want to talk about, why it is important, and what they expect to occur as a result. They keep the interest of listeners by explaining what the message means and how it affects them.

The time and method required to introduce a topic varies according to the situation. For a routine one-on-one conversation, a manager might casually say, "Joe, let's talk about the banquet plans." But for a presentation before the local Chamber of Commerce, the manager would be much more formal: "Ladies and gentlemen, there are things you should know about the proposed legislation that will affect our business and our community."

The key points of a conversation or speech should be in a logical sequence. This will require planning and organization, especially in the case of a formal presentation. Spoken cues can help listeners focus in on what's most important. For example, a speaker might say, "The main concept I'm trying to emphasize is …" In addition, speakers should maintain eye contact with the listener, vary their tone of voice, and summarize and clarify important points.

Asking questions is one effective way that speakers can ensure that listeners understand. Asking questions will keep listeners interested and encourage them to carefully consider what is being said. The final summary of a conversation or speech should repeat the main ideas and indicate what the speaker wants the listener(s) to do as a result of the communication.

## Think About the Details

When engaging in a conversation or making a more formal speech, speakers should think about more than the content of the message; they should also pay attention to how they are delivering the message. For example, if the volume of a manager's voice is too high, listeners may feel that he or she is pushy or overbearing; conversely, when a manager speaks too quietly, listeners may feel that the manager is nervous or unassertive, or may not hear the message at all because they can't make out the words. On most occasions speakers should try to speak in a normal voice that is neither too loud nor too quiet.

The pitch or tonal level of one's voice is most effective when it comes naturally. Trying to use a pitch that is higher or lower than a normal pitch can make a person's voice sound artificial.

Managers should vary the tone of their voice according to the situation. They might use a stern tone when disciplining an employee for the third time and probably would speak gently to a nervous new employee. In general, a manager who speaks too warmly may sound insincere, and those who speak too coldly will likely offend nearly everybody. Managers should avoid both extremes.

The pace at which managers speak may be revealing. If it is too quickly, others may not understand what is being said or may think the manager is anxious or very busy. If a manager speaks too slowly, listeners may find it difficult to follow the message as their minds wander or may think that the manager is indecisive or uneasy.

## Speaking on the Job

Several guidelines are helpful for speaking in any work situation. Managers should plan and organize what they want to say and stick to the main points without digressing or introducing unnecessary information. They should provide enough accurate information to support the points being made.

It is important for managers to gear the message toward the listener and use understandable language so that the message is easy to follow. Managers should pause occasionally to allow the listener to ask questions or even ask the listener questions to check for comprehension. Whenever possible, managers should maintain appropriate eye contact, not only when speaking with just one person but also when addressing groups.

Watching the listener's body language to see how the message is being received is a good habit for managers to cultivate. In addition, managers can ask questions to confirm whether they are correctly reading the receiver's body language.

Gestures are another consideration when speaking. Hand, head, and upper body movements can be used to effectively emphasize key points in a talk. (Note: body language will be more fully discussed later in the chapter.)

## Formal Presentations

Formal presentations require planning and organization. Managers should begin their planning by asking what they want to accomplish with their presentation. Presentations can be informative, persuasive, or something in between. Informative presentations explain a topic, and persuasive presentations try to convince an audience about something. Determining whether the purpose is to inform or persuade helps managers prepare for the presentation.

Different audiences require different presentation approaches. Managers should consider four things when analyzing the audience, especially for a presentation off-site to an outside group:

• What values are important to them?

- Why do they need the information being presented?

- What constraints might prevent guests from doing what is wanted or understanding what they should understand?

- What is the audience's demographic profile, including ages, income levels, and occupations?

**Three Parts of a Presentation.** A presentation should have an introduction, a main body, and a conclusion. The introduction should get the listeners' attention, gain their interest, and communicate the presentation's purpose. Here are some ways to begin a presentation:

- Show how the information relates to the audience.

- Explain your competency (knowledge or experience) to speak on the subject.

- Refer to something unusual to capture the audience's attention, or refer to something familiar to establish a bond with the audience.

- Reassure the audience about the presentation's importance.

- Use a quotation from someone else to focus attention on the topic.

While we have discussed the introduction first, good presenters do not always begin to prepare a presentation by writing the introduction. Instead, the introduction is often made from the presentation's content, so many speakers work from the center outward. They plan the main body first, then write the introduction and conclusion.

The presentation's main body should present information in a logical sequence. Each point mentioned in the main body should support the intent of the presentation. The main body should also include the benefits the audience will likely experience as a result of accepting the presentation's main points.

Good speakers summarize information from time to time during the presentation. Some speakers prefer to summarize only at the end of their talk. Others believe that summarizing points during the presentation's main body helps prepare the audience to accept their conclusions.

Visual aids such as PowerPoints can add substantially to a presentation if used properly. Guidelines for preparing PowerPoints or other visual aids include the following:

- Keep visuals short and simple.

- Develop titles for visuals.

- As a rule of thumb, use no more than one visual for every several minutes of speaking.

- Graphs, pictures, flowcharts, etc., can often summarize information better than words on a screen.

- Set off the important points of visuals with bullets, numbers, indents, or some other method.

The presentation's conclusion summarizes information already provided. New information should not be introduced at the end of the session.

**The Presentation Environment.** A poor environment can ruin an otherwise great presentation. Before beginning a presentation, ensure that the environment will contribute positively to the session by attending to the following:

- *Equipment:* Test computers, slide projectors, and other equipment in advance.

- *Visuals:* Go to the back of the presentation room and determine whether the planned visuals can be easily seen.

- *Flip charts:* Ensure that there is enough paper and that there are pens on hand.

- *Handouts:* Make sure handouts are easily accessible, are in the correct order, and can be easily distributed.

- *Pointers:* Make sure a pointer is easily accessible if it will be used.

- *Microphone:* Presentations to more than seventy-five people will likely require a microphone. Test it in advance and know how to use it.

- *Lighting:* Determine how to turn room lights on or off if it will be necessary to do so. Leave some light on when using overheads or slides; speaking in a completely dark room may be uncomfortable, and listeners cannot take notes.

- *Seating arrangements:* Arrange seating in the room appropriately.

**Presentation Delivery Tips.** How the presentation is delivered is frequently a key to its success. Presentation delivery tips include the following:

- *Posture:* Be relaxed and erect. Don't shift back and forth from one foot to the other.

- *Movement:* Moving nearer the audience emphasizes main points. When using a lectern, move out from behind it occasionally. Be aware of hand movements. Wringing your hands or keeping them in your pockets, "handcuffed" behind your back, or folded in front of yourself will likely detract from the presentation.

- *Orientation:* Speakers who keep their shoulders turned toward their audiences often find they are considered to be more engaging. Speaking while facing away from the audience seems awkward to listeners.

- *Gestures:* Many people "talk with their hands" when they speak. Gestures are an important form of nonverbal communication if they are used appropriately. However, quick hand movements and other visual signs of anxiety detract from presentations.

Some presenters use a video camera to tape themselves to see what they look and sound like when making a presentation. This helps them identify ways to improve future presentations.

# Listening Skills

Every day we hear sounds of every kind coming from everywhere. We hear selectively by noticing some sounds while tuning others out. Hearing is largely passive. We do not have to work at hearing something; instead, we hear automatically.

Listening, however, is not the same as hearing. To listen well, we must become involved; that is, we must decide we want to listen and focus on the sounds. Managers who are good listeners can become even better listeners, because listening is a skill that can be developed just as one can learn to speak or write better. Supervisors spend a great deal of time listening, and for optimum results they should use effective listening skills as they do so. They should listen attentively to everyone with whom they come in contact on the job.

It is important to take an active role when listening, which is completely different from the passive role taken when just hearing something. Active listening takes effort, but the benefits gained are worth the time and trouble. To cite just one benefit, employees appreciate managers who truly listen to their concerns.

## Obstacles to Listening

Obstacles to effective listening are created by many of the listener's own bad habits. For example, a listener's mind may wander when personal thoughts and ideas seem more interesting than those of the speaker's. Meetings can be "tuned out" because the information is boring or difficult. Sometimes there are distractions when a person would rather be elsewhere or is worried about work that must be done.

Perhaps a meaningful word or idea grips a person's attention so that he or she is distracted and doesn't take in what the speaker says after that. It is possible to prejudge speakers or their topics and form opinions of the speakers before they are even seen. It is also possible for listeners to miss a message if they are busy trying to take detailed notes. Distractions arise from others talking or by noises in the room. Some causes of poor listening habits are listed in Exhibit 3.

Some people try to fake attention by looking at the speaker and nodding their heads from time to time while their thoughts are somewhere else. However, speakers often catch on when this occurs. If guests or employees think a supervisor has

**Exhibit 3   Causes of Poor Listening Habits**

- Unsuitable listening environment: too much noise or too many distractions
- Allowing your mind to wander
- Thinking of something else
- Focusing on one word or idea at the expense of the whole message
- Negative reactions to a speaker's mannerisms, appearance, dress, accent, and so on
- "Tuning out" because the message is difficult or dull
- Not paying attention
- Taking too many notes
- Talking to others in the group or audience
- Lack of desire or determination to listen

a habit of not fully listening, they will think he or she doesn't care. The result: employees will stop sharing their problems, ideas, and solutions, and guests may take their business elsewhere.

Listening difficulties may also result from the difference between how fast we speak and the rate at which we listen, think, and comprehend. The average speaker says 125 to 150 words per minute. The average listener, however, can hear and understand more than twice as many words per minute. Managers should put this spare listening time to work. Rather than daydreaming, managers should become actively involved in receiving the message. They should use extra moments to review what they have heard or anticipate what additional points the speaker might make.

## A Listening Model

Exhibit 4 summarizes four stages of listening: focusing, interpreting, evaluating, and responding.

**Focusing.** Focusing involves paying attention to the speaker and concentrating on receiving the message. Four tactics that can help managers accomplish this include:

*   *Deciding to listen.* Keep your attention focused and set aside your own ideas. Concentrate on the speaker's words and message rather than his or her age,

**Exhibit 4   Four Stages in Active Listening**

**Stage 1—Focusing**
Decide to listen.
Create the proper atmosphere.
Focus on the speaker.
Show that you are paying attention.

**Stage 2—Interpreting**
Keep from judging.
Determine the speaker's meaning.
Confirm that you understand the meaning.
Show that you understand.
Reach a common understanding.

**Stage 3—Evaluating**
Gather more information.
Decide whether the information is genuine.
Evaluate the information.
Communicate your evaluation.

**Stage 4—Responding**
Learn what the speaker expects.
Consider your own time and energy.
Decide what to do.

gender, position, or manner of speaking. Listen without becoming defensive and remain open to new ideas and concepts.

- *Creating the proper atmosphere.* Make it easy to listen by minimizing outside distractions. Choose a suitable location and eliminate as many interruptions as possible.

- *Focusing on the speaker.* Establish and maintain eye contact. Give the speaker time to speak before beginning to question or comment. Concentrate while listening to the message's content. Avoid thinking about how to answer once the speaker is finished. If notes must be taken, keep them brief.

- *Showing concern.* Use appropriate nonverbal communication to show that the message is being received. When necessary, ask questions to obtain more information or ask that parts of the message that were not heard or understood be repeated.

**Interpreting.** Interpreting helps the listener to identify why the speaker is communicating. A manager should not judge but, instead, try to determine the speaker's meaning and confirm that understanding. Managers should keep personal biases out of the way.

Managers should try to think about the speaker's primary reason for speaking and consider what the speaker wants to get across. The speaker may be making casual conversation, expressing an idea, wanting to exchange information, or trying to persuade.

Managers should confirm that they understand the meaning of the message being spoken. They can do this by asking questions or paraphrasing (re-stating or re-wording) the speaker's message. They should continue asking questions until they understand the meaning of the message and show that they understand by using suitable words and body language. The goal of the interpreting stage is for the listener and the speaker to reach a common understanding.

**Evaluating.** Evaluating helps to verify that a common understanding has been reached. It also helps the listener determine whether the message is based on facts or is just the speaker's opinion. To evaluate a message, a listener should:

- *Gather more information.* Concentrate on the speaker's tone of voice and body language and on what the speaker does and doesn't say. If only general information is provided, listeners should ask for details if given the chance (this may not be possible if the listener is part of the audience at a formal presentation).

- *Decide whether the information is genuine.* Try to separate facts from opinions and assumptions but always judge the message, not the messenger.

**Responding.** Responding during a conversation should occur while the speaker talks (with nods, smiles, and so on) and after the speaker is finished (i.e., a verbal response). After the speaker is finished, the listener's response depends on:

- *What the speaker expects.* Listeners should ask questions if they are in doubt.

- *The time and energy available.* Listeners receiving requests from a peer must decide whether their plans and schedules can or should accommodate the speaker's request. Such listeners must consider their own objectives, time pressures, and energy levels. If employees are listening to supervisors, time and energy concerns must be expressed appropriately or set aside entirely, depending on the situation.

- *Decide what to do.* At the conclusion of the message, a listener must determine how to respond and then communicate that response to the speaker. The discussion should be ended in an appropriate way that includes a concluding statement that reviews any actions to be taken.

For an example of how the four stages of listening might play out in a hospitality environment, consider a situation in which a supervisor receives directives from his or her manager and disagrees with them. First, the supervisor should clarify understanding—perhaps the supervisor simply misunderstood the manager. Second, if it is not a case of a simple misunderstanding, the supervisor should clearly express his or her concerns and reservations about the directives and provide support for those misgivings. Third, the supervisor should seek feedback from the manager and, if the supervisor succeeds in persuading the manager to reconsider the directives, he or she should help the manager explore alternatives.

## Active Listening Skills

The responsibility for effective listening rests with the listener. Fortunately, there are useful active listening tactics that listeners may employ, which include providing feedback so the speaker will know if his or her message is understood. We will look at these tactics in the following sections.

**Mirroring.** **Mirroring** (restating) involves repeating some of the speaker's key words. It suggests that the listener is interested in the speaker's words and wants to understand them. Here are two examples:

**Speaker:**  I don't think I can finish this on time without help.

**Listener:**  You don't think you can finish without help?

**Speaker:**  I'm the only one on this crew who does any work.

**Listener:**  You're the *only one* of your crew who works?

Managers should be careful not to overuse mirroring, for it may become tedious or appear as if they are speaking down to the speaker.

**Paraphrasing.** When listeners **paraphrase,** they use their own words to re-state what the speaker is saying. This is useful for several reasons. First, it helps the listener clarify what the speaker is saying. It also helps the speaker, because the paraphrase reveals how the message sounds to others. Here are two examples of paraphrasing:

**Speaker:**  I don't like this job. I try to be friendly, but my co-workers don't even notice I'm here.

**Listener:**   You feel lonely here, and that makes you dislike your job. You wish everybody would be nicer.

**Speaker:**   Cindy is hard to work with. She thinks she works harder than everybody else, and now I'm assigned to work on a committee with her.

**Listener:**   You're uncomfortable around Cindy because she doesn't seem friendly and now you need to work closely with her.

Paraphrasing is another tactic that, if used improperly or too frequently, can make it seem like the listener is talking down to the speaker, especially when phrases such as "What you really mean is ..." or "What you are trying to say is ..." are used. Those types of phrases should be avoided.

**Summarizing and Self-Disclosure. Summarizing statements** condense parts of what the speaker said and stress important points. They may be used when a listener wants to: (1) focus attention on a certain topic; (2) show agreement with specific points; (3) guide the speaker to another part of the subject; and (4) reach agreement on specific points to end the conversation. Examples of summarizing statements include the following:

"If I hear you correctly, you want to ..."

"As I understand it, your main idea is to ..."

**Self-disclosure statements** show the speaker how a listener feels about what has been said. This helps the speaker to feel understood. Examples of self-disclosure statements are:

"That reminds me of something that happened to me ..."

"Other employees have noticed the same thing ..."

Self-disclosure statements can also be used to communicate disagreement with the speaker's point and to help the speaker by underscoring sensitive areas:

"I don't necessarily agree with your second point. There is another way to look at it, however ..."

**Questioning or Clarifying.** Listeners may notice some statements that seem incomplete or do not tell the whole story. In such instances, listeners should ask questions to help the speaker clarify his or her thinking. Sometimes speakers leave out important points because they are caught up in the emotions of the moment. Questioning or clarifying statements can help make the speaker's message clearer.

**Open-ended questions** allow speakers to respond in any way they would like. Listeners can use them to move along a discussion, discover a speaker's ideas, or examine a sensitive subject. Open-ended questions often begin in these ways:

"What do you think about ..."

"How do you feel about ..."

"Can you tell me ..."

"Could you describe ..."

For example, a speaker might be asked, "How do you feel about the changes made in the shift schedule?"

Listeners may want additional information about unclear statements. In most instances they should ask for specific details when the speaker has provided only general information. Specific questions begin with words like "who," "where," "when," "why," "which," and "how many." For example, a listener might ask a speaker a specific question such as, "Why do you think the guest was unhappy?"

**Motivating the Speaker to Say More.** This tactic encourages the speaker to continue talking. When motivating a speaker to say more, listeners should use neutral words that communicate neither agreement nor disagreement. The purpose is for the listener to show interest in wanting the speaker to continue. Examples include:

"Tell me more."

"Let's talk about it."

"I'd like to hear your point of view."

Speakers can also be encouraged when the listener uses **empathy**: that is, when the listener tries to see the situation from the other person's point of view. Empathy shows that the listener accepts the speaker, can relate to the experiences and feelings being presented, and wants to hear more. Listeners who want to show empathy should use words that avoid any kind of judgment, employing phrases such as:

"I know what you mean; I've had a similar experience ..."

"I understand how you feel about ..."

# Nonverbal Communication: Body Language ─────────

The spoken word is not the only means of human expression. Some people will argue that it's not even the most important one. The old saying "Actions speak louder than words" supports this view.

Nonverbal communication, which consists largely of body language, is important in day-to-day interactions. Supervisors should interpret physical signals such as facial expressions that employees, peers, and guests send in addition to the message given with words. Exhibit 5 presents some common interpretations of nonverbal messages.

Suppose a supervisor tells Bill, an entry-level employee, that she wants him to stay for an extra hour today to do a special project. Bill says, "Sure, no problem," but when Bill turns around to leave, the supervisor can see that Bill is frowning and his hands are clenched. Reading Bill's body language, the supervisor sees that Bill is probably upset about staying later today even after saying it was no problem. Bill is a good employee and the supervisor doesn't want to lose him. However, she also needs the special project completed.

The supervisor should approach Bill, because it is important to deal with the situation before it gets out of hand. It could be that his actions may relate to something outside of work. Bill should be asked about the inconsistency between what

**Exhibit 5   Common Interpretations of Nonverbal Communication Cues**

### What You Do and What It Says

| NONVERBAL MESSAGE | TYPICAL INTERPRETATION |
|---|---|
| Making direct eye contact | Friendly, sincere, self-confident, assertive |
| Avoiding eye contact | Cold, evasive, indifferent, insecure, passive, frightened, nervous, concealment |
| Shaking head | Disagreeing, shocked, disbelieving |
| Patting on the back | Encouraging, congratulatory, consoling |
| Scratching the head | Bewildered, disbelieving |
| Smiling | Contented, understanding, encouraging |
| Biting the lip | Nervous, fearful, anxious |
| Tapping feet | Nervous |
| Folding arms | Angry, disapproving, disagreeing, defensive, aggressive |
| Raising eyebrows | Disbelieving, surprised |
| Narrowing eyebrows | Disagreeing, resentful, angry, disapproving |
| Wringing hands | Nervous, anxious, fearful |
| Leaning forward | Attentive, interested |
| Slouching in seat | Bored, relaxed |
| Sitting on edge of seat | Anxious, nervous, apprehensive |
| Shifting in seat | Restless, bored, nervous, apprehensive |
| Hunching over | Insecure, passive |
| Erect posture | Self-confident, assertive |

he said and how he is acting. For example, the supervisor might say, "Bill, you said you were okay about helping with the project and now you seem upset. May I ask why?"

As this story illustrates, the words a person speaks do not necessarily tell the whole story. We communicate with more than just our words. Our nonverbal behavior can reveal our attitudes and feelings. Even though our words may say otherwise, our true feelings are usually exposed by our nonverbal expressions and actions.

## Facial Expressions

Our facial expressions are the most common nonverbal communication we use, and they reveal a lot about our attitudes. Most people look at the listener's face when they are talking. Have you ever felt uncomfortable trying to talk to someone wearing sunglasses? Think also about how much easier it is to understand speakers when their faces can be seen. By watching facial expressions, we can know whether someone is happy, sad, angry, or confused.

Facial expressions are not always completely reliable. For example, a smile does not always indicate happiness. It can communicate anger, nervousness, defensiveness, or embarrassment, among other emotions.

The more people catch our eye and hold it, the more likely we are to pay attention to them. For example, a speaker who maintains eye contact with the audience is likely to be considered a good speaker. The reverse is also true: a speaker who looks at the floor or over the heads of the audience is likely to appear nervous and possibly unreliable.

We generally suspect that people who avoid eye contact are uneasy or perhaps lying about something. Alternatively, they may be uninterested or nervous. An assertive, confident person is likely to look into a listener's eyes, while a passive, unassertive person may avoid eye contact.

## Posture and Body Movement

A person's slumped shoulders usually communicate depression or sadness. An anxious person may move stiffly and tensely and have a grim facial expression, with his or her lips pressed tightly together and a wrinkled brow. Tense people may avoid eye contact and may stand or sit with their arms folded tightly. A relaxed person, on the other hand, generally sits and stands comfortably and gestures naturally.

A person's walk can give clues to his or her general nature. For example, a determined person will walk firmly and steadily, while an impatient, aggressive, or busy person often walks quickly. A shy, uncertain person may walk hesitantly. New guests may be uncertain as they enter the hotel's lobby, and their hesitant steps reveal that they could use some assistance or reassurance.

When speaking before a group, managers should walk toward the group to emphasize a particular issue. When managers want to de-emphasize a point or decrease tension, they should walk away from the group.

## Gestures

Gestures often reveal a lot about a person's feelings and attitudes. For example, an employee who chews his or her lips or fingernails, or repeatedly folds and unfolds a tissue, may be nervous. People may also reveal their nervousness with repetitive movements, such as swinging their feet or drumming their fingers. Repetitive gestures may also indicate impatience or uncertainty as well as nervousness.

One of the most common body language signals is when we cross our arms in front of our chests. We may use this gesture to close off the rest of the world and form a shield between ourselves and a hostile environment. For example, an employee may tightly fold his arms across his chest when a manager is discussing a performance problem. Crossed arms may also indicate anxiety or disagreement, but it is important to consider the entire context. For example, a person may simply be more comfortable sitting with his or her arms crossed.

## Body Language on the Job

Suppose you want to discipline an employee in your office. To assert your position of authority, you should sit in a chair behind your desk, while the employee sits in a chair in front of the desk. The desk serves as a barrier between you and the employee, and shows you are in charge. However, if you want to establish a more informal atmosphere, you might move your chair to the employee's side of your desk to decrease the physical and psychological distance between the two of you. This will put you and the employee on a more equal footing.

No matter what your attitude, it will show in your nonverbal behavior. If you resent an employee, it may be difficult for you to hide it. Instead of trying to conceal it, it is often better to modify your attitude. Try to find something you can admire about the employee, and then your genuine warmth will come through in your body language.

Some forms of body language send different messages in different cultures. Many supervisors facilitate the work of diverse work forces and interact with guests from different cultures. Therefore, it is important to ensure that your body language sends the right message. In some cultures, for example, it is considered improper to show the bottoms of your shoes while sitting. In others, direct eye contact is considered a challenge to the other person. People in some cultures consider it an unclean practice to touch others with one's left hand. Learn as much as you can about the employees you supervise and the guests you serve in order to avoid communication problems caused by cultural differences.

# Writing Skills

Writing is a difficult form of communication for many people to master. However, supervisors must know how to write well. The importance of writing skills increases as a manager rises to higher levels of responsibility. For example, supervisors may write memos to employees, reports for their boss, and clear, concise comments on performance appraisal forms. In contrast, higher-level managers may write letters to vendors and attorneys about matters involving high-dollar purchases and legal matters.

## Clear Writing Is Important

Supervisors must be able to express themselves effectively in writing. The messages or reports they write represent themselves and their organizations (especially if the writing will be seen by people outside the organization). Clear and organized writing is a product of the writer's clear and organized thinking. The opposite is also true: a poorly written and disorganized communication results from disorganized thinking.

A manager's written words represent him or her not only now but in the future, as any written communication can be filed away and saved. Even memos can serve as lasting reminders of a manager's writing abilities. Well-written reports suggest that the supervisor is an efficient and organized person.

Developing an outline typically is the first step in drafting a concise and well-written document. Managers should take a few minutes to list the main points to emphasize and then place those points in a logical sequence. Then they can begin the first draft, which will serve as the foundation for the finished document. Managers should go through the document several times and revise it as necessary, especially if it is important and formal. Even the best writers spend much of their time revising.

Good writers make it as easy as possible for their readers to understand their messages. Writing for easy reading doesn't come easily; however, it is a skill that can be learned.

## Business Writing Techniques

Good business writing clearly communicates information as briefly as possible to the intended readers. This requires proper grammar, spelling, and punctuation. Before they begin writing, effective writers:

- *Have a specific reader or audience in mind.* A memo to employees about vacation schedules can be far more informal than a memo to a manager about a budget issue. Know to whom you are writing, and gear your tone, language, and level of writing to the readers.

- *Know the objective.* Determine the topic and stick to it. Identifying a specific purpose for writing will help keep your thoughts and your writing clear.

- *Decide what information is essential to include.* This may involve reviewing files and speaking to others in addition to careful thought. However, supervisors typically do much of their writing without research. In any event, determining exactly what information should be included will make the writing task easier.

- *Decide how to present the information.* The best way to do this for a formal and important document is to make an **outline,** which is a list of significant points placed in logical order. When creating an outline, managers should write down the major points and, beneath them, list the supporting minor points:

  1. Major point
     A. Minor point
        i. Sub point (if any)
        ii. Sub point (if any)
     B. Minor point

  2. Major point
     A. Minor point
     B. Minor point

Managers should look at the initial outline carefully. The first outline is a good place to start but there is often a better way to organize the points than the order in which they were first put to paper (or computer screen). As they revise the outline, managers should keep to the objective and sort all the points into a logical order that supports the objective. Using an outline usually makes writing tasks easier and faster. Outlines are valuable tools because they require the writer to organize his or her thoughts. As a manager's writing skills improve, outlines may become briefer and easier to develop. However, no matter how skilled a manager becomes at business writing, it is helpful to prepare some type of outline every time something must be written, even if it is a short mental outline for an informal memo.

Good business writing requires specific and active language. Specific nouns express meanings more powerfully than general or abstract nouns. For example, it is livelier and more specific to say "I met with Terry, Sue, Steve, and Alonzo about Tuesday's banquet plans" than "I met with four supervisors about the banquet."

Use verbs in the **active voice**: the subject of the sentence does the acting. Notice the difference in the following examples:

**Passive**     The decision was made by George.

**Active**     George made the decision.

**Passive**     The employee handbook was revised by the committee.

**Active**     The committee revised the employee handbook.

**Passive**     The employee was praised by the supervisor.

**Active**     The supervisor praised the employee.

## Plain English and Short Sentences

Readers are more likely to understand a written document if the writer uses simple and familiar words and concise sentences. Make sure you understand each word as well. If you have doubts about any word, select another that you are more familiar with.

When writing, managers should use the same types of words they use when they speak and concentrate on informing readers, not on impressing them. Examples of showy words (and their plain English substitutes) include:

- Ameliorate (help, improve)
- Ascertain (find out, learn)
- Commence (begin, start)

- Endeavor (attempt, try)
- Optimal (best, finest)
- Peruse (read, study)

Short sentences are easier to read and understand than long sentences. However, not all sentences should be short, because that could be dull. A good plan: alternate long sentences with short ones.

As a general rule, limit sentences to no more than three typed lines; longer sentences contain more information than readers can easily absorb. How can long sentences be avoided? Begin by breaking a single long sentence into smaller, stronger statements by removing the words "and" and "but." Consider the following example:

> Your readers are more likely to understand your writing if you use simple words and sentences, and you should make it a point to use words that are familiar to your readers, always making sure *you* clearly understand each word, too, and if you have doubts about any word, you should always choose another that you are more familiar with.

This example is a long-winded version of the opening paragraph of this section. The fairly simple original sentences became one long complicated sentence with the addition of the words "and" and "but" in certain places. Take the time now to reread this section's opening paragraph. Then reread the long-winded, rewritten version. Isn't the original, simpler paragraph easier to understand?

Since your co-workers and other businesspeople will probably want to read your memos and other written business communications as quickly as possible, consider using the **inverted pyramid** style of writing. Newspaper reporters put their most important information at the beginning of their stories and leave less important details for the final paragraphs because they know many readers will not read the entire story. Similarly, managers should put what's most important at the beginning of their documents.

Managers should make sure every paragraph deals with a single topic. Each paragraph should begin with a strong **topic sentence** (main point) that tells what the paragraph is about. A short, simple topic sentence is stronger and easier to understand than a long one. In fact, a lengthy topic sentence may blur the intended message, so that its effectiveness may be lost.

A one-idea topic sentence limited to 1½ typed lines stays in readers' minds. The topic sentence becomes a guideline, and the writer then logically develops the rest of the paragraph. A briefly stated topic sentence also delivers clear information to the reader that gets immediately to the point. Examples of topic sentences include:

- "There are three reasons to do this; they are ..." (list them and explain them in the paragraph).

- "We have developed a new schedule plan that will ..." (review the revised plan in the paragraph).

- "The meal did not meet the guest's expectations because ..." (discuss the guest's disappointment in the paragraph).

Once you have written the topic sentence, focus on the rest of the paragraph. The remaining sentences should relate to and support the point made in the topic sentence. A topic sentence is usually more general than the sentences that support it. It may be helpful to think of a topic sentence as a generalization which needs supporting evidence. Other sentences in the paragraph will supply that evidence by providing details or back-up material. Each paragraph, then, will look something like this: Topic sentence. Detail. Detail. Detail. Detail.

## Memos

The proper length of a memo depends on its purpose. It is important, however, to keep all business documents as short as possible. As with all writing, memos should be clear, concise, and to the point. Exhibit 6 presents a sample format to use for memos (it is also useful for e-mail communications).

If the memo is long, it should be broken up into sections highlighted with headings and sub-headings. A memo's tone may be friendly, informal, and casual when it is written for co-workers. A more formal tone is necessary when writing a cover memo for an important report or when writing to a higher-level executive. (A document checklist like the one shown in Exhibit 7 can help managers make their documents the best they can be.)

**Exhibit 6    Sample Memo Format**

---

You may want to use the following sample format for memos that you write.

**MEMORANDUM**

TO:      Your Reader

FROM:  You

DATE:   Today's

RE:       Subject

Paragraph 1: Contains a clear, direct topic sentence. This paragraph **states** why you are writing. It might also explain what you want readers to do when they finish reading.

Paragraph 2: Contains the most important proof or details supporting Paragraph 1. Alternatively, it may be about another subject entirely, presented with its own clear topic sentence.

Paragraph 3: Contains less important evidence or material, supported with less detail. Again, it may address a different subject.

Final Paragraph: Acknowledges the reader's time. Requests action or repeats an earlier request.

---

**Two Versions of One Memo.** Two versions of a memo are presented in Exhibits 8 and 9. As you read the two versions, think of the writing principles you have read about in this chapter and decide which version is better before reading further in the text. We hope you quickly came to the conclusion that Version B is the best version of this memo.

*What is wrong with Version A?*

- It includes unnecessary history and detail.
- It uses too many "big" words such as inaugurated, ameliorate, cognizant, myriad, utilize, apprised, erroneous, dispensed, repercussions, and propitious.
- It doesn't get right to the point.
- There is excessive use of the passive voice.
- Its most important paragraph is the last one rather than the first one.
- It sounds too formal and pretentious.
- It is too long (it contains more than 200 words).

*What is right about Version B?*

- The most important paragraph appears first.
- It gets to the point immediately.
- Its words and sentences are easy to understand.
- It is clear, direct, and concise.
- It tells busy employees exactly what to do.
- Its tone is appropriately informal but still courteous.

**Exhibit 7  Document Checklist**

1. *Is it organized well?*
   - Did I write with my readers in mind?
   - Did I determine my objective before beginning to write?
   - Did I decide which important information to include?
   - Did I make an outline first?
   - Do I sort my ideas in a logical order?
   - Will my reader immediately know what I am writing about?
   - Does each paragraph contain a topic sentence?
   - Do other sentences in each paragraph support the topic sentence?

2. *Is it clear?*
   - Does it clearly communicate my message?
   - Do I use plain English?
   - Are my words specific? Do they mean what I think they mean?
   - Do I use concrete nouns, rather than abstract nouns?

3. *Is it concise?*
   - Do I use active verbs?
   - Are my words strong and to the point?
   - Do I use words both my reader and I understand?
   - Do I include only what my reader needs to know?
   - Are my sentences limited to three typed lines?
   - Have I eliminated unnecessary instances of *and* and *but*?
   - Have I used the inverted pyramid style of writing?

4. *Is it accurate?*
   - Is all the information in the memo/letter correct?
   - Do I use proper grammar, spelling, and punctuation?
   - Do I refer to dictionaries and grammar texts when I am uncertain?

5. *Is it courteous and friendly?*
   - Do I use positive expressions?
   - Is my writing free of bureaucratic, pretentious, and legalistic language?
   - Do I use words like "please" and "thank you"?
   - Is my tone appropriate?

- It uses language the writer probably uses when talking.
- It is short (well under 100 words).

## E-Mail

E-mail is used today for purposes previously achieved by regular mail, office memos, and telephone conversations. However, important differences do exist between these forms of communication. For example, while telephone calls may be traced and some may be recorded, *all* e-mail messages are recorded, stored,

**Exhibit 8   Document A**

---

## Document A—Original

TO:      All employees

FROM:   Chris Greene

DATE:   February 15, 20XX

RE:      Time sheets

In January the Accounting Department, because it met with difficulty processing employee paychecks on time, inaugurated an improved program devised to
ameliorate the process and get the checks out on time. Many steps were taken by
Accounting to get the process to the much-improved point at which it presently is.
These steps included redesigning the time sheets, which were double-sided and
designated Form T-300, and are now single-sided and designated Form T-310. As
you know, the time sheets had to be turned in to yours truly by 3 P.M. Wednesdays,
and then signed by me, and delivered to Accounting.

I am cognizant of the fact that myriad members of my staff are still utilizing the old
time sheets, Form T-300, instead of the new time sheets, Form T-310. I have been
apprised that your persistent use of the erroneous time sheets will have unfortu-
nate repercussions. It will doubtlessly result in the misfortune of your hours not
being processed and your paychecks not being dispensed in time.

Therefore, take judicious note of our company's revised time sheet, a copy of
which is affixed to this memo. In the future, please see to it that you utilize the new,
improved time sheet so that you will be paid in as propitious a manner as possible.

---

**Exhibit 9   Document B**

---

## Document B—Improved

TO:      All employees

FROM:   Chris Greene

DATE:   February 15, 20XX

RE:      Time sheets

Please remember to use the new version of the time sheet (copy attached). In
January, Accounting announced that the revised single-sided time sheet takes the
place of the old, double-sided time sheet.

Using the new time sheet correctly will ensure your getting your paycheck on time
every payday. Please fill out your weekly time sheet completely, sign it, and give it
to me by 3 P.M. each Wednesday.

---

and traceable. E-mails never disappear entirely; even deleted messages can be retrieved from back-ups and can usually be traced to their origin.

In short, e-mail is not a private form of communication. Once you send an e-mail, it's out of your control. With some office computer systems, the e-mail administrator can read any and all e-mail messages. Some hospitality operations monitor employee e-mail messages and have a policy about the types of messages that can be sent. A good rule to keep in mind is that if your e-mail is safe enough to be printed and posted on your property's bulletin board, it is safe enough to send. (Note: the reverse is also true! If it's not safe enough for a bulletin board for all to see, don't send it!)

You'll never know how many people actually read an e-mail that you send because it could be forwarded many times. Therefore, managers should never send confidential information or send or forward e-mails containing libelous information or defamatory, offensive, racist, or obscene jokes or remarks.

Many e-mail systems have a "blind copy" function that enables you to send an e-mail with copies sent to others without the original recipient knowing about it. This function can be useful when you want to protect the privacy of those receiving a group e-mail. However, blind copies of your e-mail could be used to spread gossip or embarrass the recipient (or even yourself) when those receiving the blind copy pass it on to others.

**Sending E-Mails.** The subject line of an e-mail should be a short, specific identification of the message's topic so readers can quickly determine the importance of the message. Also, readers may use the subject line to help them recall the content of the message. Avoid subject lines that are too informal. Recipients may think the e-mail is spam and delete it without reading it. Some users have anti-virus software programs that automatically delete or flag e-mails with informal greetings.

E-mail messages should be short and to the point, normally less than one printed page or the length of a computer screen, because many people do not like to scroll through long e-mails. If a long e-mail is necessary, include a short summary, how quickly you expect a response, and even a brief table of contents if the e-mail is extremely long. In every case, the e-mail should address a single topic; switching topics can frustrate and confuse readers. If you have two or more separate topics to address, send separate e-mails. If lengthy, critical information must be included, send it as an attachment and use the e-mail text to describe the contents or importance of the attachment.

E-mail messages are frequently printed. Typos that may be forgiven on a screen are likely to be annoying to others and embarrassing to you when seen on paper. Most e-mail programs can spell-check outgoing mail.

E-mail has become a convenient way to send files such as documents, spreadsheets, graphics, and pictures. However, don't attach unnecessary files. Large files may take up a lot of space on mail servers and impair the performance of the e-mail system.

Before sending a large file, be sure the recipient can receive it. You may have to break up the file into smaller attachments and send a series of e-mails. When receiving attachments, it's best to save them to your hard drive as soon as possible and then delete the message and attachment from your mail box.

**Replying to E-Mails.** Senders generally expect a quick response to their e-mails. Reply to e-mail messages as soon as possible, preferably within twenty-four hours. If you can't reply within a day, send a message telling the person when you will respond. It is usually best to respond with the "reply" function and not start a new e-mail message. The reply function retains the original message as a "string" and often helps the person you are answering place your response in the context of their original message. Attempt to make your reply immediately understandable without referring the recipient to the original e-mail or to an e-mail string.

In some situations, it is necessary and appropriate to use the "Reply to All" function. This keeps everyone on the initial e-mail list up-to-date with your reply. More often, it is not necessary to clog everyone's inbox with lengthy e-mail threads. Use this function with care. Reply only to those who need to hear what you have to say.

Forward messages only to appropriate recipients. Never forward messages with personal content in them without obtaining permission from the author. If, before forwarding an e-mail, you edit the message, be sure to explain what you have done.

# Important Workplace Communication Issues

Effective communication procedures are very important in maintaining and improving positive relationships among staff members. Managers who consistently use the basic communication practices discussed in this chapter will be well on their way to enjoying the benefits that accrue when managers and employees work together as teams to attain goals. Basic communication skills are also important when planning and participating in negotiation sessions of all types.

## Relationships Between Employees

Supervisors model the behaviors they expect from the organization's employees when they treat their employees the way that they (the managers) would like to be treated—and as they expect employees to treat the property's guests. Managers can also reinforce desired behaviors when they engage in positive coaching, telling employees when they "catch them doing something right," and developing a practical rewards system for successful employees. Training and professional programs are useful ways to show employees that they are appreciated and that the organization's managers want them to be successful. These developmental efforts help the organization and its members at the same time they benefit manager-employee relationships.

Effective managers communicate a clear vision of where they want to lead their employees. They talk frequently about how to move toward the organization's vision, and they request input from their employees along the journey. They prepare their employees for the work to be done, establish performance guidelines and procedures, and recognize that employees do not need to be micro-managed. In other words, managers prepare their employees, point them in the right direction, and allow them to perform.

Managers who have a positive attitude avoid judging others and are more accepting of those on their staffs. They quickly resolve conflicts with a plan of action that involves discussion with the affected employees. These managers help employees find pride and happiness in their work by treating them with genuine respect. They do this by paying attention to their employees, listening to them, and responding according to their employees' needs. Good managers seek to understand and accept their employees' personal and cultural differences because they know this encourages a professional relationship that focuses on achieving goals.

Managers who are effective communicators are better leaders in their organizations. They can present ideas, improve working relationships, and tactfully disagree, when necessary, while continually moving others toward the organization's goals. They can make excellent oral and written presentations, they can negotiate for "win-win" conclusions, and they use their interpersonal skills to improve the working relationships between themselves and their employees and between employees in different departments. As they do so, they model desired performance by maintaining consistency between what they say and what they do.

Managers can communicate with their staffs through scheduled meetings, e-mail, employee newsletters, and other methods to keep everyone current with changes and challenges. They should have an "open door" policy and strive to talk with employees when employees want to talk, not when the managers "get around to it." Managers should, whenever possible, address employee-related situations themselves and involve those at higher organizational levels only when necessary.

In addition to encouraging open communication, the best managers clearly communicate and explain the organization's policies and culture to their staff members. Their goal: to reduce the possibility that employees will make assumptions, communicate about them throughout the "**grapevine,**" and create communication obstacles that will be difficult to overcome.

Suggestions to improve relationships with specific employees include the following:

- Be positive and not judgmental.

- Gather as much information as possible to understand the situations that are creating the conflict.

- Resolve conflicts when they first occur. A thorough discussion, development of a mutual plan to address the problem, and working together to resolve it are useful tactics.

Managers should accept the responsibility to establish and maintain cooperative interpersonal relationships with each member of their employee team. They should not discuss employee-related problems with other employees, but only with other managers as part of the property's progressive discipline process.

Effective managers try to find solutions to employee problems rather than blame employees or rationalize that the workplace would be improved if one or more employees were not part of the team. They also recognize that problems represent growth opportunities, and they work with employees to manage the problems that arise.

# Technology and Communication

Technology has dramatically changed how we communicate in our personal and professional lives, and it has even revised the ways we think and talk about the process. Communication that does not involve talking can occur instantly, and this fact is changing what we communicate. For example, people have historically used communication media to transfer big chunks of information infrequently (think paper-based letters and reports); now, smaller amounts of information can be sent much more frequently (think messages on Twitter and Facebook). Increasingly, many people are in contact with many other people almost constantly all around the world. Once a communications device (computer, smart phone) has been purchased and the monthly fee for voice and data transfer paid, the further cost to communicate is typically nothing; this may be driving the trend of people sharing many small bits of news about almost anything at any time. The technology/communication phenomenon is so great that many people reallocate their budgets to give priority to communication expenses.

## Revolutionary Communication Changes

Changes in communication have been revolutionary (not evolutionary) since the 1990s. It began with e-mail messages on computers that some persons did (and some still do) read only once or twice a day. In contrast, for many people today these messages are checked and read many times each hour on mobile phones and other devices. Instant messaging alternatives have, within just a few years, brought down message receipt and response times from several days or even weeks (letters) to hours (e-mail) to virtually instant communication (minutes, if not seconds).

The goal of any type of communication is to be understood, and there can be many obstacles to overcome when the communication process takes place online. In recent years many discussions have occurred about how communication alternatives (for example, face-to-face meetings versus virtual meetings held online, the use of a telephone versus instant messaging for one-on-one conversations) affect understanding. These are important concerns, because the Internet has forever changed how people communicate.

Most of us are familiar with and are probably users of Internet calling services such as Skype that allow people to create a video phone with a computer, webcam, and headset. Blogs are now a common way for people to broadcast ideas very widely and very quickly, and, typically, to receive message responses on an ongoing and often real-time basis. Blogs allow people to inform others or to learn from others about an incredibly wide variety of topics helpful in one's profession or of interest to one on a personal level.

Interactions with other people for both professional and social reasons are a prime reason why online social media outlets are becoming so popular. Connections among people in these online spaces involve personal and professional conversations, attendance at training workshops, and the instant sharing of news and other information.

Today, news from the world's trouble spots is shared globally by those who are there. This massive and ongoing output informs others, and also shapes the reactions of those in charge and those around the world who have become aware of the news.

The Internet allows people to communicate in numerous ways on social sites such as Facebook and in virtual environments where they can represent themselves with a personal profile or an avatar. People have communication options ranging from text and voice chat to public message boards and/or private messaging. Still other nontraditional communication channels exist that allow users to express themselves in creative ways; examples of such channels are YouTube for movies and Flicker for photos.

Online communication broadens the methods through which people provide information to others. For example, traditional communication methods involved only voice, body language, and text exchanges. Now people can integrate these methods, and communication no longer must be confined to one method at a time. A person can post a blog message to a professional group, transmit tweets (140-character messages sent through Twitter) to a family member, send an instant message to another person, and begin a Skype call at almost the same time. Moving between these and other media alternatives is quick and easy. The choice of method(s) basically depends on the person with whom one wants to communicate, the length and nature of the message, and the amount of time that can or should be spent during the interaction. The ability to do this multi-tasking is becoming more seamless almost every day as new communication tools and applications are introduced.

**More About Communication Changes**

Television, radio, newspapers, and magazines are able to reach out to many people but, with a few exceptions such as newspapers' "letters to the editor" and call-in radio shows, they are mostly one-way communication channels. People cannot usually respond to the message sender through these communication media, nor can they communicate with each other. Today, web-enabled social media outlets like Facebook and Twitter allow a different type of communication. People can send and receive messages and communicate with many people at the same time. The mobile phone made communication between people almost instantaneous from almost anywhere, so today there are numerous kinds of conversations happening at multiple levels all the time.

People such as bloggers, posters on Facebook, and broadcasters on YouTube have the ability to influence many people, and the roles of centralized communication channels such as public relations and marketing teams in organizations are changing. Any employee can easily communicate with the external world via powerful social media channels, so media policies are now increasingly necessary to guide employees about what they can and cannot discuss beyond the organization.

The choice of so many different available media allows users to determine which to select, based, in part, on the amount they want to make the communication more personal and the extent of interaction desired with the message receiver. Let's look at five examples of ways people communicate using the many alternatives open to them today:

*(continued)*

*(continued)*

- Twitter is often an excellent choice for sending and receiving short and publicly viewable messages. Its public reply feature provides an easy means for people to interact with public figures and with others they do not personally know. Tweets can, therefore, be a starting point for the possibility of more direct communication.

- After a relationship is established through public communication, the next step may be a direct message within a social network. This provides a private connection that is probably preferable to e-mail because it can only come from people you follow.

- E-mail allows for more in-depth communication, can be easily forwarded, and can be sent to many people at once. If it is used skillfully, it is a great means of communication.

- The use of a phone allows one to hear a person's voice, which provides greater context for communication than written words. A phone allows for immediate back-and-forth communication and is more private than the earlier communication methods mentioned.

- Face-to-face communication was historically the entry point of relationships but, today, often evolves at later stages of a relationship after people have communicated in other ways.

Technological innovations in communication media will continue to be rolled out to the public at a fast pace. There is no question that technology has changed how and why people communicate. Many of these impacts have and will continue to affect hospitality and other business organizations. Successful supervisors will embrace these changes rather than fear or avoid them. As they do so in a planned and organized way, they and their properties will benefit.

## Relationships Between Departments

Hospitality organizations with many or even just a few departments can suffer from inter-departmental communication challenges. Communication can suffer when there are personal conflicts between managers in different departments who do not see the importance of communicating with managers in other departments. Problems also occur when the organization's standard operating procedures do not address the need for departments to communicate with each other.

Problems can also arise when department personnel blame each other for the property's problems. For example, marketing and sales personnel might believe that, if the physical facilities were better maintained and if higher-quality services and amenities were provided, it would be easier to increase business volumes. At the same time, the property's department managers may believe the marketing and sales team does not plan and implement creative programs that are equal to or better than their competitors' programs.

Several strategies can be used to improve inter-departmental communication:

- A process should be in place in which personnel in each department identify exactly what information they need that is generated by or dependent upon another department. Once identified, employees within affected departments can design procedures and/or systems to provide this information. Standard operating procedures can also be revised to identify where information should flow between departments and outline ways to facilitate that flow.

- Departmental meetings can be held to identify factors that hinder cooperation between departments.

- Property-wide events can be scheduled that allow managers, supervisors, and employees from all departments to get to know each other. It's possible that even in small hospitality operations, some employees may not know each other. For example, employees working on the front desk in the morning may rarely if ever see staff members who work the front desk's evening shift.

- Supervisors can use **cross-functional teams** to address issues. This problem-solving approach occurs when employees from different departments provide input to the resolution of problems that may impact those in other departments.

- Managers can encourage employees to volunteer for projects that help the local community or a civic-service group, or even plan and undertake property-sponsored projects to help local causes or organizations. While participating in these worthwhile endeavors, employees who may not interact very much at the property can get to know each other better.

## Negotiations

Just as with all organizations, negotiations are a part of the hospitality world and can range from high-level negotiations involving top managers and important property-wide issues to informal, casual negotiations between managers or other staff members trying to resolve minor challenges that come up while they are performing their everyday jobs. The negotiation process helps the involved parties reach an agreement about something while bargaining for advantages in line with their own interests. Successful negotiators know the importance of effective communication and compromise during the negotiation process.

When managers negotiate with others, there are three possible outcomes:

- An agreement is reached.

- The negotiation is unsuccessful but the parties agree to continue negotiating at some future time.

- The parties "agree to disagree" and the negotiation process ends with no agreement.

The best negotiators understand that a long-term relationship between the parties is not possible when one party "wins" and the other "loses." Negotiations with "win-win" outcomes are generally the best.

The success or failure of most negotiations is influenced by the negotiators' skill levels and by the extent to which their personalities are compatible. Three other factors include each negotiator's expectations about the other party's intentions, the extent to which the negotiators are committed to their positions, and their ability to use persuasion to influence the other party and move them toward an agreement.

Effective negotiators are effective communicators. They are excellent speakers and listeners, and they can organize their thoughts before expressing them. They know how to use facts, they can build good interpersonal relationships, and they are effective decision-makers.

There are three basic elements to any formal negotiation session:

- *Preparation.* Managers should find out as much as possible about the situation before beginning a negotiation session, whether the negotiation will involve bargaining to reach a final sales price for an equipment item or attempting to resolve a dispute between staff members. They must also have an ideal outcome in mind; this will help guide the preparation process. Details must be thought through and priorities set. For example, a long-term warranty on an equipment purchase may be more important than fast delivery. Before negotiations begin, managers should identify their final fall-back position—that is, the point beyond which they will not compromise.

- *The negotiation session.* It is important that the manager negotiates with someone who has the authority to make a decision. In a purchasing situation, for example, this may be a vendor's representative, or it may be the sales manager, or even the company's owner.

  All negotiation sessions have a beginning, middle, and end—that is, a period where introductory remarks are made, the heart of the session in which the most serious discussion takes place, and a conclusion during which an agreement is finalized if the negotiation session went well, or arrangements are made to continue the negotiations if an agreement was not reached. Hopefully, the dialogue will be maintained on a professional level throughout all three stages and will prove helpful to both parties. The negotiation session is when the manager's communication skills such as questioning, listening, and observing become very important. The appropriate use of body language is another important communication skill when negotiating.

- *Follow-up to the negotiation.* Final steps in the negotiation process include confirming "who promised to do what and by when." A written summary of the negotiation session may be useful, as well as a self-evaluation of how the property manager could have improved his or her performance. These documents may be beneficial when the manager prepares for future negotiations.

Successful negotiators are patient. They do not typically accept the first offer, and their goal is to give up something of lesser importance in order to gain something of greater importance. They want to learn the other party's position before they indicate their own. Successful negotiators stay focused on their goals, they know the facts about the situation from their pre-session preparation, and they are aware of all of their options—including the option of ending the negotiation session without an agreement.

 **Key Terms**

**active voice**—In the active voice, the subject of the sentence does the acting. The active voice is usually stronger because it is more direct and uses fewer words than the passive voice.

**cross-functional team**—A group of employees from different departments that provides input to the resolution of inter-departmental problems.

**downward communication**—The passage of information from an organization's higher levels to its lower levels.

**empathy**—The ability to see circumstances from the other's viewpoint or to understand the other's feelings.

**feedback**—The reaction of a listener or reader to the verbal and nonverbal communication of a speaker or writer. Feedback may evaluate something the speaker/writer said or did, and may provide corrective information.

**grapevine**—An informal communication network within an organization.

**inverted pyramid**—A style of writing that many newspaper reporters and other writers use; it involves putting the most important information at the beginning of a written piece and leaving less important details for the final paragraphs. Reporters write with the knowledge that readers may skip closing paragraphs or that editors may delete them to fit available space.

**lateral communication**—The passage of information between peers at the same organizational level.

**mirroring**—Repeating a speaker's key words to show the speaker how they sound. Mirroring indicates the listener's interest in the speaker's words and desire to understand them. Mirroring helps both the listener and the speaker determine the importance of the key words the speaker uses. Also called restating.

**nonverbal communication (body language)**—The facial expressions, gestures, and body movements a person uses, including eye contact and posture. Our body language may contradict our words or reveal information we don't intend to reveal. We can hear certain types of nonverbal communication, such as laughter, weeping, whistling, or tone of voice.

**open-ended questions**—Questions that permit free, unstructured responses. Such questions are broad and encourage responses of more than just a few words.

**outline**—A list of significant points helpful when writing a memo, letter, or report. An outline helps the writer organize his or her thoughts before actually starting to write.

**paraphrasing**—Using your own words to restate what a speaker just said, or to reflect the content of the speaker's message as well as the feeling behind the content. Paraphrasing helps the listener clarify to him- or herself what the speaker is saying. It also helps the speaker, because a paraphrase reveals how the speaker's message sounds to the listener.

**self-disclosure statements**—Statements you can use to show a speaker how you feel about what he or she said. When you report experiences or feelings similar to the speaker's, it shows the speaker that he or she is not the only one to think or feel a certain way.

**summarizing statements**—Statements that condense parts of what the speaker said and stress important points. Summarizing statements are used to focus attention on a certain topic, to guide the speaker to another part of the subject, and to reach agreement on specific points in order to end the conversation.

**topic sentence**—A sentence that contains the main point of a paragraph and shows what a paragraph is about. Using the topic sentence as a guideline, a writer can logically develop the rest of the paragraph.

**upward communication**—The passage of information from an organization's lower levels to its higher levels.

 **Review Questions**

1. What are three types of business communication?

2. What are some of the commonly believed myths about communication?

3. What are some barriers to effective communication?

4. How can managers become more effective speakers?

5. What are some common obstacles to listening?

6. What are some active listening skills?

7. How can knowledge of nonverbal communication (body language) help managers on the job?

8. How can managers make their business writing more effective?

9. What are some special considerations to keep in mind when sending e-mails?

10. What are some interpersonal communication skills that can help managers more effectively deal with workplace communication issues?

 **Internet Sites**

For more information, visit the following Internet sites. Remember that Internet addresses can change without notice. If the site is no longer there, you can use a search engine to look for additional sites.

Editorial Service
www.editorialservice.com/11ways.html
Eleven ways to improve business writing skills.

Writing Help Central
www.writinghelp-central.com/index.html
Shaun Fawcett's website offers tips, advice, pointers, information, and templates for all types of business writing.

HyperGrammar
www.uottawa.ca/academic/arts/writcent/hypergrammar/
The Writing Centre at the University of Ottawa offers an online reference for developing grammar, punctuation, and writing skills.

The University of Western Ontario
www.sdc.uwo.ca/writing/index.html?handouts
Student Development Services provides easy-to-use, helpful information on a variety of topics related to effective writing.

E-Mail Replies
www.emailreplies.com
This site explains how to send effective e-mail replies. It discusses why e-mail etiquette is necessary, lists e-mail etiquette rules, and explains how to enforce these rules by creating a company e-mail policy.

Yale University Library
www.library.yale.edu/training/netiquette/index.html
Guidelines for e-mail etiquette.

# Chapter 3 Outline

The Supervisor and Human Resources
Learning from Employee Turnover
Making Jobs Easier to Fill
  Flex-Time
  Compressed Schedules
  Job Sharing
Internal Recruiting
  Develop a Career Ladder
  Inventory Employees' Skills
  Cross Train Employees
  Post Job Openings
External Recruiting
  Friends/Relatives of Employees
  Work-Study Programs
  Networking
Technology and Recruiting
  Potential Concerns
Interviewing Applicants
  Beginning the Interview
  Conducting the Interview
  Questioning Techniques
  Closing the Interview
  Following Up
The Selection Decision
The Supervisor and Human Resources
  Planning
  Short-Range Approach
  Long-Range Approach
  Supervisor's Role

# Competencies

1. Describe how supervisors work with the human resources department to recruit new employees. (pp. 69–72)

2. Explain how supervisors can make vacant positions easier to fill. (pp. 72–74)

3. Identify the advantages and disadvantages of internal recruiting. (pp. 74–77)

4. Identify the advantages and disadvantages of external recruiting. (pp. 77–79)

5. Review the role of technology in employee recruitment. (pp. 79–83)

6. Describe what supervisors should do before, during, and after interviewing applicants. (pp. 83–93)

7. Explain how supervisors can contribute to human resources planning. (pp. 93–95)

# 3

# Recruitment and Selection Procedures

LARGE OPERATIONS generally have **human resources departments** that advise and assist other departments. Human resources specialists can help you (as a supervisor) define, identify, and recruit the types of employees your department needs. Human resources staff is involved in many aspects of every employee's work at your property. Examples include activities and responsibilities related to wage and salary compensation, benefits, employee relations, training programs, performance reviews, company policies and procedures, and motivation.

As a supervisor, you must understand the basic policies and procedures that human resources staff use when recruiting and selecting job candidates. If you understand how the human resources department operates, you will more likely know how to work with it to meet your needs.

Attitudes toward human resources personnel, such as, "My work would be much easier if they sent me good employees"; "What do I know? They're the specialists!"; and, "They don't care about my problems!" are common in some operations. You play a very critical role in recruitment efforts because you must explain the basic skills and abilities needed to perform the job effectively.

You direct your employees' activities. You must select the applicants most qualified for particular positions and give careful attention to the process through which individuals join your company. This might sound simple, but it is often difficult because of the many other daily demands on your time.

## The Supervisor and Human Resources

Most supervisors work in **line department** positions. A line department, also called an operating department, directly provides products and/or services to guests. Human resources specialists perform a **staff department** function. They are technical specialists who serve in an advisory role and provide direct support to you and other supervisors, managers, and employees.

The human resources department is responsible for helping you find the most qualified applicants for open positions. The final selection of an applicant should rest with you and your boss in the line department. You, in turn, must provide information that will help the human resources department do its job. If members of the human resources department understand exactly what you need, they will have an easier time screening out applicants who do not qualify.

Open channels of communication help establish cooperation. Also, human resources department personnel need time to recruit applicants. While occasional emergencies occur, you will often have advance notice of expected openings. Give this information to the human resources department as soon as possible. By following all policies and procedures your property requires, you can help ensure that your requests are handled completely and in an orderly manner.

You can help human resources department staff members by providing current and accurate job descriptions and job specifications. A **job description** is a written summary of the duties, responsibilities, working conditions, and activities of a specific job. While formats for job descriptions vary throughout the industry, Exhibit 1 presents a sample job description for a restaurant server. If you work for a large property, the human resources department will help you prepare job descriptions.

A **job specification** is a selection tool that lists the critical knowledge, skills, abilities, and experience that employees need to perform a specific job adequately. For instance, if a cook must read and adjust recipes, the job specification for this position should include those skills. Exhibit 1 shows possible job specification information for a restaurant server.

Sometimes human resources employees use outdated job information when recruiting because the requesting department fails to submit current job descriptions. When this happens, a big difference might exist between how the job is described to applicants and what the work is actually like. Job specifications must likewise be accurate. As tasks, related duties, and necessary equipment change, so do the skills needed to effectively perform the job. The human resources department must know about these changes to make the best possible placements.

Find out what basic recruitment procedures your property uses. Employee recruitment is the process by which qualified applicants are sought and screened to fill currently or soon-to-be open positions. The process involves announcing or advertising job openings and evaluating applicants to determine whom to hire. As noted earlier, you should be directly involved in recruiting and selecting your staff because you have first-hand knowledge about each job in your department. Moreover, you will have to work closely with new employees as you train and supervise them.

Human resources personnel should refer only the top applicants to you for follow-up interviewing. After you interview them, the human resources staff can help you make the final hiring decision. Your department, not human resources, should extend employment offers to a candidate. The employee/supervisor relationship begins at this point.

In addition to recruiting, human resources personnel can help screen all applicants, establish employee records, and provide general property orientation. Further, they might help you develop and implement appropriate training programs. You must cooperate with human resources to develop a fully productive department.

You might be able to suggest where and how to recruit potential employees. For example, you might know that many of your good employees came from a particular school or vocational training program. Suggest these sources to human resources. In addition, tell current employees about position openings. They might

**Exhibit 1    Sample Job Description: Restaurant Server**

**Position Title:** Restaurant Server

**Reports to:** Dining Room Manager

**Tasks:**

1.   Greets guests and presents them with the menu; informs guests of specials and menu changes; makes suggestions and answers questions regarding food, beverages, and service.

2.   Takes food and beverage orders from guests and relays orders to kitchen staff and the bartender as appropriate.

3.   Ensures that all food and beverage items are prepared properly and on a timely basis; communicates with the host, buspersons, kitchen staff, and the bartender; and coordinates his or her assigned station to ensure guest satisfaction with the food and beverage products and service.

4.   Serves courses from kitchen and service areas promptly and properly presents them to guests.

5.   Observes guests to ensure their satisfaction with the food and service, to respond to any additional requests, and to determine when the meal has been completed.

6.   Totals guest bills and accepts payments or refers guests to the cashier or host as appropriate.

7.   Assists buspersons with stocking side stations, removing soiled dishes and flatware from tables at the conclusion of each course, transporting soiled items to the dishwashing area, and cleaning and resetting tables.

**Job Specification:**

**Education:**      High school graduate or equivalent; must be able to speak, read, write, and understand the primary language(s) of the work location; must be able to speak and understand the primary language(s) of the guests who typically visit the restaurant; must be able to perform simple mathematical calculations.

**Experience:**     Should have first-hand knowledge of the sequence of service and basic dining room procedures; experience as a busperson helpful; must be guest-sensitive and possess a sense of timing to serve different courses at the proper time.

**Physical:**       Must be able to move quickly and stand for periods of up to four (4) hours; must have a good sense of balance and be able to lift and carry trays and bus tubs that frequently weigh up to 25 pounds.

know eligible individuals who would like to apply, and they might also have ideas about other recruitment sources.

If your property does not have a human resources department, you could be involved in initial interviewing and reference checking. If your property has a human resources department, you (and perhaps your boss) should interview top candidates the department sends to you. It is extremely important to meet with applicants to discuss job-related matters and to answer any questions they might have about the workplace in general.

## Learning from Employee Turnover

Effective recruitment and selection procedures help bring the best applicants to the job; the skillful use of basic supervisory principles helps retain these employees. However, given the high **turnover** rates at many properties, there will always be some staff members who terminate employment for a variety of reasons. In addition, the property itself might initiate separation, perhaps because of an employee's performance.

Follow consistent procedures when employees leave. Through **exit interviews** you or others might be able to figure out why employees leave. When employees feel they have nothing to lose, they are much more likely to be honest about why they are resigning.

The exit interview should be conducted by someone other than the employee's immediate supervisor. A resigning employee might be more honest with a human resources specialist or the manager from another department. A sample format for an exit interview is shown in Exhibit 2. Conducted properly, exit interviews can help identify organizational problems. Also, you might learn information that will improve work conditions and reduce turnover rates. Information from these interviews can lead to major improvements in the way your organization deals with its employees.

## Making Jobs Easier to Fill

Your department will have an easier time locating qualified candidates if it makes working at the property as attractive as possible. To achieve this end, supervisors can take certain actions, including setting up alternative work schedules that meet the needs of the department and the employees. Options include flex-time, compressed schedules, and job sharing.

### Flex-Time

Flex-time lets employees vary their times of arrival and departure. Each shift usually has a period of time during which all employees must be present. Perhaps the other hours can be flexible. For instance, if the hours between 10 A.M. and 2 P.M. are usually very busy, flexible starting hours might be from 7 A.M. to 10 A.M. Flexible ending hours could be scheduled after 2 P.M. The actual schedule will depend on each employee's status (for example, full-time or part-time), allowed breaks, and specific business volumes for the work shift.

## Exhibit 2 Sample Exit Interview Form

**EMPLOYEE EXIT INTERVIEW**

We would like our organization to be an outstanding place to work and would sincerely appreciate your frank appraisal and honest answers to the following questions. This report is confidential.

Name

Supervisor      Department

I. Please indicate below the reason you decided to leave.

| | | | |
|---|---|---|---|
| 1. ☐ Another Job | 7. ☐ Dissatisfied with Company |
| 2. ☐ Dissatisfied with Supervisor | 8. ☐ Salary |
| 3. ☐ Leaving City | 9. ☐ Transportation |
| 4. ☐ Released | 10. ☐ No chance for Advancement |
| 5. ☐ Short Time Temporary | 11. ☐ Lack of Work (Boredom) |
| 6. ☐ Return to School | 12. ☐ Other (Explain below) |

II. 1. Was your job accurately explained to you at the time of your employment? ☐ Yes ☐ No
2. Did you receive accurate job training? ☐ Yes ☐ No
3. Was your pay adequate for the job you were doing? ☐ Yes ☐ No
4. When difficult problems came up in your work, or things went wrong, how free did you feel about asking questions?

     ☐ Not Free At All      ☐ Reasonably Free
     ☐ Immediate Supervisor      ☐ Completely Free
          Hard To Approach

5. What is your opinion of the Company's general working conditions?

     ☐ Good      ☐ Fair      ☐ Poor

6. Did you understand the importance of your job? ☐ Yes ☐ No
7. How long did you work with us? _____ Years _____ Months
8. Did you feel a part of the Company? ☐ Yes ☐ No
9. What did you like about your job?

10. How would you rate your Supervisor?

     ☐ Does Excellent Job      ☐ Below Average
     ☐ Satisfactory      ☐ Poor

11. Is there anything the Company could have done, other than salary, to make your stay a more lasting one?

12. Is there anything else you would like to say?

     Employee's Signature

Interviewer_____ Date_____
Comments: _____

Flex-time schedules allow staggered work shifts that are directed by the changing work needs during each shift. For example, one employee might start at 7 A.M. and leave at 3:30 P.M. Another could begin at 10 A.M. and finish at 6:30 P.M. Such an arrangement can improve employee morale and performance. It could also benefit the department because the need for overtime pay might decrease. These schedules do require that supervisors give careful thought to ensuring the correct number of employee hours is scheduled during each work shift's "peaks and valleys."

## Compressed Schedules

**Compressed schedules** let employees work the number of hours in a standard workweek in less than the usual five days. For example, full-time employees might work four ten-hour days. Unlike flex-time schedules, compressed work schedules do not change. However, many employees would rather take an extra day off with a compressed work schedule than work flexible hours. Benefits of compressed schedules can include enhanced recruiting power, decreased absenteeism, and greater employee satisfaction.

## Job Sharing

In **job sharing,** two or more part-time employees assume the responsibilities of one full-time job. The job sharers can each be responsible for all duties of the job, or they might divide duties between themselves. The job sharers usually work different hours each day or on completely different days.

Job sharing can reduce burnout, absenteeism, and turnover. In addition, it provides for job continuity. If one participant leaves, the other can pick up the slack and also train a newly hired staff member. Furthermore, the participants might be willing to fill in for each other on sick days or during vacations. Finally, both might work extra hours when your property is busiest.

Before you decide to adopt job sharing for your department, you'll need to make several preparations. These include assigning responsibility for specific tasks, deciding how to evaluate the employees, and ensuring the job sharers and their work standards are compatible. In addition, while a job sharing program offers many advantages, the property must consider the program's effect on the costs of fringe benefits before adopting it.

# Internal Recruiting

Your property might use various recruiting techniques to fill jobs quickly with qualified applicants. One tactic is **internal recruiting.** The benefits of internal recruiting include improved employee morale and motivation, and ready access to a skilled pool of applicants already familiar with the property.

Internal recruiting gives you an opportunity to reward good employees with new job responsibilities, while simultaneously opening up lower-level positions for new employees. You can give your current employees opportunities to develop new and existing skills. Implementation of some of these techniques is within your reach. Exhibit 3 lists some of the advantages and disadvantages of internal recruiting.

**Exhibit 3   Advantages and Disadvantages of Internal Recruiting**

**Advantages**

- Improves the morale of the promoted employee.

- Improves the morale of other employees who see future opportunities for themselves.

- Managers can better assess the abilities of internal recruits, since their performances have been observed over time.

- Internal recruiting for supervisory and management positions results in a succession of promotions (one to fill each vacated job), which reinforces the "internal career ladder."

- The cost of internal recruitment is lower than the cost of external recruitment.

**Disadvantages**

- Internal recruiting promotes "inbreeding."

- Internal recruiting can cause morale problems among those employees who were skipped over for promotion.

- Internal recruiting can have political overtones; some employees attribute internal promotions to friendships with managers and supervisors.

- Filling a gap in one department through internal recruiting may create an even more critical gap in another department.

Steps you can take to implement procedures for internal recruiting include:

- Develop a career ladder.
- Inventory employees' skills.
- Cross train employees.
- Post job openings.

## Develop a Career Ladder

Working with the human resources department or with your own boss, you might be able to develop a career ladder program specific to your property. With this program, an employee who consistently meets or surpasses performance standards can train for progressively more responsible positions. Good employees are hard to find. You can encourage them to stay by offering advancement opportunities. **Lateral transfers** from one section or department to another at the same level of responsibility are also possible.

Advantages of internal promotions following a career ladder track include improved employee morale and productivity. As employees see themselves and others being promoted to higher levels of responsibility with better pay, their feelings about themselves, their work, and their employer improve. As a result, employees might stay with the property longer. Also, lateral transfers send the message to employees that your property cares about their development and supports their efforts to broaden their work experience.

## Inventory Employees' Skills

Successful internal recruiting relies on accurate and up-to-date lists designed to evaluate the skills of current employees. Some properties actually have a higher number of skilled employees than managers and supervisors realize. This is because no one has taken the time to develop skills inventories. You can take the initiative. For example, during performance evaluations, you can ask employees if they have skills they are not using to their full potential. Perhaps you could assign employees to jobs elsewhere in your department when opportunities to use their skills arise. If employees are not given opportunities to use their professional skills, they might become less interested in their current jobs. Eventually, they might leave the property. To avoid this unwanted turnover, notify other departments if you think your employees would be better off in alternate positions within the property.

Working with your staff, you should be able to anticipate the ability of current employees to acquire new skills. Even though a property might have a firm policy of filling positions only with qualified individuals, some current employees might be able to earn these qualifications through training and acquire the necessary skills to do a more responsible job.

## Cross Train Employees

Whenever possible, train your employees to do more than one job in your department. Both your department and your employees will benefit from such **cross training.** You will have well-rounded employees who can substitute for others when you are short-handed. The employees, in turn, acquire valuable skills, increasing their value to you and to the property. In addition, employees will feel more challenged and valued as a result of their expanded skills and capabilities. With the shortage of qualified applicants, cross training is becoming increasingly critical to the success of many properties.

Remember to train current employees, not just new ones. Training is most effective if it is offered continuously. Most positions are complicated, and requirements for positions might change. Use continuous employee development programs to improve the skills of employees who might deserve promotion. Moreover, employees promoted to new positions will probably need additional training to carry out their new responsibilities.

## Post Job Openings

Posting job openings might reduce the property's turnover at some levels. Some employees might want to transfer to another department or into yours, or wish to step into higher positions. Employees applying for other jobs within your property or company deserve the same courtesy and respect you give outside applicants.

If the job goes to someone else, truthfully explain your reasons to other employees who applied. Try to understand and respond to your employees' needs. If employees do not qualify for open positions, help them develop skills that can prepare them for future openings.

Post job openings for all employees to see, making information available to everyone. Internal recruiters should post open positions as soon as they learn about them. When practical, the property should maintain internal job postings for a certain time before advertising for outside applicants. Choose a posting location visible to all employees, such as the department bulletin board or the property's employee dining area. If your property has a blog or intranet system, use these or other electronic alternatives as well.

When open positions are effectively announced, your employees will be aware of opportunities. However, unnecessary human resources paperwork might result if job requirements are not clearly stated. This is because unqualified employees might apply and then need to be processed. Another way to communicate job openings is for higher-level management to inform other supervisors about open positions and ask them to provide the names of qualified employees to human resources or the requesting department.

# External Recruiting

In addition to internal recruiting, your property should have strategies for recruiting outside applicants. Because they offer different insights, they will help your property stay up to date, and might introduce creative and better ways of doing things. New employees can contribute fresh ideas to your department. Exhibit 4 presents some of the advantages and disadvantages of external recruiting.

Three common sources of externally recruited employees are:

- Friends/relatives of current employees
- Educational work-study programs
- Networking

## Friends/Relatives of Employees

There are advantages and disadvantages to employing friends and relatives of current staff members. One advantage is that current employees already understand the job requirements and know what it is like to work for the property. If employees are impressed with the workplace, they might recruit their friends. Also, if current employees are good workers, they might have friends and relatives of the same caliber.

One disadvantage is that, if several friends or family members work for the operation, what affects one might affect them all. For example, if one member of the group is reprimanded, the entire group could react negatively.

## Work-Study Programs

Many high schools and colleges offer work-study or **internship programs.** These programs let students acquire practical work experience while earning school

**Exhibit 4    Advantages and Disadvantages of External Recruiting**

**Advantages**

- External recruiting brings new people with new ideas into the company.

- Recruits from the outside can often provide news about how and what competitors are doing.

- External recruits can provide a fresh look, which sometimes reinforces the reasons current employees work for you. Consider, for example, the value of an external recruit saying such things as "You keep your kitchen much cleaner than they do at XYZ club where I used to work" or "The helpful attitude of employees here certainly makes this a more pleasant place to work than my old job."

- External recruiting sometimes avoids many of the political problems associated with internal recruiting.

- External recruiting serves as a form of advertising for the property and reminds the public of your products and services.

**Disadvantages**

- It is more difficult to find a person who are good fit with the property's culture and management philosophy when recruiting people who are external.

- Internal morale problems can develop if current employees feel that they have no opportunity to move up in the organization.

- It takes longer to orient external recruits than it does internal recruits.

- External recruiting can lower productivity over the short run because external recruits usually cannot produce as quickly or effectively as internal recruits.

- When employees believe that they could have done the job as well as the external recruit who was hired, political problems and personality conflicts can result.

credits. Participation in internship programs helps you find good temporary employees who might eventually join your department permanently. Many students would like to continue working for the same company once they finish their studies. Moreover, if satisfied student interns report positive experiences to their schools, your property might be able to choose from a larger, better pool of candidates in the future. Work-study programs also show your property's support for community involvement.

The educational arms of national trade associations, including the American Hotel & Lodging Educational Institute, have developed high school curricula that prepare students for the adult working world before they graduate. The programs link what students learn in the classroom with on-the-job experiences. Practical classroom interaction then reinforces skills learned at the workplace.

For more information about educational work-study programs, contact your state's lodging or restaurant association.

## Networking

**Networking** is another potential source of good candidates. Your network could include your friends, former teachers, professional contacts, and peers in civic/professional associations and at other companies. You might decide to cultivate relationships with others as well. For instance, high school and college teachers and advisers can recommend students who would enjoy working in your department. In addition, consult with vendors or service people who work with your property. They often know many skilled people who might make good employees. Many areas have trade, civic, or professional associations you could join to broaden your network.

Strengthening your network requires regular and ongoing communication with your contacts. The important thing is to keep contacts aware of you and your property.

Exhibit 5 lists possible traditional strategies your property can use to recruit applicants. In addition, your property might contact state employment services, single parent organizations, and veterans groups. Sources of employees for external recruiting efforts are limited only by your own imagination.

# Technology and Recruiting

Just as it changed the ways individuals communicate in their personal lives, technology has changed the ways hospitality properties recruit employees. In the not-too-distant past, companies announced job vacancies in "low-tech" manners like newspaper ads (remember the "help wanted" section?), signs, and college or community job fairs. Companies also used (and continue to use) word-of-mouth networking (i.e., encouraging current employees to let their families and friends know about job openings).

Increasingly, companies are using electronic networking to recruit employees. This and other high-tech networking tools became available starting in the mid-1990s. Instant messaging and e-mail are becoming the preferred means of communicating with some applicants about appointments, questions, and decisions regarding job application results. Electronic networking also includes outlets like hospitality company websites, which might offer background information about their organizations, as well as employment sections that visitors can access for information about job openings and work environments. Some company websites include blogs, as well as sections where current employees tell their stories. Such features help personalize the businesses. Websites might also give visitors the chance to sign up for company or human resources employment newsletters that provide information about job vacancies.

An increasing number of hospitality organizations have Facebook (www.facebook.com) pages, which position the properties within their communities, generate new customers, maintain existing customers, and offer information about employment opportunities. Some organizations establish dedicated Facebook groups for job hunters. Such resources provide information about best practices for career progression, tips for doing well in employment interviews, and information about the organizations' corporate cultures. Facebook's "search"

**Exhibit 5    External Recruiting Strategies**

## RECRUITMENT STRATEGIES

1. **Youth**
   *Schools, Vo-Techs, Colleges*
   — Meet with counselors
   — Speak to classes
   — Sponsor work study programs
   — Participate in career days
   — Invite classes to tour hotel

2. **Minorities**
   — Meet with representatives from minority community agencies and invite them for lunch and tour of hotel
   — Advertise in minority newspapers
   — Visit schools in minority neighborhoods
   — Visit youth centers and place notices there

3. **Persons with Disabilities**
   — State Rehabilitation Agencies
   — National Alliance of Business
   — Private Industry Councils
   — National Association of Retarded Citizens
   — Goodwill Industries
   — Other local agencies

4. **Women**
   — Local organizations which assist women in transition
   — Bulletin board notices in supermarkets, libraries, YWCAs, exercise centers
   — Displaced Homemakers organizations
   — Craft centers
   — Child care centers

5. **Older Workers**
   — AARP Senior Employment Services
   — Senior Citizen Centers
   — Retirement communities and apartment complexes
   — Retired military

6. **Individuals in Career Transition**
   — University evening programs
   — Referrals
   — Teachers
   — Laid off workers from other industries
   — Speak at community functions

7. **Lawfully Authorized Immigrants**
   — Ads in foreign language newspapers
   — English as a Second Language classes
   — Citizenship classes
   — Refugee resettlement centers
   — Employee referrals

Courtesy of Radisson Hotel Corporation, Minneapolis, Minnesota feature lets visitors type the word "jobs" and uncover information about companies, people, and groups sharing employment information.

Twitter (www.twitter.com) is another useful non-traditional recruitment method. This website lets hospitality recruiters use 140 characters to "get the message out" about open positions. They can also receive inquiries from potential applicants. One of Twitter's advantages is the fact that those seeking work take the first step and might suggest those who are most interested in the position. Through Twitter, recruiters can also uncover background information that supplements the information applicants provide on their résumés.

Numerous employment websites exist, including general business sites like Monster (www.monster.com). One hospitality-specific website, Hcareers (www.hcareers.com), is a leading online jobs board where employers can post job openings and search a résumé database (see Exhibit 6). Websites like Linkedin (www.linkedin.com) are also helpful tools, especially for recruiters filling vacancies for managers and higher-level positions. A recruiter who uses Linkedin can contact individuals in his or her network and ask for referrals; the recruiter can also ask current employees to use their own electronic networks to spread the word about job vacancies. In addition to its job recruitment capabilities, Linkedin (and related sites) are useful tools for currently employed individuals seeking other career opportunities.

## Potential Concerns

Recruiters who use electronic media should consider potential complications. For example, if recruiters use social networks like Linkedin and Facebook to fill positions, do their companies risk lawsuits from potential applicants who allege discrimination because the companies overlooked candidates who did not belong to these networks? Not all potential applicants use electronic media to the same degree, so social media users might not reflect general population demographics in terms of race, age, gender, disability, etc.

Another concern is how, if at all, recruiters should use the information they learn from social media websites to make selection decisions. For example, should a recruiter access Facebook to obtain non-job-related perspectives about individuals who have inquired about or applied for positions? Some recruiters might do this—but should they?

Suggestions for using technology to recruit employees include:

- Consider technology a recruitment tactic that supplements—not replaces—traditional methods. For example, continue using employee referral programs.

- Maintain comprehensive records regarding hiring practices.

- Dismiss information learned through social media that is not relevant to the job.

- Remember that recruiters cannot use information about race, gender, marital status, etc., regardless of the methods through which recruiters learned this information.

- Don't ask for access to applicants' passwords for social networking sites.

## Exhibit 6   Recruiting Online

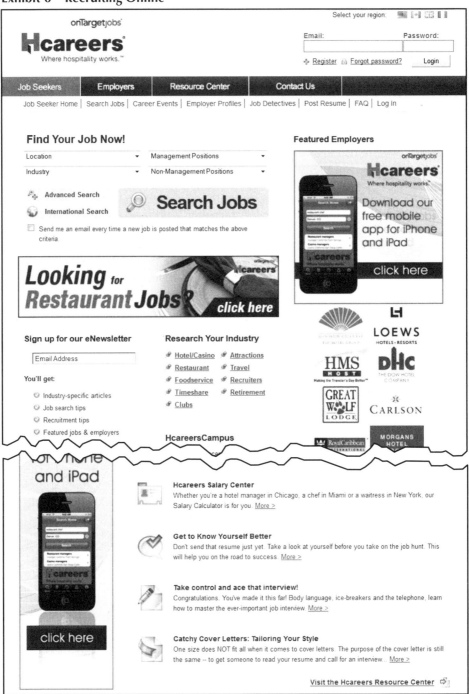

Source: www.hcareers.com

- Use electronic tools to determine what current and potential employees are saying about your organization and its work environment. If employees consistently report negative information, address the reasons for this situation.

Remember that the best use of technology in recruiting is to spread good news about the company, announce job openings, and communicate with potential and actual job applicants.

# Interviewing Applicants

The employment interview should give the applicant a good idea of what it would be like to work for your company. Once new employees start working, their general morale and productivity are affected by whether the job and the operation live up to their initial expectations. Therefore, it is important to give each applicant a truthful impression of the position and property.

In many properties, a human resources department representative screens **application forms** and conducts a first interview with each promising applicant. This first interview often includes specific questions pertaining to the application form, such as, "Are you able to work during our evening shift, which begins at 3:00 P.M.?" and, "I notice you worked at one of our properties in another city; how did you like that?"

The human resources representative determines which applicants most fit the position criteria, then refers them to the line department. Before you interview each candidate, meet with the human resources representative who previously interviewed him or her. This will help you obtain general information regarding issues you might want to follow up on during your meeting with the applicant. Also take time to review the employment application before meeting with the applicant. The form typically includes information about the applicant's employment history, educational background, work and personal references, and other data.

Questions on application forms must relate to **bona fide occupational qualifications (BFOQs)**. In almost all cases, questions that require applicants to reveal gender, age, birthplace, race, marital or family status, sexual preference, religion, military record, or convictions or arrests not related directly to the job at hand are illegal. Asking applicants for photographs and religious, military, and other specific types of references might also be illegal.

Look at the handwriting on, and neatness of, the application form. Also, look for normal career and wage/salary advancements. Consider the application a record of the applicant's employment history. Pay special attention to unexplained gaps of employment. Note which areas you wish to explore further. Exhibit 7 contains a list of questions to consider when looking over an employment application. Use a separate piece of paper to record your thoughts once the interview ends. Do not write on the application because it is a legal document that may be reviewed by outside agencies.

## Beginning the Interview

Be yourself and show your personality when conducting an employment interview. This will help the applicant do the same. The interview should be relaxed,

**Exhibit 7   Previewing an Application: General Observations**

- Is the application neat and clean—or messy, with erasures and misspellings?

- Did the applicant follow instructions?

- Is the handwriting acceptable for the job in question? Writing that goes above and below the lines may indicate poor dexterity or vision or limited education. Keep in mind that many people today are more practiced with keyboarding than handwriting

- Are there any omissions such as gaps in employment? These may indicate that the applicant has something to hide. They should be explored carefully.

- Does the signature match the handwriting? People who read and write poorly, or not at all, sometimes obtain an application, take it home, and have someone else fill it out for them. Be careful, though, as this may be considered a reasonable accommodation under the Americans with Disabilities Act.

- How long was the person employed in each previous job? If the length of employment gets shorter with each job, the applicant may have an intensifying problem.

- Do job responsibilities or pay rates indicate a career that is going up, staying at the same level, or going down?

- Do job choices indicate strong preferences for certain types of work?

professional, and private. Choose a setting where you will be neither distracted nor interrupted. If you conduct your interview in an office, put the applicant at ease by sitting on the same side of the desk. Do not sit with the desk between you. If possible, conduct the interview in an area close to the site where the new employee will be working. Take preferred applicants on a property tour before concluding the interview to provide them with a better understanding of the workplace and the job they would be doing.

Greet the applicant promptly and put him or her at ease. Introduce yourself, smile, make eye contact, and shake hands. Begin the conversation by discussing something of interest to the applicant, perhaps a hobby or favorite sport listed on his or her application form; this will help both of you relax. If the application lists the person's interests, talk about them. Alternatively, you might ask an applicant who is new to the area how he or she likes it. After a friendly introduction, begin discussing the job.

State the purpose of the interview. If you are conducting a several-minute screening interview, say so at the beginning. Similarly, if you expect the interview to be longer, let the applicant know. List the topics the interview will cover. For example, you might explain that you will review the application and discuss the job, provide an overview of the property, answer the applicant's questions, and describe the next step in the employment process.

## Conducting the Interview

Use a conversational tone and speak to the applicant without talking down to him or her. You should control the topics discussed and the direction of the interview, but allow the applicant to set the pace. If the applicant is shy or speaks slowly, the pace will be slower.

If your property has no human resources department and you conduct the first interview, verify early in the conversation whether the applicant fulfills the job's primary requirements. Then indicate that, within the first three days of work, all new employees must prove that they have the legal right to work in the United States. Mention any other qualifications that must be verified before hiring, such as minimum age for serving alcohol.

Finally, make sure that the job meets the applicant's needs in terms of pay and benefits, working hours and conditions, and type of work desired. You can cover these topics quickly at the beginning of the interview or by reading the application beforehand. It will also be helpful to show the applicant a copy of the job description as you review the required job tasks. If the needs of the applicant and the property do not match up, politely end the interview. Remember that an applicant who really wants a job might agree to anything to obtain it, even if the job clearly is not suitable. This applicant, if hired, would probably quit as soon as he or she obtained a more suitable job.

To begin questioning, ask about the applicant's job expectations. Why did the applicant apply and what type of work does he or she desire? Encourage the applicant with your own facial expressions and body language. Nod your head, maintain eye contact, and lean toward the applicant.

Carefully note the applicant's appearance, mannerisms, alertness, personal grooming standards, self confidence, and how well he or she communicates verbally and nonverbally. How an applicant communicates during a job interview might indicate how he or she will communicate on the job.

Eye contact is important. Shifting or inconsistent eye contact during the interview might indicate the applicant will be just as uncomfortable maintaining eye contact with guests or fellow employees. How often does the applicant smile during the interview? Does the applicant slouch or sit erect? Slouching is often a sign of disinterest; sitting up straight suggests alertness and involvement. Does the applicant sit with arms crossed? This might indicate the applicant is uncomfortable or defensive. Uncrossed arms help create open and relaxed communication.

Listen carefully as the individual responds to questions. If the applicant hesitates before answering a question, he or she might be uncomfortable with the topic. Listen for vague responses or changes in subject, which could indicate the applicant's desire to hide something. Listen to the applicant with sincerity and interest. If the applicant asks questions, be honest and direct so you don't lose credibility.

Ask questions in one major topic area at a time. Thoroughly discuss the applicant's work experience, for instance, before discussing education or personal history.

## Questioning Techniques

One common questioning technique uses two steps. The first step asks for specific information and usually begins with the words who, what, where, which, or when. The second step addresses the same subject by asking why or how. For example, you might ask, "Which job position was your favorite?" After the applicant responds, you could ask, "Why was it your favorite?"

Alternatively, ask for a list instead of a single answer. You might, for example, ask questions such as, "What are the best things about your restaurant job?" or, "What are your three finest characteristics?" After hearing the list, ask which single characteristic is strongest.

Another questioning technique asks the applicant to make comparisons. For example, rather than asking what it was like to work with a certain chef, ask the applicant, "How did working with this chef compare with working with the chef at your previous job?"

Other interview techniques can address the applicant's behavior in specific, job-related situations. These questions are more pointed and probing than traditional interview questions. For example, rather than asking if an applicant can work under pressure, you might ask, "At your last job, how did you handle the pressure when you were short-staffed?"

These questions are not meant to elicit "right" or "wrong" answers. Instead, this technique focuses on how applicants behaved in situations that might arise as they perform the job for which they are applying. Such question can help you assess how well the applicant's responses fit the skills needed for the job.

Whatever techniques you use, carefully listen to the applicant's answers. If they seem illogical or unreasonable, ask for more information. If answers are incomplete, encourage the applicant to go on by re-stating the answer as a question, such as, "You didn't really like your job, did you?" Use other responses such as "Really," or "I see." Commenting instead of asking questions will help maintain a conversational tone. Finally, you could simply say nothing when the applicant pauses. In all likelihood, the applicant will understand that you want to hear more information.

An applicant's unsatisfactory answer might be due to his or her uncertainty about what you're asking. In such a case, you might wish to explain the question by suggesting some answers from which the applicant can choose. You could ask, "Did you leave that position because of the salary, the benefits, or because you had to work nights and weekends?"

**Open-ended questions** are broad and ask for responses of more than just a few words. Examples of open-ended questions include:

"What do you like and dislike about your present job?"

"Can you describe a typical day on your last job?"

"What do you look for in a position?"

Open-ended questions offer several advantages. For instance, they enhance your opportunity to obtain meaningful information from the applicant. In addition, open-ended questions are easier to answer, are not threatening, and communicate your interest in the applicant. However, open-ended questions take more time to answer. Exhibit 8 lists open-ended questions that might help you develop a complete interview format. Any question can give you insight into the applicant's character and abilities, depending on how the applicant responds.

**Exhibit 8    Sample Open-Ended Recruitment Interview Questions**

**Education-Related Questions**

1. What subjects did you enjoy the most (or the least) in high school (or college)? Why?
2. What did you learn from your high school (or college) experience that is important today?
3. How did you feel about the importance of grades in high school (or college)?
4. Did you have any part-time jobs while attending high school (or college)? Which jobs were the most interesting? Why?
5. What extracurricular activities did you participate in during high school (or college)?

**Employment-Related Questions**

1. What job pressures did you experience in previous jobs? Why?
2. What kind of people do you like (or dislike) working with? Why?
3. What were the main advantages (or disadvantages) of your last job?
4. Why are you considering changing jobs?
5. Do you prefer working alone or in groups? Why?
6. What do you like most (or least) about working in a guest service position?
7. Why are you qualified to work in a guest service position in our organization?

**Goal-Related Questions**

1. What are your career goals in the next two years? In the next ten years?
2. What are your salary goals and objectives?
3. How do you evaluate this organization as a place to help you achieve your career goals?
4. Who (or what) influenced you the most in regard to your career goals?
5. What are your expectations regarding a new job?
6. If you are successful in 1 year (5 years, 10 years), what will be happening?
7. Of all the results that you have achieved in your life, which are you the most proud of? Why?

**Self-Awareness-Related Questions**

1. Which of your good qualities are most outstanding? Which of your qualities need the most improvement?
2. What qualities do you have that would help you deliver superior guest service in our organization?
3. Are you a self-motivated individual? Explain why.
4. How do you react to criticism from an employer? A guest? A staff member?
5. Have you engaged in any self-improvement activities? What were they?
6. What is your definition of superior guest service?

Probing with open-ended questions helps you better understand an applicant's responses. For example, if an applicant answers "good natured" to the question "What is your greatest strength?" find out more. Your role in the interview is to explore what the applicant means. Probe for meaning by asking questions such as:

"Tell me more about what 'good natured' means to you."

"In what ways is your good nature your greatest strength?"

"Please describe what you mean by good natured."

Don't use probing questions that can be answered "yes" or "no" (i.e., "Are you good natured?"). You will usually have only one attempt at probing to follow up an applicant's response to a question. If the applicant doesn't offer more information, move on to the next question.

**Closed questions** call for very brief responses. Use closed questions—usually with "yes" or "no" answers—when you want to verify facts or quickly cover a topic. Learning to ask and analyze closed questions requires little training. Less time is needed for the question and response, and answers are often easy to jot down. Finally, you can more easily control the length of the interview. However, closed questions typically generate less information than open-ended questions, and they don't allow the applicant to provide additional information. Overuse of closed questions provides less information than might be needed, and can lead to poor hiring decisions.

Make sure your questions are appropriate and relevant to the applicant and the job. Several categories of questions should be completely avoided because they can violate the applicant's lawful rights. Exhibit 9 lists samples of lawful and unlawful pre-employment questions. Make sure you and your property know the current laws in your area because these categories often vary according to state, and might change from year to year.

Generally, avoid topics that will produce information that, by law, should not enter into employment decisions. These topics relate to the applicant's birthplace, age, religion or creed, race or color, height and weight, marital status, sex, national origin, citizenship, memberships in lodges and religious or ethnic clubs, and arrest records. However, in most states, it is legal to ask about conviction records or whether any felony charges are pending against the applicant. It is illegal to ask questions specifically of one sex but not the other. For example, it is illegal to ask female applicants about child-care arrangements if you do not ask male applicants the same question. If a question is legitimately job-related, however, you must ask it of both male and female applicants. Important points for supervisors to keep in mind when interviewing applicants include:

- Only ask questions that relate directly to the job.

- Do not ask applicants questions that could be seen as discriminatory, such as questions about race, national origin, or religion.

- Do not ask applicants about their family lives. Their family lives have no bearing on whether they qualify for the job.

## Exhibit 9   Pre-Employment Inquiry Guide

| SUBJECT | LAWFUL PRE-EMPLOYMENT INQUIRIES | UNLAWFUL PRE-EMPLOYMENT INQUIRIES |
|---|---|---|
| NAME: | Applicant's full name. Have you ever worked for this company under a different name? Is any additional information relative to a different name necessary to check work record? If yes, explain. | Original name of an applicant whose name has been changed by court order or otherwise. Applicant's maiden name. |
| ADDRESS OR DURATION OF RESIDENCE: | How long a resident of this state or city? | |
| BIRTHPLACE: | | Birthplace of applicant. Birthplace of applicant's parents, spouse, or other close relatives. Requirement that applicant submit birth certificate, naturalization, or baptismal record. |
| AGE: | *Are you 18 years old or older? | How old are you? What is your date of birth? |
| RELIGION OR CREED: | | Inquiry into an applicant's religious denomination, religious affiliations, church, parish, pastor, or religious holidays observed. An applicant may not be told "This is a Catholic (Protestant or Jewish) organization." |
| RACE OR COLOR: | | Complexion or color of skin. |
| PHOTOGRAPH: | | Requirement that an applicant for employment affix a photograph to an employment application form. Request an applicant, at his or her option, to submit a photograph. Requirement for photograph after interview but before hiring. |
| HEIGHT: | | Inquiry regarding applicant's height. |
| WEIGHT: | | Inquiry regarding applicant's weight. |
| MARITAL STATUS: | | Requirement that an applicant provide any information regarding marital status or children. Are you single or married? Do you have any children? Is your spouse employed? What is your spouse's name? |
| SEX: | | Mr., Miss, or Mrs. or an inquiry regarding sex. Inquiry as to the ability to reproduce or advocacy of any form of birth control. |
| CITIZENSHIP: | Are you a citizen of the United States? If not a citizen of the United States, does applicant intend to become a citizen of the United States? If you are not a United States citizen, have you the legal right to remain permanently in the United States? Do you intend to remain permanently in the United States? | Of what country are you a citizen? Whether an applicant is naturalized or a native-born citizen; the date when the applicant acquired citizenship. Requirement that an applicant produce naturalization papers or first papers. Whether applicant's parents or spouse are naturalized or native-born citizens of the United States; the date when such parent or spouse acquired citizenship. |
| NATIONAL ORIGIN: | Inquiry into languages applicant speaks and writes fluently. | Inquiry into applicant's (a) lineage; (b) ancestry; (c) national origin; (d) descent; (e) parentage; or (f) nationality. Nationality of applicant's parents or spouse. What is your mother tongue? Inquiry into how applicant acquired ability to read, write, or speak a foreign language. |
| EDUCATION: | Inquiry into the academic, vocational, or professional education of an applicant and the public and private schools attended. | |
| EXPERIENCE: | Inquiry into work experience. Inquiry into countries applicant has visited. | |
| ARRESTS: | Have you ever been convicted of a crime? If so, when, where, and nature of offense? Are there any felony charges pending against you? | Inquiry regarding arrests. |
| RELATIVES: | Name of applicant's relatives, other than a spouse, already employed by this company. | Address of any relative of applicant, other than address (within the United States) of applicant's father and mother, husband or wife, and minor dependent children. |

*This question may be asked only for the purpose of determining whether applicants are of legal age for employment.

*(continued)*

**Exhibit 9**   *(continued)*

| SUBJECT | LAWFUL PRE-EMPLOYMENT INQUIRIES | UNLAWFUL PRE-EMPLOYMENT INQUIRIES |
|---|---|---|
| NOTICE IN CASE OF EMERGENCY: | Name and address of person to be notified in case of accident or emergency. | Name and address of nearest relative to be notified in case of accident or emergency. |
| MILITARY EXPERIENCE: | Inquiry into an applicant's military experience in the Armed Forces of the United States or in a State Militia. Inquiry into applicant's service in particular branch of United States Army, Navy, etc. | Inquiry into an applicant's general military experience. |
| ORGANIZATIONS: | Inquiry into the organizations of which an applicant is a member excluding organizations, the name or character of which indicates the race, color, religion, national origin, or ancestry of its members. | List all clubs, societies, and lodges to which you belong. |
| REFERENCES: | Who suggested that you apply for a position here? | |

Source: Michigan Department of Civil Rights, Lansing, Michigan.

- Do not promise terms of employment. Even pointing out examples of employees who have worked at the property for long periods could be considered an indirect promise of long-term employment.

- Do not, under any circumstances, ask about personal relationships because these questions could be construed as sexual harassment.

## Closing the Interview

Before ending the interview, allow the applicant to ask questions about the property or to further explain applicable skills and experiences. What the applicant says will give you further insight into his or her personality, requirements, and concerns.

Be prepared to answer questions that applicants might ask, such as:

- Who would supervise me?

- Can you describe a typical day at work for me?

- What are advancement opportunities?

- What kind of training do you offer?

- What do you like most about working for this company?

If you decide an applicant should be hired, you might be tempted to shorten the interview to save time. Instead, talk about the goals of the property and your department. Explain your company's successful products and services. Discuss the importance of the job for which the candidate is applying. Finally, because people like to work for successful operations, represent your company as being selective about whom it hires.

Explain the job accurately and thoroughly; describe what you expect of the employee and why. Mention any aspects of the position that might be unusual, such as the use of non-typical equipment and compressed workweeks. If the applicant seems surprised and confused, explain the situation carefully; before you extend a job offer, try to assess whether the applicant still appears interested.

If you don't extend a job offer during the interview, let the applicant know when you will contact him or her. In first interviews or screening interviews, say that a hiring decision will be made within a few days. Once you decide whom to hire, you should notify all applicants of their status.

If you are not going to hire the applicant, say so. Say something like, "We're pleased so many qualified applicants have applied." Then, end the interview decisively. Explain why the applicant won't be considered and thank the applicant for his or her interest.

The sample interview evaluation form presented in Exhibit 10 can be adapted to the requirements of different positions. You can use this form to evaluate the strengths and weaknesses of applicants you wish to consider after they have been interviewed. An applicant's score is assigned as follows:

- The applicant scores zero if he or she meets an acceptable level of skill in a given area or if the skill is not directly job-related.

- The applicant scores plus one or plus three according to the degree to which he or she surpasses the acceptable level of skill in a job-related area.

- The applicant scores minus one or minus three according to the degree to which he or she fails to meet the acceptable level of skill in a job-related area.

Every applicant possesses strengths and weaknesses. An interview evaluation form ensures that shortcomings in one area do not reduce an applicant's chances for further consideration.

## Following Up

After you interview candidates who seem especially promising, try to find more information about them. Analyze the information they supplied on their application forms and during interviews. Check the references the candidates provided. (This is normally a function of the human resources department.) Failing to conduct a thorough reference check can leave a company open to negligent-hiring lawsuits. **Negligent hiring** is commonly defined as an employer's failure to exercise reasonable care in the selection of its employees. Employers can be sued for not taking reasonable precautions to protect guests and employees from the actions of employees.

One note about reference checks. Many people—such as employers—who are asked about previous employees provide limited, if any, information. One reason is the fear that, if an applicant is not hired because of the information given, the applicant might claim that the reference provided defamatory information. (Defamation involves saying something false to ruin another's reputation.) For this reason, many employers will report only the beginning and ending dates of employment. (Similarly, talk with your manager about the type of information, if any, you should provide to employers seeking information about your previous employees.)

Some hospitality organizations administer selection tests to candidates. Some of these tests—such as those relating to honesty, aptitude, or psychological issues—are controversial because they might not be relevant to the job for which the employer is hiring. In some cases, courts have ruled that such tests discriminate

**Exhibit 10   Sample Interview Evaluation Form**

Applicant Name _____   Position Evaluated _____   Date _____

| | Poor Match | | Acceptable | Strong Match | |
|---|---|---|---|---|---|
| | −3 | −1 | 0 | +1 | +3 |
| **RELEVANT JOB BACKGROUND** | | | | | |
| General background | | | | | |
| Work experience | | | | | |
| Similar companies | | | | | |
| Interest in job | | | | | |
| Salary requirements | | | | | |
| Attendance | | | | | |
| Leadership experience | | | | | |
| **EDUCATION/INTELLIGENCE** | | | | | |
| Formal schooling | | | | | |
| Intellectual ability | | | | | |
| Additional training | | | | | |
| Social skills | | | | | |
| Verbal and listening skills | | | | | |
| Writing skills | | | | | |
| **PHYSICAL FACTORS** | | | | | |
| General health | | | | | |
| Physical ability | | | | | |
| Cleanliness, dress, and posture | | | | | |
| Energy level | | | | | |
| **PERSONAL TRAITS** | | | | | |
| First impression | | | | | |
| Interpersonal skills | | | | | |
| Personality | | | | | |
| Teamwork | | | | | |
| Motivation | | | | | |
| Outlook, humor, and optimism | | | | | |
| Values | | | | | |
| Creativity | | | | | |
| Stress tolerance | | | | | |
| Performing skills | | | | | |
| Service attitude | | | | | |
| Independence | | | | | |
| Planning and organizing | | | | | |
| Problem solving | | | | | |
| Maturity | | | | | |
| Decisiveness | | | | | |
| Self-knowledge | | | | | |
| Flexibility | | | | | |
| Work standards | | | | | |
| Subtotals | | | | | |

**TOTAL POINTS** _____

against minorities. Pre-employment tests may be used only if the employer can prove they are accurate predictors of job performance.

Many companies find it safer to avoid this problem by using tests that only relate directly to work issues. These tests relate to skills necessary for performing specific jobs. For example, if you need an experienced food server, you might ask applicants to demonstrate how to carry a loaded service tray or how to answer guest questions. Similarly, you might ask experienced room attendants to demonstrate the method for properly cleaning bathrooms or making beds. First-level supervisors are often best qualified to observe and analyze the results of these and related selection tests.

Your property may require applicants to take medical examinations before they are hired. If new employees will handle cash on the job, the property might wish to bond them. (**Bonding** is a type of insurance that reimburses the company for thefts by employees who misuse company funds.)

Other tasks might prove helpful during the selection process. For example, you might conduct follow-up interviews. Sometimes supervisors claim they are too busy to interview a lot of applicants, and ask the human resources department to "send one or two of the best applicants." The entire selection process will work to your advantage if you make recruiting and interviewing the best candidates one of your highest priorities.

## The Selection Decision

When deciding whom to hire, consider input from all concerned parties, including the human resources department. Providing enough time to interview several potentially qualified applicants will increase your chances of finding the right person for the job. This is a much better plan than recruiting only one person and modifying the selection process in a desperate attempt to fit the job to the applicant.

Many employees resign within their first months of employment. Such resignations could indicate that either the property's selection procedures or the orienting/training procedures are inferior. In extreme cases, both procedures are inadequate. It is part of every supervisor's job to ensure all applicants and new employees form accurate impressions of their jobs and the organization.

## The Supervisor and Human Resources Planning

Due to limited economic resources and a failure to plan ahead, your property might not consider recruiting applicants until a vacancy occurs or another problem arises. Of course, there will be times when an employee quits without notice or when business increases unexpectedly. Until this happens, you probably have no idea that you need additional staff members. In emergencies, time pressures might prohibit use of many effective employee selection procedures. When a position opens under emergency circumstances, it might be necessary to hire someone without using the careful evaluation process this chapter describes. Such a practice is not recommended, though, and should be used only when a careful applicant selection process is not possible.

Many of our industry's human resources problems—such as turnover, lack of training, and absenteeism—result from a lack of planning for human resources needs. If you are a first-line supervisor, you might play only a small role, if any, in determining human resources policies within your property. However, you can help employees adjust to their jobs and perform efficiently in the shortest possible time if you organize the jobs well and design effective training programs.

## Short-Range Approach

A simple, short-term approach to planning for human resources needs involves maintaining an active file of potentially eligible, pre-screened applicants. If individuals apply for jobs when none are available, request that they complete application forms and participate in preliminary interviews. This practice builds an applicant file that can form the basis for recruitment efforts as openings occur. For example, if there is an urgent need for an experienced front desk employee, contact those with applications on file to find out if they are still interested in the position. From your file, develop a **call-back list** of all talented applicants who are interested in positions in your department. Keep another list of former employees who might be willing to help on a temporary basis. It is a good idea to call good employees who left your organization a month or two after they depart. They might be interested in returning to work for you.

## Long-Range Approach

Top-level managers might prefer long-range approaches in planning for human resources needs. These plans help ensure an adequate number of qualified people will be available when you need them. Such approaches become important when key staff members leave, if the property's business volume grows, or as the property takes steps to comply with affirmative action/equal opportunity programs.

Human resources planning should be ongoing. Your property should modify plans as changes occur. As the organization's human resources needs evolve, top-level managers should assess the number and type of positions required, and also review recruiting, selecting, training, and evaluating activities. When used effectively, long-range planning considers peak business times and periods of high turnover. With information like this, plans can be made to hire additional staff in anticipation of these predictable trends.

## Supervisor's Role

Supervisors can use basic procedures to undertake human resources planning within their own departments. It is important that you, as a supervisor, understand your department's long- and short-range goals and the strategies designed to attain them. Then, match these with your present employees' skills. If you understand the organization's goals, you can assess future needs for employees.

Ask yourself how many of your current employees will be available in the next six months or the next year, as well as how many new staff members you will need. Recognize that you will need to consult specialists in the human resources department for help in planning. Maintain effective communication channels with human resources staff. Also, you must understand and evaluate those procedures for which you are responsible. How well is your department meeting its performance goals? Have strategies to attain them changed? Do you need to take corrective actions to bring your department more in line with established goals and plans?

Remember that your responsibilities start long before employees are on the job and ready to work. Developing the groundwork for finding the best employees is difficult; it doesn't just happen. You must look beyond the current shift, month, and budget period and consider the time span the organization uses for long-range planning. What are your organization's goals? How do they affect you and your employees? Once you know the answers to these and similar questions, you are ready to help plan the department's strategies. This will prepare you to deal with many routine aspects of the human resources process.

## Key Terms

**application form**—A form used by companies to obtain background and other information from prospective employees.

**bona fide occupational qualifications (BFOQs)**—Qualifications on the basis of which employers are allowed to legally discriminate during selection and promotion.

**bonding**—A type of insurance that will reimburse the company for thefts incurred by employees who misuse company funds.

**call-back list**—Names kept by a supervisor of all talented internal and external applicants who are interested in positions in the supervisor's department. The list may contain names of former employees who might be willing to help out on a temporary basis.

**closed questions**—Questions calling for very brief responses, usually requiring yes or no answers. These are used to verify facts or cover much information quickly.

**compressed schedules**—Alternative work schedules that allow employees to work the equivalent of a standard workweek in less than the usual five days. A typical adaptation is a workweek consisting of four ten-hour days.

**cross training**—A form of training in which employees are taught additional skills to fill the requirements of more than one position.

**exit interview**—A meeting between an employee leaving the organization and a supervisor or manager from the organization; this person is usually not the employee's immediate supervisor. The meeting is held to discuss aspects of the job, the company, and the employee's reason for leaving.

**flex-time**—A system of scheduling work hours that allows employees to vary their times of starting and ending work. There is usually a period of time during each shift when all employees must be present.

**human resources department**—Persons in this department help supervisors define, identify, and recruit the type of employees they need, among other tasks.

Human resources staff members are involved in many aspects of every employee's work with an organization.

**internal recruiting**—A method organizations use to fill jobs quickly with applicants from within the organization.

**internship programs**—Arrangements between a school and an employer that allow students to obtain actual work experience, often while earning school credit.

**job description**—A written summary of the duties, responsibilities, working conditions, and activities of a specific job.

**job sharing**—An alternative work schedule that allows two or more part-time employees to assume the responsibilities of one full-time job. The participants might be responsible for all duties of the job, or they might divide duties among them.

**job specification**—A selection tool that lists the knowledge, skills, abilities, and experience that employees need to perform a job adequately.

**lateral transfer**—The transfer of a current employee from one section or department to another at the same level of responsibility.

**line department**—A department that directly provides services or products to guests.

**negligent hiring**—An employer's failure to exercise reasonable care in the selection of its employees.

**networking**—The use of personal contacts such as friends, peers at other properties, business associates, vendors, service personnel, and others to help locate potential applicants for job openings.

**open-ended questions**—Questions that permit an applicant to respond in a free, unstructured way. Such questions are broad and ask for responses of more than just a few words.

**recruitment**—The process by which qualified applicants are sought and screened to fill currently or soon-to-be open positions. The process involves announcing or advertising job openings and evaluating applicants to determine whom to hire.

**staff department**—A department that provides support and advice to line or operating departments; see "line department."

**turnover**—With regard to staffing, the rate at which an organization or work unit loses employees.

## Review Questions

1. How do line departments and human resources employees work together to recruit new employees?

2. How can exit interviews help improve recruiting and selection methods?

3. What can your property do to make open positions easier to fill?

4. What internal and external recruiting techniques can you use when staffing your department?

5. What sources of potential employees can you draw from to staff your department?

6. What preparations should you make before interviewing job applicants?

7. What should you do to properly conduct an employment interview?

8. What questioning techniques can you use when interviewing job applicants?

9. How should you end a job interview?

10. What short- and long-range approaches can your property take in planning for human resources needs?

## Internet Sites

For more information, visit the following Internet sites. Remember, that Internet addresses can change without notice. If the site is no longer there, you can use a search engine to look for additional sites.

Employment Screening Resources
www.esrcheck.com

Hcareers.com
www.hcareers.com

HR-Guide.com
www.hr-guide.com

RecruitingBlogs.com
www.recruitingblogs.com

Society for Human Resource
  Management (SHRM)
www.shrm.org

TradePub.com
associates.tradepub.com/
?pt=cat&page=Hr

## Case Study

### Hobson's Choice: Finding the Best Server for the Job

Bill Hobson, general manager of McFitzhugh's, an independent, casual dining restaurant, was working late on a Thursday night, reviewing the interview notes he had gathered for a server opening he had to fill right away. On Monday, his assistant manager, Gretchen Jensen, conducted the first round of interviews and eliminated seven of the applicants. This morning Bill personally interviewed the remaining three candidates and this afternoon he asked the staff who had met them for their own impressions. Bill had told each candidate that he would let them know his decision by 3 o'clock Friday afternoon.

But the decision was not as easy as he had anticipated. Each candidate had arrived for the interviews well-groomed, well-dressed, and on time. They all had either some restaurant experience or hospitality education. Even so, none was an obvious choice for the job; each person came with his or her own strong points and weak points. Bill hoped that by going over his second-interview notes one more time he would at last be able to make a decision.

Because service skills and availability already seemed a given for these three candidates, Bill had focused on a series of questions designed to find out how well each applicant would fit in with the McFitzhugh's team. How well would they hold up under pressure? Were they able to laugh at themselves? Did they have customer-friendly, team-friendly personalities? To find out, Bill had developed four specific questions:

1. "How well do you think you work with people?"
   Although most of the McFitzhugh's team is made up of people under the age of 25, they have various education, family, and lifestyle backgrounds. They don't all share the same work ethic. Yet when they are on the job, everyone has to work smoothly together if they are going to successfully serve their guests. There is no room for lone rangers or prima donnas.

2. "What is the funniest thing that has happened to you in the last week?"
   Bill knew that some people scoffed at the importance of a sense of humor, but he had found that a positive and constructive sense of humor can be an invaluable asset when problems or stressful situations arise. And guests enjoy a pleasant, smiling server who can laugh along with them.

3. "Can you tell me about a time when you weren't treated fairly? What did you do?"
   The answer to this question would help Bill know whether the applicant could be cool under pressure—when the kitchen makes a mistake on an order, when two servers are out sick on a busy night, when guests refuse to be pleasant no matter what you do, and so on.

4. "Has your personality ever helped you out of a tough situation? "
   Over the years, Bill had hired more than his share of job applicants who described themselves as "people persons," but were unable to relate well with people who spoke, dressed, or acted differently than they did. When high-tension situations arose, they were flustered—or worse. McFitzhugh's needed servers who could relate well to a wide variety of guests and coworkers and diffuse even difficult situations comfortably.

Now Bill turned to the notes Gretchen had prepared for him after her initial interviews.

Applicant 1, Preston Clark, had impressed Gretchen with his knowledge of the hospitality industry. "This guy knows more of the terminology than I do!" she wrote on a page in the same folder with his application. He was currently a student in the hospitality program of a local community college, and his professors had nothing but glowing comments about his academic proficiency. He had no previous hospitality experience, although he emphasized his position as a "movie theater clerk" on his application.

Applicant 2, Gwen Farrell, had told Gretchen that she had been a stay-at-home mom since she and her husband moved to town from another state and her son was born. But now she was ready to start earning a second family income again. Previously, she had worked for seven and a half years as a server in a well-known casual-dining franchise in Texas. "Shy and nervous at first," Gretchen had noted, "but soon got comfortable and really opened up."

Applicant 3, Charity Lambert, had graduated from college three years ago and worked as a restaurant server ever since. The details weren't immediately clear on Charity's application, but Gretchen had learned that she had worked at three different restaurants in as many years. "Very bubbly and relaxed," Gretchen penciled in the notes section of the application. "Seems extremely customer-service oriented."

After refreshing his memory about Gretchen's perceptions, Bill shifted his attention to his own interviews from this morning. Studying his notes, he replayed the conversations in his mind.

"Tell me, Preston, how do you think you work with people?"

"Oh, I work great with people," the young man responded. "To be honest, I've never met anyone yet who didn't like working with me."

"OK," Bill said, taking notes. "If I asked what was the funniest thing that has happened to you in the last week, what would you say?"

"That's easy. It would have to be when Professor Mickelson—he's teaching a seminar on the gaming industry—that's what they call gambling now, you know—anyway, he's telling us something about the win percentage for slot machines, and he got the number wrong! Anyway, I'd been doing some extra reading and looking at sites on the Web, so I knew right away that he had blown it. Everybody else was apparently clueless. So I corrected him in front of the whole class. My friends and I are still laughing about that."

Bill nodded, writing. "Tell me about a time when you weren't treated fairly. What did you do?"

"That's another easy one. Once, I was supposed to work the 4:00 to 10:00 shift at the theater on a Saturday afternoon. I left my house on time, but I ended up getting stopped by a train. So I found a phone, called in, and said I'd be late, and they said 'okay,' but when I finally got there, the manager told me the popcorn machine had to be cleaned. I mean, right. Like nobody else could clean that. I think I got the bum job because I was late, but it wasn't fair."

"So what did you do about it?"

"Well, I cleaned it, of course—but since I was only twenty minutes late, I only worked on it for twenty minutes. It's usually a 45- to 50-minute job, but that's only fair, right?"

Bill went on. "Has your personality ever helped you out of a tough situation?"

"Yes, I believe it has. In one of my classes, we had been divided into teams of seven people each. Well, on my team, three of us seemed to be doing all the work for the whole group. The other four weren't contributing much of anything. So the other two people I was working with were getting really frustrated. They talked about just working on their own thing and letting the other four sink. Since I knew the professor wouldn't go for that, I talked to them, got them to voice their concerns to the other four, and eventually work things out so we could finish the assignment."

He turned to Gwen Farrell, Applicant 2. When he asked how well she worked with people, Gwen noted that she had some problems working with young people in the past.

"Could you explain?"

She answered that some of her young coworkers had been concerned more with talking with their friends than doing their jobs. "I'm sure there are lots of good young people out there, but in my experience they don't always have a good understanding of what it means to deliver great service. Sometimes they just want to be entertained, rather than go the extra mile for excellence."

"What's the funniest thing to have happened to you during the last week?" he asked next.

"I was waiting in the car to pick up our son from preschool when my husband called on the cell phone. Well, the reception wasn't very good, so he suggested I get out of the car. What I forgot was that I had locked the doors while I was waiting—and doing that arms the car alarm. I pulled hard on the door handle and set the alarm off. So, my husband is hollering through the static on the phone, my son is coming out of school wondering why his mother is calling all this attention to herself, and someone inside the school was already on the phone to the police!"

Bill next asked Gwen about being treated unfairly, and she mentioned that she had once offered to switch shifts with another server at the restaurant where she used to work. Gwen worked the other woman's shift and the woman thanked her profusely for trading. But when it came time for her to work Gwen's shift, she said her child was sick and she couldn't do it. "You know, her child probably was sick," Gwen said, "but I felt that she should have worked something out so she could be there. I ended up working that shift for her, but I decided right then and there that, if I ever had a child to look after, I would make arrangements to ensure I met my work responsibilities."

Finally, Bill asked, "Has your personality ever helped you out of a difficult situation?"

"Once I carded a customer who was actually 42! His wallet was out in his car, and he was pretty indignant—not only because he was going to have to go get his I.D., but because I'd even asked for it in the first place. When he came back, I had to smile when I saw his birth date. 'Well,' I told him, 'you sure seem young at heart to me.' Apparently, that was exactly what he wanted to hear. He was a great customer after that."

Now to Applicant 3, Bill thought. Charity Lambert had not made the best first impression. As they shook hands, Bill could not help noticing that she was wearing too much makeup and perfume. But that could easily be adjusted, he told himself. ("Believe me, Bill, she didn't dress like that when I interviewed her," Gretchen assured him this afternoon.) She did have good experience, though, a bright smile, and an outgoing personality that seemed tailor-made for a restaurant server.

"How well do you think you work with people?" Bill asked, settling into his four important questions.

"Well, I think I work great with people," Charity said. "I love meeting all the different customers and making sure their visit is a memorable one. In fact, you should probably be aware that lots of customers seem to move with me from restaurant to restaurant. I think I'm good for business."

"What's the funniest thing that's happened to you in the last week or so?"

Charity bit her bottom lip. "That's a tough one. Well, this was probably a month ago, but I was working at Kilby's downtown, and I had this huge tray loaded with an order for a table of six and there was this spill right by the coffee station and—whoosh—down I went! Oh, but now that I think about it, that probably wasn't all that funny at the time."

"Tell me about a time when you weren't treated fairly, and what did you do about it?"

"Wow, these are great questions. Oh, I know. I had this one job where I was working with about five other servers all the time, and they got mad at me because they said I was spending too much time at customers' tables. I don't know what they thought I should have been doing. I mean, the whole point of the job is customer service, right?"

"So what was your response?"

"I just tried to ignore them."

"Has your personality ever helped you out of a tough situation?"

"Well, I don't want to brag, but I think it has. I've heard that traffic cops really like to pick on people who drive red cars, and that's true because they're constantly harassing me about speeding or something. Anyway, when they pull me over, I'm usually able to be charming enough so that they just let me off with a warning instead of a ticket."

Bill set aside the interview notes and applications, leaned back in his chair, and took a deep breath. "Well," he said to himself, "I think that settles it." Leaning forward, he made a notation in his planner to call his new server tomorrow morning.

## Discussion Question

1. Based on the information provided, which applicant do you think Bill Hobson hired, and why?

---

Case Number: 3491CB

The following industry experts helped generate and develop this case: Christopher Kibit, C.S.C., Academic Team Leader, Hotel/Motel/Food Management & Tourism Programs, Lansing Community College, Lansing, Michigan; and Jack Nye, General Manager, Applebee's of Michigan, Applebee's International, Inc.

This case also appears in *Managing Service in Food and Beverage Operations,* Fourth Edition (Lansing, Mich.: American Hotel & Lodging Educational Institute, 2012), ISBN 978-0-86612-358-7.

# Chapter 4 Outline

# Competencies

1. Describe the ways in which learning styles and adult learning needs affect the training process. (pp. 103–110)

2. Explain the function of training within an organization, and explain the supervisor's role in training. (pp. 110–112)

3. Review activities that are required before training can begin. (pp. 112–116)

4. Identify the tasks performed in each step of the four-step training method. (pp. 116–121)

5. Discuss the need to evaluate the results and the costs/benefits of training. (pp. 121–123)

6. Explain the ways in which the orientation process affects new employees and the hospitality organization. (pp. 123–131)

# 4

# Training and Orientation

TRAINING PREPARES EMPLOYEES to complete their jobs effectively. It provides the knowledge and skills that employees need to work at proper performance levels. Training also helps introduce changes or new procedures to experienced employees.

During an employee's time with an organization, his or her most memorable day is often the day he or she starts working. Staff members can frequently remember what happened throughout their first days on the job. When employees begin working, they are often very enthusiastic and highly motivated. They want to do their jobs correctly, and they want to meet their new employers' expectations. This period of excitement is the time when you, as a supervisor, can begin building positive relationships with new employees in your department. By doing so, you will help the employees become a part of your team as they learn to perform effectively on the job.

While new employees experience initial excitement, some of them also find their first days to be awkward and even stressful. A significant amount of employee **turnover** occurs within new employees' first months on the job. High turnover during the early periods of employment often suggests that the recruiting process, the orientation process, or the training process—or all three—might be inadequate. Inadequate orientation and training programs might make new employees believe their supervisor does not care for them, and that they have not chosen a good place at which to work. It is this negative view, which can quickly overcome a new employee's positive feelings, that proper orientation and training programs are designed to counter.

## All About Learning

One definition of **training** is "any activity that results in learning." **Learning** is defined as the gaining of knowledge or skills through experience or study. If people perform differently after training than they did before training, learning has taken place. The effectiveness of employee training programs stems from the extent to which trainers recognize and apply basic learning principles, including those related to adult learning.

Employees must be motivated to learn. In other words, they learn best when they *want* to learn. Because the desire to learn involves a personal interest to do so, trainers must consider the ways in which they can motivate trainees. One important first step is to try to understand what most people expect from training, then relate training to the trainees' interests and needs.

All employees—and adult learners—want:

- *Professional growth, not grades.* Some employees have had bad training experiences. Compliment and encourage employees during training. If criticism is necessary, provide it positively and privately.

- *Practical training.* Show employees how they can use and benefit from the information and skills presented during training.

- *Job-related training.* Be sure that training directly relates to employees' jobs.

- *Appreciation of their past experiences.* Let employees know that you value their experiences and knowledge. Make training an extension of their experiences.

- *Comfortable, relaxed training.* Training will be more successful if you foster an informal atmosphere. Treat employees as professional coworkers and make training fun.

- *Participation.* Employees don't want to be lectured; they want to be actively involved in training. Exhibit 1 explains the reasons employees' participation in their own training is so important.

## Learning Styles

People learn in different ways. The unique way in which a person uses his or her senses to learn is called a **learning style.**

**Visual learners** learn best by *seeing.* They like information that is presented visually, such as in writing or with graphics, pictures, demonstrations, and charts. Visual learners:

- Are more likely to take notes.

- Often close their eyes to visualize or remember something.

- Benefit from illustrations and presentations that use color.

**Exhibit 1   How People Learn**

People remember:

10 percent of what they read.

20 percent of what they hear.

30 percent of what they see.

50 percent of what they see and hear.

70 percent of what they talk over with others.

80 percent of what they use and do.

95 percent of what they teach others.

Source: Clayton Lafferty, *Supervisory Skills Manual* Plymouth Mich: Human Synergistics, 1982, page 44.

- Find something to watch if they are bored.

- Like to see what they are learning.

**Auditory learners** learn by *hearing*. They learn best when listening to someone talk about a new idea or when discussing it with another person. Auditory learners:

- Hum or talk to themselves or others when bored.

- Might prefer to read out loud to help remember important points.

- Remember by "talking about" the information to themselves.

**Tactile learners** learn by *doing*. They want to actively and physically participate in their learning. They learn best when they have opportunities to *practice* the material. Tactile learners:

- Need to be active and take frequent breaks.

- Speak with their hands and with gestures.

- Remember what was done, but might have difficulty recalling what was said or seen.

- Find reasons to tinker or move about when bored.

- Rely on what they can directly experience or perform.

- Enjoy tasks that involve working with materials.

- Communicate by touching.

It might be unrealistic to evaluate each employee's learning preference individually, but one can assume that a diversity of learning styles exists within a group of workers. Approximately 30 to 40 percent of people are primarily visual learners, 20 to 30 percent are primarily auditory learners, and 30 to 50 percent are primarily tactile learners.

Supervisors should be aware of their own learning styles and become comfortable with other learning styles. To determine what learning style you might have, take the quiz in Exhibit 2.

When you train, don't use only the techniques that appeal to your personal learning style. Switch styles several times during a session. Have brightly colored markers and highlighters on hand. Track major points on a flip chart as the session progresses. If you seem to be losing trainees' attention, switch the methods through which you convey information.

## Factors Affecting the Learning Process

Many factors can affect a person's ability to learn. As a supervisor, you should always remember that people are individuals who have different levels and types of abilities and needs. Their backgrounds differ in terms of capabilities and life experiences.

Training programs must be flexible and consider participants' individual differences. An important step toward dealing with individual differences is to be

**Exhibit 2 Learning Styles Quiz**

For these questions, choose the first answer that comes to mind. Don't spend too much time thinking about any one question.

1. When you study for a test, would you rather:
   - ☐ a) read notes and look at diagrams and illustrations
   - ☐ b) have someone ask you questions or repeat facts silently to yourself
   - ☐ c) write things on index cards and make models or diagrams

2. Which of these do you do when you listen to music?
   - ☐ a) daydream (see things that go with the music)
   - ☐ b) hum along
   - ☐ c) move with the music, tap your foot, etc.

3. You are about to learn a new computer program. Would you rather:
   - ☐ a) read the manual that came with it
   - ☐ b) ask a friend to explain it to you
   - ☐ c) sit down at the computer and begin to experiment with the program's features

4. You have just entered a science museum. What will you do first?
   - ☐ a) find a map showing the locations of the various exhibits
   - ☐ b) talk to a museum guide and ask about exhibits
   - ☐ c) go into the first exhibit that looks interesting

5. Would you rather go to:
   - ☐ a) an art class
   - ☐ b) a music class
   - ☐ c) an exercise class

6. Which are you most likely to do when you are happy?
   - ☐ a) grin
   - ☐ b) shout with joy
   - ☐ c) jump for joy

7. When you tell a story, would you rather:
   - ☐ a) write it
   - ☐ b) tell it out loud
   - ☐ c) act it out

8. What is most distracting for you when you are trying to concentrate?
   - ☐ a) visual distractions
   - ☐ b) noises
   - ☐ c) other sensations like hunger, tight shoes, or worry

**Exhibit 2**   *(continued)*

9. If you were at a party, what would you be most likely to remember the next day?
   - ☐  a)   the faces of the people there, but not the names
   - ☐  b)   the names but not the faces
   - ☐  c)   the things you did and said while you were there

10. When you see the word "dog," what do you do first?
   - ☐  a)   think of a picture of a particular dog
   - ☐  b)   say the word "dog" to yourself silently
   - ☐  c)   sense the feeling of being with a dog (petting it, etc.)

11. What are you most likely to do when you are angry?
   - ☐  a)   scowl
   - ☐  b)   shout or "blow up"
   - ☐  c)   stomp off and slam doors

12. When you aren't sure how to spell a word, which of these are you most likely to do?
   - ☐  a)   look it up in a dictionary
   - ☐  b)   sound it out
   - ☐  c)   write it out to see if it feels right

13. You are about to purchase a new television. Other than price, what would most influence your decision?
   - ☐  a)   reading the details about it
   - ☐  b)   the salesperson telling you what you want to know
   - ☐  c)   playing with the controls

14. You want to visit a friend but you don't know his or her address. Do you want your friend to:
   - ☐  a)   draw you a map
   - ☐  b)   tell you the directions
   - ☐  c)   pick you up

15. Do you prefer a trainer or teacher who likes to use:
   - ☐  a)   handouts, charts, slides
   - ☐  b)   discussion, guest speakers
   - ☐  c)   field trips, practice sessions

16. Which are you most likely to do when standing in a long line at the movies?
   - ☐  a)   look at posters advertising other movies
   - ☐  b)   talk to the person next to you
   - ☐  c)   tap your foot or move around in some other way

*(continued)*

**Exhibit 2**   *(continued)*

When you're done, total your a's, b's, and c's.

If you scored mostly a's, you may have a visual learning style. You learn by seeing and looking. Visual learners benefit from the use of visual aids in training.

If you scored mostly b's, you may have an auditory learning style. You learn by hearing and listening. Auditory learners benefit from the use of discussion and paraphraing in training.

If you scored mostly c's, you may have a tactile-kinesthetic learning style. You learn by touching and doing. Tactile-kinesthetic learners benefit from the use of exercises, activities, and role-play in training.

Source: Adapted from www.usd.edu/trio/tut/ts/style.html.

aware of basic factors that affect the learning process. These factors could affect how trainees learn, which itself can affect your training approach. Individual differences include **demographics,** diversity issues, **disabilities,** educational levels and literacy, job experiences, and the trainer's delivery style.

You can adapt your training style to accommodate a trainee's special needs. Begin by understanding that diversity in the workforce is the rule, not the exception. Sometimes differences such as age, gender, race, or disability can affect the judgment of the trainer or the trainee. It is illegal to discriminate against a trainee because of these differences. Be sensitive to how you present information. Don't make comments that can be viewed as belittling a trainee's background or special circumstances. Have patience and use demonstration and participation techniques whenever possible to help communicate the training messages.

Know about your available training resources. You might find it necessary to maintain a list of translators who can assist when language differences present a learning barrier. Develop a list of employees at your property who have special skills (such as knowledge of foreign languages or sign language) that can assist in training. Know the areas of your property accessible to employees with disabilities. Also, know about tools like video that you can use to train employees who cannot read.

Be aware of special needs. When training employees with disabilities, make an effort to schedule training in easily accessible areas. Make requests in advance for special services such as translators, and schedule training around the availability of these resources. Spend more time with trainees who have less job experience.

Alter your delivery style to fit the learning styles of trainees. Make an effort to observe trainees and understand the ways in which they remember information; then, adapt your training program to meet their learning needs.

## Adult Learning Needs

When you were in school, you might have had teachers who stood in front of the class and lectured for long periods of time. This style might work for children and adolescents, but most adults do not learn well in this type of environment.

Adults have special learning needs, and do best when their "teachers" tailor training to address those needs. Because most employees in the hospitality industry are adults, they want to be treated as adults—not as children.

For adults, self motivation is the best incentive for leaning. The information should be something the trainee needs to know, and the trainee must be ready to learn. Adult learners want training that is life-, task-, or problem-centered. As trainees learn to immediately apply new knowledge, skills, or aptitudes, the learning process is reinforced. You know that trainee participation and involvement in training sessions are the keys to those sessions' effectiveness. Therefore, you can design the training format so that it includes interactive techniques like role plays, case studies, and games. You can also give trainees the opportunity to discuss applications of principles emphasized during the learning exercises.

People learn best and remember longer when a presentation or training activity does not exceed their **attention spans.** Trainers often feel they must cover everything in one session. Training is much more efficient and effective when it spans short sessions that focus on a few skills or knowledge areas. For example, four one-hour sessions are usually better than one four-hour session. During longer sessions, trainers must use a variety of techniques to keep participants' interest. As training time increases, trainers should incorporate breaks to refresh participants.

People learn skills best when trainers present steps in a consecutive **sequence of instruction.** For example, front desk employees should know guest room types and rates before they learn the guest registration process. You can ensure progress by making sure each step is easy to master. Trainees benefit when you first show them the method they should use to fully complete a duty; then, you should break down the duty into its component steps. Trainees usually perform individual steps better if they have a general overview of the entire task. The trainee should learn basic steps before more complex variations.

People learn at different rates of speed. Some trainees learn faster than others. When a trainee does not learn quickly, be patient and try to determine the cause. Impatient or irritated trainers can destroy a trainee's confidence and slow his or her progress even more. Some trainers teach too much too fast, forgetting that employees might not have the same background, education, or experience that the trainers have. Each employee will progress at his or her own **learning rate,** so a trainer should avoid measuring a trainee's performance against other trainees.

People learn information faster and remember it longer if it is repeated several times. Training to perform a task is most effective when each **repetition** provides a different way of looking at the same situation or concept. Reinforce the most important points by stating the same thing in several different ways, and by having trainees explain their understanding in their own words. A rule of thumb is that every key principle should be repeated two or three times during the training session. Complex skills that are hard to master might require as many as five or six repetitions.

People learn best when they want to learn. The actual amount of learning that takes place depends largely on the trainee's internal **motivation** to learn. Trainees might want to know, "What's in it for me?" As a trainer, you should state the objective of the training at the beginning of the session and show trainees the advantages of learning the subject or skill. Trainees are less likely to want to learn if they don't see an immediate need for the training. They are also more motivated to learn and apply new skills when you offer feedback, praise, and encouragement. Trainees want to know whether or not they are doing a good job.

People learn and develop skills best by hands-on experience and active participation. For example, a person who wants to learn to prepare flambé dishes might read a book on tableside cookery and then watch a maître d'hôtel prepare a flaming dessert. However, the skill will not develop until the person actually prepares a flambé dish, ignites the liqueur, and serves the menu item to guests. When trainees don't get chances to practice, they might learn the required knowledge, but they won't necessarily have the ability to apply that knowledge on the job.

## All About Training

In the hospitality industry, most training involves the three S's: standards, service, and safety. Training employees about job standards means demonstrating and providing information about:

- The specific tasks the employee must complete to be successful in his or her job.
- The acceptable standards of performance for job tasks.

Effective service training should include:

- An overview of hospitality and the factors that make it different from other industries.
- How guest feedback is used as a measure of service.
- The difference between **external customers** (guests) and **internal customers** (coworkers and other departments), and the importance of providing service to both.
- **Behavior modeling** of appropriate service behaviors.

Safety training involves teaching employees to:

- Maintain their own safety.
- Maintain guest safety.
- Recognize safety hazards.
- React during an emergency.

Most employees undergoing training want to know how the training will benefit them. It is your job to help trainees understand the ways in which the tasks for which you are training them fit into the "big picture" of their job, their department, and their property. If employees "buy in" to the training, they will be more motivated and will ultimately learn more and perform better on the job. Exhibit 3 shows some of the benefits that training affords trainees, the property, and guests.

Supervisors can use a variety of training methods to provide information and feedback to employees. Depending on the size and training needs of your property and department, you might not have much control over the ways in which

**Exhibit 3    Benefits of Training**

The good news is that training benefits *everyone.*

Benefits to the Trainee:

- Prepares employees to do their jobs effectively
- Improves self-confidence
- Improves motivation
- Improves morale
- Prepares for promotion
- Reduces tension and stress
- Provides an opportunity to succeed

Benefits to the Property:

- Increases productivity
- Reduces costs
- Builds a strong employee team
- Decreases safety hazards
- Creates a better image
- Builds repeat business
- Increases referrals
- Attracts potential employees
- Decreases absenteeism
- Reduces turnover

Benefits to Guests:

- Provides high-quality products
- Provides high-quality services
- Makes their visit more pleasant
- Makes them feel they are getting their money's worth
- Provides a safer visit

you deliver training. However, you should understand the benefits and limitations of each training method for those times when you must use them.

## Group Training

Group training is conducted by a trainer for a number of employees at the same time. It is particularly useful when you must provide the same information or skills to several employees at once.

Group training can be more interactive than one-on-one training, as employees benefit from the expertise and experiences of their trainer and other trainees. However, group training also requires significant planning, and trainers might encounter difficulty controlling the learning that takes place.

When training a group, your primary responsibility is to encourage participative learning and mutual problem solving. Use your leadership skills to produce a high level of individual employee involvement. When working with a group, encourage creative expression and teamwork, summarize discussions, and remain neutral and objective.

## One-on-One Training

**One-on-one training** is a method for training individual employees. It can take place before, during, or after a shift, on or off the job. It gives trainees individual attention and immediate feedback. One-on-one training can be individualized to the specific needs of the employee being trained.

On the negative side, one-on-one training offers little opportunity for interaction with other trainees; trainers also encounter difficulty ensuring that each trainee receives the same information.

## On-the-Job Training

**On-the-job training** is conducted at the work site. It can be more cost-effective than **off-the-job training** because on-the-job training usually takes place during normal business hours and in actual work settings. It provides the maximum amount of realism. It also addresses a trainee's specific needs and is an especially effective form of one-on-one training.

However, if not carefully planned, on-the-job training can interfere with or slow down normal business operations. Also, trainees who receive on-the-job training might not be exposed to all aspects of the job. Instead, they can learn about only activities that occur when training takes place. Because training is fast-paced, the trainer often has no time to provide feedback, repeat important steps, or explain the reasons why certain procedures are followed. On-the-job training can also cause problems if the trainer does not perform the job correctly. In such cases, trainees are likely to perform in the same manner as their trainers.

## Off-the-Job Training

Off-the-job training is conducted away from the work site, often in a conference room or private office. It can be used for either group or one-on-one training.

# Before Training Begins ———————————————————

Trainers must be selected before training can begin; in fact, they might be responsible for developing or modifying the training program they will deliver. In addition, trainers must have knowledge of job tasks and the ways those tasks should be performed because that information will drive training content.

## Qualities of Effective Trainers

When employees know how to do their jobs well, everyone's job is easier. This makes you look better as a supervisor. Fewer emergencies and conflicts occur because employees who know their jobs are more likely to head off problems before they arise.

Good trainers:

- Have self-confidence.

- Are patient.

- Are flexible.

- Enjoy teaching.

- Are respected by trainees.

- Have a good sense of humor and use it as a training tool.

- Get along well with different types of people.

- Display a consistently positive attitude.

- Are enthusiastic about training.

- Have a positive attitude toward their department and property.

- Have a personal commitment to excellence in all areas of performance.

- Have a working knowledge of job skills and procedures.

- Make decisions and solve routine job-related problems.

- Effectively organize work tasks and accomplish duties on time.

- Interact well with other departments.

- Listen well.

- Have good communication skills.

- Spend the time necessary to properly train employees.

- Understand the qualities of effective employees and model those qualities.

- Encourage trainees to think about how the training applies to their jobs.

- Persuade trainees to set training goals for themselves.

- Invite trainees to ask questions.

- Invite trainees to find better ways to do things.

- Praise even the smallest successes.

- Encourage and support trainees.

- Share personal experiences and even mistakes with trainees.

- Reward employees for training achievements.

## Understanding the Job

Before training begins, you must know what trainees need to learn. The answer seems easy enough: they must learn what they need to do their jobs. But how do you decide *exactly* what they must do and how they must do it? Many properties use task lists and job breakdowns to establish these guidelines.

A **task list** tells *what* tasks an employee in a certain position must perform. When you prepare for training, keep in mind that the task list tells you what tasks a trainee should be able to perform after he or she has completed training.

Each task on a task list has its own **job breakdown** that tells *how* to perform the task. The job breakdown lists the task's steps, the manner in which the trainee should perform each step, and the level of quality he or she should seek when performing them.

Many properties have task lists and job breakdowns for each position. If your property does, and if the lists and breakdowns are current, you will have an easier time planning your training sessions. See Exhibit 4 for a sample task list and job

**Exhibit 4   Task List**

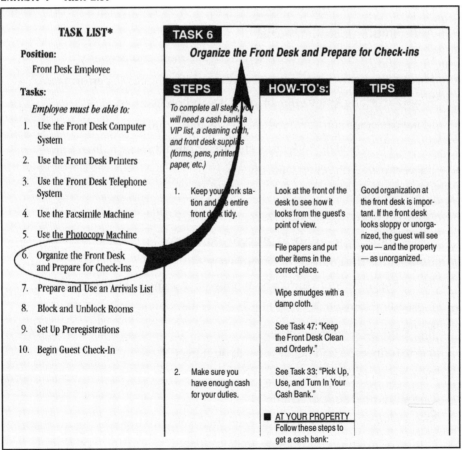

breakdown, and Exhibit 5 for an illustration of the ways job breakdowns can be used to train new employees and retrain experienced employees.

A **job description** generally defines a task and its requirements. By defining the job, the job description indicates the most important tasks that employees must perform. The job description can be used in several ways. It can be used to:

- Prepare for training by identifying the tasks a trainee should be able to perform after training is complete.

- Orient and train a new employee so that he or she understands the position's basic responsibilities.

- Evaluate the employee's job performance

## Training from Experience

In addition to using task lists, job breakdowns, and job descriptions, you also have your own personal experience to draw upon. You were most likely selected as a supervisor because of your expertise and skill in performing the jobs for which you are now providing training. Because you are familiar with and skilled at these job(s), you are better able to:

- Communicate steps for performing required job tasks

- Provide feedback

**Exhibit 5    Training with Job Breakdowns**

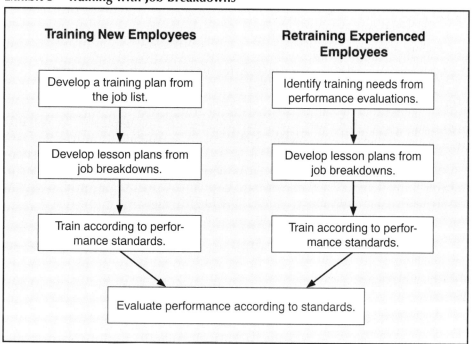

- Answer questions
- Evaluate trainee performance

## Training to Standards

You and your property must have employees who can do their jobs at a level that meets basic quality and quantity standards. This means you will have to know how well a trainee should be able to complete each job task when he or she finishes training. You should become familiar with these standards before training begins and train the employee so that he or she can do the job task to the desired performance level.

These same standards can be used on an ongoing basis to evaluate the employee's performance on the job. Job standards are significant tools that help improve performance throughout the employee's career.

# Four-Step Training Method

Many trainers use a four-step training method to train both new and experienced employees. The four-step training method is a basic model that can be used to implement an on-the-job training program. The model is general enough to be used in group training programs as well.

The steps in the four-step training method are:

1. Prepare to train
2. Conduct the training
3. **Coach** trial performances
4. Follow through

Exhibit 6 contains a checklist of activities for the four-step training method.

## Step One: Prepare to Train

Many supervisors think they know the skills required of employees so well that they can teach them to others without thought or preparation. However, it is easy to forget important details if training is approached without adequate trainer preparation. The training session will be most effective if the trainer is skilled in the area being taught. The trainer should be willing to follow the job breakdowns closely so that the skills are presented in a logical sequence. When this is done, the trainees are better able to understand and remember the steps necessary to perform the job.

Planning for training involves preliminary steps that are taken to answer the following questions:

### *Who?*

- Who should be involved in the training?
- How many trainees will be involved in the training?

**Exhibit 6    Four-Step Training Method Checklist**

When you use the four-step training method, you may wish to use the following checklist:

*Step One: Prepare to Train*

- ☐ WRITE  training objectives.
- ☐ DEVELOP  step-by-step plans.
- ☐ DECIDE  on training methods.
- ☐ PREPARE  a training schedule.
- ☐ SELECT  the training location.
- ☐ PREPARE  the training area.

*Step Two: Conduct the Training*

- ☐ PREPARE  the trainees.
- ☐ BEGIN  the training session.
- ☐ DEMONSTRATE  the steps.
- ☐ AVOID  jargon.
- ☐ TAKE  enough time.
- ☐ REPEAT  the steps.

*Step Three: Coach Trial Performances*

- ☐ LET  the trainees practice.
- ☐ COACH  the trainees.

*Step Four: Follow Through*

- ☐ COACH  a few tasks each day.
- ☐ CONTINUE  positive support.
- ☐ CORRECT  the trainees when necessary.
- ☐ EVALUATE  the trainees' progress.
- ☐ GET  the trainees' feedback.

- Who will be responsible for the trainer's and trainees' ongoing job duties during the training session?

## What?

- What topics should be covered?
- What are the employees' expectations for the training?
- What audiovisual aids and equipment will be needed for the training?
- What other materials will be needed for the training?

## When?

- When should the training take place?
- When will training be least likely to interfere with business operations?
- When will trainees be most alert?

## Where?

- Where should the training take place?
- Is the training space available or do I need to reserve it?

## How?

- How should the training be conducted?
- How will employees' special needs be met during training?

The following suggestions can help you as you prepare to train:

1. *Write training objectives.* Training **objectives** state what a trainee should know or be able to do after training. Remember that task lists, job breakdowns, and job descriptions will help you at this point. Your goal is to have the trainee do the tasks at the performance level set by you or the property. Training objectives need to be updated or adjusted whenever there are changed procedures or the information needed for a position or situation changes.

2. *Develop step-by-step plans.* In order to make the best use of the training time available, prepare a detailed plan about how you will help the trainees learn the knowledge and skills required for each task. This will be a step-by-step plan of what you're going to do in training.

3. *Decide on training methods.* As a trainer, you will need to determine the best way for the trainee to learn the information and skills you're going to present during training. Will you demonstrate? Will you have the trainee watch another employee do the task? Will the trainee practice the actions? Often, the training method depends on who, what, where, and how many are being trained.

4. *Prepare a training schedule.* Decide how long each training session will take. Schedule training during times of low business volume. You'll also need to determine trainee and property needs when preparing a training schedule.

5. *Select the training location.* If possible, train employees at the work stations where they will be working. Make sure the trainees are standing or sitting where they will actually be performing the task; otherwise they might watch you do the work from a reverse angle, which will confuse them when they try to do the task themselves. As a trainer, you'll also need to ensure that if training is conducted in a meeting room, the room has appropriate ventilation, space, and lighting, as well as comfortable seating.

6. *Prepare the training area.* Set up all materials and equipment in the training area before the session begins. Be sure the equipment is in working order.

Preparations include making sure the room is set up to enhance the training that will take place. Room temperature is another consideration. Materials and equipment should be prepared in advance and checked to make sure they work correctly.

## Step Two: Conduct the Training

Once the trainer and trainee have been prepared for training, the actual process can begin. Sea World Adventure Parks in Orlando, Florida, uses the concept of T.R.A.I.N. to help trainers remember the basics for presenting training. It stands for:

**T**each by showing.
**R**epeat until comfortable.
**A**sk questions.
**I**mitate work conditions.
**N**ote good performance.

Some suggestions for conducting the training include:

1. *Prepare the trainees.* Motivate your trainees to learn. Do this by showing how their job fits into the overall operation and why their role is important. Let the trainees know the benefits of the training, such as helping them do their jobs better. Explain the session's training objectives.

2. *Begin the training session.* It is important to start on time and take breaks as necessary. First, establish the learning objectives. Then, explain each step you will cover and tell why it is important. Be sure the trainees understand the standards and know that those standards will be used to evaluate their performance. Make sure you provide a consistent and standardized delivery from person to person and from class to class.

3. *Demonstrate the steps.* As you explain the steps, demonstrate them. Be sure the steps are arranged in the order they should be completed. Encourage trainees to ask questions whenever they need additional information.

4. *Avoid jargon.* **Jargon** is language that is technical or specific to an industry, such as "edible portion" in the kitchen or "ADR" at the front desk. Use words that new employees in the hospitality industry or at your property can understand. They can pick up the jargon later. You might want to provide your trainees with a list or "dictionary" of terms used at your hotel.

5. *Take enough time.* Go slowly and carefully. Explain and show each step thoroughly. Be patient if trainees don't understand right away. Don't let your training go more quickly than the trainees can understand.

6. *Repeat the steps.* Go over all the steps as necessary so that employees completely understand the process. When you show a step the second time, ask the employees questions to see if they understand. Repeat the steps as many times as necessary.

## Step Three: Coach Trial Performances

After the trainee feels he or she knows how to perform a duty or task in an acceptable manner, the trainer should let the trainee perform the procedure alone. This is a **trial performance.** Trial performances involve having the trainee try the steps alone while the trainer watches and provides feedback.

Suggestions for **coaching** trial performances include:

1. *Let the trainees practice.* When the trainees appear to understand each step, ask them to demonstrate and explain the steps. You might let trainees practice in on-the-job situations, or by using activities, exercises, role plays, or case studies. Such "practices" help you ensure trainees actually understand the material. Don't complete the tasks for trainees.

2. *Coach the trainees.* Praise trainees when they perform correctly. Gently correct them when they don't. Review the proper procedures again. Be sure trainees can perform each step and explain its purpose before you move on to the next step.

## Step Four: Follow Through

This step can be a part of—or immediately follow—the training session. In either case, to gain further speed and accuracy, the trainee should continue to perform the new duties on the job after his or her trial performance. **Follow through,** even if it is informal, provides you with useful information about training effectiveness.

Supervisors need to recognize that successful training doesn't end with the formal training session. They must check to see if the trainees have carried their training experience over to the workplace. Supervisors should give feedback to employees about how they are doing and remind them that the things they learned in training are valuable and necessary on the job.

Some suggestions for following through include:

1. *Coach a few tasks each day.* Trainees can't handle too much information at once. Limit a session's information to what a person can understand and remember. Then conduct additional training sessions for the remaining information.

2. *Evaluate the trainees' progress.* Ask yourself whether the trainee learned and whether the trainee is applying what he or she has learned. If the trainees haven't learned or aren't applying what they've learned, you'll need to provide further training and practice. Evaluation might or might not take place immediately after training. Some follow-up evaluation might take place at 30-, 60-, or 90-day intervals.

3. *Continue positive support.* Let the trainees know when they perform well and what they are doing correctly after training. **Positive feedback** boosts confidence levels, reinforces good work habits, and increases motivation. Employees need to know that someone noticed they are doing a good job.

4. *Correct the trainees when necessary.* If trainees are not meeting performance standards, first compliment them on the tasks they are doing correctly, they show them how to correct their bad habits, and explain why. **Corrective feedback** is used to show employees what they can do to work more effectively

and confidently. It helps employees develop good work habits and it increases motivation. Tell trainees where to seek help if you won't be available. Employees need to know that someone cares whether they do a good job. Many managers and trainers fail to correct their employees because they don't want to offend them. However, not correcting employees when necessary sets them up for failure, which might lead to poor guest service.

5. *Get the trainees' feedback.* Let the employees evaluate the training they received. This can help improve your training efforts, both for them and for other trainees. See Exhibit 7 for questions you can ask trainees to solicit information about training.

# After the Training

Two important activities remain after training is completed. The training process must be evaluated and its costs and benefits assessed.

## Training Evaluation

Once you have completed a training session, you must find out whether the training was successful. Evaluating the results of a training program might not be a formal part of your job as a supervisor; however, the best trainers want to know if employees are taking the knowledge and skills they learned in training and using them on the job. Successful supervisors realize that sometimes training doesn't work; to help make future sessions more successful, these supervisors attempt to understand the factors that created training problems.

Exhibit 8 contains observations you might make about employee performance after training is complete.

## Costs/Benefits of Training

Training, like almost any other business activity, has costs associated with it. However, these costs can be outweighed by the benefits associated with having

**Exhibit 7   Training Evaluation Questions**

Ask trainees such questions as:

- Was the training program helpful?
- What part was most helpful?
- How could we improve the program?
- Were you encouraged to ask questions during the training?
- Did you feel ready to be left alone on the job after the training?
- Do you feel comfortable in your position?
- Are there any areas of your training that you feel need to be repeated? Which ones?

**Exhibit 8    Training Measurements**

| Observation | Possible Reason | Possible Solution |
|---|---|---|
| Employee stumbles over material he/she appeared to master in training. | Not enough practice during training for long-term retention. | Allow more time for "hands on" practice during training. |
| Employee appears confused both in training and on the job. | There were barriers to communication or instruction, or the training was unclear. | Look for ways to simplify the points you make. Teach tasks in simple, step-by-step increments. |
| Employee encounters unfamiliar situations not covered in training. | Training is incomplete. | If it's a fairly common situation, add information that covers it to the training. |
| Employee repeats incorrect behaviors he/she demonstrated during training. | Not enough coaching or feedback during training. | Provide constructive feedback and coaching during training to guide trainees to correct performance. |
| Employee does not consistently apply information that was covered during training. | Trainee might be confused about when to perform certain tasks. | Make sure trainees know not only *what* to do but also *when* to do it. |
| Employee does not appear to care if he/she does the job correctly. | Trainee is not motivated to perform correctly. | During training, help trainees feel that they are part of a team. Spend more time helping them see how their job affects others. |

well-trained employees. This is called **return on investment.** A properly trained employee is likely to be more productive and to remain employed at your property for a longer period of time (and, consequently, to be less expensive) than is a poorly trained employee. Well-trained employees, then, are good investments.

The costs of training include:

- Salaries of the trainer and trainees.

- Facilities.

- Equipment.

- Materials such as training resources.

- Training supplies.

- The possibility of more errors and less productivity during the initial training period.

- Other miscellaneous expenses, such as refreshments during training breaks.

  Costs are also incurred if employees are not properly trained:

- More mistakes, which can cost the property time and money, and create dissatisfied guests

- Lower productivity, which can result in increased staffing needs

- Lost revenue due to poor guest service

- High turnover, which leads to increased recruiting efforts and other hiring costs

# Orientation

**Orientation** is the process of introducing new employees to the property and their jobs. New employees should be given a thorough orientation that begins the first day they arrive for work. Many new employees arrive with a great deal of enthusiasm about their positions. This enthusiasm presents an ideal opportunity for supervisors to foster pride in the organization and its goals.

## The Importance of Orientation

Orientation introduces new employees to your property and to their positions. Additionally, an orientation program also creates an employee's first impression of the staff, the supervisors, the property, and the company.

When employees start their first day of work, they're nervous, but they're also excited. What they think about the property begins with orientation. Greet new employees with an exciting, well-planned orientation program and they'll feel valued and welcome.

Employee turnover in the hospitality industry often averages as much as 200 to 300 percent per year. Statistically speaking, this means that the entire staff of some properties is replaced two to three times per year! Fortunately, this rarely happens. Instead, the percentages reflect extremely high turnover rates for employees in their first 30 days, balanced with lower rates for other employees who stay at the property longer than 30 days.

At one hotel, for example, more than half the turnover occurs within the first 30 days of staff members' employment. More often than not, employees who resigned within 30 days of being hired simply got off to a bad start. For them, the stress of starting a new job was simply too great.

That's why making a good first impression during orientation is so important. New employees' decisions to stay or leave are often based on their experiences during orientation and the first training sessions.

The orientation period is especially important because it can help relieve the anxiety many new employees experience. However, simply orienting employees to their new environment is not enough. It is also important to establish a good employer/employee relationship.

A well-planned and organized orientation will help a new employee get off to a good start in a new job. The orientation communicates the feeling to the employee that management cares, and it helps build the foundation of a successful professional and personal relationship.

If this attitude is also conveyed in training and in performance evaluation, the employee will develop positive attitudes and is likely to become a productive worker. Establishing **rapport** helps new employees by providing a reference point as they begin to model their relationships as well as their task behaviors.

Employees need to know that their presence in the organization is important and that their performance makes a positive contribution to organizational goals. The orientation process is also a time when employers and employees begin to establish trust in one another.

In addition to reduced turnover, numerous other benefits accrue from employee orientations. For example, they:

- Satisfy the new employee's need to know about where he or she will be working.
- Improve morale and contribute to employee motivation.
- Increase employee commitment through an introduction to the company's mission and philosophy.
- Communicate expectations to the employee.
- Show how individual jobs fit into the overall company mission.
- Help put the new employee at ease.

## Types of Orientation

Orientation programs differ from property to property. They differ in who conducts the program, how long the program runs, how formal it is, and what information is presented. In general, however, new employees should be given two types of orientation. A **general property orientation** is used to orient new employees to the organization and to the property as a whole. The **specific job orientation** focuses on organizational and departmental topics related to job performance.

As a supervisor, you will need to determine and understand your role in your property's orientation program. This means that you should:

- Know whether you are responsible for conducting both general property and specific job orientations or only the specific job orientation.
- Introduce new employees to their job and to the property.
- Provide the information and materials the employee needs to succeed.
- Understand that an orientation program needs support from *all* levels of management to be truly successful.

Exhibit 9 contains a sample checklist that can help you plan an orientation.

## General Property Orientation

A general property orientation helps new employees learn about the whole organization and its values and philosophy. It also helps the employees understand the value of their positions to the organization.

**Exhibit 9    New Employee Orientation Checklist**

Name of Employee:_____    Position: _____

Department:_____    Supervisor: _____

For each item below, place a check in the box and record the date the activity is completed or the information is provided.

*Part I — Introduction*

☐ _____ Welcome to the new position (give your name, find out what name the employee prefers to be called, etc.)

☐ _____ Tour of the property

☐ _____ Tour of department work area

☐ _____ Introduction to fellow employees

*Part II — Discussion of Daily Procedures*

☐ _____ Beginning/ending time of work shift

☐ _____ Break and meal periods

☐ _____ Uniforms (responsibilities for, cleanliness of, etc.)

☐ _____ Assignment of locker

☐ _____ Parking requirements

☐ _____ First aid and accident reporting procedures

☐ _____ Time clock or sign-in log requirements

☐ _____ Other (specify): _____

*Part III — Information about Salary/Wages*

☐ _____ Rate of pay

☐ _____ Deductions

☐ _____ Pay periods

☐ _____ Overtime policies

☐ _____ Completion of all payroll, withholding, insurance, and related forms

☐ _____ Other (specify): _____

*Part IV — Review of Policies and Rules*

☐ _____ Safety

☐ _____ Punctuality

☐ _____ Absenteeism

*(continued)*

**Exhibit 9** *(continued)*

☐ _____ Emergencies

☐ _____ Leaving work station

☐ _____ Packages

☐ _____ Fires, accidents, and emergencies

☐ _____ Maintenance and use of equipment

☐ _____ Illness

☐ _____ Use of telephone/cell phones

☐ _____ Smoking/eating/drinking

☐ _____ Vacations

☐ _____ Other (specify) _____

*Part V — Employee Handbook/Related Information*

☐ _____ Received and reviewed

☐ _____ Review of employee appraisal process

☐ _____ Review of organizational chart

☐ _____ Review of job description

☐ _____ Review of department's responsibilities

☐ _____ Review of all benefit plans

☐ _____ Discussion of performance standards

☐ _____ Discussion of career path possibilities

*Part VI — Miscellaneous Orientation Procedures*

(Review all other areas covered with the new employee)

☐ _____ _____

☐ _____ _____

☐ _____ _____

☐ _____ _____

☐ _____ _____

I certify that all of the above activities were completed on the date indicated.

Employee: _____ Date: _____

Trainer: _____ Date: _____

General property orientation at many large properties begins with a meeting of new employees conducted by human resources department personnel. Information covered generally includes the following:

- Welcome by the general manager
- Welcome by major department directors
- Video or electronic presentation or handouts about the organization's philosophy and the role the employee plays in helping meet the property's mission and goals
- Distribution of manuals and other materials
- Review of policies and procedures
- Discussion of benefits
- Discussion of guest and employee relations
- Completion of personnel forms
- Tour of the property

In addition to conducting a general orientation meeting, some managers let new employees stay overnight at the property and eat at the property's restaurant (both at the property's expense). This lets new employees get a feel for the level of service the property provides and how the property operates.

To understand your role in reinforcing a general property orientation, you must know the benefits a general orientation provides to both the company and the new employee.

Benefits of general orientation to the company:

- Provides a consistent message to all new employees
- Helps employees know they are working for a great company
- Introduces management
- Provides a memorable first impression of the company
- Builds a strong foundation of company values and philosophy
- Presents business goals and priorities
- Provides an opportunity to succeed
- Introduces the team approach at all levels in the organization
- Lowers turnover

Benefits of general orientation to the employee:

- Provides an understanding of the company's expectations about their performance
- Helps employees understand the value of their positions
- Builds self-esteem
- Helps employees realize they are important to the operation

- Provides structured learning about the company and the job
- Establishes early commitment to being a member of the team
- Builds a foundation for employee motivation

It is important to understand the role of a supervisor in reinforcing the general property orientation, regardless of whether the supervisor conducts it. The supervisor's role includes:

1. *Supporting your property's mission statement.* First, a supervisor must understand the **mission statement** of the company and the property. A mission statement is a brief statement explaining why the company exists and its overall goals. A well-defined mission statement rallies members around a shared vision of what the team stands for and what it strives to accomplish.

2. *Linking the general property orientation to the trainee's job.* A supervisor provides the link between the general property orientation and the specific job orientation by explaining how the departments work together. This might involve a tour of the property to help new employees see the various departments and their interactions. The new employee needs to meet fellow employees and learn his or her role in the organization.

3. *Helping new employees identify internal customers and external customers.* An effective orientation program also helps the new employee identify internal customers *and* external customers. In the hospitality industry, for example, guests are the external customers. Internal customers are staff members of departments and functional areas affected by processes that contribute to the making of a product or the delivery of a service.

## Specific Job Orientation

As a supervisor, you will be much more involved in specific job orientation than in general property orientation. Your success in conducting specific job orientation depends on how well you've prepared for it. Be ready to give your new employees the information they need to be confident, and let them know you're proud to have them on your team.

During specific job orientation, the focus shifts from organizational and departmental topics to those directly related to job performance. Employees are introduced to:

- The responsibilities outlined in their job description.
- Immediate needs such as safety information and key policies and procedures.
- Portions of the handbook relating to their job, the work environment, and the location of equipment.
- Their department's relationship to other departments.

The specific job orientation should represent the best of what the department has to offer and show the new employee exactly where he or she fits into the department. The supervisor can reinforce this message by emphasizing how the employee's job helps the company's operation. The employees should clearly understand the importance of their position in relation to the company's mission statement.

New employees are taken on a tour of the department and are introduced to the people with whom they will work and interact. The department's policies and procedures are discussed, including those related to work hours, time-clock operation and payroll, breaks, smoking, employee dining, and so on.

Specific job orientation provides benefits to both the department and the new employee.

Benefits of specific orientation to the department include the following:

- Provides consistency in employee training and development
- Helps employees ensure quality service and meet guest expectations
- Ensures that required standards will be maintained
- Provides consistency in staff performance
- Ensures staff capability
- Helps the department run more smoothly

Benefits of specific orientation to the employee include the following:

- Instructs the employee how to do the job correctly
- Builds self-esteem due to feeling of accomplishment
- Builds high morale
- Creates team fellowship and cooperation
- Helps employee become productive more quickly

## Orientation Activities

The culture of an organization will often dictate the type of activities chosen for the orientation. One organization might use a fast-paced, fun orientation, while another might emphasize the elegance of the property and the dignified nature of the employees. The format and activities chosen will also vary depending on how many employees are being orientated and how much information needs to be passed along.

Common types of orientation include group sessions, individual sessions, self-orientation, and mentor sessions. Each type has its advantages and disadvantages, depending on the property's circumstances. These advantages and disadvantages are listed in Exhibit 10.

Once the type of orientation that works best for the property is chosen, you need to decide which activities to include. Orientations can be as simple as one-on-one discussions or as elaborate as several multimedia presentations with panel discussions afterwards. Some common activities to include in an orientation are:

- Tour of the property
- Discussion/overview session

**Exhibit 10   Types of Orientation**

| Type of Orientation | Description | Advantages | Disadvantages |
|---|---|---|---|
| Group session | Two or more new employees are oriented at the same time. | • Saves time for the people conducting orientation.<br>• Helps new employees form a team.<br>• Provides consistency for all new employees. | • Can be difficult to schedule.<br>• Provides little individual attention.<br>• May not answer questions of all employees. |
| Individual session | A manager meets individually with the new employee to conduct orientations. | • New employee can set the pace of the orientation.<br>• Easy to schedule.<br>• Gives individualized information to each new employee. | • Can be time-consuming for the presenter if there are a lot of people who must be oriented.<br>• Does not ensure that all new employees receive the same information. |
| Self-orientation | The manager gives the orientation material to the new employee and tells the new employee to call if there are questions. | • Saves time for those conducting the orientation.<br>• Allows new employee to set the pace of his or her learning. | • Does not provide for any face-to-face question-and-answer period.<br>• No one is able to explain especially complex or sensitive issues unless the employee asks about them.<br>• Can leave the new employee feeling slightly insecure. |
| Mentor session | An experienced employee is paired with the new employee and helps the new employee learn whatever is necessary. | • Starts an ongoing relationship that can be beneficial to both parties.<br>• Gives the new employee ongoing support.<br>• Helps the experienced employee brush up on skills and knowledge. | • Orientations lack consistency.<br>• Quality of orientation depends upon the mentor selected.<br>• Time-consuming on the part of the mentor and the new employee. |

- Meal
- Slides or media presentation
- Panel discussions
- Distribution of printed material
- Question/answer session

## Orientation Evaluation

Like any other training program or process, orientation programs should be evaluated for success. Some people think of orientations as dull but necessary activities in which employees spend a day or two filling out forms and taking tours. Many managers have complained that orientations, especially general orientations, are ineffective and that employees do not learn from them.

Yet, when an orientation program is effective, the results are very measurable and beneficial to the property. Turnover is reduced, employees are more committed to the property, and team relationships are formed more quickly.

Simple forms of evaluation might involve having employees fill out evaluation forms after orientation or talking to new employees informally to ask what information given during the orientation was most helpful and what would have been helpful to include that wasn't.

 **Key Terms**

**attention span**—The length of time a person can concentrate on a topic or activity.

**auditory learners**—People who learn by listening or hearing.

**behavior modeling**—Demonstrating the same behaviors that you expect trainees to learn.

**coach**—To advise, guide, or direct trainees as they master new skills.

**coaching**—The process of providing positive or corrective feedback to an employee.

**corrective feedback**—Showing employees what they can do to work more effectively and confidently.

**demographics**—Characteristics that help define a group of persons.

**disabilities**—Physical or mental impairments that substantially limit one or more major life activities.

**external customers**—People outside an organization who purchase a product or service produced by the organization. In the hospitality industry, for example, guests are the external customers.

**follow through**—The process of providing additional support, encouragement, and evaluation upon completion of a training program.

**general property orientation**—Orientation that introduces a new employee to the organization and the property as a whole.

**internal customers**—Staff members of departments affected by processes that contribute to the making of a product or the delivery of a service.

**jargon**—Technical language specific to a job or industry, such as "ADR" (average daily rate) at the front desk.

**job breakdown**—Information that tells how to perform each task on a task list.

**job description**—A definition of a job and its requirements detailing the most important tasks that must be performed.

**learning**—Gaining knowledge or skills through experience or study

**learning rate**—The speed at which an individual is able to learn.

**learning style**—The unique way in which a person uses his or her senses to learn.

**mission statement**—A brief statement explaining why the company exists and its overall goals.

**motivation**—Desire to learn.

**objectives**—The purpose of a training program; objectives usually outline what the trainee is expected to know or do at the end of the training.

**off-the-job training**—Training conducted away from the work site.

**on-the-job training**—Training conducted at the employee's work site.

**one-on-one training**—Training that you conduct individually with a single employee.

**orientation**—The process of introducing new employees to the property and their jobs.

**positive feedback**—Letting employees know when they perform well and what they are doing correctly.

**rapport**—Relation marked by mutual trust, harmony, and friendship.

**repetition**—Saying information or demonstrating a task more than once.

**return on investment**—A measurement of the benefits of training in relation to the costs.

**sequence of instruction**—The order in which information is presented to trainees.

**specific job orientation**—Orientation that introduces new employees to their department and their specific role within the department and the property.

**tactile learners**—People who learn by touching or doing.

**task list**—A list of every task that an employee in a certain position must perform.

**training**—Any directed activity that results in learning.

**trial performance**—Opportunity for a trainee to practice a task or skill after it has been demonstrated by the trainer or supervisor.

**turnover**—The rate at which employees leave a property and are replaced.

**visual learners**—People who learn by looking or seeing.

 **Review Questions**

1. How do learning styles affect training?
2. What learning needs do most adults have?
3. What are advantages of group training and one-on-one training?
4. List four training methods and define each of them.
5. What qualities does a good trainer have?
6. What are the four steps in the four-step training method?
7. What are the two types of orientation?
8. What are advantages of effective orientation programs?

 **Internet Sites**

For more information, visit the following Internet sites. Remember that Internet addresses can change without notice. If the site is no longer there, you can use a search engine to look for additional sites.

American Hotel & Lodging Educational Institute
www.ahlei.org

The American Society for Training and Development
www.astd.org

Learning Ware
www.learningware.com

The Thiagi Group
www.thiagi.com

Trainers Warehouse
www.trainerswarehouse.com

# Chapter 5 Outline

Productivity Standards
    Determining Productivity Standards
    Balancing Quality and Quantity
Planning Staffing Requirements
    Fixed and Variable Labor
    Developing a Staffing Guide
Forecasting Business Volume
    The Nature of Forecasting
    Base Adjustment Forecasts
    Moving Average Forecasts
The Staffing Guide as a Scheduling Tool
The Staffing Guide as a Control Tool
    Variance Analysis
    Budgetary Control
Labor Scheduling Software
Monitoring and Evaluating Productivity

# Competencies

1. Identify the consequences of overstaffing and understaffing. (p. 135)

2. Explain how supervisors determine productivity standards. (pp. 136–141)

3. Explain how supervisors plan their staffing needs and develop a staffing guide. (pp. 141–145)

4. Forecast business volume using the base adjustment forecasting and the moving average forecasting methods. (pp. 145–151)

5. Explain how supervisors use staffing guides as labor scheduling and labor cost control tools. (pp. 152–159)

6. Describe the features and functions of software applications for scheduling and labor control. (pp. 159–163)

7. Identify procedures supervisors can use to monitor and evaluate productivity. (pp. 163–165)

# 5

# Managing Productivity and Controlling Labor Costs

THE HOSPITALITY INDUSTRY is **labor-intensive**; people, not machines and computers, produce and deliver the products and services that guests desire. Hospitality operations commonly spend 30 percent or more of their revenue to meet payroll costs. This fact underscores the importance of the supervisor's role in managing **productivity** and controlling labor costs. No hospitality operation of any size, or containing any number of operating units, can afford unproductive employees and wasted labor hours.

Assume that a hospitality operation's profits equal 8 percent of the revenue it generates from the sale of products and services. This means that, for every dollar of revenue, the operation earns a profit of eight cents. Also assume that supervisors who engage in poor scheduling practices create overstaffing that generates $500 in unnecessary labor costs every week. How much additional revenue must the operation generate to cover the $500 it wasted in higher-than-necessary labor costs?

The answer is *not* $500. Revenue must also pay for food, labor, and other operating costs, as well as mortgage or lease payments, taxes, and many other expenses. Therefore, the $500 in excessive labor costs must come out of the operation's profits. To maintain an 8-percent profit level, the operation must earn back the $500 it lost in profit by generating additional weekly revenue of $6,250 ($500 divided by the .08 profit requirement).

If that sounds like a lot of money, it is! If a hotel's average daily rate was $150, the first 42 rooms rented each week would generate only the revenue required to make up for the lost profit ($6,250 in revenue divided by a $150 room rate equals approximately 42 rooms). If a restaurant had a customer check average of $25, the 250 customers who dined there during the week would spend enough money to generate the profit needed to make up the $500 in lost profits ($6,250 in revenue divided by an average $25 check equals 250 customers).

The results of understaffing a department can be just as disastrous. While having too few employees to serve guests might decrease labor costs in the short term, over time it will likely increase turnover and decrease profits. The stress of constantly working short-handed will prompt employees to quit. When performance standards are not consistently met, revenues and profits will decrease due to guest dissatisfaction and lost business.

135

This chapter focuses on the supervisor's responsibility to schedule the correct number of employees, with the right skills, at the right time each day. The chapter presents step-by-step procedures that can help hospitality supervisors:

1. Develop productivity standards based on established performance requirements.

2. Construct a staffing guide based on productivity standards.

3. Create employee work schedules by using the staffing guide with business forecasts.

4. Increase productivity by appropriately revising performance standards.

# Productivity Standards

**Productivity standards** define the acceptable quantity of work to be done by trained employees who perform their work according to established performance standards. **Performance standards** explain the quality of the work that must be done. For example, the productivity standard for housekeepers in a housekeeping department establishes the time it should take a trained housekeeper to clean one guestroom according to established performance standards. That time assumes the housekeeper has been properly trained and has the required equipment, tools, materials, and supplies to do the job. The productivity standard for a food server might establish the number of guests a trained staff member can serve while meeting performance standards.

Performance standards vary according to the unique needs and requirements of each hospitality operation. Therefore, it is not possible to identify productivity standards that apply throughout the industry. Supervisors must balance quality (performance standards) and quantity (productivity standards) in relation to the volume of business and the level of service their departments provide.

For example, housekeeper duties vary widely among economy/limited-service, mid-range-service, and world-class-service hotels due to differences in room sizes and furnishings. Therefore, the productivity standards for housekeepers also vary among these types of properties. In fact, within the same hotel, the productivity standards for housekeepers might vary according to the different types of rooms that must be cleaned.

## Determining Productivity Standards

A supervisor begins to establish productivity standards by answering the question: How long should it take for an employee to perform a specific task according to the department's performance standards?

Assume that a housekeeping supervisor at the St. George Hotel determines that a fully trained housekeeper can meet performance standards by cleaning a guestroom in approximately 30 minutes. Exhibit 1 presents a sample productivity standard worksheet and shows how a productivity standard can be established for full-time housekeepers. Calculations within the exhibit consider the time needed for beginning- and end-of-shift duties, a 30-minute unpaid lunch break and two paid 15-minute breaks. The exhibit shows that the productivity standard

**Exhibit 1    Productivity Standard Worksheet—Housekeepers**

---

**Step 1**
**Determine how long it should take, on average, to clean one guestroom according to the department's performance standards.**

Approximately 30 minutes*

**Step 2**
**Determine the total shift time in minutes.**

8.5 hours × 60 minutes = 510 minutes

**Step 3**
**Determine the time available for guestroom cleaning.**

| | |
|---|---|
| Total Shift Time............................................................ | 510 minutes |
| Less: | |
| Beginning-of-Shift Duties .............................................. | 15 minutes |
| Morning Break (paid) ..................................................... | 15 minutes |
| Lunch Break (unpaid) ..................................................... | 30 minutes |
| Afternoon Break (paid)................................................... | 15 minutes |
| End-of-Shift Duties......................................................... | 15 minutes |
| Time Available for Guestroom Cleaning.......................... | 420 minutes |

**Step 4**
**Determine the productivity standard by dividing the result of Step 3 by the result of Step 1.**

$$\frac{420 \text{ minutes}}{30 \text{ minutes}} = \begin{array}{l} 14 \text{ guestrooms} \\ \text{per 8-hour shift} \end{array}$$

\*    Since performance standards vary from property-to-property and even within properties, this figure is used for illustrative purposes only. It is not a suggested time figure for cleaning guestrooms.

---

for housekeepers is to clean 14 guestrooms per eight-hour shift. Similar observations and calculations would be made for other positions in the housekeeping department, such as for inspectors, housepersons, and lobby attendants.

A dining room supervisor can also determine productivity standards by observing and tracking the time it takes for several fully trained employees to perform tasks according to performance standards. As with productivity standards for housekeepers, the productivity standards for dining room positions vary according to the style of service and the specific menu items served during different meal periods. Exhibit 2 presents a worksheet that a supervisor can use to determine a productivity standard for food servers. The worksheet provides columns for data and observations on the work of a single server over five lunch shifts. For each lunch shift, the supervisor records the following data:

- Number of guests the server served

- Number of hours the server worked

**Exhibit 2   Productivity Standard Worksheet—Food Servers**

**Position Performance Analysis**

Position: _____Service_____   Name of Employee: _____Joyce_____

Shift: _____A.M.—Lunch_____

| | 4/14 | 4/15 | 4/16 | 4/17 | 4/18 |
|---|---|---|---|---|---|
| No. of Guests Served | 38 | 60 | 25 | 45 | 50 |
| No. Hours Worked | 4 | 4 | 4 | 4 | 3.5 |
| No. of Guests/Labor Hour | 9.5 | 15 | 6.3 | 11.3 | 14.3 |
| Review Comments | Even workflow; no problems | Was really rushed; could not provide adequate service | Too much "standing around"; very inefficient | No problems; handled everything well | Worked fast whole shift; better with fewer guests |

General Comments

*Joyce is a better than average server; with all the tasks that service personnel must do in our restaurant, approximately 10 guests per labor hour can be served by one server. When the number of guests goes up, service quality decreases. When Joyce really had to rush, some guests waited longer than they should have had to. When the number of guests per labor hour dropped and Joyce was not busy, there was a lot of unproductive time.*

Suggested Meals/Labor Hour
(for this position): _____10_____        Performance Review by: _____W. Brown_____
                                                                Restaurant Manager

- Number of guests served per hour worked
- Comments concerning how well the server performed according to performance standards

    The exhibit shows that on April 14, Joyce served 38 guests during a four-hour shift. Joyce takes no breaks during four-hour shifts, so she served 9.5 guests per hour worked (38 guests divided by four hours of work). Over a five-day period, the supervisor observed her work and then recorded comments relating to her efficiency.

    Before calculating a productivity standard for this position, the supervisor would have completed worksheets for several trained servers who worked similar lunch shifts. In our example, the supervisor determined a productivity standard of 10 guests per labor hour. That is, in the supervisor's view, trained servers should be able to serve 10 guests for each hour worked without sacrificing established performance standards. Similar observations and calculations would be made for other dining room positions, such as hosts, buspersons, bartenders, and bar servers.

**BEST PRACTICE**

# GRAND THEME HOTELS

## The Creation of a Process to Track and Control Labor Costs

### Description

**The Practice:** Grand Theme Hotels conducted a series of "time and motion" studies for most of the hourly positions in the company's four properties to determine exactly how long each task (e.g., check in, check out, cleaning an occupied room, cleaning a check-out room, serving a meal) required. Supervisors and managers prepare schedules according to those targets.

**Why the Practice Was Developed:** According to Mark Kane, general manager, the purpose of identifying time requirements for each operational task was to reduce labor costs in a tight labor market.

### Execution

**The Approach to Implementation:** Once Grand Theme made the decision to initiate a time and motion study, an outside organization, Synchronamics, was hired to measure the time required to perform each aspect of a specific job. For example, in the bathroom, Synchronamics observed how long it took to change towels and to clean the bathtub/shower, toilet, countertop, and floor. Many measurements were taken of the same tasks, using different housekeepers on different days in different areas of the hotel, to derive an average number of minutes for the total job of cleaning a guestroom. Nearly all operational tasks underwent the same careful scrutiny to derive an average time for completing each task in the hotel.

The hourly employees affected by the study were involved in each step of the process from the beginning. Meetings were held to explain the what, why, and how of the process. The employees were told that they would share in whatever savings the company realized as a result of this practice. Task times were discussed with the employees, and they were given the opportunity to voice any disagreement. When the disagreements were justified, adjustments in the times were made.

The time and motion study provided some surprising results. For example, Grand Theme Hotels discovered that the average number of minutes required by a housekeeper to clean a room is about 20 minutes, including travel time, rather that the "standard" 30 minutes. Grand Theme Hotels adjusts this average time requirement up and down depending on the type of hotel (three-star versus four-star), and the amount and style of furniture in the room. Housekeepers were rewarded $75 for the first month of the program for meeting their production quotas; now they are awarded $50 per quarter. All rooms are inspected periodically to make sure the quality does not suffer, and some housekeepers have more rooms inspected than others. All, however, have at least two rooms inspected. In addition to the above, housekeepers are allowed to "buy" rooms when the need arises.

*(continued)*

**Best Practice**   *(continued)*

> The process is closely tracked. In housekeeping, for instance, a report is generated that shows cost per room, hours per room, and dollars per hour for each different level of the department, which makes it easy to spot when actual labor costs vary from targeted labor costs. Variances in these expenses are discussed immediately.
>
> Labor costs are also reduced by the environmentally sound practice of changing sheets in stayover rooms every third day, and changing only those towels left on the floor of the bathroom. A brochure in the room explains how many thousands of gallons of water are saved, as well as how many hundreds of pounds of detergent do not enter water reserves.
>
> ### Outcomes
>
> **Success of the Practice:** Grand Theme Hotels has achieved the productivity standard (or better) since implementing the program. In addition there is greater consistency in the performance of tasks.
>
> **Benefits for Customer:** For guests, the quality and consistency of standards are now better. Mr. Kane explained that in the two years that he has been with Grand Theme Hotels, he has received only one letter from an unhappy guest related to the program.
>
> ### Insights
>
> **Advice and Observations:** Mr. Kane advises involving all the employees in the entire process, making sure they are heard, and including their input in the program. He also suggests sharing the benefits with the employees. He notes that upkeep and tracking are essential, team meetings need to be held every day, and feedback needs to be given daily. Individuals who need retraining should get it as soon as possible.

Source: Laurette Dubé, Cathy A. Enz, Leo M. Renaghan, and Judy A. Siguaw, *American Lodging Excellence: The Key to Best Practices in the U.S. Lodging Industry* (Washington, D.C.: American Hotel Foundation, 1999), pp. 112–113.

With slight alterations, Exhibit 2 can be used to determine productivity standards for other hospitality positions, such as cooks, pantry workers, front desk agents, cashiers, and reservationists. For example, a productivity worksheet for a lunch cook would have space to record the number of meals prepared, the number of hours the cook worked, and the number of meals prepared per hour worked. Similarly, a worksheet for day-shift front desk agents would have space to record the number of check-ins and check-outs processed, the number of hours the agent worked, and the number of check-ins and check-outs processed per hour worked.

## Balancing Quality and Quantity

Supervisors must effectively balance productivity standards and performance standards. For example, if quality expectations (performance standards) are set too high, the quantity of work that can be done accordingly (productivity standards) might be unacceptably low. Overtime pay for current employees and/or the scheduling of additional staff might be needed to ensure that all work gets completed. However, the increased labor expense of scheduling additional staff might then exceed the department's budgeted labor expenses.

On the other hand, if quality expectations are set too low, the quantity of work that can be done will increase, and labor expenses might then be lower than the department's budget. While this might seem like a positive outcome, low performance standards might not meet the expectations of guests. Complaints from guests about poor service can affect an operation's future profits in at least two significant ways:

- Repeat business declines as dissatisfied guests choose not to come back.

- New business suffers as negative word-of-mouth advertising from dissatisfied guests drives away potential guests.

Balancing quality and quantity expectations results in realistic productivity standards. Savvy hoteliers agree that value (product and service quality relative to the price paid from the guests' perspectives) must be the starting point from which quality and quantity staffing decisions must be made. These productivity standards should form the basis for budgeting the department's labor expense and for planning staffing requirements.

# Planning Staffing Requirements

The first step in planning staffing requirements is to determine which positions within the department are fixed and which are variable relative to changes in business volume. Once this is determined, productivity standards can be used to develop a staffing guide for variable staff positions.

## Fixed and Variable Labor

**Fixed staff positions** are those that must be filled regardless of the volume of business. Many of these positions are salaried and managerial in nature, and include department managers, assistant managers, and some supervisors. The actual number and type of fixed staff positions will vary from property-to-property.

Because fixed labor is the minimum amount of labor needed to operate the lodging or food service facility regardless of business volume, it represents the minimum labor expense. During slow business periods, labor expense should be kept as low as possible. Therefore, several times during the year, top managers should review the amount of fixed labor needed in each department. During this review, managers might consider the following temporary actions to reduce labor expense during slow business periods:

- Eliminate or curtail a particular service. For example, reduce the hours of dining room, concierge, or valet parking service.

- Assign salaried staff duties normally performed by hourly employees. For example, an assistant restaurant manager might be stationed at the host stand to seat guests and take reservations. Some operations use this tactic routinely to reduce variable labor hours and related costs, but doing so has its downside as well. The salaried manager who must work these hours still must find time to do the other tasks he or she would normally do at this time. Adding excessive hours to the schedules of salaried employees can affect their morale and contribute to turnover.

- Adjust tasks performed by hourly staff. For example, given the proper cross-training, a front desk agent might also function as a cashier and/or reservationist during times of low business volume.

Each of the above and other possible ways to temporarily reduce labor costs must be carefully considered and planned. Ideas should be obtained from the employees who will be affected by them. In addition, supervisors should ensure that all affected employees are trained to perform additional duties and that no actions taken will reduce the quality of guests' experiences.

The number of **variable staff positions** to be filled on any given day will depend on the expected volume of business. For example, the number of front desk agents scheduled to work will increase as the expected number of morning checkouts and afternoon/evening check-ins increases. In the housekeeping department, the number of housekeepers, housepersons, and inspectors needed will depend primarily on the number of rooms occupied during the previous night. Similarly, the number of kitchen and dining room staff members scheduled to work will depend on the number of guests expected for breakfast, lunch, and dinner.

## Developing a Staffing Guide

A **staffing guide** indicates the number of labor hours that must be worked by persons in variable staff positions as the volume of expected business changes. When a fairly reliable forecast of business volume has been made, a supervisor can properly schedule the correct number of employees to work each day. Exhibit 3 shows a sample staffing guide for housekeepers. This staffing guide uses the 30-minute productivity standard identified in Exhibit 1. If the hotel is forecasted to be at 90 percent occupancy, there will be 225 rooms to clean the next day (250 rooms × 0.9). It will take a total of 113 labor hours to clean them (225 rooms × 0.5 hours, rounded to 113). At 80 percent occupancy, there will be 200 rooms to clean (250 rooms × 0.8). It will take 100 labor hours to clean them (200 rooms × 0.5 hours).

**Exhibit 3   Sample Variable Labor Staffing Guide for Housekeepers**

| Productivity Standard = 30 minutes/room | | | | | | | | | | | |
|---|---|---|---|---|---|---|---|---|---|---|---|
| Occupancy % | 100% | 95% | 90% | 85% | 80% | 75% | 70% | 65% | 60% | 55% | 50% |
| Rooms Occupied | 250 | 238 | 225 | 213 | 200 | 188 | 175 | 163 | 150 | 138 | 125 |
| Housekeepers' Labor Hours (rooms only) | 125 | 119 | 113 | 107 | 100 | 94 | 88 | 87 | 75 | 69 | 63 |

While the above calculations are easy to make, a significant amount of experience and judgment is required to translate the number of hours in the staffing guide into the actual number of housekeepers' hours that should be scheduled. First, a hotel may have rooms of different sizes, bedding configurations, and amenities such as kitchenettes and furnishings. Each of these factors affect the time required to clean them. To complicate the scheduling decision even further, the same room may take significantly more or less time to clean on some days. Consider the implications of the following:

- The room is occupied for one night by one person who arrives late and departs early.

- The room is occupied by a family who spend significant time in it.

- The room is a stayover with no bedding changes.

- The room is occupied by a person who wishes to work in it all day and just requests some fresh face cloths and coffee packets.

**Determining the Number of Employees.** The staffing guide helps a supervisor determine how many employees to staff. For example, when the hotel is at 90 percent occupancy, the staffing guide in Exhibit 3 indicates that there will be 225 rooms to clean. Dividing 225 rooms by the 14 per eight-hour shift standard in Exhibit 1 indicates that it will take the equivalent of 16 full-time housekeepers to clean those rooms (225 rooms ÷ 14 = 16.07, rounded to 16). This number is expressed as **full-time equivalents** or **FTEs**. The *actual* number of housekeepers scheduled to work on any given day will vary depending on the number of full-time and part-time employees the supervisor schedules to work. In this example, the supervisor might schedule 16 full-time housekeepers who clean 14 rooms each, but he or she might instead schedule 12 full-time housekeepers who clean 14 rooms each and eight part-time housekeepers who clean about seven rooms each in four-hour shifts. Many combinations of full-time and part-time employees (as well as the number of hours part-time employees work) can be scheduled to meet the 14-room per FTE productivity standard.

When calculating the number of housekeepers needed on a given day, supervisors generally take into account a variety of factors. These include the variables in rooms and occupancy uses such as those discussed earlier. In addition, supervisors might schedule more labor hours than indicated by the staffing guide to cover the estimated number of employees who call in sick or who will otherwise be unavailable to work all or some of their scheduled hours on a given shift.

Another important adjustment relates to the effect of turnover on productivity. If a department has a high turnover of employees, the supervisor rarely has a complete staff of fully trained employees. The staffing guide's productivity ratios assume a fully trained staff. High turnover in a department can create a situation in which 30 percent or more of the staff at any time is in some stage of training. This means they will be unable to perform at the speed and efficiency demanded by the productivity ratios used in the staffing guide.

In these cases, supervisors must either constantly over-schedule labor hours or revise the staffing guide to reflect more realistic productivity ratios based on the performance levels of under-trained employees. These factors illustrate that the ideal ratio of housekeepers to rooms (one to fourteen in our example) is a good place to start, but that ratio must often be modified to fit different situations in the same property.

**Estimating Labor Costs.** What are the estimated labor costs for housekeepers if the staffing guide is followed? We determined in Exhibit 3 that it will take about 113 hours to clean 225 rooms. Can we simply multiply the housekeepers' wage rate by 113 hours? As shown in Exhibit 4, the answer is no. Recall from Exhibit 1 that a full-time employee spends seven hours each shift cleaning rooms, but also spends 30 minutes each shift on beginning- and end-of-shift duties and another 30 minutes each shift on paid breaks. This means the employee is paid for one hour in addition to the time spent cleaning rooms. Looking only at room cleaning time will understate the labor costs. Exhibit 4 includes these non-room-cleaning hours in line 5. If a hotel offers its housekeepers paid lunch periods, that time would also have to be included in the calculation.

The number of FTEs needed for any given occupancy is determined by dividing the number of occupied rooms by the 14-room-per-FTE standard. In our example, we determined that the hotel needs 16 FTEs at 90 percent occupancy. Each of the 16 FTE employees will work roughly one hour of non-room-cleaning hours, so 16 hours must be added to the room cleaning hours.

Once you have determined the total labor hours expected, multiply that total by the average wage rate of the employees. (If greater precision is required, you might need to perform the calculation separately for each employee and total the results.) Exhibit 4 assumes the average hourly rate for all housekeepers is $13. At 90 percent occupancy, total expected wages (hourly rate × number of hours worked) is 129 hours × $13 or $1,677). Note that the hourly rate excludes the cost of fringe benefits because those costs are carried in a separate labor expense account.

**Exhibit 4    Labor Hours and Costs: Staffing Guide Standards for Housekeepers**

| Productivity Standard = 30 minutes/room | | | | | | | | | | | |
|---|---|---|---|---|---|---|---|---|---|---|---|
| 1 | Occupancy | 100% | 95% | 90% | 85% | 80% | 75% | 70% | 65% | 60% | 55% | 50% |
| 2 | Rooms Occupied | 250 | 238 | 225 | 213 | 200 | 188 | 175 | 163 | 150 | 138 | 125 |
| 3 | Labor Hours (rooms only) | 125 | 119 | 113 | 107 | 100 | 94 | 88 | 87 | 75 | 69 | 63 |
| 4 | Employees (FTE) | 18 | 17 | 16 | 15 | 14 | 13 | 13 | 12 | 11 | 10 | 9 |
| 5 | Labor Hours (Other) | 18 | 17 | 16 | 15 | 14 | 13 | 13 | 12 | 11 | 10 | 9 |
| 6 | Total Labor Hours (lines 3 + 5) | 143 | 136 | 129 | 122 | 114 | 107 | 101 | 99 | 86 | 79 | 72 |
| 7 | Average Hourly Rate | $13.00 | $13.00 | $13.00 | $13.00 | $13.00 | $13.00 | $13.00 | $13.00 | $13.00 | $13.00 | $13.00 |
| 8 | Housekeepers' Wages | $1,859 | $1,768 | $1,677 | $1,586 | $1,482 | $1,391 | $1,313 | $1,287 | $1,118 | $1,027 | $936 |

Regardless of the combination of full-time and part-time employees who are eventually scheduled to work, the total expected wage expense according to the staffing guide should be roughly $1,677 when the hotel is at 90 percent occupancy.

A more fully developed staffing guide than the one shown in Exhibits 3 and 4 would provide similar calculations for other variable staff positions in the housekeeping department.

With such a tool and reliable occupancy forecasts, the supervisor can effectively and efficiently schedule the correct number of labor hours for each variable labor position within the department.

Supervisors with unionized work forces must incorporate a wide range of restrictions into a staffing guide. It is not uncommon, for example, for a labor contract to stipulate the minimum and maximum hours that a union member can work per shift. The tasks that can be done may also be specified; for example, a housekeeper may not be able to assist employees in other positions. Overtime restrictions for unscheduled labor hours and the number and timing of work breaks might also be addressed in the union contract.

**Staffing Guides and the Budget.** The staffing guide used by supervisors to schedule variable labor must be developed in a way that attains budget goals. It would not, for example, be reasonable for a housekeeping department's budget to permit an average of $1,850 per day in variable wages for housekeepers to clean a specified number of rooms when the staffing guide, if carefully followed, would permits $2,100 in variable wage costs to clean that number of rooms each day.

Staffing guides and operating budgets share one important common goal: they both must reflect the quality of products and services that managers believe are important for the hospitality operation's guests. Operating budgets are revised at least annually in most properties. Staffing guides, unless needing to reflect significantly revised standards, very different products and services, or vastly different procedures to attain them, are revised less frequently. Therefore, annual budgets typically incorporate financial information driven by carefully developed and monitored operating plans expressed in staffing guides or, as noted above, require staffing plans to be altered as significant budget assumptions are made.

# Forecasting Business Volume

No matter how precise the department's staffing guide, accurate labor scheduling depends on the reliability of forecasts that predict the volume of business for a particular month, week, day, or meal period. Forecasting in large hospitality properties is often the responsibility of a committee made up of representatives from key departments. In small properties, the general manager and/or designated supervisors might prepare the necessary forecasts.

Many hospitality organizations develop monthly, ten-day, and three-day forecasts of business volume. The supervisor uses the monthly forecast to generate initial work schedules for employees in the department. The ten-day and three-day forecasts are used to fine-tune the work schedules and to anticipate increases or decreases in business.

---

## Budget Development Affects Scheduling Practices

Managers in some properties develop weekly budgets and combine them to yield an annual budget. Other managers develop monthly budgets and combine them to generate their annual budget. Knowledge of how budget numbers are developed can help schedule planners use staffing guides. If weekly budgets are available, a planner might determine the average wage cost for a specific position by dividing the weekly budgeted wage by the number of days the operation is open to determine the average daily wage. This can be then be compared with the wage that will be incurred when the staffing guide is used.

Wise supervisors know that fewer hours should be scheduled when forecasted business volume is low, and more hours are required as planned business volume increases. This double-check between the staffing guide and the budget is helpful because even the best budgets cannot accurately estimate business revenues and expenses for a week that is a year or more into the future when the budget is developed. The actual revenue and expenses incurred to generate it is the best measure of control effectiveness, and staffing guides and operating budgets must work together to best meet financial goals without sacrificing quality in the process.

---

Exhibit 5 presents a sample form that rooms division managers can use to develop ten-day forecasts. Note that the form in Exhibit 5 is first used to estimate the total forecasted rooms (row 9). It does this by estimating departures (row 2) because they represent rooms that can be resold. Reservations made by groups and individuals (rows 3 and 4) increase the number of rooms needed. It also estimates the number of reservations that will be received after the forecast is completed (row 5) and the expected number of walk-ins (row 6). Then, by considering the total arrivals (row 7) and stayovers (row 8), the total forecasted number of rooms to be sold can be determined (row 9).

The total number of forecasted rooms (row 9) is multiplied by a multiplier based on the average number of guests per occupied room on the same day for the last three weeks. This calculation yields the forecasted number of guests who will be in the hotel (row 11) for each day in the ten-day occupancy forecast.

This form can also be used to report the actual number of rooms occupied, taken from the daily report for the actual date (row 12); the difference between the forecasted and the actual number of rooms occupied on each day is also reported (row 13). A final row (15) is used to provide explanations about significant variances.

Exhibit 6 presents a similar ten-day forecast form that food service managers can use to indicate the forecasted (F) and actual (A) number of meals in each of the hotel's food and beverage outlets. Note that this information—and reports about it—are very easy to generate using modern point-of-sale (POS) systems.

Exhibit 7 presents a sample three-day forecast for guestrooms to revise predictions made on the hotel's ten-day forecast (see Exhibit 5). As you review Exhibit 7, note that the number of occupied rooms from the previous night is reduced by the number of expected and early departures and is increased by the number of

**Exhibit 5    Sample Ten-Day Forecast Form**

**Ten-Day Occupancy Forecast**

Location _____    # _____    Week Ending _____

Date Prepared: _____    Prepared By: _____

To be submitted to all department heads at least one week before the first day listed on forecast.

| | Fri. | Sat. | Sun. | Mon. | Tues. | Wed. | Thur. | Fri. | Sat. | Sun. |
|---|---|---|---|---|---|---|---|---|---|---|
| 1. Date and Day (start week and end week the same as the payroll schedule) | | | | | | | | | | |
| 2. Estimated Departures | | | | | | | | | | |
| 3. Reservation Arrivals—Group (taken from log book) | | | | | | | | | | |
| 4. Reservation Arrivals—Individual (taken from log book) | | | | | | | | | | |
| 5. Future Reservations (estimated reservations received after forecast is completed) | | | | | | | | | | |
| 6. Expected Walk-ins (% of walk-ins based on reservations received and actual occupancy for past two weeks) | | | | | | | | | | |
| 7. Total Arrivals | | | | | | | | | | |
| 8. Stayovers | | | | | | | | | | |
| 9. TOTAL FORECASTED ROOMS | | | | | | | | | | |
| 10. Occupancy Multiplier (based on number of guests per occupied room for average of the same day for last three weeks) | | | | | | | | | | |
| 11. FORECASTED NUMBER OF GUESTS | | | | | | | | | | |
| 12. Actual Rooms Occupied (taken from daily report for actual date to be completed by front office supervisor) | | | | | | | | | | |
| 13. Forecasted Variance (difference between forecast and rooms occupied on daily report) | | | | | | | | | | |

14. Explanation (to be completed by front office supervisor and submitted to general manager; attach additional memo if necessary)

APPROVED: _____    DATE: _____
          General Manager's Signature

unexpected stayovers and unoccupied rooms. These calculations yield the number of rooms available for sale. To that number, the supervisor adds the number of expected arrivals, walk-ins, and same-day reservations and subtracts the number of "no-shows" to yield the number of occupied rooms.

**Exhibit 6    Sample Ten-Day Forecast—Food Service**

**TEN-DAY VOLUME FORECAST—FOOD**

Date Prepared —————————
Week Ending —————————

Restaurant ————————————
(LOCATION)

| | DATE | | | | | | | | | | | | | | | | | | | | | |
|---|---|---|---|---|---|---|---|---|---|---|---|---|---|---|---|---|---|---|---|---|---|---|
| | DAY | THUR. | | FRI. | | SAT. | | SUN. | | MON. | | TUES. | | WED. | | THUR. | | FRI. | | SAT. | | Totals |
| | | Previous Week | | | | | | | | | | | | | | | | | | | | |
| **FOOD DEPARTMENT** | | F | A | F | A | F | A | F | A | F | A | F | A | F | A | F | A | F | A | F | A | F | A |
| Dining Room | | | | | | | | | | | | | | | | | | | | | | | |
| Breakfast | | | | | | | | | | | | | | | | | | | | | | | |
| Lunch | | | | | | | | | | | | | | | | | | | | | | | |
| Dinner | | | | | | | | | | | | | | | | | | | | | | | |
| Total D.R. Covers | | | | | | | | | | | | | | | | | | | | | | | |
| Coffee Shop | | | | | | | | | | | | | | | | | | | | | | | |
| Breakfast | | | | | | | | | | | | | | | | | | | | | | | |
| Lunch | | | | | | | | | | | | | | | | | | | | | | | |
| Total C.S. Covers | | | | | | | | | | | | | | | | | | | | | | | |
| Banquet | | | | | | | | | | | | | | | | | | | | | | | |
| Breakfast | | | | | | | | | | | | | | | | | | | | | | | |
| Lunch | | | | | | | | | | | | | | | | | | | | | | | |
| Dinner | | | | | | | | | | | | | | | | | | | | | | | |
| Total Banquet Covers | | | | | | | | | | | | | | | | | | | | | | | |
| Room Service | | | | | | | | | | | | | | | | | | | | | | | |
| Total R.S. Covers | | | | | | | | | | | | | | | | | | | | | | | |
| TOTAL FOOD COVERS | | | | | | | | | | | | | | | | | | | | | | | |

SPECIAL COMMENTS
(i.e., types of groups—V.I.P., etc.)

**F = Forecast**
**A = Actual**

At that point, the occupancy percentage (i.e., the number of occupied rooms divided by the total number of rooms in the hotel) can be determined. The expected house count is found by multiplying the forecasted number of occupied rooms by the multiple occupancy percentage, which is determined based on experience.

Because forecasts directly impact the supervisor's ability to properly schedule labor, many hotel supervisors monitor reservations throughout a given day, update forecasts, and make modifications to employee schedules as needed. For example, the number of reservation cancellations on a given day will lower the number of labor hours needed in housekeeping for the following day. Likewise, an unexpected increase in reservations on a given day will increase the number of labor hours needed in housekeeping for the following day.

## The Nature of Forecasting

To use forecasts as effective labor scheduling tools, supervisors must understand the nature and limitations of forecasting. Forecasting deals with the future. A

**Exhibit 7    Sample Three-Day Forecast Form**

**Three-Day Forecast**

Date of Forecast: _____          Forecast Completed By: _____

Total Rooms in Hotel: _____

|  |  | Tonight | Tomorrow | 3rd Night |
|---|---|---|---|---|
| | **Day** | | | |
| | **Date** | | | |
| Previous Night Occupied Rooms[1] | | | | |
| − | Expected Departures | | | |
| − | Early Departures | | | |
| + | Unexpected Stayovers | | | |
| + | Unoccupied Rooms[2] | | | |
| = | Rooms Available For Sale | | | |
| + | Expected Arrivals | | | |
| + | Walk-ins & Same Day Reservations | | | |
| − | No-Shows | | | |
| = | Occupied Rooms | | | |
| = | Occupancy % | | | |
| = | Expected House Count[3] | | | |

[1]   Previous night occupied rooms is determined from either the actual number of rooms occupied last night or the forecasted number of rooms from the previous night.
[2]   Unoccupied rooms equals the total number of rooms in the hotel less the number of rooms occupied.
[3]   Expected house count equals the forecasted occupied rooms times the multiple occupancy percentage for the day (found on the computer report).

**Distribution:**   General Manager, Front Desk, Housekeeping, All Food and Beverage, Accounting, Sales, Banquets, Security

forecast made today is for activity during a future period, whether it is tonight's dinner sales or next year's room sales.

The time period involved is significant. A forecast today for tomorrow's sales is generally much easier to develop, and is likely to be more accurate, than a forecast today of next year's sales. The further the forecast period is from the date the forecast is made, the greater the difficulty in making the forecast. In addition, there is a greater risk that the actual results will differ from the forecast. Long-range forecasts are periodically reviewed and revised on the basis of new information obtained after the forecasts were made.

Forecasting involves uncertainty. If managers were certain about what circumstances would exist during the forecasted period, they could easily prepare forecasts. Virtually all situations that managers confront involve uncertainty; therefore, managers must gather information on which to base their forecasts and make judgments.

Assume that room sales for a major hotel are forecasted one year in advance. The manager (i.e., the forecaster) might be uncertain about competition, guest demand, room rates, and other factors. Nevertheless, using the best information available and his/her best judgment, the manager must make a forecast.

Forecasts generally rely on information such as historical data about check-ins and check-outs, group histories, weather, and special events and holidays. Historical data like past transient room sales might not be a strong indicator of future activity, but they are considered reasonable starting points.

Many computer-based property management systems and point-of-sale systems include revenue management software programs, which consider a number of factors to make forecasts. When no such tools are available, managers and supervisors involved in forecasting should modify their forecasts when current factors make historical information less useful for the future time period. For example, an approaching snow storm might have a major impact on hotel occupancy for a three-day period, regardless of past trends.

By their nature, forecasts are generally less accurate than desired. Managers can often improve forecasts by investing in revenue management software programs. However, slight changes should be expected between forecasted demand and actual demand on any given day.

Supervisors should monitor their reservation systems to make necessary adjustments to their three-day forecasts. In addition, long range forecasts should be revised as soon as there is a change in the circumstances on which the forecasts were based. For example, an increasingly excellent food and beverage reputation due to favorable publicity might call for reforecasting (i.e., increasing) next month's food and beverage revenue.

## Base Adjustment Forecasts

One of the simplest forecasting methods is to use the most recently collected data as the basis for the forecast. This is called the **base adjustment forecast**. For example, a food service manager's revenue projections for the current month might be based on revenue generated the previous month. To take seasonality into account, a manager might use revenue from the same month of the previous year as a base, then add or subtract a certain percentage to make the revenue goal more accurate.

For example, assume that a hotel's dining room generated revenue in January 20X1 of $150,000. The projection for January 20X2, using an anticipated 10 percent increase due to expected increases including menu selling price increases, would be $165,000, computed as follows:

$$\text{Base} \times (1 + 10\%) = \text{Forecast for January 20X2}$$

$$\$150{,}000 \times 1.1 = \underline{\underline{\$165{,}000}}$$

Although this method is very simple, it might provide reasonably accurate forecasts, especially for estimates of up to one year.

## Moving Average Forecasts

In some cases, the major cause of variations in the data used to make forecasts is randomness. Managers attempt to remove the random effect by averaging the data from specified time periods. One such approach to forecasting is the **moving average forecasting method**. This method can be expressed as follows:

$$\text{Moving Average} = \frac{\text{Activity in Previous } n \text{ Periods}}{n}$$

Exhibit 8 reveals weekly meals served for weeks 1 through 12. Using a three-week moving average, the estimate for the number of meals to be served during the thirteenth week is 1,025. It is calculated from the information in Exhibit 8, beginning with week 10:

$$\text{3-Week Moving Average} = \frac{1{,}025 + 1{,}000 + 1{,}050}{3}$$

$$= \underline{\underline{1{,}025}} \text{ meals}$$

As new weekly results become available, they are used in calculating the average by adding the most recent week and dropping the earliest week. In this way, the calculated average is "moving." It is continually updated to include only the most recent information for the last three weeks. Note that the greater the number of periods averaged, the less effect random variations will have on the forecast.

## Exhibit 8   Weekly Meals Served

| Week | Actual Meals Served |
|------|---------------------|
| 1 | 1,000 |
| 2 | 900 |
| 3 | 950 |
| 4 | 1,050 |
| 5 | 1,025 |
| 6 | 1,000 |
| 7 | 975 |
| 8 | 1,000 |
| 9 | 950 |
| 10 | 1,025 |
| 11 | 1,000 |
| 12 | 1,050 |

# The Staffing Guide as a Scheduling Tool

Sales or revenue forecasts are used in conjunction with the staffing guide to determine the "right" number of labor hours to schedule each day for every position in the department. Supervisors have found the following tips helpful when developing and distributing work schedules:

- A schedule should cover a full workweek.

- Workweeks often are scheduled from Saturday to Friday because weekend leisure business is generally more difficult to forecast beyond a three day forecast.

- The work schedule should be approved by appropriate managers before it is posted or distributed to employees.

- Schedules should be posted at least three days before the beginning of the time period for which they apply.

- Schedules should be posted in the same location and at the same time each week.

- Days off, vacation time, and requested days off should be planned as far in advance as possible and indicated on the posted work schedule. Decisions about these schedule issues should be made on the basis of policies that apply to all employees in all departments.

- The work schedule for the current week should be reviewed daily in relation to forecast information. If necessary, changes to the schedule should be made.

- Any scheduling changes should be noted and highlighted directly on the posted work schedule so the changes are not overlooked by the affected employees.

- A copy of the posted work schedule can be used to monitor the daily attendance of employees. This copy should be retained as part of the department's permanent records.

Whenever possible, work schedules should be developed to meet the day-to-day (and even hour-by-hour) demands of business volume. For example, if a large convention group is expected to check in between 2 P.M. and 4 P.M. on a particular day, additional front desk agents might be needed during those hours. Also, additional housekeepers might need to be scheduled to work earlier in the day to ensure that clean rooms will be available for the large number of expected arrivals. If the dining room attracts local business people during the lunch period, more cooks and servers might need to be scheduled during the rush time than are scheduled for other hours during the shift.

Some supervisors use a schedule worksheet to determine when employees are needed to work. Let's review how the supervisor might have completed the schedule worksheet shown in Exhibit 9. After receiving the forecast of 250 estimated guests, the supervisor checked the staffing guide and found that 18 labor hours should be scheduled for the position of assistant cook for the evening shift. Knowing that the peak hours during the dinner period are between 7:30 P.M. and

**Exhibit 9   Schedule Worksheet**

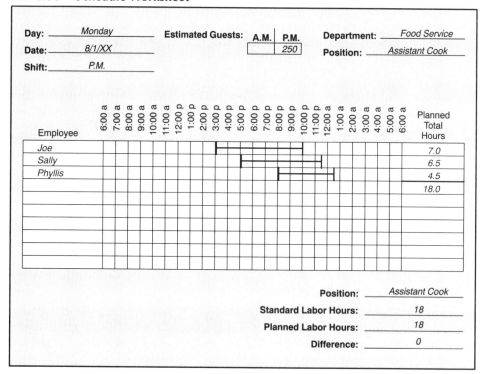

9:30 P.M., the supervisor staggered the work schedule of three assistant cooks to cover these peak hours. Joe was scheduled to work earlier to perform duties at the beginning of the shift, and Phyllis was scheduled to work later to perform duties at the end of the shift.

Not every supervisor would need to complete a schedule worksheet for each position during every work shift. In many departments, business volume stabilizes, creating a pattern of labor demands that makes scheduling relatively easy. However, all supervisors must develop work schedules that meet the particular business demands of their departments. The following sections present useful **alternative scheduling** techniques. These techniques might also meet the needs of many employees and, properly implemented, could increase staff morale and job satisfaction.

**Stagger Regular Work Shifts of Full-Time Employees.** Because the volume of business varies from hour to hour, there is no need for all employees to begin and end their shifts at the same times. By staggering and overlapping work shifts, the supervisor can ensure that the greatest number of employees is working during peak business hours.

**Compress the Work Week of Some Full-Time Employees.** For departments such as housekeeping, it might be possible to offer some full-time employees the opportunity to work the equivalent of a standard work week in fewer than the usual five days. One popular arrangement compresses a 40-hour work week into four 10-hour days. This technique can benefit lodging operations whose primary market is the business traveler. A compressed work schedule for some full-time housekeepers would meet the demands of high occupancy during the middle of the week.

**Implement Split Shifts.** A split shift schedules an employee to work during two separate time periods on the same day. For example, a day-shift dining room server might be scheduled from 8 A.M. to 10 A M to handle breakfast business and, on the same day, be scheduled from 11:30 A.M. to 1:30 P.M. to handle lunch business. This technique helps the supervisor ensure that the greatest number of employees is working during peak business hours. However, it will likely meet the personal needs of very few full-time employees (though offering split shifts to part-time employees might give them a convenient way to increase their earnings).

**Increase the Number of Part-Time Employees.** Employing a substantial number of part-time workers provides the supervisor with greater scheduling flexibility. Part-time employees can easily be scheduled to match peak business hours. Also, employing part-time workers can reduce labor costs, because the costs of benefits and overtime pay generally decrease.

**Increase the Number of Temporary Employees.** Temporary employees can also be used. Many properties keep a file of names of people who do not want steady work, but like to work occasionally. A large banquet, employee illness, or similar circumstances might create the need for temporary assistance.

While these scheduling principles are helpful, two of the most useful scheduling tools are the supervisor's past experience in developing work schedules and the supervisor's knowledge of the staff's capabilities. In many food and beverage operations, the pattern of business volume stabilizes and creates a repeating pattern of labor requirements. The more experience a supervisor acquires in relation to a specific operation, the easier it becomes to stagger work schedules, balance full-time and part-time employees, and effectively use temporary workers.

Similarly, the better a supervisor understands the capabilities of the operation's staff, the easier it becomes to schedule the right employees for particular times and shifts. For example, some servers might work best when they are scheduled for the late dinner shift, or some cooks might not perform well when experiencing the stress of a busy lunch rush where fast service is the norm. These factors can be taken into account when planning work schedules.

Whenever possible, managers or supervisors with scheduling responsibilities should consider their employees' preferences. Employees can be given schedule request forms to indicate which days or shifts they want off. These requests should be submitted by employees several weeks in advance and honored by management to the maximum extent possible.

Once the working hours for each employee are established, they should be combined in a schedule and posted for employee review and use. The posted schedule attempts to provide employees with the best possible advance notice of their work hours.

Technology can also help with the distribution of employee work schedules. For example, some hospitality organizations have an **intranet** system designed to facilitate communication among staff. An intranet is a partitioned section of the public website that is password-protected to provide staff members with timely access to important work-related information. For example, in addition to the traditional posting of employee schedules on an employee bulletin board, the schedule can also be electronically sent to employees with Internet access. As well, some hospitality operations also have one or more employee-accessible computers at the work site, and they can be used to obtain the employee schedule.

Of course, schedule plans do not always work. Employees might call in sick or fail to show up without warning. Also, the number of actual guests and the volume of meals might be lower or higher than expected. Therefore, it is often necessary to revise, post, and/or distribute modified work schedules.

Management must continually encourage employees to adhere to posted work schedules. Policies providing for on-call staff members might help protect the operation when the unscheduled absences of staff members result in a reduced number of employees. Supervisors, of course, must comply with all union, legal, or other restrictions regarding policies that require employees to call in or be available for work on days when they are not scheduled.

# The Staffing Guide as a Control Tool

Using the department's staffing guide and a reliable business volume forecast to develop employee work schedules is a sound business practice. However, it does not guarantee that the hours employees actually work will equal the number of hours for which they were scheduled to work. Managers must monitor and evaluate the scheduling process by comparing, on a weekly basis, the actual hours each employee works with the number of hours for which the employee was scheduled to work. Information about actual hours worked is usually obtained from the accounting department, from a staff member assigned to maintain payroll records, and/or from electronic payroll systems. These are discussed later in this chapter.

Exhibit 10 presents a sample weekly department labor hour report for the food service department in a hotel. Actual hours worked by each employee are recorded for each day of the week in columns 2 through 8. Actual total hours worked for each employee and for the position categories are totaled in column 9. These actual hours worked can be compared with the scheduled labor hours shown in column 10. Significant variances should be analyzed and corrective action taken when necessary.

## Variance Analysis

The sample weekly labor hour report (Exhibit 10) shows that during the week of July 14, 216.5 labor hours were scheduled for dining room employees, but the actual hours worked totaled 224.5. This indicates a variance of eight hours. Is eight hours a significant variance? Should the manager or supervisor investigate it?

To answer these questions, let's do some quick calculations. Assuming an average hourly wage exclusive of fringe benefits of $12, the variance of eight hours

**Exhibit 10   Weekly Department Labor Hour Report**

| | | | | | | | | | | |
|---|---|---|---|---|---|---|---|---|---|---|
| **Weekly Department Labor Hour Report** | | | | | | | | | | |
| **Week of:** 7/14/XX | **Department:** *Food Service* | | | **Supervisor:** *Sandra* | | | | | | |
| **Shift:** *P.M.* | | | | | | | | | | |
| **Actual Labor Hours Worked** | | | | | | | | | | |
| Position/ Employee | 7/14 Mon | 7/15 Tues | 7/16 Wed | 7/17 Thurs | 7/18 Fri | 7/19 Sat | 7/20 Sun | Total Labor Hours | |  |
| | | | | | | | | Actual | Std. | |
| DINING ROOM       1 | 2 | 3 | 4 | 5 | 6 | 7 | 8 | 9 | 10 | |
| Jennifer | 7 | — | 7 | 6.5 | 7 | 6 | — | 33.5 | 31.0 | |
| Brenda | — | 7 | 6.5 | 7 | 6.5 | 6.5 | 5 | 38.5 | 38.5 | |
| Sally | — | 5 | 8 | 7 | 8 | 10 | — | 38.0 | 36.0 | |
| Patty | 8 | 6 | 6 | 4.5 | — | — | 6 | 30.5 | 31.0 | |
| Anna | 4 | 4 | 6.5 | — | 4.5 | — | 5 | 24.0 | 22.0 | |
| Thelma | 6 | 5 | 5 | 5 | 5 | — | — | 26.0 | 24.0 | |
| Elsie | 6 | — | — | 6 | 6 | 8 | 8 | 34.0 | 34.0 | |
| | | | | | | | | 224.5 | 216.5 | |
| COOK | | | | | | | | | | |
| Peggy | 4 | 4 | 4 | 4 | 4 | — | — | 20.0 | 20.0 | |
| Kathy | 4 | 4 | 4 | — | — | 4 | 4 | 20.0 | 20.0 | |
| Tilly | 4 | — | — | 4 | 4 | 4 | 4 | 20.0 | 18.0 | |
| Carlos | — | 4 | 4 | 4 | 4 | 4 | — | 20.0 | 20.0 | |
| Sam | 4 | 4 | — | — | — | — | 4 | 12.0 | 12.0 | |
| | | | | | | | | 92.0 | 90.0 | |
| DISHWASHING | | | | | | | | | | |
| Terry | — | — | 6 | 6 | 6 | — | — | 18.0 | 18.0 | |
| Andrew | 6 | 6 | — | — | 8 | 5 | 5 | 30.0 | 30.0 | |
| Robert | 8 | 8 | 8 | 8 | — | — | 6 | 38.0 | 38.0 | |
| Carl | 5 | — | 5 | 5 | 5 | 6 | — | 26.0 | 26.0 | |
| | | | | | | | | 112.0 | 112.0 | |
| | | | | | | | | | | |
| | | | | | | | Total (all personnel) | 428.5 | 418.5 | |
| Remarks:   7/18 — Jennifer, Sally and Elsie given extra hours to learn tableside flaming | | | | | | | Difference | +10.00 | | |
| 7/19 — Sally stayed 2 hours—special cleaning | | | | | | | | | | |
| 7/20 — Tilly stayed 2 hours—cleaned storeroom shelves | | | | | | | | | | |

costs the operation a total of $96 for the week of July 14. If actual hours worked differed from scheduled labor hours at this rate for the entire year, it would cost the operation a total of $4,992 ($96 weekly × 52 weeks) in lost profits. Because no manager wants to lose any amount of potential profit, the variance is indeed significant.

The remarks at the bottom of the report address the variances in relation to each employee. If similar variances and remarks occur over a period of several weeks, corrective action might be necessary. For example, the manager or supervisor might need to do a better job at planning and scheduling necessary cleaning for the dining room and storage areas.

A weekly department labor hour report will almost always reveal differences between the hours scheduled and the actual hours worked. Generally, a small deviation is permitted. For example, if the labor performance standard for a position is 210 hours for the week, a variance of 2 percent, approximately 4.2 hours, might be tolerated. So, if actual labor hours do not exceed 214.2 (210.0 + 4.2), no investigation is necessary. If actual labor hours increase beyond 214.2, analysis and corrective action might be required.

There may be explainable reasons for a difference between standard and actual results. While management must decide what constitutes an acceptable reason, examples might include:

- Hours worked by new employees and included in the weekly department labor hour report represent training time rather than time spent on productive work.

- Out-of-order equipment such as a broken dish machine results in additional manual labor.

- New menu items or new work procedures create a training or transitional period and increase labor hours.

If these types of situations explain reasons for variances, corrective action is not needed. The supervisors and managers are aware of the problem and its cause, expected duration, and estimated cost. These reasons for variances are understood by management and are within its control.

Occasionally, problems might exist for which immediate causes or solutions are not apparent. In these situations, the manager or department supervisor could ask employees for ideas about the problem. Also, the manager or supervisor could work in the affected position for a shift or two. Unknown reasons for variances, while rare, deserve high priority to ensure that the operation is in control of labor costs at all times.

The procedures discussed so far use one week as the time period for comparing labor standards and actual labor hours. If comparisons are made too infrequently, time is wasted and labor dollars are lost before managers notice that a problem might exist. On the other hand, if comparisons are made too frequently, excessive time and money is spent in assembling data, performing calculations, and making comparisons. Some time is necessary for labor hours and costs to average out. Obviously, labor hours can be higher than established labor standards on some days and lower on other days.

When a comparison of labor standards with actual labor results indicates unacceptable variances, answering several questions might help uncover potential causes:

- Are the labor standards established by position performance analyses correct? If they are incorrect, the staffing guide itself will be incorrect. A recurring problem might call for reviewing position performance analyses and evaluating the accuracy of the labor standards used to construct the staffing guide.

- How accurate are the forecasts used for scheduling staff? Additional labor hours might have been necessary if more meals were produced and served than forecasted. If this happens frequently, the forecasting techniques should be reevaluated.

- Are employees performing tasks that are not listed in their job descriptions? These tasks might not have been considered in the initial position performance analyses that established labor standards.

- Are there new employees who do not perform as efficiently as employees did during the initial position performance analyses?

- Have factors affecting labor efficiency changed, such as menu revisions or new equipment purchases? If so, updated position performance analyses leading to revised labor standards might be necessary.

- Are personal or professional problems among the staff affecting efficiency?

## Budgetary Control

It is important that the information recorded in a weekly labor hour report be consistent with information developed for other aspects of the labor control system. For example, Exhibit 11, a department weekly labor hour and cost report, provides the same information as Exhibit 10, but it also lists hourly rates for each employee

**Exhibit 11   Department Weekly Labor Hour and Cost Report**

Week of: _7/14/XX_

Department: _Food Service_    Supervisor: _Sandra_

Shift: _P.M._

**Actual Labor Hours Worked**

| Position/ Employee | Mon 7/14 | Tues 7/15 | Wed 7/16 | Thurs 7/17 | Fri 7/18 | Sat 7/19 | Sun 7/20 | Total Labor Hours Actual | Total Labor Hours Standard | Hourly Rate | Total Labor Costs Actual | Total Labor Costs Standard |
|---|---|---|---|---|---|---|---|---|---|---|---|---|
| 1 | 2 | 3 | 4 | 5 | 6 | 7 | 8 | 9 | 10 | 11 | 12 | 13 |
| DINING ROOM | | | | | | | | | | | | |
| Jennifer | 7 | — | 7 | 6.5 | 7 | 6 | — | 33.5 | 31.0 | $7.00 | $234.50 | $217.00 |
| Brenda | — | 7 | 6.5 | 7 | 6.5 | 6.5 | 5 | 38.5 | 38.5 | 7.15 | 275.28 | 275.28 |
| Sally | — | 5 | 8 | 7 | 8 | 10 | — | 38.0 | 36.0 | 7.25 | 275.50 | 261.00 |
| Patty | 8 | 6 | 6 | 4.5 | — | — | 6 | 30.5 | 31.0 | 7.10 | 216.55 | 220.10 |
| Anna | 4 | 4 | 6.5 | — | 4.5 | — | 5 | 24.0 | 22.0 | 7.10 | 170.40 | 156.20 |
| Thelma | 6 | 5 | 5 | 5 | 5 | — | — | 26.0 | 24.0 | 7.40 | 192.40 | 177.60 |
| Elsie | 6 | — | — | 6 | 6 | 8 | 8 | 34.0 | 34.0 | 7.05 | 239.70 | 239.70 |
| | | | | | | | | 224.5 | 216.5 | | $1,604.33 | $1,546.88 |
| COOK | | | | | | | | | | | | |
| Peggy | 4 | 4 | 4 | 4 | 4 | — | — | 20.0 | 20.0 | 14.00 | 280.00 | 280.00 |
| Kathy | 4 | 4 | 4 | — | — | 4 | 4 | 20.0 | 20.0 | 14.15 | 283.00 | 283.00 |
| Tilly | 4 | — | — | 4 | 4 | 4 | 4 | 20.0 | 18.0 | 14.50 | 290.00 | 261.00 |
| Carlos | — | 4 | 4 | 4 | 4 | 4 | — | 20.0 | 20.0 | 14.00 | 280.00 | 280.00 |
| Sam | 4 | 4 | — | — | — | — | 4 | 12.0 | 12.0 | 14.10 | 169.20 | 169.20 |
| | | | | | | | | 92.0 | 90.0 | | $1,302.20 | $1,273.20 |
| DISHWASHING | | | | | | | | | | | | |
| Terry | — | — | 6 | 6 | 6 | — | — | 18.0 | 18.0 | 9.50 | 171.00 | 171.00 |
| Andrew | 6 | 6 | — | — | 8 | 5 | 5 | 30.0 | 30.0 | 9.25 | 277.50 | 277.50 |
| Robert | 8 | 8 | 8 | 8 | — | — | 6 | 38.0 | 38.0 | 9.55 | 362.90 | 362.90 |
| Carl | 5 | — | 5 | 5 | 5 | 6 | — | 26.0 | 26.0 | 9.50 | 247.00 | 247.00 |
| | | | | | | | | 112.0 | 112.0 | | $1,058.40 | $1,058.40 |
| | | | | | | | | | | | $3,964.93 | $3,875.48 |

and converts actual and standard labor hours into labor dollars. The labor dollars sections enable managers to compare actual labor costs with scheduled labor costs.

For example, during the course of each month, the manager can total the actual labor costs to date by adding actual costs from all previous weekly department labor hour and cost reports. The to-date figure can be subtracted from the total labor costs allowed by the operating budget for that month. The result indicates the amount of labor dollars left in the current month's budget. This helps managers plan future expenses and remain within the budgeted allowance for labor costs. Note that electronic systems can do these and almost any other calculations for any desired time periods. They can do so quickly and accurately, and save supervisory time that can be used for other purposes.

Alternatively, the manager could divide the actual labor costs to date by the amount of food and beverage revenue to date. This yields a to-date actual labor cost percentage, which can be compared with the budgeted labor cost percentage for the period.

The weekly labor hour and cost report can also be used to monitor overtime labor costs. Any number of situations might arise that force a supervisor to schedule overtime for some employees. However, most operations require management approval for any scheduled overtime. Unscheduled and excessive overtime costs are generally signs of poor forecasting and/or scheduling problems.

The weekly labor hour and cost report alerts the manager to all situations in which an employee's actual labor hours exceed the number of hours for which that employee was scheduled. If previous approval of a variance was not granted, the discrepancy might signal an attempt by one or more dishonest employees to steal through payroll fraud.

# Labor Scheduling Software

Scheduling the right number of employees with the right skills at the right time requires a thorough understanding of a department's functions, staff, and **demand-drivers** (i.e., the factors that affect business volume). Add to this the reality of a tight labor market in which employees expect schedules to be based upon their preferences, seniority, and union contract provisions, and you see there are quite a number of variables that must be taken into account when creating an optimum labor schedule.

Labor scheduling software packages are designed to prompt supervisors about their staffing requirements based on programming that considers the property's productivity requirements, group bookings, reservations, and other demand-drivers. The more sophisticated software packages interface with the hotel's computerized **property management system (PMS)**. This allows for constant, real-time monitoring of the conditions that affect a specific department's staffing requirements.

The key to such software's ability to aid management in optimizing the labor scheduling process is the interface with computerized systems for reservations, group histories, forecasting, and human resources data. The ability to forecast workloads based on the demand-drivers of specific departments makes a software-aided scheduling process a powerful tool for supervisors.

The procedures to develop a labor schedule in a computerized system are basically the same as when a manual system is used. First, desired productivity standards must be established. For example, a housekeeping manager might select 30 minutes as the time it should take a housekeeper to clean a room. Then the manager or supervisor must consider the factors that affect staffing requirements. Examples include the number of forecasted arrivals, departures, and stayovers for each day, the number of guests per room, and the types of rooms. Exhibit 12 provides examples of the productivity standards and demand-drivers for three hotel departments.

One of the most important features of employee scheduling software packages is the interface with the hotel's PMS. Seldom is forecasted demand identical to actual demand, and the supervisor must routinely access the reservation system to determine if adjustments to the next day's schedule are warranted. The interface enables the software to monitor in real time the reservations activity, and

**Exhibit 12    Examples of Productivity Standards and Demand-Drivers By Department**

| Department | Productivity & Performance Standards | Demand-Drivers |
|---|---|---|
| **Restaurant** | | |
| Servers | Number of Covers | Rooms Occupied |
| Bartenders | Number of Table Turns | House Counts |
| Buspersons | Average Check | Arrivals/Departures/Stayovers |
| | | Group Type/Histories |
| | | Weather |
| | | City Events |
| | | Hotel Events |
| **Front Desk** | | |
| Guest Services | Number of Check Ins | Number of Arrivals/Departures |
| Lobby Hostess | & Check Outs | Arrival/Departure Times |
| Door Attendants | | Type of Guest |
| Bell Attendants | | Group Type/Histories |
| | | Weather |
| **Housekeeping** | | |
| Room Attendants | Time to Clean a Room | Rooms Occupied |
| Housepersons | Quality Scores | House Counts |
| Floor Supervisors | | Arrivals/Departures/Stayovers |
| | | Number of Guests Per Room |
| | | Room Type |
| | | Room Attendant's Proficiency |
| | | Weather |
| | | Hotel Events |

automatically alerts the supervisor when forecasted demand significantly differs from actual demand and warrants adjustments in staffing levels.

Other demand factors can be programmed as well. Consider how the type of group and its history affect staffing requirements. A conference of health-conscious physicians will likely elicit few sales at the bar, but will increase restaurant sales of health-conscious items. A fraternal organization will likely boost beverage sales and lower food sales. These different groups with different histories will prompt adjustments to the labor hours scheduled for the bar and dining room.

Experience shows that the number of arrivals and departures is generally an insufficient predictor of staffing requirements for the front desk. A departing group of 200 guests between the hours of 9:00 and 9:45 A.M. will require a larger staff than 200 departures spread across an entire morning. The type of guest (such as leisure or corporate) will also have an impact upon the front desk's labor requirements.

Front desks might be staffed on a ratio of 1 staff member per 50 corporate checkouts, as opposed to a ratio of 1 staff member per 30 leisure checkouts. The reason for this discrepancy is that business travelers often use express check out and direct billing, while leisure guests do not. Failing to consider these and related factors can lead to unnecessary over-scheduling or under-scheduling. Through the interface with the hotel's PMS, the scheduling software can capture data needed for predicting staffing requirements quickly and accurately.

With the desired productivity standards in place and the demand-drivers selected, it takes a simple "point-and-click" of the PC's mouse for supervisors to generate the staffing requirements for their departments. Scheduling software also lets supervisors assign employees to specific work schedules based on their preferences, seniority, union contract, wage costs, and proficiency. This employee-centered scheduling approach might improve morale, reduce turnover, and create maximum flexibility when allocating a hotel's greatest resource—its people.

When the software alerts a supervisor about the need to increase staffing levels, it presents a prioritized list of employees available to work that shift. A supervisor can edit the schedule by dropping employees into the scheduling pool for call outs.

Exhibit 13 presents a sample software-generated schedule of housekeepers to work the week of September 17 through 23. Clicking on "Availability" at the bottom of the screen alerts the supervisor to the names of housekeepers available to work each day of the week. The supervisor can scroll down the list and click on the employee he or she wishes to assign to the schedule.

An important feature is the software's ability to automatically produce a labor cost summary. This allows the supervisor to make comparisons of the scheduled week's labor costs with what has been budgeted. The supervisor can review the impact of a possible schedule on the labor budget before the schedule is finalized. Once the schedule has been approved by the supervisor, an individualized schedule for the upcoming week can be printed for each employee.

Scheduling software that interfaces with payroll, time and attendance, and back office accounting packages eliminates the need to re-key data from one software package to another, saving management both time and money. Managers

# Exhibit 13   A Software-Generated Schedule by ITP's DREAM Software

**King James Hotel**   DREAM v1.0 - [King James Hotel]

Schedule  Forecast  Analyzer  Configure  Interface  Security  Reports  Help  Exit

**Department**  Rooms Division
**Services**  Room Attendants

**Schedule**
Start Date 9/17/XX   End Date 9/23/XX

## Schedule Information

| Employees | 9/17/XX(Sun) | 9/18/XX(Mon) | 9/19/XX(Tue) | 9/20/XX(Wed) | 9/21/XX(Thu) | 9/22/XX(Fri) |
|---|---|---|---|---|---|---|
| Smith Rachel | 8:30 AM - 12:30 PM / 1:00 PM - 4:00 PM | | | 8:00 AM - 12:30 PM / 1:00 PM - 4:30 PM | 8:00 AM - 12:30 PM / 1:00 PM - 4:30 PM | 8:00 AM - 12:30 PM / 1:00 PM - 4:00 PM |
| Doe Jane | | | 8:00 AM - 12:30 PM / 1:00 PM - 4:30 PM | 8:00 AM - 12:30 PM / 1:00 PM - 8:30 PM | 8:00 AM - 12:30 PM / 1:00 PM - 4:30 PM | 8:00 AM - 12:30 PM / 1:00 PM - 4:00 PM |
| French Frankie | 8:30 AM - 12:30 PM / 1:00 PM - 4:00 PM | | | | 8:00 AM - 12:30 PM / 1:00 PM - 3:00 PM | 8:00 AM - 12:30 PM / 1:00 PM - 3:00 PM |
| Rice Carol | | 8:00 AM - 12:30 PM / 1:00 PM - 3:00 PM | 8:00 AM - 12:30 PM / 1:00 PM - 4:30 PM | 8:00 AM - 12:30 PM / 1:00 PM - 4:30 PM | 8:00 AM - 12:30 PM / 1:00 PM - 4:00 PM | 8:00 AM - 12:30 PM / 1:00 PM - 3:30 PM |
| White Paula | | | 8:00 AM - 12:00 PM / 12:30 PM - 4:30 PM | 8:00 AM - 12:00 PM / 12:30 PM - 4:30 PM | 8:00 AM - 12:00 PM / 12:30 PM - 3:30 PM | 8:00 AM - 12:00 PM / 12:30 PM - 3:30 PM |
| Boyd Darla | 8:30 AM - 12:00 PM / 12:30 PM - 4:00 PM | 8:00 AM - 12:00 PM / 12:30 PM - 3:30 PM | 8:00 AM - 12:00 PM / 12:30 PM - 4:30 PM | 8:00 AM - 12:00 PM / 12:30 PM - 4:30 PM | 8:00 AM - 12:00 PM / 12:30 PM - 4:00 PM | |
| Conelly Monica | | 8:00 AM - 12:30 PM | 8:00 AM - 12:30 PM | 10:00 AM - 12:30 PM | 8:00 AM - 12:30 PM / 12:30 PM - 4:30 PM | 8:00 AM - 12:30 PM / 1:00 PM - 4:00 PM |

Availability | Day Schedule | Approve | Edit

---

### Do Employees Still Punch In?

Modern electronic systems allow supervisors to quickly develop employee schedules for their departments that meet all requirements related to business volume and the needs of employees. When a schedule is completed, it can be printed for posting on the employee bulletin board or at another location; it can also be electronically sent to employees.

The scheduling software can also be interfaced with the property's employee time and attendance system. For example, an employee scheduled to begin work at 10 A.M. and to complete work at 4 P.M. would not be able to check into the system before, for example, 9:45 A.M. or after 4:15 P.M. These systems can use finger printing or eye retina identification systems to ensure that only the employee himself or herself can check in or check out.

Modern time and attendance systems can also track hours worked and calculate wages earned on almost any basis, such as by department per hour, by employee per shift, and total wages on by-department basis for the time period covered by the employee schedule.

These features allow supervisors to quickly and accurately compare scheduled hours and labor costs with actual labor hours and labor costs on a by-employee, by-shift, or by-department basis for any time period. These and related features allow supervisors to have current information available to determine if potential problems exist and to then take quick corrective actions to address them.

---

can choose from numerous reports to make well-informed business decisions. The selected reports can be formatted by employee, by day, by shift, by department, by union contract, or by other selected factors.

Another important feature is that scheduling, payroll, and other labor databases can be made available to corporate controllers on virtual private networks over the Internet. With this easy access, controllers can quickly generate answers to specific questions and customize reports requested by managers at their individual units or properties.

## Monitoring and Evaluating Productivity

A supervisor is often evaluated on the basis of how well he or she manages the productivity of the department's employees while meeting budget. This chapter presented practical procedures with which supervisors can:

- Develop productivity standards based on established performance expectations.

- Construct a staffing guide based on productivity standards.

- Create employee work schedules by using the staffing guide in conjunction with business volume forecasts.

However, even if a supervisor carefully follows these procedures, the actual productivity of employees on a given day will rarely, if ever, correspond exactly to the established standards. This is because forecasts of business volume are themselves rarely, if ever, exact. Therefore, some variance in productivity is to be expected. For example, when the actual volume of business is greater than the forecasted volume, productivity generally increases—but only because the department is understaffed. Conversely, when the actual volume of business is less than the forecasted volume, productivity generally decreases—but only because the department is overstaffed.

The supervisor's responsibility is to minimize variances in productivity when, for whatever reason, the department is understaffed or overstaffed. Supervisors must plan for these occurrences so that appropriate action can be taken quickly the very day (or shift) that the situation arises. For example, on a day that the department appears to be understaffed, a supervisor could call in the appropriate number of full-time or part-time employees who were not scheduled to work. Part-time employees might be preferred to avoid possible overtime costs for full-time employees working an extra shift. On a day that the department appears to be overstaffed, a supervisor could check if any scheduled employees would volunteer to take the day off or work shorter shifts.

These are the kinds of adjustments that supervisors must make on a daily basis to ensure the productivity of employees in their departments. A challenge for all hospitality supervisors and managers is to be continually alert to methods that increase the productivity of employees. Understaffing the department is not an effective solution to increasing productivity.

One of the most difficult and challenging tasks for supervisors is to create new ways of getting work done in the department. Too often supervisors get caught up in routine, day-to-day functions ("we have always done it this way!") and then fail to question the way things are done. The best way to increase productivity is to continually review and revise performance standards. A five-step process for increasing productivity by revising performance standards can be used.

**Step 1—Collect and Analyze Information about Current Performance Standards.** Often this can be done by simple observation. If supervisors know what must be done to meet current performance standards, they can observe what is actually being done and note any differences. When analyzing tasks listed in performance standards for positions within the department, supervisors should ask the following questions:

- Can a particular task be eliminated? Before revising the way in which a task is performed, the supervisor must ask whether the task needs to be carried out in the first place.

- Can a particular task be assigned to a different position? For example, instead of housekeepers stocking their own carts at the beginning of their shifts, the task could be assigned to a night-shift houseperson. This could increase the productivity of day-shift housekeepers by half a room.

- Are the performance standards of another department decreasing the productivity of employees in your department? For example, the on-site laundry area might not be supplying the correct amount of clean linens your department needs. Productivity suffers when housekeepers or dining room staff must make frequent trips to the laundry area to pick up clean linens as they become available.

**Step 2—Generate Ideas for New Ways to Get the Job Done.** Generally, when work problems arise, there is more than one way to resolve them. Performance standards for many hospitality positions are complex. It is often difficult to pinpoint the exact reasons for current problems or new ideas about completing the job more efficiently.

Employees, other supervisors, and guests are important sources of information who can help a supervisor pinpoint tasks for revision. Employees who actually perform the job are often the best source for suggested improvements. Other supervisors might be able to pass on techniques they successfully use to increase productivity in their areas. Also, networking with colleagues often results in creative ideas that can be applied to other areas. Completed guest comment cards and/or personal interviews with selected guests might reveal aspects of the department that supervisors consistently overlook.

**Step 3—Evaluate Each Idea and Select the Best Approach.** The actual idea selected might be a blend of the best elements of several different suggestions. When selecting the best way to revise current performance standards, confirm that the task can be done in the time allowed. It is one thing for a "superstar" employee to clean a room or register a guest within a specified time; however, it might not be reasonable to expect an average employee—even after training and with close supervision—to be as productive. Remember, performance standards must be attainable to be useful.

**Step 4—Test the Revised Performance Standard.** Have a few employees use the revised performance standard for a specified time to closely monitor whether the new procedures increase productivity. Remember, old habits are hard to break. Before conducting a formal evaluation of the revised performance standard, employees will need time to become familiar with the new tasks and build speed.

**Step 5—Implement the Revised Performance Standard.** After the trial study has demonstrated that the new performance standard increases productivity, employees must be trained in the new procedures. Continual supervision, reinforcement, and coaching during the transitional period will also be necessary. Most important, if the increased productivity is significant, it will be necessary to change the department's staffing guide and then base scheduling practices on the new productivity standard. This will ensure that increased productivity translates to increased profits through lower labor costs.

## 🔑 Key Terms

**alternative scheduling**—Scheduling staff to work hours different from the typical 9 A.M. to 5 P.M. workday. Variations include part-time and flexible hours, compressed work schedules, and job sharing.

**base adjustment forecast**—A forecasting system that uses the most recently collected information as the basis of the forecast.

**demand driver**—Factors that influence business volume.

**fixed staff positions**—Positions that must be filled regardless of the volume of business; the minimum amount of labor required to operate a property regardless of the volume of business.

**full-time equivalent (FTE)**—A measure of staffing needs expressed as the number of full-time (40 hours per week) employees it would take to meet the need. Actual staffing may include full-time and/or part-time employees.

**intranet**—A portioned section of the public website that is password-protected to provide staff members with timely access to important work-related information.

**labor-intensive**—The situation in which employees, not machines or computers, are required to produce and deliver products and services.

**moving average forecasting method**—A method of forecasting in which historical data over several time periods are used to calculate an average; as new data become available, they are used in calculating the average by adding the most recent time period and dropping the earliest time period. In this way, the calculated average is a "moving" one because it is continually updated to include only the most recent data for the specified number of time periods.

**performance standard**—A required level of performance that establishes the quality of work that must be done.

**productivity**—Output relative to the input needed to produce products and services meeting quality standards.

**productivity standard**—An acceptable amount of work that must be done within a specific time frame according to an established performance standard.

**property management system (PMS)**—The set of application programs that directly relate to a hotel's front and back office activities. Note that "application" is a term for programs that tell a system's hardware what it is supposed to do and when and how to do it.

**staffing guide**—A labor scheduling and control tool that indicates the number of labor hours that must be worked by persons in variable staff positions as the volume of expected business changes.

**variable staff positions**—Positions filled in relation to changes in business volume; for example, as more guests are served or as more meals are produced, additional service or kitchen labor is needed.

##  Review Questions

1. Why is it impossible to identify productivity standards that would apply to all properties throughout the hospitality industry?

2. How are productivity standards determined?

3. What is the relationship between performance standards and productivity standards?

4. What is the difference between fixed staff and variable staff positions?

5. What purpose does a staffing guide serve?

6. Why is it important that the budgeted labor expense for a department be based on the same productivity standards as the department's staffing guide?

7. How does a base adjustment forecast differ from a moving average forecast?

8. How can supervisors use a weekly hour labor report to control and evaluate the scheduling process?

9. Explain how scheduling and labor control software programs can increase the efficiency and effectiveness of supervisors in managing productivity.

10. What steps can supervisors take to increase productivity by revising performance standards?

 **Case Study**

### Under Pressure

Philip knocked tentatively on his general manager's office door. "You wanted to see me, Mrs. Smith?"

"Yes, Philip, please sit down." The general manager shifted some papers on her desk and handed Philip Stone, the executive housekeeper, a copy of the labor-cost budget. "Take a look at last month's report. Notice which direction the labor costs are going."

Philip quickly scanned the report he had previously studied in detail. "They're rising by about 2 percent, almost the same as the previous months of this quarter. In fact, they've been rising at about that monthly rate for the past year."

"Yes, Philip, I'm well aware of that. But that's why we hired you. You are supposed to turn these numbers around, and now—90 days after you started—there's no change in direction at all. I need you to do something about this immediately. I can't have this creeping overhead! Get back to me tomorrow with your action plan for how you're going to make sure labor costs are reduced next month."

Mrs. Smith then stood up and opened the door for Philip to leave.

Walking back to his office, Philip considered implementing a quick job-saving solution such as giving each housekeeper an extra room to clean. As he mentally rehearsed breaking this news to the housekeeper staff, Philip noticed his office was occupied.

"Betty! Jane! What can I do for you?" Philip asked, entering his office.

"Mr. Stone, we've been meaning to talk to you for a couple weeks," Jane said, "but we didn't want you to think we were a bunch of complainers, being as this job is new to you and all."

"Why, of course not, Jane. You two are some of the hardest-working house-keepers in the department. You have the best productivity and set a wonderful example for all our other employees."

"Well, it's that productivity thing we want to talk to you about. We want to help make sure the rooms are done and done right, but you've been asking too much of us lately. We're burning out. And it's not just Betty and me. There are other employees who've been around a long time like us, and we can't keep up anymore. If you don't find a way to lighten the workload a little, you're going to kill us."

Betty chimed in, "I remember when we were expected to do only 17 rooms a shift. Now we're up to 22 rooms on a regular basis. I promise, Mr. Stone, we weren't slacking before. If we have to do more than 22 rooms, they're just not going to be clean, and I don't want a guest checking into any one of *my* rooms that isn't clean."

Philip felt a first-class headache coming on as he realized this would be a poor time to suggest housekeepers take on extra rooms or spend less time per room. "Is there something specific that you think would help?"

"Yeah," said Jane. "Give us fewer rooms to clean so we don't all get ulcers!"

"Well, ladies, your break is over, you'd better get back to work. I appreciate your coming to talk to me. I'll let you know in a couple days what I decide to do," Philip said, looking at his watch in hopes of speeding the two women out.

The two housekeepers exchanged disappointed glances. Betty shrugged and said, "OK, but you will get back to us, won't you? You're not just trying to get rid of us?"

"No. I'll get back to you by the day after tomorrow. Would that be okay?" Philip asked.

"If we don't have heart attacks first," Jane muttered as she and Betty left.

Philip sat at his desk with a sigh and pulled out his department's productivity standards. According to the information left him by the previous executive house-keeper, each room should take 26 minutes to clean. He decided to analyze how many rooms each housekeeper was actually cleaning.

After a half-hour of analyzing productivity data, Philip identified the follow-ing problems:

- Forty percent of his housekeepers were performing at the hotel's productivity standards or better

- Sixty percent of his housekeepers were each cleaning fewer than 17 rooms a day and averaging longer than 26 minutes to clean a room

- The 60 percent performing below standards were all either new hires or still in training

- The housekeeping department has had 60 percent of its personnel in training or at new-hire status for the past ten months, due to high turnover

Philip then began to outline presentations for the general manager and for his own employees. First, he decided, he would explain the cause of rising labor costs to his general manager. "I'll have to tell her that turnover and poor training are causing lower productivity. We're not hiring the right people for the right posi-tions, and then we're not bringing their productivity levels up to standards."

Philip determined he would tell Mrs. Smith she has to spend money to bring the labor-costs curve down. His suggestions included:

- Update job descriptions so new hires have more realistic expectations

- Provide more resources to the training department

- Organize training better so housekeepers come up to speed within 30 days

- Terminate new hires if they do not meet productivity standards after 30 days

- Hold weekly recruitment meetings with human resources

He hoped that, although his suggestions wouldn't please Mrs. Smith, they would illustrate that the resources needed for the short term would be less costly than steadily increasing labor costs.

Philip struggled a little more over what to tell his housekeepers. Ideally, he thought, he could encourage the more experienced 40 percent to pitch in and help bring the 60 percent up to speed. By doing just a little more now, they could reduce stress and tension in the long run. All he had to do, he thought, was convince them to give a little more a little bit longer. "At least I'm not giving them more rooms to clean," he decided.

As Philip set his presentation plans aside to go back to his daily work, he stopped and took one more look at them. "Hmmm," he thought, "Perhaps I should ask a few of my colleagues at other hotels how they would handle this."

## Discussion Question

1.  What feedback would executive housekeepers give Philip?

---

Case Number: 3382CA

The following industry experts helped generate and develop this case: Gail Edwards, Director of Housekeeping, Regal Riverfront Hotel, St. Louis, Missouri; Mary Friedman, Director of Housekeeping, Radisson South, Bloomington, Minnesota; and Aleta Nitschke, Publisher and Editor of *The Rooms Chronicle*.

# Chapter 6 Outline

# Competencies

1. List the benefits of performance evaluations and common obstacles that interfere with their effectiveness. (pp. 171–175)

2. Identify common errors to avoid when evaluating employee performance. (pp. 175–176)

3. Describe the different approaches to performance evaluations including comparative methods, absolute standards methods, and management by objectives methods. (pp. 176–182)

4. Identify the steps supervisors should take when conducting performance evaluations. (pp. 182–188)

5. Describe coaching principles and techniques. (pp. 188–192)

6. Distinguish between informal and formal coaching. (pp. 192–196)

# 6

# Evaluating and Coaching

Evaluating employee performance is one of the supervisor's primary responsibilities. There is no hard and fast rule in the hospitality industry about what exactly the supervisor's role should be. An employee's immediate supervisor may not even be the staff member who conducts **performance evaluations**. However, the employee's immediate supervisor is at least responsible for providing information that will be helpful in the review. The supervisor must also assume the responsibility to provide the employee with the proper orientation, training, and ongoing assistance to ensure that he or she has the knowledge and skills required for successful job performance. The best supervisors understand that an employee's success can depend on the quality of supervision that the employee receives.

In many organizations, the evaluation forms require the signatures of at least two levels of management. The number of employees in a department typically influences who will conduct the evaluation session. For example, in a small hotel, the front office manager (a department head) may have the responsibility to evaluate all entry-level front desk agents. In a somewhat larger hotel, a front desk supervisor may provide appraisal information to the front office manager (who is not the head of the department) to conduct the session. In a still larger property, a front desk supervisor (one of several in this position) may perform evaluation sessions for those staff members whom he or she directly supervises. While the department head ultimately is responsible for employee evaluations, the authority to conduct them may be delegated to a supervisor.

Since the evaluation should focus on employee performance, the supervisor must be familiar with exactly *what* the employee is expected to do and the agreed-upon levels of expected performance for each task. This background forms the basis for the review. The supervisor compares the employee's actual performance with performance standards. If the employee's level of performance falls below the level of expected performance, the difference between the two levels represents the improvement the employee must make.

This chapter begins by describing the benefits that performance evaluations have for the employee, the supervisor, and the property's management team. It also addresses obstacles to effective performance evaluations and notes the types of resources and training that supervisors require to conduct effective performance review sessions that avoid common errors and make the evaluation process as objective and fair as possible.

The chapter next discusses the different methods and approaches that properties commonly use in conducting employee performance reviews. The chapter also presents a list of tasks that an effective supervisor should carry out before, during, and after a performance evaluation session. During these sessions, the supervisor may determine that an employee will benefit from further **coaching.** Formal and informal approaches to coaching are presented to show how training and development can be fostered on a continual basis.

Regularly held performance evaluations remind employees of their commitment to the property's high standards of performance and productivity. Done correctly, they can yield motivated employees who will consistently meet or exceed guests' expectations. In all evaluating and coaching interactions, you will need to give your employees support and encouragement. The result should be improved employee-supervisor relationships, improved employee performance, and increased productivity.

# Benefits of Performance Evaluations

Performance evaluations benefit employees, their supervisors, and the property's management team.

Performance evaluations provide feedback to employees by letting them know how they are doing on a regular basis. Feedback during scheduled performance review sessions can prevent employee guessing and misunderstanding. Without feedback, employees might believe anything from "I must be doing very badly" to "My performance must be perfect." A well-conducted performance review session helps to identify employee strengths as well as areas for improvement. During the one-on-one review session, the supervisor typically points out the employee's strengths and compliments the employee for good performance. The compliments boost the employee's **self-esteem** (i.e., positive feelings about oneself and self-respect). Conversely, if the supervisor identifies areas for improvement, the review session can focus on the specific improvements that the employee needs to make before the next evaluation session.

Through performance reviews, a supervisor can recognize individual employees who have contributed valuable ideas about work improvement or other professional development activities. A properly conducted performance evaluation will, in part, address an employee's career plans. The supervisor can encourage the employee to consider long-range career programs and can offer helpful suggestions. Subsequent evaluation sessions can focus on specific career development strategies and the progress the employee has made since the plans were developed.

Supervisors benefit from conducting performance evaluation sessions because of an improved relationship with employees. The supervisor and the employee interact during the performance review sessions, and learn about each other in the process. The dialogue at the core of a properly conducted evaluation process can lead to understanding between a supervisor and the employee even if the evaluation is, at times, negative. Employees see that performance standards are "real" measures that, although set high, are reachable. They will understand the supervisor's commitment to monitoring compliance with the standards, and will recognize the supervisor's commitment to their success in the supervisor's providing feedback with an action plan to help employees improve.

The property's management team benefits from the information obtained during the evaluation process, which forms the basis for decisions that affect compensation, job actions, and training programs. Wages, salaries, merit increases, and bonuses are linked to job performance. Although employee unions may have critical interests in compensation matters, wage and salary adjustments should focus on job performance. Employee accomplishments and abilities recognized during the evaluation process and documented in performance evaluations can lead to promotions, transfers, and other positive job actions. Likewise, the employee's inability to perform according to property standards can lead to negative job actions. It is important that all evaluations of employee competence be done regularly and as objectively as possible.

From the information obtained during evaluation sessions, trainers and supervisors can determine the need for property-wide training programs and evaluate the effectiveness of programs already established. If the evaluation process indicates that several employees are weak in specific skill areas, the property may schedule group training sessions. Similarly, the property may authorize supervisors to schedule individualized training programs or to use coaching sessions to resolve employee problems.

## Obstacles to Effective Performance Evaluation

Obstacles to implementing effective performance evaluations stem from a number of different causes.

**Unskilled Supervisors.** Because of the busy nature of the hospitality industry, supervisors may not receive sufficient training in conducting performance evaluations. In some cases, the supervisors themselves may never have been evaluated.

An organization that requires supervisors to conduct performance evaluations—but doesn't teach them how to do it—may unintentionally send the message that such evaluations are unimportant. However, organizations will likely find that an effective performance evaluation process has a positive effect on employee productivity. Such organizations give priority to informing supervisors about the importance of the evaluation process and to training them in conducting effective performance evaluation sessions.

**Ineffective Forms.** When evaluation forms do not contain factors that relate to job performance or become too complicated and lengthy, the forms themselves may cause problems. Furthermore, some supervisors may not know how to complete the forms. Others may not know how to use the information gained in the evaluation process to plan actions that improve employee performance.

**Inadequate Procedures.** Some hospitality operations may have few, if any, organized procedures for conducting performance reviews. Supervisors or managers may conduct performance evaluations only when they wish to discipline employees—not as opportunities to gain the benefits of evaluation. Performance evaluation procedures should be standardized. For example, all entry-level employees should be assessed the same way with a focus on the performance of tasks that are identified in their job description.

**Infrequent Evaluation.** Some properties conduct performance evaluations infrequently and irregularly rather than regularly and frequently. Properties need to establish and enforce a policy relating to frequency of evaluation, such as conducting reviews quarterly or biannually. The policy can specify whether, for example, evaluations should occur using the employee's starting dates as the schedule basis or, alternatively, whether all staff members are evaluated during the same months.

**Fear of Offending Employees.** It is easy and enjoyable to congratulate an employee for outstanding performance. However, it is hard to tell an employee when performance does not meet standards. Some supervisors may fear offending those who are performing inadequately and may be less than completely honest when evaluating them. However, these supervisors defeat the purpose of the evaluation process and, therefore, miss opportunities to improve performance.

When evaluating an unsatisfactory performer, you must concentrate on criticizing the poor performance (behavior) and not the employee. The focus should be on performance standards, not personalities. Remember to make it a business decision, not a personal one. Use specific evidence, rather than general statements, to support your observations. Then, explain the specific steps the employee must take to improve performance.

Since evaluations are typically tied to wage or salary increases, employees often challenge supervisors when they receive unsatisfactory evaluations. Many employees believe their performance is better than it really is when compared with the standards. This issue highlights the importance of setting measurable (observable) performance standards, keeping accurate records, and giving the employee frequent feedback throughout the evaluation period.

**Fear of Unfairness.** Effective supervisors try to be fair in their interactions with employees. Therefore, some supervisors may be concerned that negative information surfacing in performance review sessions will become part of an employee's permanent **personnel file**. This data could affect the employee even after performance problems are resolved.

When observing employees between reviews, you may notice areas of performance that do not meet the standards. You must give the employee feedback on these areas promptly and initiate actions to improve the employee's performance. These discussions and actions must be documented. To keep these records from becoming a permanent part of the employee's file, write the information on paper and keep it in your working files. These notes will then support any unsatisfactory ratings given on the evaluation if the employee's performance does not improve. However, if performance improves and is highly rated on a future evaluation, you may decide to throw out the support notes in the working files.

Satisfactory or even outstanding performance observed between evaluation sessions should also be noted, included with your working papers, and used to illustrate and support positive **feedback** given during performance appraisal sessions.

**Failure to Follow Up.** Supervisors and managers in some hospitality operations may fill out and file performance evaluation forms, but do nothing else with them. In fact, some supervisors may fill out the forms but fail to tell employees or to even show them the forms. In order for performance evaluations to work, employees must be actively involved in the process. Furthermore, information gained in the evaluation process must be used to improve employee performance.

It is important that supervisors follow up on employee performance evaluations. The supervisor must follow up performance reviews with the necessary coaching, counseling, or re-training to help employees improve performance. It is useless to conduct and discuss evaluations with employees if the evaluations are going to be forgotten until the next review.

## Common Performance Evaluation Errors

Many supervisors receive inadequate training in how to conduct performance evaluations. This lack of training is particularly damaging in the hospitality industry because many first-time supervisors must evaluate the performance of the same employees who were once their coworkers. Training in performance evaluation systems can help supervisors make the process as objective and fair as possible. While the chance of error can never be entirely avoided, it can be reduced. The first step in reducing errors is to become aware of the more common types of errors to avoid.

- **Recency Errors.** People tend to remember best those events that happened most recently. For example, a supervisor is more likely to remember what employees did a few weeks before their performance reviews than what they did a few months before the evaluation. Unless the supervisor keeps an ongoing record, it is likely that employees will be judged only on recent performance.

- **Past-Anchoring (Performance) Errors.** Supervisors tend to rate an employee's performance close to how it was rated in the past. If an employee's ratings in the past were high, supervisors tend to rate the employee high again even if the ratings should be lower this time. The same type of error applies to evaluating employees who have been rated low in the past. Supervisors tend to continue to rate these employees low, even if the ratings should be higher.

- **Halo Errors.** These errors occur when supervisors evaluate employees positively based primarily on a single trait, behavior, or action. A typical employee will perform some tasks well, others poorly, and others about average, but the halo effect causes a supervisor to rate an employee high in all areas if the employee does well in one area that is important to the supervisor.

- **Pitchfork Errors.** These errors are the opposite of halo errors. They occur when an employee receives an overall negative evaluation based primarily on a single trait, behavior, or action.

- **Leniency Errors.** Some supervisors give more lenient ratings to employees than they deserve. For example, if ratings of 1 to 5 were given to all employees (1 = poor, 5 = excellent), we would expect that the majority of employees would be rated near the midpoint (3) on the scale. Supervisors who are more lenient than others would likely give more ratings near 5 than near 1. As a result, the ratings overall would be higher than normal.

- **Severity Errors.** Severity errors are the reverse of leniency errors. Using the previous scale, supervisors' severity errors would result in more employees receiving ratings nearer the lowest point on the scale (1) than the highest point (5).

- **Central-Tendency Errors.** Some supervisors tend to rate all employees, regardless of their performance, near the midpoint on a scale. Therefore, if this error were committed, many more employees would be rated near the midpoint (3, using the previous scale) than would be normal.

The problems caused by leniency, severity, and central-tendency errors are magnified in the hospitality industry because supervisors tend to change jobs frequently. As a result, employees in a department or work area are often rated by a new supervisor during a subsequent performance appraisal session. If the first supervisor tended to be lenient and the second severe, it would look like employee performance was going down when, in fact, no change had occurred. On the other hand, too-severe ratings from the first supervisor and too-lenient ratings from the second supervisor could result in the wrong conclusion that employees were getting much better (and possibly deserved raises and promotions) when the employees had not actually improved their performance. Central-tendency errors make employee performance evaluations subject to the same distortions: if the first supervisor tended to rate all employees in the middle of the scale, and the second supervisor tended to be more lenient, then improvement would be noted when none occurred. The reverse would be true if the new supervisor tended to be severe.

Another problem with leniency, severity, and central-tendency errors is that employees' ratings may depend on who rates them rather than on their actual performance. This can lead to injustices. Employees in one department, for example, may be passed over for promotions or career-development assignments because their supervisor tends to be severe, while employees in another department may receive raises and prized assignments simply because their supervisor is more lenient.

These problems can be minimized through a training program for supervisors that clearly explains the ratings that are used to evaluate employee performance in relation to specific job standards. The training program should ensure that supervisors understand the factors used to rate performance with whatever method and on whatever scale the organization uses.

## Approaches to Performance Evaluations

Supervisors are not likely to have significant input in determining which type of performance review system the organization or department uses. Ideally, though, upper management will have considered their input. Supervisors should have some knowledge of the different types of performance evaluation systems that exist and be aware of the potential advantages and disadvantages of each. Then they can better understand the specific system used by their organization. The following sections describe three major methods for evaluating performance: comparative methods, absolute standards methods, and the management by objectives (MBO) method.

## Comparative Methods

A comparative method of evaluating performance involves comparing employees with each other and yields a listing of employees, from best to worst. These methods have limited applicability to hospitality organizations. Frequently supervisors facilitate the work of employees who perform different tasks so it is difficult—if not impossible—to use comparative methods consistently, fairly, and objectively. Also, employees deserve a performance evaluation that focuses on the employee's ability to perform required work—not on how the employee compares with others.

**Simple Ranking Approach.** With this approach, the supervisor classifies employees in order, from the best to the worst. This is done subjectively, that is, the supervisor makes a judgment of the overall performance of each employee. Ranking should consider how consistently employees meet performance standards. Serious disadvantages of this approach include the supervisor's possible bias and the chance that comparisons will focus on personalities or relationships instead of job performance.

**Alternative Ranking Approach.** This is a modification of the simple ranking approach. First, the supervisor places the best employee at the top of the list, and the worst employee at the bottom. The supervisor then places the second best employee in the place second from the top, and the second worst employee in the second place from the bottom. This process continues until the supervisor has included all employees in the ranking list.

**Paired Comparison Approach.** This approach involves comparing each employee to each other employee specifically (on each job factor) or generally (on overall performance). The simplest way to compute the final rankings is to count the number of times an employee is rated as the better performer. Exhibit 1 shows the outcome of a paired comparison involving four employees.

**Forced Distribution Approach.** With this approach, the supervisor is permitted to rank only a certain percentage of all employees "superior" and the same percentage of employees "unacceptable." The supervisor is then forced to place a required percentage of the remaining employees in each of the other categories such as "above average," "average," and "below average." An example of employees ranked using this method is shown in Exhibit 2.

## Absolute Standards Methods

With the absolute standards method, the supervisor assesses each employee's work performance without regard to the performance of other employees.

**Critical Incidents Approach.** With this approach, the supervisor keeps a "diary" of incidents that indicate acceptable and unacceptable job performance. When using this approach, remember that the diary should be kept up to date during the entire time between evaluations. Waiting until the last minute to write something down results in entries that are inaccurate, incomplete, and unfair. Furthermore, avoid dwelling only on negative incidents. While these are important, it is equally important to consider the positive aspects of an employee's performance. A sample critical incidents format is shown in Exhibit 3.

**Exhibit 1   Results of a Paired Comparison Rating**

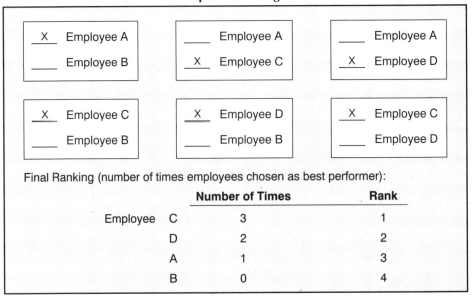

| | | Number of Times | Rank |
|---|---|---|---|
| Employee | C | 3 | 1 |
| | D | 2 | 2 |
| | A | 1 | 3 |
| | B | 0 | 4 |

Final Ranking (number of times employees chosen as best performer):

**Exhibit 2   Forced Distribution Scale**

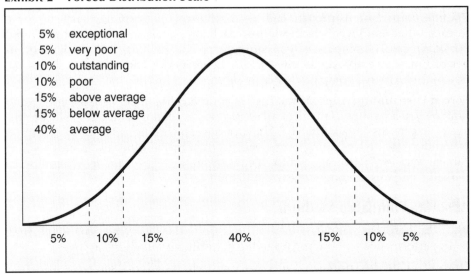

**Weighted Checklist Approach.** With this approach, supervisors and others famil-iar with departmental work flow and positions develop checklists of the tasks and duties making up each job. Each task or duty listed is weighted to represent the relative value of "good" and "bad" performance aspects. After the supervisor has completed the checklist, the values applicable to the tasks or duties that have

**Exhibit 3    Sample Critical Incidents Diary**

Instructions:    Provide examples of employee activity in regard to each of the following. Indicate positive and negative incidents.

Name of Employee: _____

| Activity | Date | Observed Activity |
|---|---|---|
| Follows Directions | | |
| Work Quality | | |
| Makes Suggestions | | |

Signature of Supervisor: _____  Date: _____

Signature of Employee: _____  Date: _____

received a check mark are added to obtain a total evaluation score—the higher the score, the better the performance. A sample checklist format is shown in Exhibit 4.

**Forced Choice Approach.** This approach requires the supervisor to select one statement (from among several) that describes how well the employee performs in relation to selected factors and tasks considered important for successful job performance. A sample format is shown in Exhibit 5. Many hospitality operations use the forced choice approach. The number of work factors addressed in this method may vary. When using this method you should consider all the specific tasks that are important to a position.

**Graphic Rating Scale.** This is one of the most widely used methods for evaluating performance. When using this method, supervisors typically rank employees on 10 to 15 factors using a point scale from 5 (highest or outstanding) to 1 (lowest or unsatisfactory). The factors used in the ratings usually contain such items as work characteristics, quality of work, quantity of work, dependability, attendance, job knowledge, and so on. The ratings can be added together to compile a score for each employee. A section for the supervisor to record comments is typically

**Exhibit 4   Sample Weighted Checklist Method**

| Instructions: | Check (✓) each of the statements that apply to the employee being evaluated. | |
| --- | --- | --- |

Name of Employee: _____

| (✓) if applicable | Activity | Scale Value |
| --- | --- | --- |
| _____ | 1. Turns off equipment when finished | 2.0 |
| _____ | 2. Keeps work area clean | 1.5 |
| _____ | 3. Gathers all work supplies/utensils needed at one time | 1.5 |

Signature of Supervisor: _____ Date: _____

Signature of Employee: _____ Date: _____

**Exhibit 5   Sample Forced Choice Method**

Instructions:   Check (✓) the box for each factor which exemplifies the quality of work performed by the employee.

Name of Employee: _____

| FACTOR | PERFORMANCE | | | | |
| --- | --- | --- | --- | --- | --- |
| | Excellent | Above Average | Average | Below Average | Unacceptable |
| KNOWLEDGE OF JOB | Understands all aspects of work | Understands almost all aspects of work | Understands basic aspects of job | Has fair job knowledge | Has poor job knowledge |
| WORK QUALITY | Very accurate and neat | Seldom makes mistakes | Work normally acceptable | Work often unacceptable | Work seldom meets quality requirements |

Signature of Supervisor: _____ Date: _____

Signature of Employee: _____ Date: _____

provided. A sample performance evaluation form using a graphic rating scale is shown in Exhibit 6.

**Behaviorally Anchored Rating Scale (BARS).** Like the graphic rating scale, a behaviorally anchored rating scale requires supervisors to rate employees on a scaled continuum. In this case, supervisors rate the dimensions of an employee's work based on specific examples of what are considered to be good and bad behaviors. Exhibit 7 shows one dimension of performance for a restaurant server. The descriptive statements to the right of the rating bar guide supervisors in their interpretations of what counts for good or bad behavior along the dimension of "Technical Competence."

## Management by Objectives Method

With comparative methods and absolute standards methods of evaluating performance, employees are often evaluated according to factors that are developed without input from the supervisor or from the employee being evaluated. With the **management by objectives (MBO)** method, the supervisor works with the employee to determine a set of goals. The supervisor and the employee first consider how the employee will reach the goals. They then work together to establish evaluation procedures. Creating an MBO plan typically consists of four steps:

1. Goals are set for the employee to reach by the next performance evaluation.

2. The employee is given time on the job to master tasks to reach goals. Strategies for training, coaching, and other developmental activities are built into the plan.

3. During the next evaluation session, the goals actually reached are compared with the goals originally set. If the employee did not reach the goals, the

**Exhibit 6   Sample Graphic Rating Scale Method**

| | Outstanding | Good | Satisfactory | Fair | Unsatisfactory |
|---|---|---|---|---|---|
| Quantity of work | ☐ | ☐ | ☐ | ☐ | ☐ |
| Quality of work | ☐ | ☐ | ☐ | ☐ | ☐ |
| Job knowledge | ☐ | ☐ | ☐ | ☐ | ☐ |
| Personal attributes | ☐ | ☐ | ☐ | ☐ | ☐ |
| Teamwork | ☐ | ☐ | ☐ | ☐ | ☐ |
| Dependability | ☐ | ☐ | ☐ | ☐ | ☐ |
| Initiative | ☐ | ☐ | ☐ | ☐ | ☐ |

Comments: _____

_____

_____

Signature of Supervisor: _____ Date: _____

Signature of Employee: _____ Date: _____

**Exhibit 7   Sample Behaviorally Anchored Rating Scale Method: Restaurant Server**

| Position: Restaurant Server | Performance Dimension: Technical Competence |
|---|---|
| 9 – | The server consistently applies all skills required for the position and is an excellent performer. |
| 8 | |
| 7 – | The server can apply most required skills and performs most assignments well. |
| 6 | |
| 5 – | The server applies some required skills and can complete most assignments. |
| 4 | |
| 3 – | The server has difficulty applying required skills and is not able to complete most assignments. |
| 2 | |
| 1 – | The server cannot apply most required technical skills and is likely to disrupt work because of this inability. |

supervisor and the employee try to understand why. The supervisor asks for the employee's views on the extent of goal-attainment and which actions to take. It is important that the supervisor meet periodically with the employee during the time allowed to accomplish the goals. The supervisor should measure progress and provide additional coaching when necessary. It is particularly helpful to set intermediate **benchmarks** to measure progress.

4. New goals and strategies for attaining them are developed for the next evaluation period.

One variation of the MBO approach is to use **job lists** (which identify **job tasks** for a given position) and **job breakdowns** (which explain how to perform each task). While these tools are usually developed for training programs, they can be very helpful for evaluating employees. The supervisor and employee agree on which specific tasks the employee performed well, and on those tasks toward which the employee must apply extra effort. Copies of the job list and job breakdown are given to the employee to help ensure that the tasks are performed correctly and up to standard.

A second variation of the MBO approach uses the job description for the employee's position as the basis for the evaluation. A copy is given to the employee and, after a review of it, the supervisor and the employee discuss the tasks in the job description on which there is disagreement regarding performance levels.

## Steps in the Performance Evaluation Process

Performance evaluation must be a two-way communication process that permits you to help the employee develop goals to reach by the next evaluation. At the

## Supervisors Must Also Be Evaluated

While this chapter addresses procedures that supervisors should use to evaluate the performance of entry-level employees, the supervisors' own work must also be assessed. Most supervisors want to know how their boss views their work, and many are interested in learning how they can better meet performance expectations. These are among the benefits of supervisory evaluation.

Many (most) of the tactics that supervisors use to evaluate their employees are applicable to the process by which managers evaluate supervisors. Large hospitality organizations with human resources departments may use these staff specialists to help develop performance evaluation procedures. For example, there are numerous responsibilities and duties that all supervisors in every department must assume. Examples include the knowledge and ability to facilitate departmental induction and training programs; to evaluate, coach, and discipline staff members; and to comply with numerous union-related, legal, and/or organizational requirements. These standards can become factors to evaluate supervisory performance in all departments. Then concerns applicable to supervisors in specific departments or work sections can be added. For example, front desk supervisors may need specialized skills to develop computerized front office reports, and head bartenders may need to know beverage inventory procedures. Supervisory performance evaluation systems that incorporate consistent factors are fairer to those being evaluated in the same way that consistent use of factors and procedures to evaluate entry-level staff members is most appropriate for them.

end of the session, you and the employee should agree about areas in which the employee is performing well, areas that need improvement, and specific action plans for improving performance. The evaluation session should not end until you and the employee have agreed on these points. Also, you should make it clear to the employee what you, as his or her supervisor, can do to help and whether interim evaluation sessions should be scheduled. When the review is over, you must complete any required paperwork. Managers frequently require performance review information for the employee's personnel file because it is often used in wage and salary decisions. See Exhibit 8 for a set of guidelines to help you conduct performance reviews. Exhibit 9 lists tasks that you should complete before, during, and after a performance evaluation session.

### Before the Session

Prepare for the discussion. Set the date and time in advance. Review the employee's job description. Gather information, such as material about job incidents that you observed, that is directly related to outstanding, acceptable, or poor performance. If appropriate, get input from others, too. List objectives you wish to accomplish. Find a private, non-threatening place to hold the interview. Plan what you're going to say, and rehearse your opening remarks.

The importance of preparation by both you and the employee cannot be over-emphasized. Exhibit 10 presents a list of questions you can give employees to help

**Exhibit 8   Guidelines for Conducting Performance Evaluations**

1. Interview in a setting that is informal, private, and free of distraction.
2. Provide a courteous, supportive atmosphere.
3. Encourage the employee to actively participate.
4. Clearly explain the purpose of the evaluation.
5. Explain problem areas thoroughly but tactfully.
6. Listen when the employee talks; don't interrupt.
7. Criticize job performance, not the employee.
8. Criticize while you're calm; never become angry.
9. Avoid confrontation and argument.
10. Emphasize the employee's strengths and then discuss areas which need improvement.
11. To set goals for improvement, focus on future (not past) performance.
12. Assume nothing; instead, ask for clarification.
13. Ask questions to gather information, not to "test" the employee.
14. Assume the employee will disagree; be prepared with documentation and/or examples.
15. Try to resolve differences; don't expect total agreement.
16. Avoid exaggerations (such as "always" or "never").
17. Help the employee maintain self-esteem; don't threaten or belittle.
18. Keep your own biases under control.
19. Work with the employee to set goals for improvement.
20. Assure the employee that you will help him or her reach the goals; mutually agree on the assistance you will provide.
21. Maintain appropriate eye contact.
22. End on a positive note.
23. Establish a time for additional evaluation if it is to occur before the regularly scheduled date.

them prepare for the review. There are two kinds of preparation you must undertake: preparing the *content* of the interview and preparing the *process*. When you prepare the content, you plan *what* topics the evaluation will cover. Process planning determines *how* the topics will be discussed.

Ask the employee to do some content planning as well and provide him or her with a blank evaluation form ahead of time. Ask the employee to review it and conduct a self-evaluation. The employee can make notes on the form or even fill it out completely. During the evaluation session, ask the employee to explain his or her self-evaluation. Then, state how you rated the employee, and explain what factors contributed to your decisions.

Asking employees to rate themselves before the evaluation session has advantages. For instance, employees are often quite accurate when rating themselves

**Exhibit 9    Supervisors' Performance Evaluation Tasks**

A wide variety of tasks must be done before, during, and after the evaluation session.

**Before the Session**

- Review the previous evaluation form and any records in the employee's personnel file about the employee's performance since the previous evaluation.
- Allow the employee to review information from the previous evaluation.
- Complete a first draft of the evaluation form for the current session. Request that the employee complete one as well.
- Schedule a time and place for the evaluation meeting.
- Prepare for the session by thinking about the results you desire and specific procedures which will achieve those results.
- Make a list of questions you have and matters you wish to resolve.
- Think about your suggestions for the employee's performance improvement and professional development plans.
- Focus the evaluation on the employee's performance, how it has changed, and how it can improve.

**During the Session**

- Create a friendly and relaxed atmosphere.
- Review the evaluation forms thoroughly; highlight areas in which the two of you agree. Be sure to note areas of disagreement as well.
- Request feedback from the employee.
- Focus on the employee's performance, not on the employee; be specific about areas of acceptable performance and areas where improvement is possible.
- Take notes about the most important points covered during the session.
- Be sure that the employee knows exactly what you expect.
- Request that the employee sign the evaluation.
- End the evaluation on a professional note and offer any possible assistance to help the employee further reach goals agreed upon during the evaluation.

**After the Session**

- Review the notes you took during the session; make any necessary changes while the interview is fresh in your mind.
- Complete any necessary forms; route copies as necessary to the human resources department.
- Give the employee a copy of the evaluation.
- Follow up; do appropriate coaching, as necessary.
- Discuss any important points with your own supervisor.

and can recognize at what level their performance has been. In addition, this helps ensure that both you and employees focus on the same topics, and that no important subject is overlooked. Bear in mind, also, that sometimes employees rate themselves more harshly than their supervisors do. This gives you an

**Exhibit 10    Questions to Prepare Employees for Performance Review**

Before conducting an employee performance evaluation, help employees prepare for the session. Ask them to think about questions like the ones listed below:

- What have I personally done to improve my skills since my last performance evaluation?
- In which areas of responsibility do I excel? In which do I fall short?
- What aspects of my position do I especially enjoy? What have been the most challenging aspects of my position?
- What were my three major accomplishments since the last performance review?
- What have I done personally to improve morale and teamwork within my department?
- How could my supervisor help me do a better job?
- How does my present position make the most of my capabilities?
- What challenges affect my ability to perform my job to the best of my ability?

Courtesy of Opryland Hotel, Nashville, Tennessee.

opportunity to provide additional positive feedback. Asking employees to rate themselves helps you spot those areas in which you agree on performance levels. You should quickly cover these areas so that you can spend more time discussing those areas in which you disagree. Giving employees an opportunity to rate their own performance also allows them to remind you of their accomplishments that you may have forgotten. Finally, this approach may help put employees at ease because they know in advance exactly what topics the evaluation session will cover.

Effective content planning offers several advantages. It helps you to appraise employee performance more objectively. With adequate, thoughtful preparation, you will be less likely to rely on suspicions and rumors, others' opinions, or your own unclear memories. Moreover, thorough content planning, when focused on facts, helps keep both you and the employee from becoming too emotional. In addition, careful planning saves time in the interview itself; you won't have to search files for facts or records if they are already assembled. Finally, in the course of your planning, you will have formulated a schedule of topics to keep the discussion organized.

When planning for the evaluation session, you decide how to introduce the content you have planned. This involves considering how you think the employee will rank himself or herself, whether and to what degree the employee will challenge your evaluation, and how you will handle the employee's resistance, among other matters.

## During the Session

As you make your opening remarks, be friendly and sincere. This will help relieve any tension that the employee may be feeling at the start of the meeting.

Clearly explain why you are holding the interview. Encourage the employee to participate, and interact positively with him or her. Make sure that the employee understands that the session will be a two-way conversation.

In many hospitality organizations, pay increases are directly related to the performance evaluation and become effective at the time the review is given. In these systems, it is a good idea to begin by stating your overall rating, what the wage or salary increase will be, and when it will take effect. Usually, the compensation issue is foremost in the employee's mind. Once you address it, you can focus more easily on the specifics of job performance. Alternatively, some organizations choose to discuss compensation in a second, separate meeting that occurs after the performance appraisal meeting.

Ask the employee to discuss previously established performance objectives (if any) and the results reached in each area. Have the employee rate his or her own performance and explain the ratings. Make sure you understand what the employee is saying. Actively listen to the employee—don't interrupt.

Next, explain your appraisal, focusing on the employee's performance rather than his or her personality. Then, explain why you appraised the performance as you did. Discuss both the employee's strengths and the areas that need improvement.

When addressing areas that need improvement, begin by describing the employee's current performance. The more specifically you can describe current performance, the less likely that the employee will become defensive. A specific statement helps reduce arguments because it describes behavior, not personality. For example, instead of saying, "You make too many errors," you could state: "There were five errors made while checking in guests last month." Or, instead of saying, "You're always late!" the supervisor could state: "Attendance records show that you've been at least fifteen minutes late five times during the last thirty days."

Next, state the expected standard of performance. Avoid general and vague statements like, "I expect you to improve your attitude with guests," or, "You've got to increase your productivity." Keep to the performance standard and state exactly what is expected in terms of guest service skills or productivity. State the performance gap, i.e., the distance between current performance and expected performance.

It is often helpful to next ask the employee to identify the cause(s) of the performance gap. Probing for the cause(s) of the performance problem is important because the employee may state causes that you haven't considered. Also, the more the employee identifies the cause(s), the more likely he or she will accept solutions to the performance situation. This keeps the discussion focused on performance and avoids confusing behavior with personalities. Ask questions like, "What do you think is the cause of this situation?" or, "What other causes do you see?" Use the word "situation" and not the word "problem." Employees tend to react less defensively when they are asked to analyze situations than when they are asked to address "problems."

Those conducting performance evaluations should recognize that, many times, employees perform at less-than-desired levels for personal reasons. Challenges concerning transportation, child care, finances, family, and substance abuse, among numerous other issues, can affect job performance. Few supervisors can be effective counselors; however, they can listen and, often, make suggestions about where employees can seek professional advice on such personal matters.

Also, ask the employee for solutions. Explore each solution to reach the ones that will correct the performance and close the gap. You should also make suggestions and build on the comments of the employee. After reaching agreement, create action plans, including goals and time frames, for improvement. Determine specific actions the employee should take to improve job performance. Avoid trying to change everything all at once. Instead, choose significant areas of performance, making sure that you and the employee agree. Then, set practical, time-oriented, and specific action plans and approaches the employee will take. Ask for and obtain the employee's commitment. Ask the employee what he or she needs from you to improve performance. If the performance evaluation discussion becomes lengthy, it may be better to deal with the performance improvement plan in a separate session. This approach gives the employee and you a chance to consider each other's input, identify improvement strategies, and focus completely on this important element of the process.

At the end of the session, summarize the performance evaluation and action plans. Schedule follow-up dates. It's a good practice to mark the dates and times for follow up on your calendar in the employee's presence. This shows him or her that performance improvement is important to you. It also clearly commits you to follow up and the employee to carry out the action plans.

Close the interview by thanking the employee and have him or her sign the evaluation form. The "thank you" is a courtesy that employees will appreciate.

## After the Session

Evaluate the interview and think about how you might have improved the session. Give the employee a copy of the final version of the written performance evaluation. Then, meet the employee on the previously determined follow-up date. Provide the employee with the appropriate help, support, and rewards for improving performance. Lastly, if the employee desires, allow him or her to ask for additional evaluation sessions, which would be held before the next "official" session.

# Coaching Overview

Coaching activities will be important between performance evaluation sessions. Through training, employees learn how and why to perform their jobs according to standards. Through coaching, employees learn how to apply what they learn in training sessions. When coaching, a supervisor persuades, corrects, and inspires employees to perform effectively. The supervisor uses positive reinforcement to achieve desired results.

Coaching may be informal or formal. **Informal coaching** is usually unplanned and conducted at the employee's actual work station. It occurs in the course of normal day-to-day operations. Supervisors use informal coaching to improve a skill, communicate specific information, correct an inappropriate behavior, confirm that a test is being done correctly, and reinforce the need to correct weak performance.

**Formal coaching** is usually conducted privately and away from the work station. It focuses on knowledge, skills, or attitudes that negatively affect a large part of the employee's job performance. A formal coaching session may also be called a performance improvement session. The supervisor should plan an agenda and keep a formal record of the session.

Coaching differs from taking disciplinary action, although it can be an early step in a progressive discipline program. Coaching is helping employees improve their performance on the job by providing feedback. If poor performance is the result of an employee not knowing how to complete a task, coaching is required. If an employee knows how to complete a task but performs poorly on purpose, then disciplinary action is generally required. Coaching also differs from **counseling,** which uses a one-on-one process to help employees solve their own, non-job-related problems. Counseling may concentrate on the employee's attitudes toward the job and the work environment. It can also involve personal problems not directly connected with work. However, personal concerns often negatively affect job performance. Personal counseling issues are usually referred to professionals trained to handle them.

In any planned coaching session, supervisors should address at least three concerns:

1. The purpose of the coaching

2. The relationship between the supervisor and the employee

3. The employee's general growth and development

Planned coaching sessions should be similar to an interview in form and approach. You should obtain facts, provide fair feedback, show understanding of the employee's feelings, and plan a course of corrective action. Planned coaching sessions help resolve problems and build supervisor-employee relationships. They also help employees to perform more effectively and productively.

Generally, coaching sessions are problem-oriented. That is, they focus on problems that the employee encounters while on the job, or on problems resulting from ineffective performance. Effective supervisors, however, recognize that coaching can help employees find pride and enthusiasm in their work. Positive coaching actions help employees to develop self-esteem. It also inspires employees to "do the right thing" and recognizes and rewards desired results. Too often, supervisors are quick to point out errors in employee performance but slow to acknowledge a job well done and thanking the employee for his or her efforts.

## Principles of Coaching

Coaching is an important supervisory activity. Employee attitudes and performance are affected by how a supervisor directs, or instructs, the supervisor's attitudes toward employees, and the supervisor's own performance. If you act as though you don't care how employees perform, they are also unlikely to care. If you expect work that meets established performance standards, that is what employees are likely to produce. Coaching is most effective when you develop a proper work environment that helps employees do their best.

**Employee Involvement.** If coaching is to succeed, employees must be actively involved in setting goals and be held responsible for meeting them. The more employees become involved in identifying problems and seeking solutions, the more committed and successful they are likely to be. Encourage employees to participate in the coaching process. Ask questions that the employee can answer to help solve problems.

**Mutual Understanding.** Both you and the employee must understand the topic being discussed. To ensure this, ask the employee to define the problem in his or her own words. Then, re-state the employee's views to see whether you have understood. If you do not do this, both of you might leave the session with entirely different ideas about the issues and their solutions.

**Listening.** The supervisor must do more listening than talking. You and the employee will likely gain more from the coaching session if you allow the employee to talk while you actively listen. Allowing the employee to describe the problem will allow him or her to make suggestions and discuss job-related issues and problems.

## Coaching Actions

Supervisors coach to improve employee behavior and attitudes. They may help employees by changing a situation, an employee's attitude, an employee's skills, or an employee's objectives.

**Changing a Situation.** The supervisor may (1) change his or her own behavior or leadership style, (2) alter the work group by encouraging employees to change their own behavior or by separating problem employees, or (3) change work resources or conditions. A supervisor making any of these changes may help an employee to modify performance.

**Changing Employee Attitudes.** A supervisor can help change an employee's attitude toward work by making sure the employee is accurately informed about company objectives, goals, plans, and challenges. In addition, the supervisor can point out how the employee can effectively perform to meet personal goals that are in line with those of the hospitality operation. Then they can provide positive feedback when the employee meets established performance standards.

**Changing an Employee's Skills.** A supervisor can help an employee learn more about the job and how to resolve common problems. This will often help improve the employee's attitude and enhance his or her self-esteem.

**Changing an Employee's Goals.** A supervisor can help employees set goals that they can reasonably meet. Supervisors should regularly review job performance standards. If standards are too high, or if employees expect too much of themselves, employees may become discouraged. Set short-range goals that employees can reach and allow them to celebrate success as they do so.

## Set Performance Goals When Coaching

The overall objective of coaching should always be to improve performance. This can best be accomplished when supervisors work with employees to establish performance goals. To be effective, performance goals must be:

- Clear and specific
- Measurable
- Time-specific
- Achievable

**Clear and Specific.** Goals must be clear and specific. Sometimes goals are not completed, or are incorrectly completed, by employees because they did not understand them. Specificity relates to the exactness of the goal. Goals such as "Do your best" or "Improve" are not specific. However, a goal such as "Consistently clean a standard guestroom in 15 minutes beginning the first of next month" is specific. Specific goals are better motivators than nonspecific goals.

**Measurable.** Goals should be stated in terms that are easy to measure. The more they are measurable, the better. For example, the goal to "Show a 10 percent decrease in guest complaints on guest comment cards over the next month" is more measurable than "Make guests happier."

**Time-Specific.** Many goals are neglected or completed unsatisfactorily because the supervisor and employee did not agree on a time limit in advance. "As soon as possible" is not specific enough. Neither is "soon," "right away," or "on high priority." Goals that include statements such as "by 2:00 P.M." "by tomorrow at noon," "by June 1," and so on establish time limits.

**Achievable.** Unattainable goals do not motivate employees. A goal such as "Increase the number of rooms cleaned per day by 30 percent before the end of the month," although specific, measurable, and with time limits, is probably not achievable. These types of goals quickly become unchallenging and de-motivating.

The number of performance goals set with an employee is important. Employees generally can work on no more than just a few performance goals at one time. This range has proven effective because there are enough goals to capture the complexity of position, but there are not so many that employees become confused or think that they are being asked to accomplish too much.

A nine-step approach to setting performance goals with employees can be used:

1. Specify the exact (specific) objective or tasks to be completed.

2. Establish attainable goals. Be sure to establish goals that will require effort, but are still attainable.

3. Specify how the employee's performance will be measured. Be specific about whether the measures will include productivity, observations of changed behavior, or other measures.

4. Specify the outcome to be reached. Establish and discuss with the employee exactly what outcome you expect.

5. Set a deadline. Remember to allow enough time for employees to learn how goals should be accomplished and to accomplish them.

6. Set priorities if there are multiple goals. Discuss and agree on which goal or goals are the most important. Use active listening skills to make sure that the employee understands the priorities.

7. Determine coordination efforts. If the employee requires the cooperation of others to attain a goal, be sure to arrange for this and explain to the employee how it will work.

8. Establish an action plan. A step-by-step action plan makes goal attainment much easier. Since the steps of an action plan often represent "mini-goals," accomplishing them can encourage employees to keep progressing toward their goal.

9. Decide when follow-up will occur. Even though a deadline has been agreed upon (step 5 above), wise supervisors check up on goal attainment activities as they evolve. They can then use additional coaching efforts to help the employee stay on track to attain the performance goal.

# Informal Coaching

When coaching is conducted informally, it is a routine part of supervision. A supervisor coaches whenever he or she talks to an employee about the employee's performance. When coaching employees informally, you should reinforce good performance, re-state or demonstrate performance expectations, and stay involved with the employees.

## Use Positive Reinforcement

The purpose of informal, everyday coaching is to point out which job behaviors meet performance standards and which do not. In cases of sub-standard performance, demonstrate correct procedures and explain why incorrect procedures are unacceptable.

When you want an employee to continue meeting established performance standards, you must observe the employee doing so and immediately compliment him or her. It's a good idea to try to "catch" an employee doing something right, and then immediately praise the employee. Positive reinforcement is most effective when it is specifically connected to correct behavior. Behavior that is positively reinforced is more likely to be repeated.

## Re-State Expectations

As you coach, expect to state and re-state your expectations to get your points across. Employees may not even try to meet desired standards unless they understand and remember your expectations. Re-stating expectations will reinforce employee learning and will also remind employees of established performance standards. Employees base their performance goals on performance standards.

When re-stating expectations, describe the gap between the employee's performance and the performance standard in a non-threatening manner. For example, avoid such statements as:

- *"YOU* did that wrong."
- *"YOU* made a mistake."
- "There were too many errors in *YOUR* work."
- *"YOU* failed!"

Instead, focus your remarks specifically on what was done improperly, and explain how it can be corrected. Always avoid even the appearance of a personal attack, an example being the "YOU" in the above statements. Whenever possible, simply describe what happened, what should happen, and what needs to be done to resolve the gap in performance.

For example: "Charles, almost everything you do when you rack dishes is good; however, it is always best to put the larger plates behind the smaller plates. Do you know why?" If Charles provides the correct response to the question (to ensure that the water that should be sprayed on the small plates is not blocked by the larger plates), you will know that earlier training has been effective. Charles does know the "what" and "why" of proper task performance. Your best response might then be, "You're correct, Charles, and we and our guests depend on you to protect us by always washing dishes in the way that ensures there will be no germs on the dishes when they are reused. Please don't use any shortcuts when washing dishes."

Conversely, if Charles does not know why the dishes should be racked a specific way, an appropriate response may be to first inform him ("Okay, as a review of the earlier training session on this topic…"), and to then state that the correct procedures must always be used: "Charles, I'm glad we could clarify this and it really is important that the correct procedures always be used. Do you have any questions about how or why the dishes should be racked as we discussed? I'm counting on you to do it correctly."

Supervisors may use an "over-the-shoulder" technique, in which they watch from a distance as employees work. The supervisor compliments the employee for tasks that the employee is doing well. Then, the supervisor tactfully corrects sub-standard performances while re-stating job expectations. Employees usually welcome positive "over-the-shoulder" coaching. They feel that their supervisors are interested in them as people, not as machines. However, supervisors should make sure that they never hang over their employees as they work. Supervisors should not crowd employees or criticize every action.

Effective supervisors make coaching a regular part of every workday with every employee. They continuously reinforce, teach, and re-teach correct procedures. Effective supervisors must master all job skills themselves or know which employees they can rely on to demonstrate or teach skills.

# Formal Coaching

Formal coaching is often conducted during interview sessions. There are two primary types of interviews used in formal coaching: directive and non-directive interviews.

**Directive interviews** are those that the supervisor directs by asking certain questions. Directive interviews are generally held to give and receive information, but they are also conducted to discuss feelings and attitudes. The success of this type of interview depends on how well the interviewer (supervisor) communicates and asks questions.

In **non-directive interviews,** problems are discussed in a less structured format that allows supervisors to analyze employee attitudes that affect job performance. The supervisor begins with general questions or statements about the problem and gives the employee freedom to discuss the issues from his or her own perspective. Non-directive interviews are generally conducted to explore the employee's feelings and attitudes.

In non-directive interview situations, supervisors sometimes find that employees try to hide or misrepresent their true feelings and do not always say what they really mean. To overcome this, provide an understanding, open-minded atmosphere. When you do, employees are more likely to say exactly what they feel. Although you may need to start the session by announcing that there is a problem, quickly give employees the lead. When employees believe that you will listen in a non-threatening way, they might be more able to discuss the problem.

Listen to the employee with understanding and acceptance. In this usage, "acceptance" indicates that you accept the employee's right to a viewpoint and that you accept the employee as a worthwhile human being. Withhold criticism of the employee without necessarily agreeing with everything the employee says. In a non-directive session, your criticism or judgment of the employee's viewpoints, statements, or attitudes will likely make the employee stop talking. Then, you may never discover the cause of a problem.

Respond briefly and positively to show understanding of the employee. Nods or simple responses such as "Yes" or "I see" help to show understanding. You will probably receive similar signals from the employee.

In addition, you might try repeating key statements that the employee makes. For instance, the employee may say, "I want my job to have more responsibility." Your non-directive response might be, "You feel that you want more responsibility." Be sincere when you say this. Say something that will be matter-of-fact and that will prompt the employee to further clarify his or her point. You could follow this re-statement with a question such as, "Could you tell me what type of extra responsibility you would like?"

## Preparing

When preparing to conduct a formal coaching session, you must first decide what you hope to accomplish. You should have a definite objective in mind. The session will be more productive if you write down exactly what information you want from the employee, what issues you will stress, and even some questions to ask.

Then, gather background information. Supervisors should know their employees; however, in large organizations, this can be difficult. In these cases, you should discover as much background information as possible about the employee, including strengths and areas that need improvement. You can do this by reviewing written performance evaluations and other records and speaking to other supervisors who work with the employee.

Before scheduling the coaching session, consult with the employee and review the weekly work schedule. The coaching session is an expanded training session, but it should not interfere with the employee's regular work. Notify the employee as far in advance of the session as possible.

It often takes extra time for an employee to feel comfortable enough to talk openly, especially when the interviewer is the employee's supervisor. In addition, this may be the employee's first chance to relate personal experiences and goals with the organization's goals. Allow the employee time to make the connection.

Be aware of your attitudes toward coaching, the session, and the employee. You should also consider the employee's attitudes. The employee's biases and behaviors may influence job performance. The session may be more productive if you try to understand how the employee feels about the coaching process and the topics under discussion.

## Conducting

Conduct the session privately, and minimize interruptions. Use an office or conference room suitable for thoughtful, productive discussion.

Establish a comfortable atmosphere. The employee must feel free to talk and express ideas. You must be willing to listen to the employee without getting angry, even if the employee questions your effectiveness. To establish a relaxed atmosphere, give the employee time to get used to the setting. Help the employee feel that he or she is relating to you as an equal. Put the employee at ease by reassuring him or her that you want to clarify the issues and work toward improvement. Show your understanding by honestly answering every comment the employee makes.

Start slowly. When the session begins, the employee may respond to your questions or statements unclearly if he or she is nervous or confused. Therefore, allow the employee extra time to think before responding. If you seem calm and patient, the employee will not feel threatened. Adjust to the employee's thinking and conversational abilities.

Describe the problem in a caring, positive way. Make it clear that your goal is to solve it rather than to blame the employee. Then the employee will be more willing to talk about the problem. Also, avoid accusing the employee and provide assurance that you realize he or she wants to do well. When you outline the problem, be as specific as you can. Discuss performance standards and explain how the employee's performance is falling short of expectations. Support your views with specific evidence or situations. Remember to focus on the performance problem, not on the employee's personality or attitude.

Ask the employee to help you solve the problem or identify its cause. If you can obtain the employee's commitment, the chances of solving the problem will be greater. Ask for the employee's help in deciding what steps to take to work out the problem. Employees who understand that you really value employee ideas are more likely to cooperate and this will help raise the employee's self-esteem.

To obtain more information, ask the employee general questions (beginning with "What," "How," "Who," and "When"). As the employee becomes more relaxed, ask more specific questions to clarify the problem. Be sure to listen and show understanding, especially when the employee seems worried or upset. Your empathy will help the employee maintain self-esteem. If you take notes, keep them brief so you can focus more fully on what the employee says and also maintain frequent eye contact. However, it is better to make your notes when the discussion is over. Be sure to store them in your working file.

In addition, you'll have ideas of your own to discuss. As you do so, remain friendly and safeguard the employee's self-esteem. Before beginning to talk about solutions, summarize the causes the two of you have identified to help ensure that you both understand all the information discussed.

When employees feel that the session is about to end, their remarks often become more pointed and significant. The last several minutes of the session may be the most productive if you pay close attention to the employee's final comments.

Ask the employee for ideas about resolving the performance problem. Taking brief notes at this time will make the employee feel good and will also produce a record of possible solutions. Such a record may prove helpful if the first remedy you try doesn't work out. When possible, use the employee's suggestions to solve the problem.

After deciding on a course of action, work together to determine exactly who must do what by a certain date. Add this information to your written record. Stress that, while you will do what you can to help the employee succeed, the employee is responsible for improving. Express confidence in the employee's ability to improve performance. This will strengthen the employee's commitment to solving the problem.

Before ending the discussion, you should schedule a follow-up session if necessary. This emphasizes that you expect the employee to solve the performance problem and that you want to track progress and celebrate success when the performance goal is attained. A follow-up discussion ensures that you and the employee will meet to explore progress and address any problems the employee continues to have. If necessary, you'll be able to plan a different course of action.

End the discussion in a positive, caring manner. Again, express your confidence in the employee's ability to solve the problem and show your support.

## Following Up

Following up does not mean concluding a coaching session with the familiar statement: "My door is always open. If you have any questions, don't hesitate to stop by and I'll help you any way I can." Supervisors who rely on this open invitation typically find that few employees ever "stop by." Following up is not the employee's responsibility—it is yours as a supervisor. You are the one who should take the initiative and observe the employee's performance on a regular basis.

Give the employee help and encouragement as he or she takes steps to improve performance. Provide further coaching or training, if necessary. Let the employee ask for additional coaching sessions, which could occur before the next "official" session. Keep written records of all sessions, especially of the improvements the employee makes.

 **Key Terms**

**alternative ranking**—Rating system in which an appraiser lists all employees and then chooses the best and worst, second-best and second-worst, and so on.

**behaviorally anchored rating scale**—Rating system in which the supervisor performing the evaluation identifies how often an employee displays desired behaviors.

**benchmark**—A standard against which progress is measured or evaluated; a point of reference from which progress is measured or evaluated.

**central-tendency error**—An error in a performance appraisal or interview that results when supervisors or interviewers rate all or most employees as average.

**coaching**—A process used by a supervisor to train and orient an employee to the realities of the workplace and to help the employee remove barriers to optimum work performance.

**counseling**—A problem-solving technique that uses a one-on-one process to help employees solve their own problems. Job-related counseling concentrates on the employee's attitudes toward the job and the work environment. Non-job-related counseling involves personal problems not directly connected to work.

**critical incident approach**—Job analysis technique based on capturing and recording actual events that occur at work that, when combined, form an accurate picture of a job's actual requirements. Useful in describing how services should be performed. Also used in training and as a measurement in certain performance appraisal systems.

**directive interview**—A session directed by the supervisor who asks specific questions.

**feedback**—The process by which the supervisor conducting a performance evaluation session informs the employee about his or her performance.

**forced choice approach**—A rating system in which appraisers select one statement from among several that describes how an employee performs relative to selected factors judged important for success on the job.

**forced distribution approach**—Evaluation method in which a supervisor ranks employees on an exact bell-shaped curve.

**formal coaching**—Coaching that is usually conducted privately, away from the work station. It focuses on knowledge, skills, or attitudes that negatively affect a large part of the employee's job performance. A formal coaching session may also be referred to as a performance improvement session.

**graphic rating scale**—Rating system in which appraisers rate employees on specific, measurable factors.

**halo error**—An error in a performance evaluation or interview that results when supervisors or interviewers rate employees based on a single positive trait.

**informal coaching**—A type of coaching that is usually conducted at the employee's work station. It occurs in the course of normal day-to-day operations. It often is conducted to improve a skill, communicate knowledge, or adjust inappropriate behavior.

**job breakdown**—Procedures that should be used to correctly perform a job task.

**job list**—A list that identifies the job tasks for a given position.

**job task**—One task (activity) that is part of a job.

**leniency error**—An error in a performance appraisal or interview that results when supervisors or interviewers rate employees too positively.

**management by objectives (MBO)**—Performance appraisal system in which a supervisor meets with each employee and sets specific goals to attain; both the supervisor and the employee meet later to assess the extent to which these specific goals were reached.

**non-directive interview**—Sessions that use an unstructured format that allows the interviewer (supervisor) to analyze employee attitudes that affect job performance.

**paired comparison approach**—A method of evaluating performance that involves comparing the performance, behaviors, skills, or knowledge of each employee with each other employee.

**past-anchoring error**—An error in a performance appraisal that results when supervisors or interviewers rate employees on the basis of previous ratings.

**performance evaluation**—A meeting held between a supervisor and an employee to evaluate the performance, behaviors, knowledge, and skills of that employee. Also referred to as a performance appraisal.

**personnel file**—A file of an employee's records used in making employment-related decisions, which is usually kept for all employees in a central location, such as the human resources department.

**pitchfork error**—An error in a performance appraisal or interview that results when supervisors or interviewers rate employees based on a single negative trait.

**recency error**—An error in a performance appraisal or interview that results when the supervisor or interviewer bases employee ratings primarily on the most recent events or behaviors.

**self-esteem**—Confident, positive feelings about oneself; self-respect.

**severity error**—An error in a performance appraisal or interview that results when supervisors or interviewers rate employees too severely.

**simple ranking approach**—Method of ranking all employees in a single list. Also called straight ranking.

**weighted checklist approach**—Rating system in which evaluators consider each employee's performance of tasks and duties according to values that have been previously assigned to each task or duty.

**Review Questions**

1. What are the benefits of conducting performance evaluations to the employees, supervisors, and management team?

2. What obstacles may interfere with effective performance evaluation programs?

3. What are some of the common errors to avoid when evaluating employee performance?

4. What are some comparative methods of evaluating employee performance? How do they differ?

5. What are some approaches to performance evaluations that incorporate absolute standards?

6. How do supervisors and employees work together to determine goals in the management by objectives (MBO) method of performance evaluation?

7. How, if at all, should supervisors handle a "good" employee's personal problems in terms of his or her job performance?

8. What steps should the supervisor take before, during, and after conducting performance evaluations?

9. How is coaching different from counseling and disciplining?

10. How can supervisors set performance goals with employees?

11. What tasks should supervisors use to conduct an informal coaching activity?

12. What should supervisors do to prepare, conduct, and follow up formal coaching sessions?

 **Case Study**

### Raising the Performance Bar

Just thirty days ago, Laverne Wilson was excited when she started her new position as executive housekeeper at the spectacular Melrose Hotel. The Melrose had enticed her away from a competing property with the promise of higher pay, greater prestige, and more responsibility. With her eye for detail, however, Laverne immediately noticed major housekeeping oversights at the hotel. In fact, on her first day at the Melrose, she was greeted by an overflowing trash can near the main entrance and cigarette butts on the lobby floor.

As Laverne reviewed guest comment cards and results from guest satisfaction surveys, the problems seemed to multiply. Guest complaints ranged from stained linens to crumpled and soiled stationery in the guestrooms. Worst of all, guest property had been reported missing from rooms on a number of separate occasions—without resolution. To top it off, guest satisfaction reports over the last six months showed consistently low ratings for the housekeeping department.

The real challenge emerged as Laverne read through the past year's performance appraisals of the housekeeping staff. Performance ratings were based on a scale of 1 to 5 (5—outstanding, 4—exceeds expectations, 3—meets expectations, 2—needs improvement, and 1—unsatisfactory). Laverne was surprised to find that virtually every housekeeping employee had received the highest performance rating. "How on earth," she wondered, "could the staff in this department receive such high ratings when the performance of each unit is absolutely substandard?"

Since she was a newcomer to the management team at the Melrose, Laverne decided to tread lightly. She first met with the general manager and asked for advice. He had been aware of the performance problems for some time and was anxious to work with Laverne to correct them. He knew the hotel would suffer financially in the long term if things didn't change, so he gave Laverne the go ahead to shake things up. While speaking with the GM, Laverne also learned of important incentive changes. To complicate her task, salary increases and bonuses would now be based on the performance not only of individual employees, but of entire units. In fact, each department's share of bonus pool funds would now be based on its overall performance. As their meeting ended, the GM added that guest satisfaction ratings would play a bigger role than ever in determining salary increases.

Laverne felt overwhelmed. How could she convince the various units in her department to improve their performance—particularly when they had been following the same routine for years? She was new to the operation and no one in her department would be very pleased with her for upsetting the way things were. Later in the day, she sat down with the human resources director, Rodney Ramirez, to express her concerns.

"Rod," Laverne began, "I have a problem. Certain units in my department are underperforming, yet the employees have been getting very high ratings on their annual performance evaluations. I need to meet with the unit supervisors, but before I do I thought I would get your input. How can I encourage supervisors to evaluate their staff more realistically and get them to make the necessary improvements in their units? I don't expect them to be happy with this news, but if things don't change, my department will be in big trouble."

Rod thought about the situation for a moment and then responded. "Yes, you're in a tough spot—especially when you're trying to upset the status quo. It's going to be difficult and you can expect resistance, but we hired you because we knew you could handle the situation. Let's work together on this. I could prepare some refresher training programs for your units, but the bottom line is that different departments in this hotel have been using performance reviews in different ways and for different purposes. To make performance reviews work in the future, you need to recalibrate them. Competencies and evaluation factors should be consistent throughout your department. To some degree you're being tougher on your employees, but you're also being fairer. Keep in mind that the changes you make will benefit our guests."

Laverne thanked Rod for his time and helpful advice and thought about what to do next. She scheduled a meeting with the supervisors from the three most troublesome units in her department: Melika Chinoy, a room inspector; Susan Duvall, the laundry supervisor; and Clarence Patterson, the public space supervisor. After a few days of preparation, she was ready to face the fire.

When they all met the following week, Laverne got right to the point. "Thank you for meeting with me today. I think you all must be aware of some problems facing our department. I called you here today because many of the problems seem to point to your units. Let me ask you—what do you think are trademarks of quality housekeeping?" Laverne sat back in her chair with her arms crossed and glared at each supervisor as she waited for their responses.

Melika was the first to speak up, "It's obvious. Clean rooms and linen, and attention to details."

Clarence added, "A nice-looking lobby and clean bathrooms."

"Right," Laverne affirmed. "So tell me why all of these guest comment cards say only bad things about the hotel? Look at this one. A guest says that the room she stayed in was filthy. Here's another complaint about stained sheets. Here's someone else who complained of a foul odor in the lobby. What are we going to do about this?"

Laverne paused. Susan's back straightened in the chair and her face seemed to harden. Melika and Clarence looked at each other. No one offered to speak.

"I want to see improvement in these areas," continued Laverne, "but, oddly enough, when I look at the performance evaluations of your staff, everyone has received a resounding ovation. How can every individual in your units receive a top rating and yet housekeeping underperforms as a department? We are only here to serve the guests of this hotel. If customers aren't satisfied—and judging from the number of complaints we've received they aren't—then we aren't doing our jobs."

Laverne paused again to observe their reactions. Melika and Clarence were visibly agitated, while Susan appeared unmoved.

Laverne decided to continue. "Each of you must reconsider your methods of appraising employees prior to the upcoming annual performance reviews. We need consistent evaluation guidelines, and they must be closely followed without exception. In other words, it's your responsibility to re-evaluate your employees and I want to see concrete improvements in their performance within the next two months. We can no longer gloss over the staff and hope for the best. You should also be aware that next year's bonuses and salary increases will be based on overall departmental performance. We get nothing if this situation doesn't improve. Now I'll listen to your comments."

Susan Duvall, the laundry supervisor, was the first to respond. "With all due respect, Ms. Wilson, you haven't been here very long. I have been here twelve years and although I agree with some of the problems you've mentioned, previous department heads never approached us in this way. We have always aimed for a cooperative work environment, and I think it is totally unfair that you point the finger at us. This employee re-evaluation stuff may be an opportunity for improvements and changes, but what about the other units in the department? Aren't they part of the problem too?"

Melika chimed in. "I think re-evaluating our employees is stupid. Like it or not, I need to keep my workers. It's a tight job market. People aren't lined up trying to get a job here. My unit will suffer if I lose people. It's easier to give them a high rating and then encourage them to do their best. I'm not going change the way I've always done things. I've got to think about my people."

Clarence, who had never been one to let his opinions go unspoken, was the most outraged. "I've been at this hotel for ten years and things have been going great—up to now. What do you expect me to do? We've got lousy equipment, and this hotel isn't up to the most modern standards, you know. The employees I work with are my friends. Why, I've known old Frank since I started here. Now I'm his supervisor and you want me to tell him his work isn't any good? Forget it. Then you tell us we won't get a raise if we don't work harder? We don't get paid enough as it is!"

## Discussion Questions

1. How could Laverne have approached the supervisors differently?

2. What steps should Laverne now take with each supervisor to ensure they improve employee performance in their units?

---

Case Number: 3567CA

The following industry experts helped generate and develop this case: Philip J. Bresson, Director of Human Resources, Renaissance New York Hotel, New York, New York; and Jerry Fay, Human Resources Director, Aramark Corporation, Atlanta, Georgia.

This case also appears in *Managing Hospitality Human Resources*, Fifth Edition (Lansing, Mich.: American Hotel & Lodging Educational Institute, 2012), ISBN 978-0-86612-396-9.

## Chapter 7 Outline

## Competencies

# 7

# Discipline

SUPERVISORS AND MANAGERS try to change employee behavior through the use of **discipline.** In a positive sense, discipline involves activities that correct, strengthen, and improve employee performance. However, many supervisors dislike and try to avoid disciplining employees.

This inaction often stems from a supervisor's hope that a problem will somehow correct itself. However, problems don't just go away. Wishful thinking allows a problem to continue beyond the time when a supervisor should have taken action to resolve it. A problem that is ignored typically gets worse. Then, employees who are aware of the problem wonder why their supervisor hasn't taken appropriate action against it.

Many supervisors do not understand how to use discipline properly and effectively. Their lack of understanding leads to actions that either work poorly or not at all. In contrast, effective supervisors learn when to act and how to involve the employee to be disciplined in identifying the cause(s) of a problem and developing a workable solution.

Normally, a supervisor will discuss a potential disciplinary situation with his or her own manager. For example, you might ask your manager to clarify whether a specific policy violation justifies disciplinary action. Many employees believe that manager input ensures a degree of consistency and fairness. In other words, a supervisor cannot make arbitrary decisions because his or her own boss is involved in the disciplinary process. Sometimes a supervisor may request that his or her manager be directly involved in a disciplinary interview. However, this is not typically advisable, because the supervisor will appear to lose authority in the employee's eyes.

If problems continue after corrective conversations and private interviews, other levels of management will become involved. For example, a supervisor might have the authority to reprimand an employee and place a written report in the employee's personnel file. However, that supervisor might not be authorized to discharge an employee without the full knowledge and approval of managers at higher organizational levels. In unionized operations, union officials are likely to be involved in most aspects of the discipline program. For example, the result of some disciplinary actions might be **mediation** or **arbitration** by an outside, impartial party.

Discipline is a management or supervisory skill that you can learn only through practice and by following basic guidelines. This chapter will help you learn to better handle disciplinary situations and keep employees productive in the process.

# Myths about Discipline

Most of the problems surrounding the use of discipline arise when a supervisor doesn't understand its purpose or the proper way to handle it. If a supervisor bases disciplinary actions on any of the following myths, discipline will be ineffective. It might, in fact, be counterproductive.

**Myth 1: Discipline Is Punishment.** This is probably the most commonly believed myth. Sometimes supervisors use punishment when they are angry or tense, or when they don't know what else to do. Some supervisors punish employees to get revenge or to show an employee "who's the boss." However, punishment is not an effective long-term improvement strategy in the workplace.

The long-term negative effects of punishment, however, may overwhelm your department. Employees who have been punished might react by hiding future mistakes or by becoming resentful and hostile. They might decrease the quality or quantity of their work. Quite often, they simply stop trying and return to work only until they can find another job. Feelings of low self-esteem replace creativity and the desire to do a good job—traits that supervisors should encourage, not suppress. Most important, perhaps, is the fact that punishment fails to deal with the problem's actual cause.

**Myth 2: Being the Boss Means People Have to Do What You Say.** Many supervisors think their employees will do everything they are told to do because they must do so. Some supervisors try to threaten and force employees to behave in certain manners. However, this approach usually results in a power struggle that no one can win. Employees make their own power plays, the supervisor responds with a greater display of power, and the struggle continues until both sides run out of ideas. A supervisor's final threat might be **termination**, but you can't fire your entire staff. If employees challenge the threat of termination and don't get fired, they've won the battle: the supervisor loses all credibility and authority.

The problems resulting from such "control by power" are similar to those stemming from the use of punishment. The causes of problems aren't identified or analyzed, and employees become defensive, rebellious, unhappy, hostile, and stubborn.

Being the supervisor doesn't make you "better" than your employees. Effective supervisors must have a personal value system that prizes high ethical principles, a belief in the dignity of employees, and a respect for employee rights. Employees who are unhappy working for an unusually strict supervisor will generally look for a job somewhere else. If a supervisor continues to use power over employees who have no other choices, the employees' hostility will contribute lower work standards and lower productivity.

**Myth 3: If You're Nice to Your Employees, They Won't Need Discipline.** Some supervisors believe they ensure employee loyalty, friendship, and productivity when they ignore mistakes and broken rules and give in to employee demands. Instead, employees learn to expect such treatment and actually lose respect for the supervisor or loyalty to the department. Employee morale and productivity will eventually suffer. Employees in other departments with stricter supervisors might experience drops in morale, too.

In addition, the overly lenient supervisor might begin to resent employees who take advantage. Such resentment might build until the supervisor lashes out in anger unexpectedly. This causes more problems to arise as employees become confused about what to expect from their supervisor. Employees might believe they're being unfairly treated because their own behaviors haven't changed, but the supervisor's behavior has.

**Myth 4: Every Disciplinary Situation Must Be Handled the Same Way.** Union contracts, labor laws, and government regulations attempt to ensure that all employees are treated fairly. However, many managers and supervisors think this means they must treat all employees in exactly the same way under all circumstances. It's true that you must be able to justify handling similar infractions differently. However, while two problem behaviors might be similar, their causes might be different—and that means your solutions may differ as well. Your choice of a disciplinary approach depends on the factors involved in a given situation.

For example, consider a dependable employee who has worked in the department for 15 years and is late twice in the same week because of a spouse's serious illness. Compare that situation to a second employee who just started, is still on probation, and who is late twice in the same week because his or her alarm didn't go off. It would be unfair to use the same disciplinary approach for both employees.

Effective supervisors enforce the spirit rather than the letter, of the policy. Keep the policy's overall purpose in mind, which is to employees improve their behavior and productivity. Be consistent but flexible within the guidelines established by the property.

Handle each situation properly and effectively from the start, maintain thorough records, and document every instance of disciplinary action. Explain the reasons behind any exceptions you make. As long as you apply the same set of goals and values to fairly assess each situation, you can address employees and challenges differently.

# The Purpose of Disciplinary Action

The purpose of disciplinary action is not to punish employees, but to modify their behavior—to close the gap between an employee's unacceptable behavior and the required performance standards. Supervisors who think of discipline as a form of punishment spend all their time waiting for employees to do something wrong. To avoid this mindset, think of discipline as a method of giving employees the opportunity to improve themselves and their behavior so that they meet department expectations. If you do this, you will be better able to discuss and then close the gap that exists between the property's expectations and employees' behavior.

Instead of acting as judge and jury, an effective supervisor considers himself or herself to be a *coach* who tries to motivate employees to perform to the best of their abilities. By adopting this attitude, a supervisor emphasizes the fact that discipline can be a positive process. This attitude also encourages a supervisor act quickly when potential issues arise, rather than putting it off as a way to avoid confrontation. When discipline is approached properly, confrontations rarely occur.

A well-planned disciplinary program helps modify employees' behaviors by providing clear-cut and well-defined consequences for improper behavior. Know your organization's policies and procedures for disciplinary action. Most organizations delegate to supervisors the responsibility for such disciplinary actions as issuing oral and written warnings. If suspension or termination is warranted, the supervisor must consult an upper-level manager or a representative of the human resources department.

When deciding which disciplinary action to take, evaluate these important factors:

- Facts and circumstances surrounding the incident
- Seriousness of the problem
- Whether the problem with the employee has occurred before
- The employee's length and quality of service

## Policies, Rules, and Procedures

One objective of discipline is to ensure employee compliance with reasonable policies, rules, and procedures. Some hospitality operations might have too many rules and regulations, often thought of as "red tape." The number and types of rules vary according to the philosophy and leadership styles of top-level managers. The rules that cause trouble and that employees often break are probably those that do not make sense to them.

Reasonable rules and regulations set guidelines within which employees must work. They also tell employees when they do and do not have the authority to make "on-the-spot" decisions. These tools are important elements in the operation's basic management program.

It is important to review policies, rules, and procedures, especially those frequently broken, to ensure that they are reasonable. If management has determined that policies, rules, and procedures are, in fact, reasonable, you should explain and justify them to employees. Staff members who understand reasonable policies and rules are less likely to break them.

Employees working in organizations with too many rules often feel as though their supervisors and managers are communicating the message, "Our employees are not smart or mature enough to discipline themselves. Therefore, we must issue rules to manage their behavior." Not surprisingly, this kind of management attitude can create problems. Employees might feel they are misunderstood or believe that management considers them untrustworthy. As a result, they might respond by becoming distrustful themselves.

Policies, rules, and procedures should apply to all employees of an operation, not just to some. They should also be written, included in employee handbooks, and explained during orientation sessions. Employees should also be informed about any major changes in policies, rules, and procedures before those changes are implemented.

## Minor Corrections to Behavior

Training, performance discussions, and discipline often overlap. Suppose you notice that one of your cooks isn't wearing a head covering. You tell the employee

## Coaching and Discipline

The definitions of "coaching" and "discipline" contain similar elements. Coaching involves, in part, "a process to help the employee remove barriers to optimum work performance." Discipline is defined, in part, as "activities that correct, strengthen, and improve employee performance." Are these terms and their related activities the same?

One way to answer this question is to regard coaching as an ongoing series of activities that encourage and reinforce proper performance. If informal conversations and more formal interviews do not result in desired performance, activities included in a progressive discipline program, such as those discussed later in this chapter, become important.

Coaching is an ongoing extension of orientation and training. When a supervisor coaches, he or she suggests areas for improvement or encourages and thanks employees for their excellent performance. When done correctly in a culture that recognizes and respects employees, coaching should be the only tool a supervisor needs. Only when other issues arise—including those stemming from ineffective supervision—will additional steps in the discipline process become necessary.

you have noticed a problem and explain the reasons he or she should always wear a chef's cap. In this case, the correction process becomes a form of coaching. You conclude the discussion by praising the employee for the work he or she is doing well, and affirm that you're glad the employee is part of the team. Even though this interaction is casual, it communicates the following messages to the employee: that your standards are high, that you're checking his or her work, and that you're confident the employee can be successful.

**Positive discipline** usually starts with this kind of casual and friendly corrective action. In fact, positive discipline is a normal part of a supervisor's day-to-day responsibilities. If you correct employees when you first spot mistakes, small errors are not likely to become major problems. For many employees, positive discipline is the only type of corrective action they need, as most employees come to work hoping to perform well, not poorly.

If, after positively disciplining an employee, you notice him or her making the same mistake, say something like, "I believe I've said this before, and here is how I'd like you to do this." Such a statement allows the employee to maintain self-esteem. Express confidence that the employee can correct the problem and learn the right way to perform. This type of feedback is similar to the training new employees receive, when they learn the "what and why" about the tasks they must complete.

Experienced supervisors know that excessive criticism is usually not beneficial when an employee can make only small improvements. It is unrealistic to expect error-free employees who always meet department standards. Constant criticism reduces employee morale and self-esteem, and causes even bigger problems. A little discipline goes a long way.

Follow up on every act of discipline, regardless of how minor it might have been. First, make a brief note about the incident and place the note in the employee incident file. A sample form is shown in Exhibit 1. Include the date and time of the incident, an explanation of the incident, and any action upon which you and the employee agree.

The note serves as a reminder that you have given the employee a chance to correct his or her behavior. If the employee successfully changes the behavior, you will be able to recognize the change and thank him or her for it. A well-documented paper trail also serves as an important means of protecting yourself, the operation, and your right to supervise. Without such records, you might encounter difficulty proving that you ever tried to correct the problem. Careful documentation helps you track important dates, facts, and patterns of behavior.

Many supervisors hesitate to document negative incidents if doing so would create a permanent written record in the employee's personnel file. This concern might be minimized if the operation's policies permit removal of such information after a certain period of time or after corrective action has proven effective. Supervisors and managers should remember that the incident file is also the best place to record positive achievements.

## Positive Reinforcement

**Positive reinforcement** tends to increase the likelihood of acceptable behavior and decrease the likelihood of unacceptable behavior. It can be a powerful tool in a positive discipline program. You cannot build a good relationship with employees if you talk to them only when they are doing something wrong. Positive reinforcement helps foster goodwill and mutual respect. Another advantage is that it costs only a few minutes of your time.

**Exhibit 1    Sample Employee Incident File**

| INCIDENT FILE | | |
|---|---|---|
| Employee Name_____ | | |
| Date of Employment_____ | | |
| Date | Time | Incident and Action Taken |
| | | |
| | | |
| | | |
| | | |
| Supervisor          Date | Employee          Date | |

Typically, supervisors are much more effective in maintaining acceptable behavior through positive reinforcement than they are in eliminating undesirable behavior after it begins. In part, this is because employees who comply with rules and work according to procedures do not need to change their behavior. Instead, a supervisor must simply motivate them to continue their acceptable behavior.

By contrast, employees whose behavior is unacceptable must change their behavior and consistently repeat desired work practices. When an employee's work behavior corresponds to expectations, you can positively reinforce him or her through praise, compensation, or other incentives. Such practices often encourage employees to exceed the expectations management places on them.

For positive reinforcement to be effective, you must offer a reward the employee finds meaningful. The reward must also be timely and frequent. A relationship must exist between the desired activity and the positive reinforcement. Positive reinforcement must also recognize group or team efforts, as one employee's work frequently depends upon that of another employee.

Praise is one of the best positive reinforcement techniques. Sincere praise is a strong reward, and people tend to repeat behavior that's been rewarded. Praise employees for trying to improve behavior. Be sincere, though, and don't overdo it. The following sentences of praise, though simple, can be very powerful:

"You learn fast."

"You're really doing a good job here."

"Keep up the good work."

"These tables look great."

"You handled that last guest really well."

"I'm proud of you."

Instead of waiting for employees to do something wrong, provide positive reinforcement for what they do right. The praise should be given in public, not in private. When supervisors create positive team environments, everyone on the team takes pride in the recognition of each member's performance. Public praise also reminds others of your expectations and helps improve their performance as well.

# Progressive Discipline

Many hospitality operations adopt **progressive discipline** programs in relation to defining the behaviors subject to disciplinary action. Some programs define behaviors in great detail and specify the disciplinary action for each type of offense. Other programs define unacceptable behaviors more generally. Progressive discipline programs use sequential steps. A sample sequence of steps might be as follows:

1.  An oral warning

2.  An oral warning, possibly followed up by a written warning filed in the supervisor's work station

3. An official written reprimand placed in the employee's file

4. A suspension of a few hours or several days with or without pay

5. A disciplinary transfer or demotion

6. A "one-last-chance" step immediately before termination

7. Termination of employment

Termination (or discharge) is typically the last step in the disciplinary process. However, termination might be the immediate and only response to very serious behaviors like violence, theft, and falsification of employment records.

Immediately before discharge, some organizations might grant an offending employee "one last chance" to correct a problem. Typically, supervisors specify exactly what the employee must do and by when. For example, consider an employee with significant performance problems who has admitted to substance abuse as the direct cause of his or her behavior. The employee might be allowed to participate in an appropriate employee assistance program. If the employee agrees, he or she might receive a specific amount of time to attend the program and resolve the problem to avoid termination.

## Discharge

When upper management is when planning procedures to be used in discharge interviews and terminations, it is generally wise to consult with an attorney to help ensure that proper procedures will be consistently used for all employee discharge situations.

The decision to discharge an employee must be weighed carefully. The following questions can serve as a helpful checklist to ensure that a decision to discharge is appropriate. A "no" answer to any of the questions should prompt further investigation before a discharge action is taken. Note that while all the factors the questions address might not be critical to a successful legal defense, they are helpful in ensuring that effective procedures are in place for the day-to-day supervision of employees:

- Did the employee know what he or she was expected to do?

- Were the rules clearly and fairly communicated to the employee?

- Did management explain why the rules were important?

- Were the rules that were broken reasonable and important to the organization?

- Is the evidence for the discharge substantial and reliable?

- Is the discipline equal to the seriousness of the offense?

- Did management make a sincere effort to identify poor performance and to correct behavior or actions?

- Are records of previous progressive discipline activities available, and do they support the discharge decision?

- Is the disciplinary action taken for the improper behavior applied consistently to all employees?

Discharges typically occur during a termination interview conducted according to established procedures. Generally, a manager conducts the interview, along with a witness, who is often another manager or a human resources representative.

## Wrongful Discharge

Many hospitality organizations have established well-thought-out discipline programs, including complete documentation and progressive discipline to avoid **wrongful discharge** lawsuits. However, these efforts are of little use unless all supervisors and managers have the proper training and carefully follow established discharge procedures. The easiest wrongful discharge case for an employee to win is the one in which rules are enforced unfairly. Unfortunately, this is the single area in which supervisors and managers make the most mistakes. Consider the following situation.

Jorge is a high performer who is well-liked by guests, managers, and fellow employees. However, he has a habit of coming to work late. Sally is a poor performer who is not well-liked by guests, managers, and fellow employees. She also has a habit of arriving late. A manager who "solves" the problem with Sally by discharging her but who does not discharge Jorge is encouraging a wrongful discharge suit. As noted previously, policies, rules, and procedures should apply to all employees, not just to some of them. On the other hand, also keep in mind that the supervisor does not necessarily have to treat the two employees exactly the same. While Jorge should be disciplined as well, it may be possible to justify a less severe form of discipline for Jorge if circumstances warrant it. Clear records might make all the difference in defending against any wrongful discharge suite Sally might bring.

# Procedures for Disciplinary Action

A supervisor generally takes disciplinary action when an employee knew and was able to do what he or she was supposed to do, but chose not to do so. Supervisors usually do not discipline employees if the employees didn't know their behavior was unacceptable, or if they were unaware that their job performance was below the supervisor's expectations. These are important concerns. Supervisors have a responsibility to ensure that employees have the information they need to perform according to job standards.

Before deciding to take disciplinary action, supervisors should ask the following questions:

- Did factors beyond the employee's control cause the problem?

- Did the employee know the performance standard, and was he or she able to meet it?

- Is the disciplinary action to be taken consistent with that previously used in the same type of situation?

Employees can do many things that cause supervisors concern. Be sure that a situation for which you will take disciplinary action warrants the time that will be required to do so. This is not to suggest that unacceptable behavior should be overlooked, but if the problem is minor, a minor form of correction such as an informal coaching discussion might be most appropriate.

In general, there are two major types of unacceptable behavior:

1.  That which results from a purposeful decision made by the employee, such as failure to follow reasonable policies and procedures and failure to follow reasonable supervisory instructions

2.  That which is beyond the employee's control due to lack of training, improper tools, poor supervision, or other conditions

In every potential disciplinary situation, supervisors should assess whether a problem's causes are within the employee's control. Unacceptable behavior that is *within* an employee's control must be managed through effective disciplinary action procedures. However, unacceptable behavior *beyond* an employee's control is really the supervisor's problem. The supervisor must do a better job of helping employees meet job requirements. This might involve, for example, retraining that covers the area or task in which the employee is performing unacceptably.

An employee who is constantly late for work or who takes too much time for breaks is troublesome for a supervisor and might affect the morale and productivity of coworkers. This employee usually knows better. In this case, the problem typically isn't a lack of knowledge about policies and regulations, and won't be resolved by coaching or retraining. Instead, some type of disciplinary action is in order.

Some supervisors believe that, once they determine disciplinary action is needed, they must resolve the situation immediately. New supervisors often believe this, and might think they were promoted to make quick decisions and take decisive actions. However, except in cases of emergencies, a supervisor should take time to analyze a situation.

Supervisors might think they know what should be done to resolve a problem. However, keep in mind that the employee is the key factor in solving the problem. Therefore, a supervisor should determine what he or she must know before making a discipline-related decision.

## Gather Facts

Before deciding if disciplinary action is required, a supervisor should gather facts about the problem. This can sometimes be a challenge because assumptions, opinions, and allegations can cloud facts.

In general, a fact is something that most people would agree is true. Facts are typically written records, statistics, photographs, and things someone (i.e., a witness) has personally seen or heard. A supervisor's role in gathering facts is similar to the task of a detective investigating a mystery: "What really happened here? What counts as the best evidence of what really happened?"

Assumptions, opinions, and allegations are often mistakenly accepted as statements of fact. As a supervisor gathers facts, he or she must confirm that they are true as stated. Test your skills at distinguishing fact from fiction by carefully reading the short story in Exhibit 2 and marking the statements that follow it. Answers are provided in Exhibit 3.

**Exhibit 2    Fact or Fiction**

Test your skills at distinguishing fact from fiction by carefully reading the short story below and marking the statements that follow either "T" (definitely true), "F" (definitely false), or "?" (not stated in the story).

> After reviewing the current disciplinary program for Heartland Restaurants Inc., Chris Brinks, the new President and CEO, ordered the immediate development of a company-wide progressive discipline process. Brinks gave three top-performing brand managers authority to spend up to $2,500 without corporate approval. Brinks sent one of corporate's best men, Miller, to benchmark the progressive discipline process used by one of their company's suppliers. Within ten days, Miller developed a highly promising proposal.

1. Brinks sent one of corporate's best men to research a supplier's disciplinary program.

   T    F    ?

2. Brinks underestimated Miller's ability.

   T    F    ?

3. Miller failed to develop a plan.

   T    F    ?

4. Miller lacked authority to spend money without corporate approval.

   T    F    ?

5. Only three brand managers had authority to spend money without corporate approval.

   T    F    ?

6. The President and CEO sent one of his best men to research a supplier's disciplinary program.

   T    F    ?

7. Three men were given authority to spend up to $2,500 each without corporate approval.

   T    F    ?

8. Brinks had a high opinion of Miller.

   T    F    ?

9. Only four people are referred to in the story.

   T    F    ?

10. Although Brinks gave authority to three of his best men to spend up to $2,500 each, the story does not make clear whether Miller was one of these men.

   T    F    ?

**Exhibit 3   Answers to Statements in Exhibit 2**

1. Brinks sent one of corporate's best men to research a supplier's disciplinary program.
   T—Stated in the story.

2. Brinks underestimated Miller's ability.
   ?—The story does not say whether Brinks did or not.

3. Miller failed to develop a proposal.
   F—The story states that he did.

4. Miller lacked authority to spend money without corporate approval.
   ?—The story does not state whether or not Miller had authority to spend money.

5. Three brand managers had authority to spend money without corporate approval.
   T—Stated in the story.

6. The President and CEO sent one of his best men to research a supplier's disciplinary program.
   ?—The story does not state that the President and CEO is a man.

7. Three men were given authority to spend up to $2,500 each without corporate approval.
   ?—The story does not state if the three brand managers are men.

8. Brinks had a high opinion of Miller.
   ?—The story suggests this, but does not specifically state it.

9. Only four people are referred to in the story.
   ?—If Miller is one of the three brand managers given the authority to spend up to $2,500, this would be true, but the story does not specify whether Miller is one of those three.

10. Although Brinks gave authority to three of his best men to spend up to $2,500 each, the story does not make clear whether Miller was one of these men.
    ?—The story does not specify whether Brinks is a man or whether he gave such authority to men.

In fairness to employees and in the best interests of the organization, supervisors should follow the principle that an individual is presumed innocent until proven guilty. With this principle as a guide, a supervisor should try to use the facts to prove that an infraction has occurred. It is important to consider all applicable circumstances. Ask questions such as:

- Did the employee knowingly break the rule?
- What were the consequences of the behavior?
- What is the employee's disciplinary record?
- Is a temporary personal problem contributing to the discipline problem?

- Is the incorrect behavior or rule violation entirely the employee's fault?
- Have the behaviors of this employee and others been overlooked in the past?

Think through the situation in detail. Determine what the facts indicate about the situation and whether additional facts are needed. Study available records. Does an observable pattern exist? Has the problem always existed, or is it recent? Are all the available facts sufficient for you to be certain about what happened? Do your boss and human resources personnel need to know what you are planning, and should they have input?

## Explore Probable Causes

A supervisor who thinks through a problem's probable causes before taking disciplinary action will identify relevant information and be prepared to meet with the employee. Exploring probable causes might not always identify the exact causes of a performance problem. However, a successful study will uncover clues to the kind of questions that the supervisor should ask an employee during his or her disciplinary meeting.

Explore a problem's probable causes by seeking answers to the following questions:

- Who are all of the people involved?
- What rules were violated?
- Is there a pattern?
- Is the problem related to any specific time or shift?
- Is the problem related to any particular time of year?
- How long has the problem existed? When did it start?
- Where is the problem occurring?
- Have any changes occurred that could have caused the problem?
- Are there other symptoms of this problem?
- How does the employee's record compare with that of others?
- Were the rules posted, published, or otherwise known to the employee?

The probable causes you might identify during this questioning process will be only tentative, for you will not have all the information until you talk with the employee. However, an exploration of probable causes will help you determine the kinds of questions you should ask the employee. The questioning techniques you use during the disciplinary session should help the employee understand the problem, identify its root cause, and develop a plan of action to satisfactorily resolve it.

## Managing the Disciplinary Process ———————————

The disciplinary process must be designed to yield benefits for the hospitality operation. Otherwise, serious problems can arise in the form of poor human relations, low job performance, potential legal or union controversies, and problems for both supervisors and staff. Employees will view discipline as a form of punishment if supervisors and managers have not established performance standards, clearly communicated expectations, and consistently and fairly enforced rules. If you experience problems disciplining employees, you might have to change your own behavior. When you are able to change yourself, you are ready to help employees change themselves.

Remember that the objective of discipline is to elicit a change in an employee's behavior, not to punish him or her. Conduct disciplinary sessions so that they determine the reasons a situation occurred and the actions that will best resolve the difficulty. The most effective way to do this is to solicit the employee's involvement and commitment to change. You cannot do this by criticizing, blaming, or attacking the employee. Exhibit 4 outlines the steps to follow in managing the disciplinary process.

A supervisor sometimes becomes disappointed with the employee and with himself or herself when a problem is not managed successfully the first time it occurs. Such a situation creates anger that the supervisor often directs toward the employee. Expressing anger toward an employee solves nothing and usually makes the situation worse. An effective supervisor develops the abilities to tell an employee what he or she (the supervisor) expects, to get the employee involved in discovering a solution, and to work with the employee on a plan of action.

**Exhibit 4   Managing the Disciplinary Process**

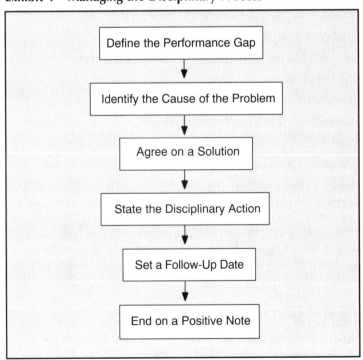

Disciplinary sessions should take place as soon as possible after the employee's inappropriate behavior has been identified, facts have been gathered, and possible causes of the problem have been explored. The disciplinary meeting should be held in as much privacy as possible, and a witness should be in attendance.

## Define the Performance Gap

At the beginning of the meeting, define the problem by describing the **performance gap** that exists between the employee's expected and actual behavior. The employee must learn exactly what he or she is presently doing that is inappropriate, improper, or incorrect. If you have had previous discussions with the employee about the same problem, summarize what actions, if any, the employee has taken to date and acknowledge any progress the employee has made.

Be specific when describing the gap in performance. Avoid statements such as, "Your performance is very poor," or "You really need to work harder," or "You've got to change your attitude." It's always easier to make general statements about "poor performance" and "bad attitudes" than it is to be specific. However, general statements are unproductive because they offer few, if any, solutions and ignore the problem's underlying causes. In addition, this tactic attacks the employee rather than his or her behavior. Remember that if the employee has a problem, it's also your problem!

Before the meeting, ask questions such as:

- "Why do I think this employee has an improper attitude?"

- "What has the employee done that makes me feel this way?"

- "What do I expect from this employee?"

Answering these questions will help you identify specific actions the employee has taken, or specific things he or she has said. Do not focus on the employee's attitude; instead, focus on the ways in which the employee's problem behavior fails to meet expectations. Don't attack the employee's personality. For example, instead of saying, "You're rude," tell the employee that, "It's rude to turn your back on a guest who's obviously coming to ask you a question."

Supervisors who concentrate on an employee's behavior instead of on the employee himself or herself help the employee maintain self-esteem. This focus may enable the employee to talk about the problem objectively instead of reacting defensively. Throughout the interview, do not threaten, argue, or display anger. These actions will move the focus of the discussion away from the objective, which is to change behavior, not to punish.

Tell the employee exactly what you expect. If the employee's behavior is inappropriate because of a company policy, rule, or procedure, say so and explain the reason for the policy, rule, or procedure. Simply saying, "Because it's policy," is not a very good justification for a performance standard. Instead, explain the policy in terms of its importance to employees. Policies should exist for good reasons. If you do not know the reasons a policy exists, learn them before the meeting. You should be able to answer questions such as:

- Why should an employee arrive to work on time?

- Why is it important for an employee to promptly return to work after breaks and lunch?

- Why are personal mobile phones not to be used at work except for personal emergencies?

Chances are that your answers to these questions will not be the same as the employee's answers.

It is always helpful for the supervisor to explain how he or she feels about the problem behavior. If the employee feels that sub-standard performance is not important to the supervisor, the employee might not take the disciplinary session seriously. Make statements like, "When I saw you turn away from the guest, I was disappointed, because guest relations are very important to our company and to me." Avoid statements like "Because *you* turned *your* back on that guest, *you* ruined the company's good reputation for guest service." By telling the employee how you feel, you encourage the employee to talk freely. You might also help the employee understand that his or her behavior is his or her problem, and that he or she is responsible for changing it.

## Identify the Cause of the Problem

Ask the employee to explain the reasons for his or her behavior. Let the employee explain his or her side of the story while you listen attentively and objectively. Encourage the employee to talk by using active listening responses, such as "Uh huh," "Go on," and "I see," or by nodding your head. Ask the employee to summarize what went wrong. The two of you should agree on the cause of the problem.

Remember, the objective is to reach agreement on the cause of the problem so that you can involve the employee in the process of discovering a solution. The objective is not to tell the employee what is causing his or her inappropriate behavior. A supervisor accomplishes very little when he or she speeds through a discussion with a quick question like, "What happened?" so that he or she can force a solution with, "OK, here's what we will do!"

You must have a sincere desire to ask and listen for all information relating to the problem. Sometimes, to identify the real problems, you will have to probe the situation: "We have reviewed this situation in the past, but nothing seems to have worked. Though we tried to analyze the cause of the problem, we may have missed it. What are other possible causes for this continued problem?"

Encourage the employee to provide more information by saying, "Tell me more about that." Ask questions like, "How did it happen?" or, "What else can you tell me about this?" Listen actively by nodding your head and saying "I see" or "Uh huh" at appropriate points. Don't interrupt. Clarify the employee's statements and responses by asking questions like, "Can you be more specific?" or "Could you give me an example of that?" or "How do you feel about that?"

Open-ended questions that start with "when" or "how" can pinpoint useful details. The least desirable questions are often personal "why" questions, such as, "*Why* did *you* do that?" A "why" combined with "you" can produce defensive behavior on the part of the employee because it focuses on personal motives.

However, "Why did they do it that way?" or, "Why did that occur?" does not normally challenge the employee because it asks for an opinion.

Avoid **loaded questions**. Suppose you asked your employee, "Couldn't you see that it was going to be a problem?" This is not really a question that attempts to seek new information. You are simply expressing your opinion in the form of a question. Rather than expressing personal views by asking loaded questions ("Wouldn't you?" "Didn't you?" "Weren't you?" "Shouldn't you?"), simply say what you think! If you are truly looking for information, ask genuine "open" questions.

## Agree on a Solution

Disciplinary action is prompted by the employee's problem, and the employee must accept responsibility for his or her actions. Keep in mind that the employee must solve the problem. The supervisor's job is to:

- Ask the employee for improvement ideas.

- Add suggestions (if any).

- Agree on a specific solution.

- Set up a timetable with specific target dates for improvement.

For many supervisors, asking for the employee's solution can be difficult. Supervisors are often promoted to leadership positions because they are good at solving problems. You might have an idea about what an employee should do to solve his or her problem, but you should first ask the employee for his or her solution.

Interact with the employee. Although one person might be able to develop several solutions to a problem, two people can often come up with many more. This is because one person's ideas can trigger new thoughts in the other. When two people "bounce ideas off each other," they can increase their chances of reaching a solution.

What is important is not so much what the employee says during the meeting, but what he or she does after the meeting to improve his or her performance. It is best if the employee suggests the solution or is a part of the solution plan. In such cases, he or she will be more likely to view the idea as a good one and to accept the responsibility of implementing the solution on the job. Good supervisors ask questions such as, "What do you think we should do about this situation?" or, "What other things could we do?"

If an employee says, "I'll just have to try harder," don't accept that as a solution. Ask additional questions to help the employee specify the actions he or she will take as a means of "trying harder." Help the employee be as specific as possible because specific goals increase his or her chances of producing results.

Ask questions like, "What do you think you can do to keep this from happening again?" and, "How can I help?" If possible, offer a choice of acceptable solutions: "Would you like to try working another shift?" or, "Do you think you need further training in guest relations?" Choices discourage power struggles.

Remember, you are not trying to *win*. You are trying to help an employee change his or her behavior.

After the employee presents one or more possible solutions, offer your own ideas, if appropriate. You can do this in one of two ways. You might make suggestions to improve the quality of the employee's solution. Even better, you can prompt the employee to improve his or her solution by asking questions like: "What would that accomplish?" or, "How do you see this being done?" or, "What can you do to help make that happen?"

## Explain the Disciplinary Action

Explain exactly what disciplinary action you will take and let the employee know that the action is effective immediately. Also explain the disciplinary action that you will take if the employee does not resolve the problem. If the employee becomes upset or angry, listen and respond with empathy. Explain that you understand how he or she feels, but be firm. Tell the employee that you are trying to correct the performance problem, not to punish him or her.

Clearly describe the future disciplinary action that will be taken if significant improvement does not occur. Be very specific. Avoid statements like, "If you don't improve, things are going to get a lot worse." Instead, state exactly what the action will be and when it will occur. If you do so, you are not threatening the employee, you are simply specifying the outcomes if the problem continues. If you must discipline the employee again for the same problem, the next step in the disciplinary procedure will not be a surprise.

## Set a Follow-Up Date

Once you have determined the disciplinary action to take, set a date for a follow-up meeting. By setting a follow-up date, you communicate your concern to the employee, and also commit yourself to the follow-up. However, you do not have to wait until a specified future time to give positive feedback to an employee who implements a solution and shows improvement. Observe the employee's behavior regularly before the follow-up date because you can provide feedback at any time. Similarly, make it clear that the employee does not need to wait until that date to discuss the problem; if the employee wants further guidance and has questions, he or she should feel free to approach you at any time during the interim.

At the end of a disciplinary meeting, write a summary of the improvement plan so that you elicit the employee's commitment and reduce the possibility of misunderstandings. A clearly stated summary should include your expectations and specific actions the employee must take for improvement.

## End on a Positive Note

The meeting should focus on the future, except in extreme circumstances (e.g., the employee is terminated during the meeting). The goal is for the employee to correct the behavior because he or she is important to your company. Offer the employee support and encouragement, and express confidence that he or she can improve. Employees often rise to the expectations of their supervisors. Shake hands with the employee when the meeting ends.

Communicate with the employee again before the day ends, even if you just talk about something else. Such a conversation lets the employee know that you do not hold a grudge and that you still value him or her.

## Key Terms

**arbitration**—A process to resolve disputes in which parties present their cases to an impartial third party who makes a (usually) binding decision.

**discipline**—In a positive sense, those activities that correct, strengthen, and improve employee performance. Discipline may involve minor on-the-job corrections, or may be built into a formal program with increasingly serious steps.

**loaded question**—An opinion stated in the form of a question; a question that contains its own answer and is asked only to express an unstated opinion. Examples include "Wouldn't you?" "Didn't you?" "Weren't you?" and "Shouldn't you?"

**mediation**—A voluntary process in which two or more people involved in a dispute work with an impartial third party to arrive at a non-binding solution. The mediator does not decide who is right or wrong; instead he or she helps the parties resolve their dispute.

**performance gap**—The difference between expected and actual employee performance.

**positive discipline**—Actions taken to reinforce desired behavior that is occurring.

**positive reinforcement**—Rewards in the form of praise, compensation, or other incentives that tend to increase the likelihood of acceptable behavior and decrease the likelihood of unacceptable behavior. For positive discipline to work, the reward must be timely, frequent, and meaningful to the affected employee.

**progressive discipline**—A program that typically involves several steps, such as: (1) an oral warning; (2) an oral warning, possibly followed by a written, filed warning; (3) an official written reprimand placed in the employee's file; (4) a suspension of a few hours or several days without pay; (5) a disciplinary transfer or demotion; (6) a "one-last-chance" step immediately before termination; and finally, (7) termination of employment.

**termination**—An ending of a worker's employment.

**wrongful discharge**—Legal action brought against an employer for terminating employees without due process or without substantial efforts to first call an employee's attention to improper work habits and to help the employee change; terminating an employee's employment without sufficient reason.

## Review Questions

1. Why should discipline not be a form of punishment?
2. Why do some supervisors dislike disciplining employees?

3. Should every disciplinary situation be handled in exactly the same way? Why or why not?

4. What is the relationship between training, performance discussions, and discipline?

5. What are common components of a progressive discipline program?

6. What can supervisors do to avoid wrongful discharge lawsuits?

7. What should supervisors consider before taking disciplinary action against an employee?

8. How might a supervisor identify the probable cause(s) of a situation that might warrant disciplinary action?

9. What are the first things a supervisor should address with an employee in a disciplinary session?

10. How can a supervisor help an employee identify the cause of, and suggest a solution to, a disciplinary problem?

 **Case Study** ────────────────────────────────────

### Explosion in the Kitchen

It was a sweltering August evening, the hottest night of the hottest summer in recent memory. It was a night when those who ventured far from air-conditioning paid a heavy price in discomfort, and it was certainly a night when no one wanted to cook. Perhaps that was why it was the busiest Saturday night of the year at the Sandstone Country Club's main dining room. Servers and cooks wilted in their uniforms as they struggled to keep up the frantic pace.

Roberto, a server who had been with the club just nine months, was having more than his share of problems. The dining room manager had already corrected him twice for improperly serving two tables. Tips had not been generous, and he'd taken a lot of grief from the cooks. Most of the diners were impatient—"Where's our food?" "Tell the chef to pick up the pace in there!"—and when Roberto dutifully went to the kitchen to check the status of orders, the cooks would brandish knives in their sweaty hands and tell him to go away.

The party that just sat down in his section was one table he didn't dare make a mistake with. Dr. Steele, his wife, and three other couples were all dressed up for a night on the town. Roberto knew that Dr. Steele was a big tipper, but he also knew the doctor was hard to please. Roberto put forth his best effort, took the order, and got it to the kitchen quickly. About ten minutes after the appetizers had been cleared, Dr. Steele stopped Roberto on his way to another table and asked him to please check on his table's order.

"Yes sir," Roberto replied and hurried to the kitchen.

When he opened the kitchen door, he had to dodge two servers charging out with loaded trays. A wave of heat enveloped him and the noise was deafening: shouted orders, dishes clattering, oven doors slamming, the hissing of steam from the dishwashing station. He located Steve through the maze of rushing bodies and yelled, "How we coming on the order for table 10?"

Steve, the assistant executive chef, looked up from stirring a boiling pot and wiped his glistening forehead with a white coat sleeve. "We've got a problem," Steve yelled back, "we've eighty-sixed that special."

"You're kidding!" Roberto wailed. Wouldn't you know it—the other seven diners had ordered something else, but Dr. Steele had ordered the whitefish special. "It's not on the board! Why didn't you tell me when I placed the order?" The cooks were supposed to write on the board any items the kitchen was out of, so the servers could stop promoting those items. If they were too busy to write it on the board, they should have said something. The stupid cooks always forget, Roberto thought, and the servers always get the grief.

"Hey, look around!" Steve jerked his head at the cooks bustling all around him. "We don't have time to baby-sit every order back here. Just go tell 'em to choose something else."

I ought to make you tell him, Roberto thought grimly as he left the kitchen. The other seven orders at Dr. Steele's table would be ready in five or ten minutes, but Dr. Steele's meal wasn't even started. The orders for the rest of the table would have to sit under heat lamps while Dr. Steele's order was prepared. No one was going to be happy at table 10; Roberto could see his big tip disappearing.

Roberto was right; no one in the Steele party looked very happy when he broke the news. Through thinly pressed lips, Dr. Steele ordered his second choice—a rack of lamb, medium-well. Roberto knew that would take a long time to cook, but he didn't want to give Dr. Steele any more bad news. Roberto practically ran back to the kitchen to get the order in as quickly as he could.

Twenty minutes later Roberto was filling the water glasses for guests at another table when out of the corner of his eye he saw Dr. Steele impatiently waving him over.

"Yes sir?"

"Listen, we've got tickets for the play tonight. How much longer is it going to be?"

"Well, Dr. Steele, it will probably be another fifteen minutes at least. It takes time to properly prepare a rack of lamb. I'm very sorry, I would have told you before, but I didn't know you needed to leave so soon."

"Well, we certainly can't wait another fifteen minutes. Do you have anything you can serve quickly?"

"I'm sure we have something you'd like, sir, let me check for you. I'm terribly sorry." As he left the table he saw Dr. Steele sarcastically muttering something to his guests.

Back into the chaos of the kitchen, weaving through servers, cooks, and bus persons, Roberto found Steve and told him that Dr. Steele wanted to change his order again. "Damn it!" Steve turned harassed eyes to Roberto. "The lamb's already half-cooked—who's going to pay for it?"

"I don't care!" Roberto said angrily. "What can you give me in five minutes?"

"I know what I'd like to give you," Steve said under his breath while he wiped his brow. "It'll have to be pasta," Steve said aloud. "Tell him the pasta primavera is good tonight."

Roberto went back to the Steele table with this news. "Oh, forget it!" Dr. Steele threw his napkin on the floor. "We're running late, and everyone else's meal is probably ruined by now anyway. We're leaving." Everybody gave Roberto dirty looks as they scraped back their chairs and left in a huff.

Roberto stalked angrily back to the kitchen, found the seven orders for table 10 under the heat lamps, and started scraping them into the garbage with savage strokes. "I hope you're happy!" he yelled at Steve's back. "Dr. Steele just left, madder than hell! Forty dollars in tips just walked out the door because you couldn't get it right!"

Steve turned suddenly and lunged across a countertop at Roberto, clutching at him. "You think it's so easy back here?!" he bellowed, his face mottled with rage. "We never get tips, just a lot of crap from jerks like you! I'm sick of your attitude!"

"Keep your hands off me!" Roberto pulled away and made what witnesses later said was "some sort of racial remark" in Spanish to Steve. Steve ran around the end of the counter, grabbed Roberto, and hurled him against a wire storage rack; pots, pans, and kitchen utensils rained down with a metallic crash. Steve was moving in to throw a punch when bystanders restrained him.

Lloyd Marlowe, Sandstone's general manager, sat at his desk Tuesday morning with two employee files in front of him and two decisions to make. Last Saturday's incident had surprised him; at least he was surprised that Steve was involved. Tension between cooks and servers was an age-old problem present in every food-service operation since the world began, but he never expected it to erupt into violence at his club.

Lloyd had been out in the dining room that Saturday night, chatting with guests, when he had heard the big metallic crash in the kitchen. When he arrived on the scene, Steve and Roberto were yelling insults at each other, held apart by what appeared to be half the club's staff. Lloyd helped restore order and resume production, then took Steve and Roberto, one at a time, to his office. He kept the interviews brief. He suspended both of them without pay for three days, told them he would take that time to review the incident, and would get in touch with them after he had made a decision on what disciplinary action to take. After escorting each of them separately to their cars and watching them drive away, he had returned to the club and pitched in to help the staff get through the rest of the evening.

The three-day suspensions gave Lloyd time to question witnesses and review Steve's and Roberto's employee files. Steve had been employed at the club for three years and had an excellent record. He was never late, always volunteered to work extra hours, and had been employee of the month four times. There were two letters in his file from guests praising him for his work at special events they had hosted. All three of his annual performance appraisals were excellent and he had received a substantial raise each time. He was well-liked by his coworkers in the kitchen; indeed, Lloyd liked him too. Steve was a key member of the staff and it would be hard to be without him, even for a short time, because the rest of August and all of September were among the busiest times of the year.

Roberto, on the other hand, had been something of a problem ever since his hire last December. He was habitually late for work, and had already passed from the oral-warning to the written-warning stage on the tardiness issue. The club had high standards and strict service procedures that Roberto was having trouble mastering. On several occasions when the club wasn't busy, he had disappeared during his shift for short periods of time; his excuse was always that he "didn't feel good." He was also something of a loner and didn't really fit in with the rest of the service staff. At times he tended to be rude to other staff members; his supervisor had noted in his file that she had met with him informally to discuss this problem. All of these issues were reviewed with him at his six-month performance appraisal (new employees received two appraisals their first year), but instead of inspiring Roberto to try harder, the appraisal seemed to embarrass and anger him. After his appraisal, his attitude took a noticeable dive. He was still careful to be polite with guests, but with his coworkers he was usually sullen and uncooperative. His supervisor kept him on, however, in part because she thought Roberto had the potential to become a good employee despite his problems, in part because the labor market was tight and servers were very hard to find.

Witnesses to the incident Saturday night emphasized how incredibly hot it had been in the kitchen and how much pressure everyone felt because of the unusually large dinner crowd. Roberto had "had an attitude" with the cooks throughout the evening, they all agreed. On the other hand, everyone also agreed that Steve had grabbed and shoved Roberto and seemed ready to throw punches. "Sure, Roberto was out of line," was the consensus, "but no more than usual, except for that last racial remark after Steve went for him." The heat and the pressure, coupled with Roberto's attitude, apparently had just made Steve lose his head momentarily.

Lloyd drummed his hands nervously on the employee files and sighed. He didn't need to review the files yet again; he needed to make some decisions. He reached for the phone. He thought to himself, "I'm going to call Steve and Roberto and tell them I'd like to see them tomorrow morning. I will make separate appointments—eight o'clock and ten o'clock." He was pretty sure what he was going to do, but this gave him one more night to sleep on it.

## Discussion Questions

1. Should Lloyd fire Steve? Why or why not? If he shouldn't fire Steve, what disciplinary action should he take?

2. Should Lloyd fire Roberto? Why or why not? If he shouldn't fire Roberto, what disciplinary action should he take?

3. What messages will Lloyd send to the rest of the staff by the disciplinary actions he takes with Steve and Roberto?

---

This case was adapted from Case Number: 3138CA

The following industry experts helped generate and develop this case: Cathy Gustafson, CCM, Hotel, Restaurant and Tourism Administration, University of South Carolina, Columbia, South Carolina; William A. Schulz, MCM, CHE, General Manager, Houston Country Club, Houston, Texas; and Kurt D. Kuebler, CCM, Vice President and General Manager, The Desert Highlands Association, Scottsdale, Arizona.

# Chapter 8 Outline

# Competencies

1. Explain how employment laws administered by the Equal Employment Opportunity Commission affect hospitality operations. (pp. 229–233)

2. Describe how important employment-related laws affect hospitality supervisors. (pp. 233–236)

3. Summarize the supervisor's role in assuring that the hospitality workplace is free of sexual harassment. (pp. 236–238)

4. Describe the supervisor's safety and security role. (pp. 238–240)

5. Discuss the special challenges of supervising a multicultural work force. (pp. 240–241)

6. Discuss ethics in relation to supervisory responsibilities. (pp. 241–242)

7. Explain the supervisor's role in combating drug abuse by employees and guests. (pp. 242–246)

8. Identify the supervisor's special role in unionized hospitality properties: why employees join unions, appropriate actions during union organizing campaigns, and how a supervisor's work is impacted when a union represents the employees. (pp. 246–252)

# 8

# Special Supervisory Concerns

**T**HE JOB OF THE SUPERVISOR in today's hospitality industry is very complex. Supervisors have to know their own jobs and much, if not everything, about the jobs of their employees. There are many laws that affect what a supervisor can and cannot do. You may think that your organization's attorneys and top-level managers are the only ones who need to keep up with these laws. Not true! In fact, if you break a law you're not aware of, you and/or your employer may still be held responsible. In addition, supervisors have to be knowledgeable about areas as diverse as guest relations, safety, security, business ethics, substance abuse, union relations, multicultural work force issues, and more.

Large hospitality operations may have specialists to help you in these areas when necessary. Small organizations may hire consultants to provide help and advice. However, all managers and supervisors must have at least a general knowledge of these special areas so that they can effectively manage potentially serious problems.

## Equal Employment Opportunity Laws

The sections that follow will give you an idea of some of the laws of which supervisors must be knowledgeable. Always check with your own supervisor if you are unsure of the legal aspects of a given situation.

Equal employment opportunity (EEO) laws and regulations are enforced by the **Equal Employment Opportunity Commission (EEOC)**. The principal impacts of these laws are presented in Exhibit 1. This exhibit addresses the EEO laws and regulations that directly relate to the issue of illegal discrimination in the private sector. **Discrimination** is the practice of treating someone differently—usually wrongly—based on a factor such as the individual's race, nationality, sex, age, or sexual orientation. When supervisors discriminate, they don't acknowledge people as individuals or relate to them according to their personal merits. Rather, they categorize people according to preconceived ideas that are often grounded in ignorance. This treatment leaves employees subject to stereotypes and prejudices from not only their supervisor, but also their coworkers and sometimes even guests. Let's review some details about the major EEO laws noted in Exhibit 1.

### Equal Pay Act of 1963

The Federal **Equal Pay Act of 1963** is administered by the EEOC. It prohibits employers from discriminating among employees in the same property on the

**Exhibit 1    Major EEO Laws and Their Implications**

| EEO Law | Major Implication |
|---|---|
| Equal Pay Act (1963) | Provides that equal pay is required for men and women if they do equal work. |
| Title VII of the Civil Rights Act (1964) | Bars discrimination on basis of race, sex, religion, color, and national origin. |
| Age Discrimination in Employment Act (1967) | Bars discrimination against people over 40. Involuntary retirement prohibited. |
| Pregnancy Discrimination Act (1978) | Prohibits discrimination against pregnant women. |
| Americans with Disabilities Act (1990) | Prohibits workplace discrimination against people with disabilities. Reasonable accommodations required to make workplace accessible for all qualified employees. |

basis of sex. Men and women must receive equal pay if they work on jobs that require substantially equal skill, effort, and responsibility under the same working conditions.

## Title VII of the Civil Rights Act of 1964

Employment discrimination at all organizational levels is prohibited by law in the United States. **Title VII of the Civil Rights Act of 1964** deals with employee selection and guarantees the right of an individual to work in an environment free from discrimination based on race, color, sex, religion, or national origin. All employees must be treated equally by both managers and co-workers. A hospitality organization may be held liable for the discriminatory acts of its employees even if company officials were unaware of those acts. Discrimination includes practices where discrimination may not have been intended, such as supervisors allowing employees to tell ethnic or racial jokes.

Supervisors must not discriminate on the basis of sex. For example, refusing to hire women because of uniform requirements involving weight or height restrictions is unlawful unless they reflect essential attributes required for performing the job. These essential attributes are called **bona fide occupational qualifications (BFOQs).** Examples of bona fide occupational qualifications include:

- Female attendants in a women's locker room

- Language requirements at an ethnic restaurant

- Polynesian dancers in a Polynesian dance revue

In each of these cases, bona fide occupational qualifications are based on the assumption that the qualification is truly mandatory. One exception would invalidate the entire BFOQ defense against a charge of discrimination. For example, it would be acceptable for a Chinese restaurant to require that all of its guest-contact staff speak Chinese. However, if a single employee is hired for a guest-contact position who does not speak Chinese, the BFOQ status is lost. In that sense, the burden of proof that a BFOQ is required rests with the employer.

Dress codes and standards for personal appearance also have discrimination implications. Men and women are allowed to dress differently, but the same general standards must apply to both sexes, and the standards must be reasonable, appropriate, and consistent. For example, if a hotel or restaurant requires food service employees to be clean shaven, this requirement should be imposed on other guest-contact employees at the bell-stand, front desk, and garage. There must be property-wide consistency in the interpretation of what is appropriate for employees; individual departments or managers must not be allowed to make contrary decisions or rules.

Religious discrimination must be avoided. You must allow employees time off for religious purposes, and you will need to make whatever schedule and other adjustments are necessary to meet these special requests. An employee's personal appearance may reflect his/her religious heritage (length of hair, for example) and personnel policies must accommodate these special circumstances.

Laws prohibit direct or indirect discrimination against individuals because of their national origin. Employees must be allowed to use their native language unless they must interact with the public in a situation where English is the only language understood.

## Age Discrimination in Employment Act of 1967

**The Age Discrimination in Employment Act of 1967** applies to persons over the age of 40. The EEOC views employees who are 40 or older as a protected group. All employment actions, including hiring, recruiting, performance appraisals, promotions, and job advertising, that affect employees who are 40 or older are subject to scrutiny. All private employers with 20 or more employees and all unions with 25 or more members must comply. Offering different fringe benefit packages to older workers, refusing to train or promote them, and mandating their retirement are all examples of illegal acts.

## Pregnancy Discrimination Act of 1978

Before the enactment of the **Pregnancy Discrimination Act of 1978**, an employer could require an employee to take pregnancy leave for a stipulated period or at a specific time in her pregnancy. Under this act, employers cannot stipulate the beginning and ending dates of a pregnant employee's maternity leave. In addition, this act prohibits employers from refusing to hire pregnant applicants as long as they can perform the major functions of the job.

This act substantially affects the hospitality industry because of the high percentage of women in its work force. The act specifically prohibits employers from discriminating against pregnant women on the basis that these women may not fit the image the company wants to project. As a result, the hospitality employer cannot require an employee to take a leave of absence simply because her appearance no longer reflects the company image. At the same time, employers cannot force a pregnant employee to perform duties other than those that she normally does. For instance, a hotel could not reassign a front desk employee to a back-of-the-house position during her pregnancy.

Other forms of discrimination are also prohibited, including limiting pregnancy benefits to married workers and discriminating between men and women regarding employee benefits. Employers who provide pregnancy benefits are required to provide the same benefits to spouses of employees. In 1993, Congress enacted the Family and Medical Leave Act, intended to establish a national leave policy. This act is discussed in a later section.

## Americans with Disabilities Act of 1990

Handicapped persons' rights to work are also protected by EEOC law. The **Americans with Disabilities Act (ADA) of 1990** stipulates that a disabled individual can't be discriminated against in hiring if he or she can perform the job and does not pose a threat to the safety and health of others. The law further stipulates that an employer must provide work areas and equipment that are wheelchair-accessible unless this is not "readily achievable" and it would be an "undue hardship" to provide such areas and equipment.

Under the ADA, an individual is considered to have a disability when he or she has a physical or mental impairment that substantially limits one or more major life activities, has a record of such an impairment, or is regarded as having such an impairment. Major life activities include seeing, hearing, speaking, walking, breathing, performing manual tasks, learning, caring for oneself, and working.

While the law does change, protected groups under the ADA may include people with disabilities that involve speech, vision, and hearing, as well as disabilities caused by mental retardation, a specific learning impediment, and emotional illness. In addition, people with diseases such as cancer, heart disease, palsy, epilepsy, multiple sclerosis, arthritis, asthma, and diabetes are protected, as are people with HIV and AIDS. Drug and alcohol addiction is considered a disability if a person participates in a supervised rehabilitation program or has undergone rehabilitation and is not currently using drugs or alcohol. The ADA also protects people who are regarded as having a substantially limiting disability. For instance, the ADA would protect a severely disfigured person from being denied employment because the employer feared the "negative reaction" of others.

Under the ADA, people with disabilities are considered qualified if they can perform the **essential functions** of the job with or without **reasonable accommodation.** Essential functions are job tasks that are fundamental. For instance, cooking skills would be considered fundamental for a cook. However, the ability to hear orders called by servers to a cook might not be considered fundamental. As a result, an operation might be required to make reasonable accommodation so that cooking positions are open to people with hearing disabilities. Reasonable accommodation refers to what employers must do to make the workplace accessible to people with disabilities. The following efforts are considered reasonable accommodations by the EEOC unless particular issues in a specific case deem them otherwise:

- Making facilities accessible—this could include constructing wheelchair ramps, widening aisles, and raising a cashier station on blocks for a person in a wheelchair.

- Restructuring jobs to eliminate nonessential functions.

- Reassigning a person to a vacant job—moving someone to another job if he/ she becomes unable to perform in an existing job.

- Modifying work schedules to allow for medical and other related appointments.

- Modifying or acquiring equipment—this may include special equipment that a person with a disability needs to perform essential job functions.

- Providing readers or interpreters for people who cannot read or who have visual impairments.

The provisions for reasonable accommodation basically stipulate that employers must make the workplace accessible and barrier-free so employees with disabilities can be hired and can access their work stations. Physical barriers such as stairs, curbs, escalators, and narrow doorways have to be modified to accommodate employees with disabilities. Elevators must have audio cues and Braille buttons for people with visual impairments.

The ADA prohibits employers from discriminating against employees and job applicants because of disability only if employers are aware that the disability exists. This means that employers are not liable for conditions of which they are unaware. However, employers must anticipate issues of reasonable accommodation because cases will arise in which employees contend that their employer should have known that they needed such accommodations.

## Other Important Employment Laws

To this point, we have been discussing federal employment-related laws regulated by the EEOC. However, several other federal government agencies also administer labor laws that affect the work of hospitality supervisors.

### Immigration Reform and Control Act of 1986

The **Immigration Reform and Control Act of 1986** is a federal law administered by the Department of Justice that is designed to regulate the employment of aliens (non-citizens) in the United States. Under this act, employers with four or more employees are prohibited from discriminating against applicants on the basis of citizenship or nationality. The act mandates that all employers—no matter how small—must verify that applicants are authorized to work in the United States. This verification must take place within three days after hire by completing the Employment Eligibility Verification Form—commonly called the **I-9 Form**. A sample the I-9 Form is shown in Exhibit 2.

Under the act and under the regulation of the Immigration and Naturalization Service, employers may rely on several documents to establish an employee's identity and authorization to work. Employers must verify an applicant's

## Exhibit 2    I-9 Form: Employment Eligibility Verification

OMB No. 1615-0047; Expires 08/31/12

**Department of Homeland Security**
U.S. Citizenship and Immigration Services

**Form I-9, Employment
Eligibility Verification**

Read instructions carefully before completing this form. The instructions must be available during completion of this form.

**ANTI-DISCRIMINATION NOTICE:** It is illegal to discriminate against work-authorized individuals. Employers CANNOT specify which document(s) they will accept from an employee. The refusal to hire an individual because the documents have a future expiration date may also constitute illegal discrimination.

**Section 1. Employee Information and Verification** *(To be completed and signed by employee at the time employment begins.)*

| Print Name.  Last | First | Middle Initial | Maiden Name |
|---|---|---|---|

| Address *(Street Name and Number)* | Apt. # | Date of Birth *(month/day/year)* |
|---|---|---|

| City | State | Zip Code | Social Security # |
|---|---|---|---|

**I am aware that federal law provides for imprisonment and/or fines for false statements or use of false documents in connection with the completion of this form.**

I attest, under penalty of perjury, that I am (check one of the following):
☐ A citizen of the United States
☐ A noncitizen national of the United States (see instructions)
☐ A lawful permanent resident (Alien #) _____
☐ An alien authorized to work (Alien # or Admission #) _____
until (expiration date, if applicable - *month/day/year*) _____

Employee's Signature                   Date *(month/day/year)*

**Preparer and/or Translator Certification** *(To be completed and signed if Section 1 is prepared by a person other than the employee.) I attest, under penalty of perjury, that I have assisted in the completion of this form and that to the best of my knowledge the information is true and correct.*

| Preparer's/Translator's Signature | Print Name |
|---|---|

| Address *(Street Name and Number, City, State, Zip Code)* | Date *(month/day/year)* |
|---|---|

**Section 2. Employer Review and Verification** *(To be completed and signed by employer. Examine one document from List A OR examine one document from List B and one from List C, as listed on the reverse of this form, and record the title, number, and expiration date, if any, of the document(s).)*

| List A | OR | List B | AND | List C |
|---|---|---|---|---|
| Document title: | | | | |
| Issuing authority: | | | | |
| Document #: | | | | |
| Expiration Date *(if any)*: | | | | |
| Document #: | | | | |
| Expiration Date *(if any)*: | | | | |

**CERTIFICATION:** I attest, under penalty of perjury, that I have examined the document(s) presented by the above-named employee, that the above-listed document(s) appear to be genuine and to relate to the employee named, that the employee began employment on *(month/day/year)* _____ and that to the best of my knowledge the employee is authorized to work in the United States.  (State employment agencies may omit the date the employee began employment.)

| Signature of Employer or Authorized Representative | Print Name | Title |
|---|---|---|

| Business or Organization Name and Address *(Street Name and Number, City, State, Zip Code)* | Date *(month/day/year)* |
|---|---|

**Section 3. Updating and Reverification** *(To be completed and signed by employer.)*

| A. New Name *(if applicable)* | B. Date of Rehire *(month/day/year) (if applicable)* |
|---|---|

C. If employee's previous grant of work authorization has expired, provide the information below for the document that establishes current employment authorization.

Source: U.S. Department of Homeland Security, Washington, D.C.

citizenship status by examining such items as a U.S. passport, certificate of nationalization, birth certificate, or Social Security card. Applicants may also be eligible to work if they possess a valid foreign passport and a U.S. employment authorization or receipt from an alien registration form. This receipt is commonly referred to as a **green card**.

While this act does not allow employers to discriminate, it does permit employers to choose or show preference to U.S. citizens or nationals over aliens. However, discharges and layoffs cannot be based on these preferences. The final provision of the act concerns a common theme in equal employment legislation: making the workplace free of discrimination. This act requires that employers not only follow the guidelines above, but provide a working environment that prohibits ethnic slurs and verbal or physical abuse related to an individual's national origin. The employer is responsible for providing a workplace free of such acts by supervisors, other employees, and non-employees.

## Family and Medical Leave Act of 1993

**The Family and Medical Leave Act of 1993** is administered by the U.S. Department of Labor. This act requires employers with 50 or more employees within a 75-mile radius to offer up to 12 weeks of unpaid leave during a 12-month period for birth; adoption; care for an ill parent, spouse, or child; or medical treatment. To be eligible, a worker must have been employed for at least 12 months and have worked 1,250 hours (or about 25 hours per week). Employers are not required to provide these benefits to the highest paid 10 percent of executives.

The right to take leave applies to men and women equally. Employers who employ both husband and wife can limit their total to 12 weeks annually. Intermittent leave cannot be taken for birth or adoption, but is available for illness. Employers must continue health care coverage while employees are on leave.

## Fair Labor Standards Act of 1938

The **Fair Labor Standards Act (FLSA) of 1938** is administered by the U.S. Department of Labor. It addresses compensation and child labor concerns that are very important to hospitality supervisors. For example, the FLSA requires that a **minimum wage** be paid to employees covered by the law (this includes most hospitality employees), and it mandates overtime requirements, including **overtime pay.**

Congress periodically revises the minimum wage, and some states set separate minimum wage rates for their residents. (In these instances, employees must pay the higher of the federal or state wage rates.)

There are numerous regulations that address the employment of young people, and documentation and permit requirements are an important part of those standards. For example, the hours that youths age 14 to 15 may work on school and non-school days, the times of their work day, and scheduled breaks are regulated. The type of positions (those that are not hazardous) are also important. Children ages 16 to 17 may work for unlimited hours in jobs that are not hazardous.

States have their own laws applicable to child labor and, as with minimum wage rates, the federal or state law that is most favorable to the affected person will be applicable.

Many supervisors manage the work performed by tipped employees. Regulations affect the extent to which tips can be included as part of the minimum wage (**tip credit**) that these employees must receive.

Supervisory implications of these compensation-related laws become a concern when, for example, employee schedules are developed, when staff who will be requested to work additional hours are determined, and when policies relating to **tip pooling** and **service charges** are determined.

## Sexual Harassment

Today, **sexual harassment** in the workplace receives significant attention and is one of the most frequent reasons for employee lawsuits. Title VII of the Civil Rights Act of 1964 and similar state laws focus on this issue.

While the laws and their interpretations may change, some principles appear established. You and/or your employer will probably be held liable for sexual harassment if an employee is deprived of a tangible job benefit—for example, if an employee is fired for refusing a supervisor's sexual advances. If (in the employee's opinion) an employee's work environment is negatively affected by the sexual harassment of a supervisor or co-worker, and if the employer knows or should have known of this conduct and does not take immediate action, the employer will probably be held liable. You and your organization could also be found liable for the harassment of employees by guests and vendors if a) unwanted activities occurred, b) you were aware of them, and c) you did not take immediate corrective actions.

Sexual harassment can take many forms; some are easier to identify than others. The EEOC identifies sexual harassment acts as unwelcome sexual advances, requests for sexual favors, or other verbal or physical conduct of a sexual nature. These acts constitute sexual harassment if:

- Employment decisions are made or threatened based on acceptance or rejection of sexual conduct.

- A person's job performance is adversely affected by sexual conduct.

- Sexual conduct creates an intimidating, hostile, or offensive work environment.

Sexual harassment does not necessarily involve sexual contact or overt sexual advances or suggestions. Harassment can occur, for example, when one employee, supervisor, or manager stares provocatively at another employee, supervisor, or manager. Graffiti, vulgar and abusive language, suggestive jokes, references to sexual activity, unwelcome or repeated flirtation, and unwelcome comments about appearance have been considered by courts of law to be forms of sexual harassment.

Workplace sexual harassment does not just occur between a male boss and a female employee. Offenders can be supervisors, co-workers, guests, vendors, or suppliers. Harassment may take the form of:

- Peer to peer harassment

- Employee harassment of a supervisor

- Men harassed by women

- Same-gender harassment

How individuals perceive and respond to particular situations plays a big role in defining harassment. What one person thinks is friendly and harmless behavior may be unwelcome or offensive to another. Sexual harassment is not:

- Normally friendly interactions

- Non-offensive joking

- Behavior that would not offend a reasonable person

Your organization must exercise reasonable care to prevent sexual harassment. General strategies include:

- A written and distributed policy statement prohibiting sexual harassment.

- A reasonable and well-publicized grievance procedure for reporting and processing sexual harassment allegations.

- Ongoing training for supervisors and managers to make sure they are aware of their responsibilities to guard against sexual harassment.

As a supervisor, make sure your employees know the organization's policy on harassment, which should be posted in employee areas. You should review this policy when orienting new employees and periodically at department meetings. Be a positive role model. Always conduct yourself in a businesslike manner. Listen to employees and observe their behavior. If you note behavior that could be offensive to others, express your strong disapproval and restate your organization's policy. Take concerns, suggestions, or complaints seriously. Keep a record of all complaints and report them to your human resources department or, if your property does not have a human resources department, your own boss. If it is your responsibility to do so, investigate each complaint immediately. Monitor and correct offensive situations as they occur. Don't wait for a complaint before correcting a situation. If there is graffiti in the workplace, have it removed.

If an employee lodges a complaint, act immediately and appropriately. Do not simply direct the employee to the human resources department. Once you receive a harassment complaint, it is your responsibility (not the employee's) to follow through to ensure that the complaint reaches the appropriate manager. Keep the facts and other information concerning the issue private. Do not discuss the situation with others unless you are conducting an investigation into the complaint. If you are investigating a complaint:

- Interview the accuser, the accused, and any witnesses.

- Establish and maintain a professional tone for each interview.

- Obtain detailed answers to the "who, what, when, where, and how" questions that are specific to the investigation.

- Whenever possible, protect everyone's privacy by maintaining confidentiality.

Take corrective action by stopping the harassment. Failure to take corrective action in response to sexual harassment places you at risk of contributing to the harassment environment. Correct the effects of harassment and ensure the harassment does not recur. Disciplinary measures should be proportionate to the seriousness of the offense and consistent with the discipline administered in similar situations. Measures to stop the harassment may include:

- Oral or written warning
- Transfer or reassignment of the harasser (not the victim)
- Demotion
- Reduction of wages
- Suspension
- Discharge

Follow up by immediately reporting back to the victim about the actions you have taken. Also, after an appropriate period of time, check with the victim to make sure the situation has been corrected and retaliation has not occurred. Follow up with the accused to reinforce improved behavior or to counsel further, if necessary.

## Safety and Security Concerns

Supervisors have a significant role to play in their property's safety and security programs. A primary concern of every hospitality operation is to protect the health and well-being of employees and guests. This is best done through efforts to prevent accidents and by promptly investigating problems that do occur.

Hospitality operations must comply with regulations established by the **Occupational Safety and Health Administration (OSHA).** This federal agency is responsible for developing and managing regulations and standards for employee safety and health in the workplace. In many states, a state agency may administer workplace safety regulations. Applicable personnel inspect businesses and have the authority to issue citations to those who are not in compliance with safety and health requirements.

There are a number of ways you can assist in a property's safety program. Observe employees as they work and correct any unsafe practices immediately. Make sure first aid kits are well stocked and conveniently located, and that employees know where they are. Check work areas for safety hazards on a regular basis. Inspections must be continual, not put off until "we have more time." Promptly correct any problems identified during inspections, such as leaky pipes or employees incorrectly working with hazardous equipment. Keep records of all inspections and actions taken to fix problems.

Take an assertive role in alerting your boss to potential safety problems in the workplace. Maintain safety records and promptly complete all required reports. If your firm has a safety committee, serve on it and consider its recommendations.

You should also motivate employees to make safety a priority at work (see Exhibit 3). Train employees to perform their job tasks in a safe manner. Encourage them to report all accidents and injuries and take prompt follow-up action when necessary.

Ideally, you and your employees should be trained in first aid techniques. Food service supervisors and employees should be trained in the **Heimlich**

**Exhibit 3  Sample Safety Rules for Employees**

---

### SAFETY RULES AND REGULATIONS

1. All fires and accidents must be reported immediately.
2. Any unsafe act or condition must be brought to the attention of your supervisor immediately.
3. Smoking is permitted only in designated areas.
4. No running, horseplay, or fighting is permitted anywhere on the property.
5. If you are unfamiliar with an assigned task, check with your supervisor before beginning it.
6. Do not operate hazardous equipment if you are unauthorized to do so or if you do not know how to safely operate it.
7. Use of alcohol or drugs is prohibited. Those reporting for work in an intoxicated condition are subject to immediate discharge.

---

maneuver—a first aid technique that involves exerting pressure on a choking person's diaphragm to dislodge an obstruction in the windpipe. Exhibit 4 suggests procedures for aiding choking victims.

Several people at the property should be trained in cardiopulmonary resuscitation (CPR)—a technique to provide artificial circulation and breathing to someone whose heart or lungs have stopped because of a heart attack or some other health threat.

**Exhibit 4  Procedures for Aiding Choking Victims**

---

1. Send someone for help, but don't wait for assistance to arrive.
2. Ask the victim if he or she can talk. If the victim is conscious but unable to make a sound, you can be reasonably sure he or she is choking.
3. Using a napkin to get a firm grip, pull the victim's tongue forward as far as possible. This should lift the obstruction into view.
4. Using your index and middle fingers like tweezers, grasp the obstruction and pull it out.
5. If this fails, use the Heimlich maneuver: Stand behind the victim and wrap your arms around his or her waist, allowing the head and arms to hang forward. Make a fist with one hand and clasp it with the other hand. Place your hands against the victim's abdomen just above the navel and below the rib cage. Press in forcefully with a quick upward thrust. Repeat several times. This pushes the diaphragm up, compressing the lungs, and may force the object out of the windpipe. This procedure may be used on children and adults. Infants and toddlers should be held upside down over the arm of the rescuer and struck between the shoulder blades. After the obstruction is removed, restore breathing by artificial respiration if necessary. Keep the victim warm and quiet. Seek medical help.

For details about and drawings of steps in the Heimlich manuever, go to: www.heimlichinstitute.org/choking.php

---

Safety is as much an attitude as it is a set of rules and procedures. Many of the cuts, slips, burns, and falls that happen to employees and guests can be prevented and the severity of many others can be reduced if you constantly look for potential problems and take immediate action to prevent them.

You also have a role to play in keeping your property secure. You must know exactly what to do when there is a threat or an occurrence of a fire, severe storm, bomb threat, or other emergency. During an emergency, every moment is critical. You must know what actions to take and how to guide your employees and guests through the crisis. It is critical that you know details about and train your employees to carefully follow the property's safety procedures if/when emergencies arise.

Your role in property security programs includes helping to guard against the unlawful acts of others. To protect employees and guests, you should be trained in guestroom security, including key control; control of the building's perimeter (grounds and entrances); and the protection of assets: money, employees' and guests' personal effects, equipment, inventories, and so forth.

Your employees are an important part of your organization's security team. Alert employees can help prevent events that may threaten lives or property. You should train your employees to:

- Report suspicious activities or persons anywhere on the property.

- Avoid confronting a suspicious individual. Instead, they should go to a secure area and call you or another designated person for help.

- Report drug paraphernalia or other suspicious items they see while working.

- Make sure posters, tent cards, and other security information for guests is available and properly located.

## Supervising a Multicultural Work Force

Today, food and lodging properties in the United States employ many people from cultures and ethnic groups with unique values and attitudes. The resulting diversity creates significant challenges and opportunities for supervisors.

Many supervisors do not know how to manage people whose backgrounds are significantly different from theirs. They may believe in inappropriate stereotypes—for example, that all people in a particular ethnic group are overly aggressive. They may be insensitive to cultural differences and lack the ability to effectively interact with those whom they supervise. Communication problems can involve language difficulties as well as actions. For example, being honored as "employee of the month" may be embarrassing for employees from some ethnic groups.

Several principles can help you get maximum effort from employees no matter what their cultural background is. Keep in mind that ideas about the value of work differ among cultures. Definitions of what is socially acceptable differ from culture to culture also. Be careful with humor and jokes because it is often difficult to anticipate how people will react to things that you, with your unique background, believe to be funny. Words and phrases have different meanings; one phrase may be complimentary to one group and insulting to another. Recognize that members of ethnic groups are often victims of racism and stereotyping. Finally, keep in mind that trying to force members of different cultural or ethnic groups to conform to your "norm" is often unproductive.

Training can help you become a better multicultural supervisor. You should make an honest attempt to understand the basic values and beliefs of various ethnic groups represented by your employees and try to modify your management strategies accordingly. Recognize the numerous benefits to a diverse work force and help everyone to be a contributing member of your hospitality team. Otherwise, tensions and misunderstandings may plague your work group, and you may be continually fighting problems such as low productivity, high absenteeism, and turnover.

# Ethics

**Ethics** involve standards about what is "right" and "wrong." Some organizations create a code of ethics for their personnel. This code helps employees decide between right and wrong when called on to make tough decisions at work. Professional associations may develop ethical guidelines for their members. Unfortunately, ethical codes and guidelines tend to be general in nature and may not be very helpful when it comes to the day-to-day decisions and actions of supervisors. There are few, if any, absolutes when it comes to making an ethical decision. While federal, state, and local laws and a firm's policies establish guidelines for a supervisor, there are still many "gray areas" not covered by laws or regulations in which you have latitude.

Let's look at a common situation in the hospitality industry. An employee arrives a half hour late for work with a reasonable excuse and asks you to (1) rewrite her schedule so that it appears she wasn't late, and (2) extend it a half hour so she can receive full pay. If there is no company policy or rule that dictates what to do in this situation, the decision is yours to make. What should you do? On the one hand, the employee has a good reason for being late, will still work a full shift, and needs the full pay. On the other, the company expects employees to arrive on time and you and your hospitality team needed her for the half hour she missed, not for the half hour she's now requesting. What should you do? There may be no "right" or "wrong" answer to this question. And, in that sense, this situation is like many others where ethical questions arise (see Exhibit 5).

Opportunities to cheat your guests provide other examples of ethical dilemmas that arise in the hospitality industry. You know it's against truth-in-menu laws but you also know you probably won't get caught—so is it acceptable to use frozen chicken rather than fresh chicken in a recipe when the menu specifies fresh chicken? Is it okay to advertise a special sales package with "limited availability" when only a few guests can be accommodated and the main objective of the ad is to sell guests on other, more expensive, packages?

Some supervisors may post restrictions involving ethical decisions in conspicuous places like on the employee bulletin board or in the company newsletter. This tactic can often help supervisors make decisions in questionable situations. As well, many hospitality operations have a **code of ethics** that provides guidance for employers confronted with problems demanding ethical decisions.

**Exhibit 5   Ethics Quiz for Supervisors**

1. You drop some loaves of bread on the floor in the kitchen; you do not have time to prepare new ones. No one will know if you pick them up, re-plate them, and serve them. What would you do?

2. You want to buy some products used by your property for personal use. You talk with the salesperson, who says, "I can get you those items at no cost if you'll make some additional purchases for your property." What would you do?

3. One employee is an excellent worker; another is your friend who is not as good. There is an opportunity for you to promote one of your employees in the near future. What would you do?

4. As a sales supervisor, you have booked a function room for a small party and now have an opportunity to sell the room to a larger group that will generate significantly higher revenue. There is no other place to put the small group. What would you do?

5. You supervise a friend who is unable to perform to required standards. According to company policy, you should meet with the employee to discuss the situation and write a report about his shortcomings for his personnel file. What would you do?

6. You are in charge of receiving products for the hotel. Through a delivery error, a larger quantity of products is received than is entered on the delivery invoice; the property will need to pay only the smaller amount unless the supplier is notified of the error. What would you do?

7. You are writing a report for the general manager to advise her about which company the hotel should select to replace an expensive water-heating system. One supplier's representative offers you a free weekend of hunting if you "put in a good word for our product." What would you do?

Regardless of the extent to which policies, rules, and regulations exist, there will always be gray areas in which you will need to make a decision. Your boss and other upper managers expect you to put the long-term interests of the organization ahead of any other considerations.

## Substance Abuse

**Substance abuse** problems are all around us. Many of us see these problems daily in our communities and in the properties where we work. The drug problem is significant among all age groups, particularly young adults. Employees who abuse drugs—including alcohol—cost their firm in many ways. Drug-abusing employees are not as productive as those who are drug-free. Drug abusers use more sick time and have a much higher accident rate than drug-free employees. Income is lost when guests do not return to a property because of a bad experience with one or more intoxicated employees. A substantial percentage of industrial deaths or injuries can be traced to employee substance abuse.

Drug abuse is not limited to entry-level employees. Staff at all organizational levels may abuse drugs and may pose a hazard to themselves and others.

Unfortunately, hospitality industry supervisors frequently neglect the problem of drug abuse among their employees. Reasons include:

- Difficulty in estimating the scope and cost of the problem
- The thought that what employees do off the job is not the supervisor's concern

- Difficulty in identifying employees with substance abuse problems
- Difficulty in estimating the effects of substance abuse on job performance
- The view that "everybody" does drugs
- Uncertainty about whether to refer employees to treatment centers
- Potential for lawsuits by employees accused of substance abuse

What can you do to combat drug use among employees? First, you must become aware of how many—if any—of your employees are abusing drugs. Unexplainable changes in attendance, discipline or performance problems, and unusual outbreaks of temper are all signs that an employee may be using drugs. Exhibit 6 lists other appearance, mood, behavior, and job performance characteristics frequently associated with substance abuse.

**Exhibit 6    Behaviors and Characteristics Associated with Possible Substance Abuse**

| PERSONAL | JOB PERFORMANCE |
|---|---|
| *Appearance* | *Absenteeism* |
| • Sloppy | • Multiple instances of improper reporting of time off |
| • Inappropriate clothing | • Excessive sick leave |
| *Mood* | • Repeated absences that follow a pattern (Fridays and Mondays; absence on days following days off) |
| • Withdrawn | • Leaving work early |
| • Sad or depressed | • Excessively late in the morning, or when returning from breaks |
| • Mood swings (high and low) | • Peculiar and increasingly improbable excuses for absences |
| • Suspiciousness | • High absenteeism rate for colds, flu, gastritis, general malaise, etc. |
| • Extreme sensitivity | • Frequent unscheduled short-term absences, with or without medical explanation |
| • Nervousness | • Frequent use of unscheduled vacation time |
| • Frequent irritability with others | *On-the-Job Absenteeism* |
| • Preoccupation with illness or death | • Unusually large amounts of time spent away from job work site |
| *Actions* | • Frequent trips to water fountain or restroom |
| • Physically or orally assaultive | • Long breaks |
| • Unduly talkative | *Accidents* |
| • Exaggerated self-importance | • More than the usual number of accidents on the job |
| • Rigidity—inability to change plans with reasonable ease | • More than the usual number of accidents off the job |
| • Making incoherent or irrelevant statements on the job | |
| • Over-compliance with any routine, making the routine a ritual | |
| • Frequent argumentativeness | |
| • Frequent outbursts of crying | |
| • Excessive use of the telephone | |

Confronting an employee about a drug problem is never easy. To avoid complaints of slander (injuring a person's reputation) or discrimination, make sure that your talk with the employee concentrates on lowered job performance and other measurable or observable job-related factors. Avoid accusations or general comments about substance use or abuse. Exhibit 7 summarizes some of the principles important in identifying and dealing with substance-abusing employees.

Several elements are necessary in an effective program to manage substance abuse. First, an appropriate company policy for dealing with the threat is required. While this will be developed by top-level managers with advice from legal counsel, you will be required to communicate it to your employees. Exhibit 8 illustrates a typical policy. Companies can also create employee assistance programs that try

**Exhibit 7    Summary of Guidelines for Supervisory Action in Suspected Substance Abuse Cases**

- Know whom to notify when you suspect an employee of substance abuse.
- Watch for strangers who visit the employee frequently or at odd times.
- Try to determine whether the change in the employee's behavior is caused by a reason other than substance abuse.
- Before meeting with the employee, make sure you know your property's substance abuse policy.
- Become familiar with substance abuse (employee assistance) programs offered by your company and/or the community. In most cases, offer this information only if the employee asks for it.
- Meet with the employee at a formal review session. In most situations it's best to have your boss or some other person present at the meeting.
- Assure the employee that the meeting and what is said during the meeting will be kept confidential.
- At the meeting, focus on the employee's decline in job performance. Have written documentation of job performance problems available to back up your statements.
- Don't get involved with the employee's personal life or try to analyze the employee. Unless you are a trained counselor, do not try to counsel the employee at all.
- Don't moralize. Be factual and specific—not judgmental—about the problems you see.
- Be firm and formal yet have a considerate attitude.
- Explain in very specific terms what you want the employee to do to remedy the situation.
- Troubled employees manipulate others by emotional pleas and defensiveness; don't get caught in this trap.
- With the employee's input, decide on the amount of time appropriate to correct the situation.
- Only talk about possible disciplinary measures if you're willing and able to do what you say.
- If your boss was not present at the review session, discuss the employee's case with him or her. Explain your intended plan of action and ask for advice.
- Try to involve your boss at each step of the process. At the very least, keep him or her fully informed.

**Exhibit 8    Sample Company Substance-Abuse Policy**

**Sample Company Policy Statement: Abuse of Alcohol and Drugs**

(Name of Company) recognizes that the future of the company depends upon the physical and psychological health of all its employees.

The abuse of alcohol and drugs threatens both the company and its employees. Commonly abused or improperly used drugs or substances include the following: alcohol, painkillers, sedatives, stimulants, and tranquilizers, in addition to such illegal substances as marijuana, cocaine, heroin, etc.

It is the responsibility of both employees and the Company to maintain a safe, healthful, and efficient working environment. Therefore, the Company has adopted the following policy:

1. The possession, use, or sale of alcohol, unauthorized, or illegal drugs, or the misuse of any legal drugs on Company premises or while on Company business continues to be prohibited and will constitute grounds for termination of employment.

2. Any employee under the influence of alcohol or drugs that impair judgment, performance, or behavior while on company premises or while on Company business will be subject to disciplinary action, including termination of employment.

3. The Company has a number of jobs that pose special safety considerations to employees, such as use of moving machinery, transportation of goods and persons, and the handling of chemicals. The Company will require all employees whose jobs involve special safety considerations to be tested periodically for use of drugs. Positive test results may result in the withdrawal of qualification to work on those jobs.

4. All prospective employees will be tested for use of drugs before being hired. Positive test results will be considered in employment decisions and may result in the withholding of medical qualification for employment.

5. It is the responsibility of each employee to report promptly to his or her supervisor the use of any prescribed medication that may affect judgment, performance, or behavior.

The Company will institute such procedures as are required to effectively enforce this policy. This may include the requirement that employees cooperate in personal or facility searches when the presence of drugs or alcohol is indicated and performance is impaired or behavior is erratic. Refusal to cooperate with these procedures may subject employees to discipline and/or termination of employment.

The Company has developed an Employee Assistance Program (EAP) and strongly encourages employees to use the program for help with alcohol or drug-related problems. It is each employee's responsibility to seek assistance from the EAP prior to reaching a point where his or her judgment, performance, or behavior is negatively affected.

Any provision of this policy in conflict with applicable law in any jurisdiction will be modified to comply with such law.

to restore employees to their former productivity levels by providing measures to help employees free themselves of chemical dependency.

You have a duty to report any illegal activity that occurs in a hotel's guestrooms or public areas. If your employees, in the course of their required work activities, see guests who may be abusing or selling drugs, they should notify you immediately. You must then alert your boss. If there truly is a drug problem, the next step is to alert the appropriate law enforcement agency.

How much cooperation to offer police in conducting searches is largely dependent on whether a search warrant has been issued. In the absence of a search warrant, you should provide the police with information only about the guest's automobile registration. A search warrant should be produced before you release folio information (telephone call information, room charges, etc.) or allow access to guestrooms. However, if police are in "hot pursuit," there is no need for them to present a warrant for room entry.

How do you know if guests might be dealing in drugs? The U.S. Department of Justice suggests 14 potential indicators of criminal activity (see Exhibit 9). If you or any of your employees observe any of the indicators listed in the exhibit, you should report them to your superiors immediately.

# Unions

**Labor unions** have successfully organized numerous large hospitality properties located in large metropolitan areas. While the lodging and food service industry is labor-intensive, its employees are spread among thousands of operations throughout the country. Traditionally, labor unions have not organized small, scattered properties because it's not economically feasible to do so.

While you may think that this section is applicable only to supervisors now working in unionized properties, this is not necessarily true. First, your career

**Exhibit 9   Indicators of Criminal Activity**

1. Guests checking in without prior reservations, paying cash and extending the length of their stay on a day-to-day basis. Guests who check out prematurely or at an unusual time of the day or night.
2. Guests visiting from cities considered to be "source" cities—Los Angeles, Miami, San Diego, Orlando, and others—who exhibit one or more of the other indicators listed below.
3. Guests from foreign countries whose luggage and/or personal effects are not consistent with their length of travel or stay.
4. Guests displaying large amounts of U.S. currency. These individuals will generally pay cash for their lodging, meals, and expenses on a day-to-day basis.
5. Guests whose general appearance does not fit with their clothing or general attire—i.e., seedy in appearance yet wearing expensive clothing or jewelry.
6. Several guests checking into different rooms, requesting different floors, and later meeting in one room with excessive communication between the rooms.
7. Unusual foot traffic to and from a guest's room. The guests have late-night visitors and a high volume of telephone communication.
8. Drug-related paraphernalia found in a guest's room. Examples include plastic baggies, scales, rubber bands, money wrappers, empty luggage, and large amounts of currency.
9. Guests who exhibit unusual behavior such as never leaving the room, constant use of the "Do Not Disturb" sign, and refusal of cleaning services.
10. Unusual alteration of room furnishings or tampering with room fixtures.
11. Guests who use pay telephones instead of the telephones in their rooms or cell phones.
12. Guests whose registration information does not fit the driver's license and other identification they carry or whose registration information is scant or vague.
13. Packages containing white or brown powder substances. Any unusual chemical odors.
14. Evidence that a guest may have a firearm including loose ammunition cartridges, empty handgun holsters, and empty ammunition containers.

Source: U.S. Justice Department.

may take you to a unionized property. Second, many of the principles discussed in this section can be useful in dealing with all employees, not just those who are members of a union.

## Why Join a Union?

Employees who join unions usually have several reasons, including:

- *Inattentive management.* Employees usually turn to unions because their managers are not responding consistently to their issues and concerns.

- *Increased bargaining power.* Individual employees believe they have little power in an organization. Often, they think their only bargaining tool is threatening to quit. Unions present an opportunity for employees to make group demands.

- *Desire for self-expression through a third party.* Unions allow employees to communicate their concerns, feelings, and complaints to management through an organized structure. Many employees think a third party will represent them more fairly than their employer will.

- *Minimizing favoritism.* With union bargaining agreements, fewer management decisions are based on personal relationships. Treatment based on seniority as a top priority is a common practice of employee unions.

- *Social reasons.* Employees are influenced by the attitudes and behaviors of their peers. They associate with people they like and the desire to "go along with the crowd" becomes important.

- *Concerns about advancement opportunities.* If employees believe they cannot receive reasonable pay increases, better jobs, and greater professional status, they often turn to employee unions for assistance.

Most hospitality employees do not belong to unions. There may be other reasons for this besides the fact that existing unions do not try to organize small properties with relatively few employees. Some employees may distrust unions because of past experiences, because they want to control their own destinies, or because of perceptions that unions encourage lower productivity. Some employees want to represent their own interests to management—they would rather work things out by themselves. Other employees, especially those aspiring to management positions, identify with management. Even though employees are protected by various laws, some employees may be anti-union out of fear that they will be punished if they join a union.

## Structure of Unions

A **local** is a union's basic unit of organization. For example, a union local may represent all persons working in a specific trade in a city, or it may represent only union members within a specific property (which is prevalent in the hospitality industry).

Most unions have a president. Normally, the union president has a regular job at the property, is paid by the employer, and uses some time from the job—in addition to personal time—for completing union duties. Typically, union stewards are elected in each department to represent the employees of that department. Unions carry out contract negotiations, build memberships, charge dues, administer grievances, manage the union bargaining agreement, and conduct strikes or other work actions when necessary.

## Impact of Unions on Management

Once a union represents hospitality employees, management's options in dealing with individual employees are altered. Managers no longer can make one-sided decisions or deal individually with employees. They must closely follow all requirements imposed by the union bargaining agreement. Regardless of an employee's skill or ability, managers must give equal treatment to employees in the same job classification. Seniority becomes the most important determinant of management actions regarding promotions, schedule preferences, and other personnel decisions.

## Collective Bargaining

Collective bargaining involves (1) negotiations between employers and unions when union contracts are up for renewal, and (2) day-to-day negotiations between employers and unions over routine situations or problems. Most union contracts in the hospitality industry involve a single property dealing with a single union. A single hospitality operation also may have separate bargaining agreements with a number of different unions. For example, a large urban hotel may have agreements with ten or more separate employee unions.

Union agreements or contracts are typically negotiated for three or more years. Preparing for contract bargaining is difficult and time-consuming. Managers must gather information about wage rates, fringe benefit practices, and the firm's current financial position. Analysis of the current contract's provisions and speculation about new union demands also must be addressed. Management and union representatives meet during negotiations, bargain in good faith, reach decisions, and write down what they agree to. While there are many topics that might be negotiated, Exhibit 10 lists those typically covered in union bargaining agreements.

## Union Organizing Campaigns

As a supervisor, you can have an impact on whether your employees want to join a union. This section reviews actions you can and cannot take during a union organizing campaign. Your property will need competent legal advice when it faces possible unionization, and the following information provides general guidelines only.

There are many actions you can take to affect the outcome of a union organizing campaign. All employees should be encouraged to vote, for example. In many cases union advocates could be out-voted if the "apathetic majority" that opposes unions took the time to vote. Under the direction of higher-level managers, you can also:

**Exhibit 10   Topics Typically Covered in Union Bargaining Agreements**

1. Union recognition
2. Union security
3. Management security
4. Wages and benefits
5. Strikes and lockouts
6. Duration of agreement
7. Union dues procedures
8. Union representation
9. Duties and responsibilities of union stewards
10. Grievance procedures
11. Seniority rights
12. Probationary periods
13. Promotions and job openings
14. Leaves of absence, vacations, and sick leave
15. Discipline and discharge procedures
16. Hours of work, scheduling, and overtime
17. Prohibition of discrimination
18. Safety concerns
19. Meals, uniforms, and dressing rooms
20. General provisions including breaks, layoffs, and posting of jobs

- Inform your employees of employee benefits that equal or exceed industry averages.

- Relate management's past successes in dealing with employee grievances.

- Indicate how management has developed and improved benefits and working conditions.

- Inform employees about management policies that favor them.

- Publicize details about the union of which your employees may be unaware.

- Describe disadvantages of union membership.

- Explain that even if the union wins the election, it still must bargain with management. In other words, union organizers may not be able to deliver all they promise.

- Remind employees that all sides lose when there is a strike.

- Tell employees that they do not need to vote for the union even if they have signed a union authorization card to hold the election.

- Point out statements made by the union that management feels are untrue.

There are actions that by law you cannot take during a unionizing campaign:

- You cannot promise benefits to employees who vote against the union and you cannot make any type of threat (a layoff, for example) to employees who vote for the union.

- You cannot withhold benefits from union organizers.

- You cannot discriminate against employees because of their pro-union activities, including subjecting pro-union employees to unfair working conditions to which other employees are not subjected.

- You cannot attend union organizing meetings or attempt to secretly determine which employees are participating.

- You cannot grant unscheduled wage increases, special benefits, or concessions to employees during the pre-election period.

- You cannot keep employees from wearing union buttons unless the buttons are extremely large or are considered in poor taste.

- You cannot stop union organizers from soliciting employee membership during their non-working hours as long as they do not interfere with the work of other employees.

- You cannot hold private meetings with employees to discuss unions or the upcoming election, nor can you question employees about their union activities.

- You cannot ask employees about how they intend to vote.

- You cannot meet with employees within 24 hours of the election.

- You cannot refuse to recognize the union if it's chosen to represent the employees.

## Working with the Union

Once hospitality employees have unionized, the relationship between you and your employees will change. You must continue treating all employees fairly and consistently, but you will likely find that some of your authority has been eroded. You must comply with all contract provisions, even those you don't agree with or particularly like. Most importantly, you cannot discriminate against employees who join the union (see Exhibit 11).

Perhaps the most frustrating change may be that you can no longer interact directly with your employees on matters covered by the union contract. Instead, your employees' union steward acts as an intermediary. Therefore, the relationship between you and the steward is very important.

**Stewards and Supervisors.** You and the steward are in unique positions within a hospitality operation. Both of you rank between employees and higher management. As a supervisor, you have to represent management to your employees and represent your employees to management. In the same way, the steward represents higher union officials to employees and vice versa. In these positions, you and the

**Exhibit 11   After Unionization**

Many laws prevent discrimination against unions and their members. Some restrictions that apply to supervisors include:

1. You cannot interfere with, restrain, or coerce employees from exercising their right to participate in union activities.

2. You cannot fire, demote, or discipline employees solely because of union activities.

3. You cannot refuse to hire employees because of pro-union sentiments.

4. Special benefits cannot be given to employees who do, or do not, participate in the union.

5. You cannot interfere with the management of the union.

6. There are limits on the degree to which you can participate in employees' union activities. Generally, the lower the organizational level, the greater the amount of union activity which is permitted.

7. You cannot transfer or lay off employees for anti-union reasons nor can you refuse to reinstate employees after strikes if they otherwise are eligible to be rehired.

8. You cannot fire or discriminate against employees who file grievances or testify in any union proceedings.

9. You cannot refuse to bargain with union representatives if you are part of management's bargaining team.

10. You cannot refuse to provide the union with information it needs to bargain intelligently.

11. In cases where there is more than one union at your property, you cannot show favoritism, link benefits to membership in a union that is sanctioned by the employer, or give financial aid to any union.

12. Any anti-union activity by you or any employee should be considered a violation of the law.

steward may share similar types of pressures and experience similar conflicts of loyalty. Therefore, try to view the union steward as someone who is in a tough position, just as you are, and try to work together rather than making him or her the enemy. You both have the responsibility to understand, interpret, and enforce the union contract while protecting management and employee rights. This can be accomplished more easily with less possibility of frustration, misunderstandings, and anger if you can establish and maintain a good working relationship with the steward.

**Grievances.** If the steward agrees, an employee may file a formal grievance when he or she is not satisfied with the way you have resolved a complaint. While a different grievance process is outlined in every union contract, certain components of the process are typical.

In most grievance procedures, you first meet with the steward and employee to resolve the problem. If you can't resolve it, your boss or another manager may meet with the union's grievance committee to reach an agreement. If unsuccessful, top managers meet with the grievance committee to search for a solution. If necessary, top management can discuss the problem with high-level representatives at the union's national or international offices. If resolution is impossible at this level, the matter then goes to **mediation** or **arbitration.** With mediation, the two sides meet with an unbiased third party—a mediator—who reviews the dispute and gives advice on how to resolve it. The parties involved in the dispute do not have to take this advice. Arbitration involves meeting with an unbiased third party—an arbitrator—who reviews the dispute and makes whatever decisions he or she believes are necessary to resolve it. The parties in dispute must then abide by those decisions.

As you can see, an employee's complaint can develop into a serious grievance that can take much time and money to resolve. It's in the best interests of you and your company to resolve employee complaints before they become grievances that must be handled according to provisions of the union contract.

**Management Rights.** Management rights may be limited to those that are expressly included in the union contract. A list of basic rights that management must protect includes the rights to schedule and allocate overtime; to establish, change, and enforce work rules, policies, and procedures; to discipline and fire employees; to develop or change work schedules as needed; to adjust or change job tasks; to increase workloads of staff members when necessary; and to have jobs performed by employees that management believes are qualified.

Other management rights that should be protected include the rights to assess the employees' eligibility for merit increases and job promotions, to require tests for employment, to set work standards, and to close down departments or the entire property if a strike occurs.

Management rights should belong to and be retained by the organization. Unfortunately, these basic rights can be jeopardized during contract negotiations or day-to-day bargaining. Practices that can diminish these rights include careless wording of contracts and failure to understand the implications of contract wording.

Exhibit 12 provides information about a major hospitality labor union.

## 🔑 Key Terms

**Age Discrimination in Employment Act of 1967**—Legislation that made it illegal to discriminate on the basis of age. U.S. citizens age 40 and over are protected by this act.

**Americans with Disabilities Act (ADA) of 1990**—Legislation that requires commercial operations to remove barriers to persons with disabilities in the workplace

**Exhibit 12    UNITE HERE Labor Union**

UNITE HERE was formed in 2004 and is a major labor union representing members in U.S. and Canadian hotels, food service, gaming, and other organizations.

To review UNITE HERE's website, go to www.unitehere.org.

To see information about this union's hotel-related activities, go to www.hotel-online.com (enter "unite here" into the site's search box).

and to provide facilities for customers with disabilities. It is called the "Bill of Rights" for persons with disabilities because it prohibits job discrimination against people with disabilities.

**arbitration**—A method of settling a dispute between managers and union representatives in which the parties meet with an unbiased third party—an arbitrator—who reviews the dispute and makes whatever decisions he or she feels are necessary to resolve it. The parties involved must abide by those decisions.

**bona fide occupational qualifications (BFOQs)**—Qualifications that reflect essential attributes required for performing a job.

**code of ethics**—A statement that provides guidance when decisions with ethical concerns must be made.

**discrimination**—The practice of treating someone differently—usually wrongly—based on a factor such as the individual's race, color, religion, nationality, sex, age, or sexual orientation.

**Equal Employment Opportunity Commission (EEOC)**—The federal agency established by Title VII of the Civil Rights Act of 1964 that enforces laws against employment discrimination.

**Equal Pay Act of 1963**—Federal law that requires equal pay for men and women who do substantially the same work.

**essential functions**—Job tasks that are fundamental.

**ethics**—Standards about what is "right" and "wrong." It is sometimes referred to as choosing between the better of two "rights."

**Fair Labor Standards Act (FLSA) of 1938**—Legislation that prescribes standards for wages and overtime pay for the employment of young workers. It also establishes guidelines for tip and meal credits and for uniform purchases.

**Family and Medical Leave Act of 1993**—Legislation that requires employers with 50 or more employees to provide 12 weeks of unpaid leave for employees after the birth or adoption of a child; to care for a seriously ill child, spouse, or parent; or in the case of the employee's own serious illness.

**Heimlich maneuver**—A first aid technique that involves exerting pressure on a choking person's diaphragm to dislodge an obstruction in the windpipe.

**green card**—Documentation issued to an alien who has been granted permanent U.S. citizenship.

**I-9 Form**—Form used to verify citizenship of applicants and employees as required by the Immigration Reform and Control Act of 1986.

**Immigration Reform and Control Act of 1986**—Legislation designed to regulate the employment of aliens in the United States, and to protect employees from discrimination by the employer on the basis of citizenship or nationality.

**labor union**—An organization of workers formed for the purpose of advancing its members' interests in respect to wages, benefits, and working conditions.

**local**—A union's basic unit of organization.

**mediation**—A method of settling a dispute between managers and union representatives in which the parties meet with an unbiased third party—a mediator—who reviews the dispute and gives advice on how to resolve it. The mediator's advice does not have to be taken.

**minimum wage**—The lowest compensation for an employee based on regulations of the Fair Labor Standards Act or state law (whichever is the highest).

**Occupational Safety and Health Administration (OSHA)**—A federal agency responsible for developing and managing regulations and standards for employee safety and health in the workplace.

**overtime pay**—The number of work hours after which the Fair Labor Standards Act requires additional pay (typically 1.5 times the normal hourly rate) to be paid to employees.

**Pregnancy Discrimination Act of 1978**—Civil rights legislation that prohibits discrimination by the employer on the basis of pregnancy.

**reasonable accommodation**—A modification to a job or work setting that, under requirements of the Americans with Disabilities Act, will allow an otherwise qualified applicant or employee with a disability to apply for or perform a job.

**sexual harassment**—Sex discrimination prohibited by Title VII of the Civil Rights Act of 1964.

**substance abuse**—The consumption of drugs (including alcohol) to the point where an individual's health and personal and professional lives are negatively affected.

**tip credit**—The amount that tips are allowed to supplant wages when minimum wage laws are determined.

**tip pooling**—A system in which tips received by employees are combined and then shared among eligible employees.

**Title VII of the Civil Rights Act of 1964**—Legislation that prohibits discrimination on the basis of race, color, religion, sex, or national origin.

**service charge**—A fee added to a guest's bill by the employer and then distributed to the employees in the manner determined by the employer.

 ## Review Questions

1. How do equal opportunity laws affect a hospitality organization?

2. How do wage and hour laws affect supervisors?

3. What are bona fide occupational qualifications (BFOQs)? What are some examples of BFOQs found in the hospitality industry?

4. What is sexual harassment?

5. What is the supervisor's role in safety and security programs?

6. A multicultural work force presents what kinds of challenges to supervisors?

7. What are examples of ethical concerns that may confront supervisors in hospitality operations? How should they be addressed?

8. What are some signs that an employee may be abusing drugs?

9. What is the best way to confront an employee you suspect is abusing drugs?

10. Why do employees join unions?

11. What are some management "do's and don'ts" in a union organizing campaign?

12. What is the difference between mediation and arbitration?

# Chapter 9 Outline

What Is a Work Team?
Types of Work Teams
    Simple Work Team
    Relay Work Team
    Integrated Work Team
    Problem-Solving Work Team
Building an Effective Team
    Mission
    Commitment
    Temperament
    Accountability
    Skills
Stages of Team Development
    Forming
    Storming
    Norming
    Performing
    Adjourning
The Supervisor as Team Leader
    Supervisors as Role Models
    Interpersonal Skills
    Keep Hope Alive
Special Work Team Concerns
    Social Loafing
    Teams that Never Perform
The Future of Work Teams

# Competencies

1. Define a work team and distinguish work teams from work groups. (pp. 257–258)

2. Describe types of work teams and identify essential building blocks for an effective work team. (pp. 258–264)

3. Explain the stages of team development. (pp. 264–268)

4. Describe issues supervisors should be aware of as they assume the role of team leader. (pp. 268–271)

5. Summarize special work team concerns and discuss the future of work teams. (pp. 271–276)

# 9

# Team Building

Hospitality industry supervisors use resources—employees, money, time, equipment, work procedures, energy, and materials—to produce goods and services for guests and profits for their organizations. One of the best ways to accomplish these tasks is to create high-performance work teams.

Why are work teams effective? As one industry veteran put it, "None of us is as smart as all of us." The collective wisdom and productivity of a good team always outperforms even the most talented and motivated individual. Teams can overcome organizational barriers and increase communication within and among departments. Interdepartmental teams tear down the "functional silos" within an organization and get people talking to each other.

As a supervisor, you might be committed to the team concept and want to implement team-building activities in your department. However, team building must start with top-level management. Because teams can plan non-traditional approaches to work and can cross department lines, managers at the organization's highest level must be excited about and support the team concept for it to be most effective.

## What Is a Work Team?

There are many ways to define a **work team.** Here is a good working definition: a group of staff members who build trust and commitment within the group and work together to achieve common organizational objectives.

If staff members don't know how to work together, they are limited by the scope of their individual skills. However, if they work together as a coordinated group whose members effectively communicate and trust each other, and are committed to achieving a common purpose, they can accomplish great things. Two forces in the hospitality industry create the need for work teams: organizational demands and guests' demands (see Exhibit 1). These demands often tend to oppose each other. In general terms, the organization wants to maximize profits by keeping costs down and prices up, while guests want to maximize the value they receive in the products and services they purchase. Not surprisingly, this exerts an upward pressure on costs and a downward pressure on prices.

Caught in the middle are supervisors and employees who work for the organization but are employed to please the guests. They must ask and answer two questions: "What do I have to do to make my numbers?" and, "What do I have to

**Exhibit 1    Why Do Supervisors Need Teams?**

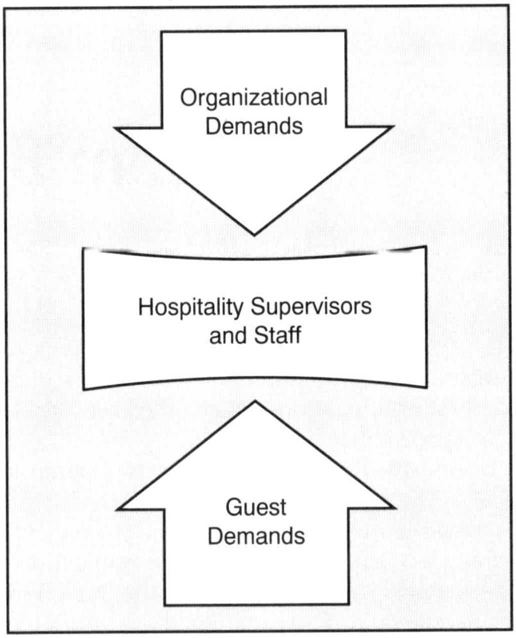

Teams help hospitality staffs meet the sometimes conflicting demands of their organization
and their guests.

do to ensure my guests have positive experiences and return so that I can continue
making my numbers?"

Supervisors must deal with the sometimes-conflicting demands of their organizations and guests. An effective way to do this is to develop work teams that
deal with the day-to-day challenges that come up on the "battleground" of conflicting demands a hospitality workplace creates on a daily basis.

# Types of Work Teams

One way to classify work teams is by their purpose.

## Simple Work Team

A **simple work team** is a group of employees with similar skills who are brought
together because there is more work to do than one person can complete in the
allotted time. For example, when a hotel isn't busy, one front desk agent can handle the work; however, when many guests want to register at the same time, one
front desk agent is not enough. Therefore, a supervisor must schedule other front
desk agents, who work as a simple team to handle the increased workload. Other
simple work teams include food servers, kitchen cooks, and housekeepers. Notice
that all members of a simple work team tend to be from the same work area or
department.

## Work Teams and Work Groups

In many hospitality organizations, people do not really work as a team. Instead, they are part of **work groups** whose members tend to consider their jobs in isolation from the jobs of fellow work group members. They focus on doing their own jobs well, but don't consider how their jobs interconnect with those of coworkers or how employees help define the guest experience. They are not committed to an overall goal or to each other.

In contrast, members of a work team think, "We're all in this together." Communication, trust, commitment, and clearly identified goals can transform work groups into work teams.

A simple work team performs best when every member is well trained. If one front desk agent has trouble checking in guests, he or she will slow the registration process. Such a situation underscores one of the most important responsibilities of a supervisor: he or she must ensure that employees know how to do their jobs. Top management often recognizes and rewards supervisors who nurture and maintain high-performing simple work teams.

## Relay Work Team

In a relay race, runners take turns sprinting around the track with a baton; each runner must successfully hand off the baton to the next runner before that runner can continue the race.

A **relay work team** works in much the same way (see Exhibit 2). For example, the order-taker and cook at a quick-service restaurant form a very simple relay team. The order-taker must take the order correctly and pass it along to the cook.

**Exhibit 2    Sample Relay Work Teams**

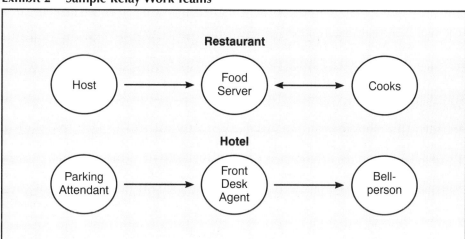

Hospitality organizations have many relay work teams; these are just two examples.

The cook must prepare the order correctly and pass the food back to the order-taker, who gives the order to the guest. Mistakes can and do happen even with this simple two-person relay team, and the problems that are created can upset guests and affect other employees.

A similar simple relay team can be found in a fine-dining restaurant, where guests' food orders are more complicated. After the host seats the guests, the server must take the guests' orders correctly, recording guest preferences ("I'd like my steak medium-rare, please, but with a warm center!") and variations from standard menu items ("Can I get your house salad without onions?"). The server must then successfully communicate these orders to the cooks in the kitchen. The cooks must prepare the food to order, and give it to the server in a timely manner. The servers and cooks form small relay teams that work together on guests' behalf to make sure every meal meets or exceeds guest expectations.

All hospitality organizations have relay work teams, whether or not they acknowledge them. Every employee is part of at least one relay team, and might be on several. Therefore, the jobs all employees perform take on added importance because employees' work (whether good or bad) affects the organization.

Some supervisors do not explain to their employees that they (the employees) are members of relay teams. These supervisors also do not explain that the employees' work has an effect on both external customers (i.e., guests) and internal customers (i.e., fellow employees).

When a member of a relay work team treats a guest well, he or she "hands off" a satisfied guest to the next team member, who is more likely to have a pleasant experience with the guest. For example, a guest who has been enthusiastically greeted and given efficient valet service by the parking attendant approaches the front desk much differently than does a guest who has been given a curt "hello" and indifferent service. When team members treat guests poorly, they might hand off an irritated, angry, or disappointed guest to their co-workers, whose jobs then become more difficult.

Back-of-the-house or non-guest-contact staff members are also part of a property's overall relay team. Housekeepers, for example, are part of the team because guestroom cleanliness plays an important role in forming guests' overall impressions of the property. In fact, each person who works in a hospitality operation is a member of one big relay team because everyone has an impact, either directly or indirectly, on a guest's experience.

## Integrated Work Team

An **integrated work team** brings together people with various specialized skills to accomplish an overall task or goal. One example of an integrated work team is a group of hotel employees who plan a successful business meeting. A team consisting of a sales manager, the food and beverage director, the rooms manager, and the head of maintenance plan and coordinate the activities of their various departments and employees, who themselves create a successful meeting experience for the client's group.

The sales manager communicates the client's needs and makes sure the plans that other team members propose will meet those needs. The food and beverage director must delegate the planning of meals and refreshment breaks for attendees. The rooms manager must plan for the group's arrival, make sure the correct rooms are blocked, and take care of any special requests, such as VIP amenities for the meeting planner's room. The head of maintenance might plan and manage audiovisual equipment the group needs, and might help set up meeting rooms. Members of this integrated team must not only be competent in their own areas of expertise, they must also be good communicators.

## Problem-Solving Work Team

As the name implies, a **problem-solving work team** solves problems. These teams might arise when a problem is so large or complicated that it is beyond the ability of any one person to solve. These types of problems often stem from breakdowns in one or more of the simple, relay, or integrated work teams within an organization. Sometimes the cause of a problem has not been identified; in such cases, the problem-solving work team's first task is to isolate the cause. The team might brainstorm, list all the difficulties people are encountering, and try to determine whether the challenges have an overall theme or similar causes

Some organizations have permanent problem-solving teams that meet on a regular basis to brainstorm and solve problems. Other organizations don't form problem-solving teams until a problem arises. If a significant number of guests arrives at the front desk with inaccurate reservations, for example, a hotel might form a team of front desk agents, reservationists, and information systems specialists to figure out what's going wrong and how to fix it.

Regardless of whether the problem-solving team is a permanent or an impromptu one, the basic process of solving a problem is usually the same.

# Building an Effective Team

Supervisors must be aware of the basic building blocks or requirements that produce an effective team. The basic team-building blocks are mission, commitment, temperament, accountability, and skills.

## Mission

An old saying says, "If you don't know where you're going, any road will take you there." Teams run into problems when they don't know where they are going or what they are supposed to accomplish. This is why every team needs a purpose-driven mission statement. Team members should understand that what they do on a daily basis is important to the team and the organization as a whole. For this reason, supervisors should work with their teams to craft a mission statement that relates to the overall organizational mission.

To be worthwhile, the mission statement should contain measurable objectives that the team can track so that the team will know whether it is accomplishing its mission. If the team discovers it is accomplishing its mission, members should try to stay on target. If the team is not on target, members must determine what they can do to get on track.

## Commitment

A team cannot recruit and retain committed members unless it has agreed-upon values. Otherwise, the team might find it difficult to encourage staff members to commit their time and energies to the team and its mission. For example, honesty should be a team value. If a team member says he or she will do something and then doesn't do it, other team members might lower their own commitment—a situation that hampers the team's overall performance.

Another team value that enhances commitment might be lifelong learning. As members increase their knowledge, they become more valuable to the team and to each other—a situation that ultimately increases their commitment to the team and its mission. Lifelong learning might include training classes offered by the human resources department, night school, trade magazines, conferences, and so forth. Team members who continue learning might eventually find that they do not have to work as hard to accomplish the team's mission as they once did because they work smarter, not harder.

Teams can embrace other values to increase member commitment; these values include integrity and a strong work ethic. The team's supervisor should help members identify and pursue these values.

## Temperament

Have you ever been a member of a team that was cohesive, focused, and generally fun to be on? Conversely, have you ever been on a team that was passive, argumentative, and confused? Which one would you rather supervise? Teams develop temperaments based on the mix of personalities or behavioral styles of their members. If supervisors can identify the basic behavioral styles of their team members, they can better help all members form a more positive and productive team.

People with different behavioral styles exert different influences on a team's temperament. For example, some team members might be competitive and crave power. They often want to be the team leader because they are firm, forceful, confident, and decisive. People who desire power also like to take risks. If a team has many members with these characteristics, the team might be confident and capable of attaining performance objectives. However, the team might also find itself held hostage over questions as to who will run it.

A second type of team member prefers stability to risk. They care greatly about their relationships with others. They will rarely say or do anything that could hurt someone's feelings, even when it means sacrificing personal needs and wants. Such team members promote team harmony and tend to be good conflict mediators, which helps to create a team with a caring temperament. However, the danger exists that, to preserve harmony, such team members will not play active roles if other members are more dominant and express opposing views.

A third type of team member is outgoing, optimistic, and enthusiastic, and they like to be at the center of the action. Such team members have lots of ideas and love to talk. They can be fun to work with because they tend to look at the lighter side of things. A team with a majority of these members might have a fun temperament. However, such a team might also find itself distracted from its work.

A final type of team member is self-controlled, cautious, and logical. Thinkers prefer analysis to emotion, love clarity and order, and can help a team think through a decision even when other members want to rush to an early conclusion. However, these group members might also influence a team to analyze its decisions to such a degree that the team ultimately achieves nothing.

Supervisors who want to create efficient teams should attempt to identify the behavioral style of each team member. Then they can make adjustments by adding or removing members with certain behavioral styles, in order to achieve the right mix of members for effectiveness.

## Accountability

Accountability is a key building block for effective teams. If supervisors do not hold all team members equally accountable for fulfilling their roles and responsibilities, the team's overall performance will suffer. Out of respect for members who do their best to make the team better and the organization stronger, supervisors must identify ineffective team members and correct the situation. Otherwise, team morale and performance will suffer. Top performers might question, "Why should I do my best when others don't bother and get away with it?" These top performers might weaken their efforts, or ask for a transfer to another team, which would further weaken the team's performance.

## Skills

All team members should possess four basic skills. The first skill is the ability to communicate well. If team members truly practice active listening, they will likely reduce instances of miscommunication and the problems it causes. Think of all the problems that teams deal with on a daily basis simply because their members do not properly communicate. Good communication is especially critical for simple, relay, and integrated teams. If a server (member of a relay team) communicates the wrong order to a cook, he or she could place a dish in front of the customer that might not only be incorrect, but even dangerous if the customer has food allergies. To avoid these mistakes, supervisors must ensure that team members properly communicate.

The next skill all team members should possess is the ability to solve problems. Team members should try to identify problems and suggest solutions. If they see a problem and it is within their power to address it immediately, they should do so, and notify their supervisor about needed actions or procedure changes. If team members cannot solve the problem themselves, the supervisor can facilitate a problem-solving process with them.

The third skill is flexibility. Members should have the flexibility to form nonroutine duties or responsibilities that are not significantly different from their job descriptions. This is especially true when an opportunity exists to meet or exceed the needs and expectations of guests or fellow team members. Inflexible team members who maintain an "it's not my job" attitude do a disservice to themselves, their teams, and their hospitality organizations. Supervisors should encourage such team members to change their attitudes or find other teams.

The last skill team members should possess is the ability to manage conflict. Conflict is inevitable because people are different from one another! Everyone has a unique blend of feelings, attitudes, and thoughts. Because team members view the world differently, conflict will occur from time to time. Often, a supervisor's first step in successfully managing team conflict is to realize that it is normal, and that there is no need to panic. The next step in managing conflict is to acknowledge it when it happens. To ignore a conflict or wish it would go away is unproductive. The third step for resolving team conflict is to use agreed-upon procedures to address it, so that the team can move on. Too many teams are frozen in time, unable to move forward because of past conflicts. Supervisors must ensure that, once a conflict has occurred, it is addressed immediately and handled amicably. Then, members can put it behind them and move on for the benefit of the team and the good of the organization.

## Stages of Team Development

Good teams do not develop overnight; they must go through several developmental stages before they become productive. One common way to describe team development is to break it down into five stages: forming, storming, norming, performing, and adjourning (see Exhibit 3).[1]

**Exhibit 3   Stages in Team Development**

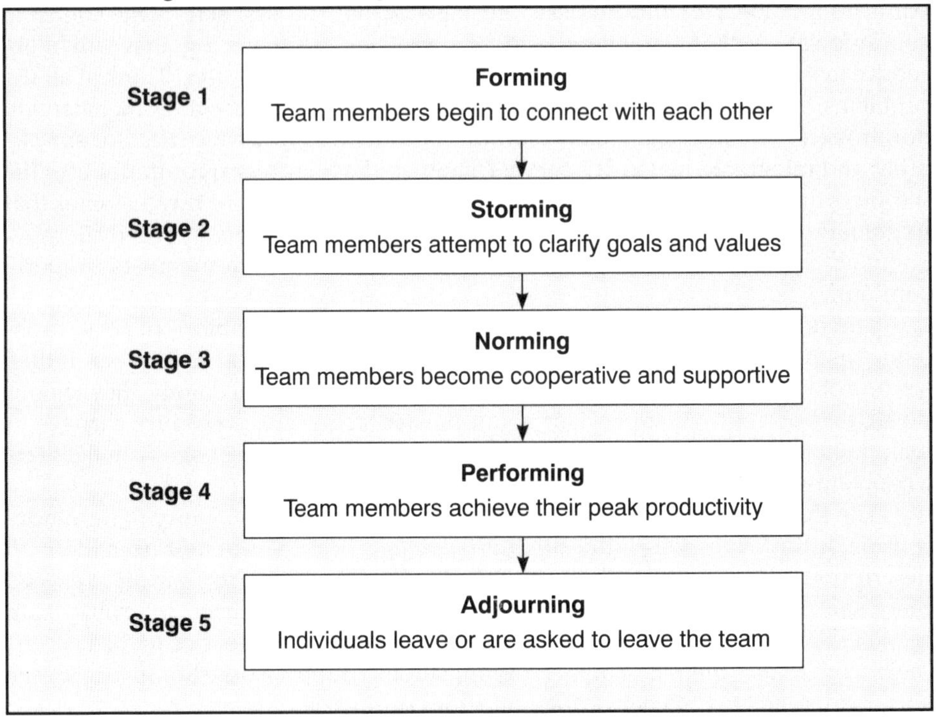

**Stage 1**
**Forming**
Team members begin to connect with each other

**Stage 2**
**Storming**
Team members attempt to clarify goals and values

**Stage 3**
**Norming**
Team members become cooperative and supportive

**Stage 4**
**Performing**
Team members achieve their peak productivity

**Stage 5**
**Adjourning**
Individuals leave or are asked to leave the team

Every type of team—simple, relay, integrated, and problem-solving—goes through these developmental stages, though the amount of time a team spends on each stage depends on the specific team and its members. Some teams quickly move through the first three stages and in performing; other teams move through the first three stages more slowly and take more time to become productive.

Ultimately, the supervisor must determine the team's location on the development/performance scale and do what is needed to help the team advance more quickly to the high-performing stage. A supervisor should also be prepared for teams that never make it past the "I'll do just my job" working group stage. The supervisor might find it beneficial to disband such teams and start over instead of wasting time trying to move the team's original members to perform.

## Forming

The **forming** stage of team development occurs when the team is first brought together and members start to connect. During this stage, members are concerned about fitting into the team and are wondering what their roles will be. Some might worry about their ability to contribute to the team. Other questions that might occur to new team members include:

- Why am I on this team?
- Can I trust the other members of this team?
- What are the rules?
- What's really important to this team?

During this first stage of team development, individuals test various behaviors and are more concerned about establishing relationships with other team members and learning "what this team thing is all about" than they are with achieving team goals or performing assigned tasks. Communication within the team is often polite and tentative as members guardedly get to know each other. Anxiety tends to be high, productivity low.

The supervisor's responsibility during a team's forming stage is to help employees transition from individuals to team members. A supervisor might do this in several ways. He or she might ask the team to create its own code of conduct or mission statement. Setting up administrative details such as formats for team meetings can also help members start thinking of themselves as a team.

## Storming

**Storming** is the second stage of team development; during this stage, members attempt to clarify the team's goals and values. It is called "storming" because this is usually the stage during which conflict first occurs. The politeness of the forming stage gives way as team members try to determine each other's roles. Some members might become frustrated as their initial expectations about the team and the ease with which it would work together give way to the realization that the team might not have an easy time accomplishing its tasks. Because the team has not yet established its norms, one or two members might try to dominate the others.

Members sometimes become defensive or blameful during this stage if they are not pleased with the team's progress. Team members might ask themselves some of the following questions during the storming stage:

- Who is really in charge of this team?
- How are we going to resolve the conflicts that occur?
- How can we keep department politics out of the team process?
- Why aren't some team members really listening to others?

At this stage, the team has not yet developed a common purpose or committed to its tasks or goals. A dip in the team's performance and in the productivity of each team member might occur, perhaps in part because team members are distracted by the hard work of finding their individual places while also molding the team into a cooperative unit.

During the storming stage, some supervisors give up on the team concept without really giving their teams a chance to become more productive. Supervisors should stay calm and try to manage the conflicts so that they do not become counterproductive or destructive. Supervisors should also encourage open communication and interaction among team members. By providing positive feedback for productive behaviors and focusing members on the team's tasks and goals, a supervisor will be better able to guide his or her team through the storming stage.

## Norming

During the **norming** stage, the team begins to act like a team. It establishes its own norms, ways of conducting business, and patterns of communication and behavior. By now, conflicts have been resolved, and team members better appreciate the group's diverse perspectives and personalities. Roles have been established, the team's purpose and goals have been clarified, and team members generally feel more comfortable about the team and their place on it.

At this stage of development, the team is ready to perform the tasks or achieve the goals for which it was created. At this point, the supervisor should step back from the leadership role he or she assumed during the forming and storming stages, and begin to facilitate the team's efforts.

## Performing

In the **performing** stage, team productivity is high, as is trust among members, who speak freely to each other. Members tend to avoid conflicts, and take pleasure from being on the team because they can see themselves making progress toward their goals. At this point, the team can be said to be a "real team." Members are committed to a common purpose and hold themselves mutually accountable for achieving team goals.

Some teams become high-performance teams whose members are committed to their own and the hospitality organization's success. Supervisors who want to determine if their teams are high-performance teams can take the quiz in Exhibit 4.

Supervisors help performing teams by ensuring the organization provides the resources the teams need. The supervisor serves as the communication link

**Exhibit 4    Do You Supervise a High Performance Team?**

**Supervisors:** Answer the following questions concerning your work team(s).
(Fill out the quiz separately for each work team.)

Yes [  ]  No [  ]    1.  We meet together regularly to discuss common goals, solve problems, or work together on a designated task.

Yes [  ]  No [  ]    2.  We promote a comfortable and relaxed atmosphere when we meet.

Yes [  ]  No [  ]    3.  We are committed to a common purpose.

Yes [  ]  No [  ]    4.  We strive to reach common goals.

Yes [  ]  No [  ]    5.  We take pride in what we accomplish together.

Yes [  ]  No [  ]    6.  We communicate openly and honestly with each other.

Yes [  ]  No [  ]    7.  We share ideas with each other.

Yes [  ]  No [  ]    8.  We use effective listening techniques.

Yes [  ]  No [  ]    9.  We respect and support each other.

Yes [  ]  No [  ]   10.  We show appreciation to each other.

Yes [  ]  No [  ]   11.  We work together to build a climate of trust.

Yes [  ]  No [  ]   12.  We embrace conflict but disagree with each other in a nonthreatening and productive way.

Yes [  ]  No [  ]   13.  We stay loyal to each other.

Yes [  ]  No [  ]   14.  We encourage a diversity of ideas and opinions.

Yes [  ]  No [  ]   15.  We encourage creativity and risk-taking.

Yes [  ]  No [  ]   16.  We constantly learn.

Yes [  ]  No [  ]   17.  We look for ways to improve ourselves.

Yes [  ]  No [  ]   18.  We stay flexible and open to change.

**Answer Key:** If you answered "no" to any of these questions, you do not have a high-performance work team. Your group may have the potential to become one, but staff members have not yet made the commitment to the team concept and to each other that it takes to become a high-performance work team.

between the team and the rest of the organization. Many tasks formerly performed by the supervisor are now the responsibility of other team members.

## Adjourning

Unfortunately, **adjourning** and its negative consequences are a way of life in many hospitality businesses. Adjourning occurs when a staff member leaves his or her team and, consequently, changes the team dynamic, which itself negatively affects the team's performance. Adjourning is an aspect of the work team experience that supervisors must be prepared to manage.

There are two types of adjourning. The first occurs when the departure of the team member will ultimately be good for the team even though the team's productivity will suffer in the short term. Perhaps the team member didn't like the job, team, or organization and couldn't be turned around despite the supervisor's best efforts. These team members often leave on their own, though supervisors sometimes must remove them from the team.

The second type of adjourning is bad for the team. It occurs when one of the team's top performers leaves the team. This situation can be troublesome because team members might fear lowered performance. Typically, top performers leave a team because: (1) they have been promoted; (2) they have taken a job with another organization; or (3) they have a personal issue that forces their resignation.

The loss of a top performer especially hurts the team, but any loss has an initial slowing effect. The new team member who replaces the former member must learn and appreciate the team's established norms and goals. He or she also must build trust in the rest of the team, as well as earn their trust. These requirements will lower the team's productivity for a period of time, the length of which depends on factors like the new team member's abilities and personality.

The loss of a team member affects not only the team, but the entire organization. For example, adjourning team members leave their simple teams and their relay teams (and they may have been on more than one). They also might have been part of one or more integrated teams and problem-solving teams.

Suppose that when Jose, the head bartender at the Golden Gardens Hotel, leaves, his loss is felt by members of his simple team: the other bartenders and his supervisor who invested time to train him. Members of his relay teams (including cocktail servers, buspersons, dining room hosts, room service employees, and security personnel) are also affected. In addition, Jose was part of an integrated team that planned receptions with alcoholic beverage service, and a problem-solving team that addressed ways to increase "secret-shopper" scores among the bartending staff.

You can see how the departure of just one person can affect many work teams. Multiply that impact by the turnover rates many hospitality organizations experience, and you can see why turnover is a significant problem for the industry.

# The Supervisor as Team Leader

Supervisors must be team leaders. They do so by developing their team's (and each team member's) capabilities so that the team can function effectively without constant input from the supervisor. An effective supervisor must be able to do every job performed by members of his or her simple team, and should help when necessary.

To develop an effective team, the supervisor must do what he or she can to ensure the team is ready and willing to address its responsibilities. Ultimately, such efforts will benefit the supervisor because a high-performance team can give him or her more time to devote to other tasks.

## Supervisors as Role Models

Effective team leaders must be passionate about exceeding guests' expectations while meeting the organization's goals. You can't have a bad day when you're the

> ## What About Power?
>
> Many supervisors see themselves assuming the weight of responsibility to "make things happen" each day on the front line, but believe that they have limited power within the organization.
>
> Power can be looked upon in two ways. There is hierarchical power that accrues as one moves up the organizational ladder. There is also personal power that comes from an individual's knowledge, skills, and personal characteristics. Supervisors have a great deal of personal power for one reason: *they know how to get things done.* They know how the organization really operates, how the daily work actually gets accomplished, and who the key players are. The best supervisors either know the answer already or know where they can get it.

leader. You cannot build a team spirit if you are constantly complaining about the organization, your boss, your job, or your guests. Employees admire and respect positive, energetic people who are passionate about their work.

Supervisors are not better than their staff members, but they must set the tone. Too many supervisors don't live the values or culture of their organizations and then wonder why their employees "don't get it." Some supervisors share problems and stories other staff members have told them in confidence, then wonder why they have a staff that likes to gossip. Even simple things done correctly can help set the right tone for team members and build a supervisor's credibility.

For example, if the organization has a no-smoking policy for its staff, team members should never catch the supervisor smoking at work. If the organization has a dress code, the supervisor must always follow it. If the organization has a rule that employees must leave the premises after their work shifts are over, supervisors shouldn't be eating and drinking at the bar after their shifts.

Part of being a role model is knowing when a celebration is appropriate and, if it is, how to conduct it. Every significant team accomplishment should be celebrated with an event like a pizza party or something else the supervisor has determined that all team members will appreciate.

## Interpersonal Skills

The hospitality industry is a people industry; supervisors must be able to relate to their guests and staff members.

**The Importance of Connecting One-on-One.** Supervisors will not be optimally effective in dealing with team members until they get to know each team member individually. It's hard to get the most out of employees until some sort of personal bond has been established.

If the supervisor interviews team members before they are hired, this connection can begin during the interview process, with questions such as, "What do you do in your spare time?" and even, "Do you have a pet?" You can learn a lot about a person with questions that provide clues about who the person really is. You may discover that Applicant A spends all of his spare time playing video games and doesn't like animals. Applicant B volunteers at a local homeless shelter and has a dog that is getting old and requires special care, but she's happy to provide it because the dog is like a member of her family.

Whom would you rather hire? Organizations today want to hire energetic, engaged people who are involved with their communities and doing something with their lives. "Hire the smile" is how it is sometimes put; it's easier to teach people how to check in a guest or serve food to a diner than it is to teach them how to smile.

If supervisors have no role in hiring or are transferred to properties where they don't know anyone, they still must meet and spend a little time with each staff member. It's always best to attempt one-on-one connections with staff members.

One way supervisors can connect with staff members is to practice "management by walking around" (MBWA). Supervisors should routinely visit with as many staff members as possible on a daily basis and ask them how things are going. Supervisors should ask general questions like, "What are we not doing that we *should* be doing to make our team or your job better?" and, "What are we doing now that we should *not* be doing?"

Asking these types of questions shows respect for staff members and what they are thinking. Most employees respond positively to supervisors who show genuine interest in their opinions. Once a supervisor gathers information, he or she must act on it, even if the only action is to explain to a staff member the reasons a particular idea won't work. If a supervisor never takes action, employees will believe the supervisor is not interested in their input, and they will stop talking. Asking staff members for ways that policies, procedures, the team, or the organization can be improved is a good way for supervisors to make strong personal connections with their staff members.

Connecting one-on-one doesn't mean that supervisors must be everyone's buddy or even spend time away from work with them. However, the supervisor must interact with staff enough that he or she can identify each worker's basic personality and motivators.

**Treat Employees as Mature Adults.** Does it make sense to hire the most mature and responsible people you can find, then turn them into your dependents? Of course not. When addressing situations that don't really need supervisory input, supervisors shouldn't constantly tell their staff members, "Come see me," or, "You should have checked with me first."

Some supervisors spend a lot of time resolving disagreements among staff members. Instead, they should empower their employees to resolve their own problems when possible. Supervisors should listen to complaining staff members, then let them address their own issues.

Supervisors can apply the following questions and responses to almost any problem situation a staff member mentions:

1. "What do you think the problem really is?" (This encourages the staff member to think through what is actually going on.)

2. "What are some ways you can address this problem?" (This encourages the staff member to come up with his or her own solutions.)

3. "Those sound great!" (This validates the staff member's solutions. Even this simple validation might give staff members the reinforcement they need to build confidence in their own problem-solving abilities.)

4. "Pick the solution that you think will work best, try it out, and get back to me." (This implies that you are confident in the staff member's ability to pick the most appropriate solution, and it reassures the staff member that you are interested in the outcome.)

This is not a course of action designed to let supervisors avoid situations in which they should be involved. For example, if staff members overreact to common job stress, the supervisor should get involved. However, simple disagreements among staff members are not problems in which the supervisor should get involved, unless those problems start to affect guest service. Most of the time, the best approach is to let staff members solve their own problems.

## Keep Hope Alive

Building teams, being a role model, checking your troubles at the workplace door day after day, inspiring your staff, and keeping the boss happy can make a supervisor's job seem overwhelming. That's why supervisors must find a way to "keep hope alive," as one veteran supervisor put it. Supervisors must nurture themselves so that they can build and maintain resources needed to lead their teams.

Supervisors need emotional support from their bosses, other supervisors, and individuals outside the organization, including family and friends. Anything that nurtures one's spirit is useful in the daily struggle to stay hopeful, helpful, and positive in the workplace.

Supervisors often work long hours. However, they must find balance in their lives. They should make their leisure time count by spending it on activities they enjoy—anything that makes them feel good and develops them as a person. Taking care of yourself is one of the best ways to stay sharp and ensure you have something to give when you go back to work.

# Special Work Team Concerns

The term **social loafing** refers to the inclination on the part of many people to not work as hard when they're on a team as they would if they were not on a team. Another work team concern is the team that never quite comes together. We will discuss these two concerns in the following sections.

## Social Loafing

Social loafing can occur on any type of work team: simple, relay, integrated, or problem-solving. Many people will not try as hard when others are around to help them with a task. This is a classic problem in team-building, and one that supervisors must address. If they do not, resentment on the part of the team's more productive members builds to the point at which the team's overall productivity suffers or the team itself becomes ineffective.

How can supervisors reduce social loafing? First of all, supervisors can try to utilize people in ways that best suit their personalities. For example, a supervisor would likely ensure better results if he or she placed an outgoing, social person in charge of planning a team celebration, and a detail-oriented "thinker" in charge of team minutes. People who are suited to their jobs tend to be more productive.

Another way to reduce social loafing is to use quantitative and qualitative measurements to keep tabs on each individual's productivity within the team. Such measurements can reveal who is working hard and who isn't. Examples of quantitative measures for simple teams include number of rooms cleaned per day and number of tables waited on per meal shift. The property's productivity standards often include target productivity goals and baseline figures for each position.

Qualitative measures are more subjective, but no less important. Is the employee attentive and involved on the job or during team meetings? What is his or her body language telling you? Is the team member slouched down in the chair during team meetings, with eyes wandering around the room while others are talking? Or is the team member leaning forward, intently listening to each speaker and providing comments when appropriate?

Social loafers demonstrate the classic 90/10 rule; that is, supervisors will spend 90 percent of their time dealing with the 10 percent of their team members who cause problems. As one veteran supervisor put it, "This is where supervisors really earn their paychecks; it's the true test of how well they manage their people." Supervisors *must* either reform the social loafers or remove them from the team. If not, the team's producers will take notice and productivity might suffer. The team's respect for the supervisor will probably drop as well.

Supervisors who remove social loafers from the team are sending important messages to other team members: "I appreciate your efforts to be good workers. I can see the difference between a good worker and a bad one. Just as I value and reward good work behaviors, I am willing and able to discipline those who do not demonstrate good work behaviors." Exhibit 5 shows a process supervisors can follow to confront and reduce the number of social loafers on their teams.

While determining the reasons a team member is loafing, supervisors sometimes discover areas that need improvement, either in the organization or in the supervisor's management style. Social loafing often suggests another problem: the hospitality operation or the supervisor failed to connect with the person and excite him or her about the team or the organization as a whole. Talking honestly with a social loafer can sometimes reveal surprising information that the supervisor can use to modify his or her approach with other team members and new hires. For example, the team member might reveal that a personal problem is contributing to his or her drop in productivity or lack of interest in work. Serious personal problems are beyond the ability of most supervisors to deal with effectively, and they shouldn't try to do so; in such cases, the supervisor should refer team members to the organization's employee assistance program. If the organization does not have such a program, the supervisor should direct employees to counseling services and support groups in the area.

The supervisor might have to ask the team member some difficult questions: "Can you bounce back from this situation, or is this going to affect your ability

**Exhibit 5    Ways to Reduce Social Loafing**

1.  *Confront the loafer.* Tell the loafer that you know he or she is loafing: "Your productivity and your involvement with the team is lower than the productivity and involvement of your teammates."

2.  *Produce the evidence.* Present the facts—qualitative as well as quantitative—to the loafer.

3.  *Get agreement.* Get the loafer to agree with you that his or her loafing is a problem.

4.  *Look for the underlying cause(s).* Ask the loafer, "What's behind this problem?" Remember that a problem identified is a problem half-solved.

5.  *Work together on a solution.* Once the underlying cause or causes have been identified, work with the loafer on finding or creating a solution. Make sure that the solution is measurable.

6.  *Coach the loafer.* Once the loafer begins to put the solution into practice, help him or her with any advice necessary to keep the loafer on track.

7.  *Encourage the loafer.* Cheer on the loafer as his or her performance improves.

8.  *Reward the loafer.* When the loafer has achieved the solution or has reached the performance goals that you set with him or her, take the loafer out to lunch or in some other way reward him or her. This brings closure to the episode and helps the loafer feel that he or she has returned to your good graces.

to do your job for some time to come?" Supervisors should be prepared to offer options to the team member. Perhaps time off, paid or unpaid, is appropriate, or perhaps the team member can assume another job. Supervisors should try to accommodate team members with current challenges who have been good workers in the past and seem likely to become good workers again.

Sometimes loafers are not meeting expectations because they are simply unhappy in their jobs or unwilling to meet the property's work standards. In such cases, for the good of the organization, team, and even the employee, the supervisor should ask the employee to resign or begin the termination process.

## Teams that Never Perform

In contrast to teams that suffer a dip in productivity or performance at first and then recover, some teams never become high performers. You know a team is in trouble when:

* Members can't describe the team's mission, purpose, or goals.

* Decisions are made by the supervisor and other formal leaders, with little meaningful involvement from other team members.

* Team meetings are formal or tense.

* There's a lot of talk but not much communication.

* There's a lot of effort but not much accomplishment.

- Trust is low; team members are not open with each other.

- Team members blame others on the team.

- Disagreements are aired in private after meetings.

- Confusion or disagreement exists regarding roles or work assignments.

- The team is overloaded with the same personality types; that is, there's not a good mix of people.

What can a supervisor do in such cases? The solutions depend on the type of team.

With a simple team, supervisors can do several things with team members who are not performing to standard: provide more training, meet one-on-one to determine what is wrong, or work one-on-one alongside the employee while he or she is doing the job. The supervisor could also ask behavioral questions to encourage critical thinking and/or reveal training issues, such as, "When guests lose their room keys, what should be done?"

With a relay team, supervisors must ensure that employees realize that the quality of their work affects other employees. One of the best ways to nurture a relay team is to hold meetings during which employees from different departments explain how the quality of their work affects other employees or departments. One way to do this is to have employees list the steps that guests takes as they moves through the hospitality operation, and determine which steps they affect. For example, if housekeeping employees still do not understand how their jobs relate to those at the front desk, additional basic training is needed. This might also be a good time to conduct an attitude check. Employees who do not care how their job performance affects others should be prime targets for progressive discipline as established by the human resources department.

With an integrated team, supervisors might try team-building exercises. Perhaps team members do not trust each other; trust-building exercises could quickly correct the situation. Perhaps team members are not properly trained for their jobs and more training is in order. Poor communication can always cause a breakdown in an integrated team; in such a case, basic training in communication skills might prove effective.

With a problem-solving team, supervisors must make sure the team uses effective problem-solving procedures to deal with the work-related problems that often affect simple, relay, and integrated teams. If no formalized problem-solving procedures exist, the supervisor might provide training in problem-solving techniques. All too often, personality problems among team members prevent problem-solving teams from working effectively together. In such a case, the supervisor must learn about these personality conflicts and try to eliminate them.

Supervisors must also be prepared for the possibility that employee turnover might be needed because some team members will likely not perform as expected. A supervisor must follow his or her organization's disciplinary procedures so that employees receive every chance to improve before termination. Even though no supervisor enjoys terminating employees, but turnovers can send a message to remaining employees that the organization takes its work standards seriously. These terminations can ultimately increase employee morale because employees who won't or can't perform their jobs to standards can no longer affect the team's performance.

# The Future of Work Teams

In recent years, some hospitality organizations have formed "empowered" work teams. These are work teams that have some measure of authority to set their own goals and address problems that they (not management) select. In the future, some organizations will take work teams another step forward and let their teams direct themselves.

A **self-directed work team** hires and fires its members, sets wages, makes recommendations about raises, creates work schedules, and ensures that team members adhere to those schedules. Self-directed work teams might also approve vacation time for team members, set work policies, and evaluate and redesign work procedures. In other words, self-directed work teams make many decisions formerly reserved for supervisors and managers. These teams are also responsible for "making their number" (i.e., doing their part to meet the organization's financial goals).

Self-directed teams demonstrate a significant change from the way organizations did business in the past. The teams themselves might create additional organizational changes. For example, if an organization's structure no longer make sense, self-directed teams might modify it or even completely abolish parts of it. As another example, a work process that seems reasonable to supervisors and managers might not make sense to a self-directed team. Consequently the team might change the order of the process's steps, combine some steps, or eliminate some steps altogether.

What does this mean for supervisors? Will they still have jobs in the world of self-directed work teams? The answer is "yes," but their jobs will be different from what they are now. In the future, supervisors might not know what their roles and responsibilities are until their teams define them! Almost certainly, supervisors will no longer be mostly concerned with command and control issues. The emphasis will be reversed: supervisors will be mostly coaches, mentors, and facilitators.

Today, continuing education is an option for supervisors who want to improve themselves. In tomorrow's hospitality industry, constantly learning will be a requirement. Supervisors will have to keep acquiring knowledge so that they can continue serving as resources for their self-directed teams.

Today's supervisors hire team members; tomorrow's supervisors might recruit applicants for self-directed teams which themselves interview and hire candidates. The team might or might not ask the supervisor for advice concerning the final hiring decision, but the supervisor must be ready with knowledge and experience to share. When a conflict arises that a self-directed team cannot solve on its own, the team might call on the supervisor to mediate the conflict.

Although self-directed teams will have the power to give raises, the team might consult the supervisor on the ways in which a raise given to a particular team member might affect that member's performance and the team's dynamics. Self-directed teams, after researching a productivity problem (perhaps with the supervisor's help), might decide that new equipment is needed; the team might then ask the supervisor to research various equipment options and get back to the team with the information so that the team can make a final decision.

The change to self-directed work teams will not be an easy one. Organizations currently undergoing the process cite many obstacles, including the fact that everyone is outside their comfort zone. Some supervisors and managers feel threatened by the new autonomy of staff members, while some staff members are frightened by their new responsibilities. However, the rewards of such a system can be great: lower administrative costs, greater job satisfaction (for supervisors and managers as well as employees), and better customer service. As one observer has indicated, "Self-directed teams are not perfect; however, they are generally better than the alternatives!"

## Endnote

1.  The first four stages were initially discussed by Bruce Tuckman ("Developmental Sequence in Small Groups," *Psychological Bulletin* 63 (1965): 384–399.). The fifth stage, adjourning, was added a few years later (Bruce Tuckman and Mary Jane Jensen, "Stages of Small Group Development Revisited," *Group and Organizational Studies* 2 (1977): 419–427.

## Key Terms

**adjourning**—The act of individuals who choose to leave a work team or who are asked to leave the team by their supervisor.

**forming**—The first stage of work team development, in which team members start to connect with each other; it is characterized by politeness, guarded communication, and anxiety on the part of team members, as well as low productivity.

**integrated work team**—A group of staff members with specialized skills, brought together to accomplish an overall task or goal.

**norming**—The third stage of work team development, during which relationships become cooperative and supportive as team members learn that they can work together as a cohesive unit. The team becomes more productive during this stage.

**performing**—The fourth stage of work team development, during which a team achieves its peak productivity; individual members share the desire to achieve the team's common goals and appreciate each other's individual contributions toward that end.

**problem-solving work team**—A group of staff members brought together to solve a problem, because the problem is so large or complicated that it is beyond the ability of any one person to solve it.

**relay work team**—A group of staff members connected by the necessity to perform tasks in sequence or to provide services to guests in sequence. Everyone within a hospitality organization can be seen as part of one big relay team.

**self-directed work team**—A group of staff members that enjoys much autonomy; it hires and fires team members, creates work schedules, and sets work policies.

In short, it makes many of the decisions formerly reserved for supervisors and managers.

**simple work team**—A group of staff members with similar skills, brought together because there is more work to do than one person can complete in the required time.

**social loafing**—The tendency for individuals to expend less effort when working collectively than when working individually.

**storming**—The second stage of work team development, characterized by conflict within the team as members push boundaries and challenge authority. Member interaction becomes less polite and more confrontational, and productivity remains low.

**work group**—A collection of staff members that does not form a cohesive unit or work toward common goals. Members of a work group tend to think of themselves as individuals and worry only about their own jobs; they do not think of the group as a whole or how their jobs interconnect.

**work team**—A group of staff members who build trust and commitment within the group and work together to achieve a common organizational objective.

 ## Review Questions

1. What distinguishes a work team from a work group?

2. What is a simple work team? a relay work team? an integrated work team? a problem-solving work team?

3. What are some of the essential building blocks of an effective work team?

4. How do the forming, storming, norming, and performing stages of team development help build highly productive work teams?

5. What is "power" and how much power should supervisors have?

6. How can supervisors be effective role models?

7. What is "social loafing," and how can supervisors combat this problem?

8. What can supervisors do when teams don't perform?

9. How might teams function in the future?

 ## Internet Sites

For more information, visit the following Internet sites. Remember that Internet addresses can change without notice. If the site is no longer there, you can use a search engine to look for additional sites.

Acumen & Human Synergistics
www.acumen.com

Teambuilding Inc.
www.teambuildinginc.com

Center for Collaborative Organizations
www.workteams.unt.edu/

## Case Study

### Turning Department "Heads" into a Management Team

Alec Levine had been the general manager of the Purvis Hotel for about six weeks, long enough to know that the hotel's managers were not going to enjoy today's department head meeting, or as he had begun to call it, the management team meeting. He wasn't looking forward to discussing the letter he had received from a disgruntled guest, but reminded himself that the letter might provide the perfect opportunity to open the staff's eyes to some important ideas about working together as a team.

The expressions on the managers' faces looked, in turn, concerned, angry, and defensive as they perused the copy of the letter Alec handed out as they entered the meeting room. Alec looked around the table. Food and beverage manager Edgar Hamilton, sales manager Keisha Washington, rooms manager Luis Gallardo, revenue manager Stuart Miller, human resources manager Li Fong, and engineering manager Ray Dorsett finished reading and turned expectantly to Alec.

"I'd like to make this letter from Cecilia Worthington the subject of today's meeting," the general manager began. "I'll read it first, then we'll discuss what happened." He cleared his throat and began to read:

> Dear Mr. Levine: On Saturday, June 18, my daughter, Angela, was married. We had the reception, including a sit-down dinner, at your hotel. Many of our family members and friends also stayed at the hotel. I had high expectations for a flawless experience, given your property's reputation and all the cooperation we received during the wedding's planning and preparation. Instead, what should have been the happiest day of my daughter's life was filled with frustrations and disappointments. Here's what happened to us:
>
> 1. When we met with your sales manager, Keisha Washington, she assured us that we would be able to have the reception in the Starglow Room. We especially wanted that room because of its beautiful ocean view and the balcony where our guests could enjoy the sea breeze. We were so pleased when Ms. Washington checked and told us that room was available. She was very helpful. However, the room we got had an ocean view, but no balcony. While I was chagrined by that problem, I was appalled that my complaints were answered with the comment, 'Why are you complaining? You got an ocean view.' Is this what you call customer service?
>
> 2. The person who helped us reserve a room block for the wedding party and our families was most helpful, as well as friendly and courteous. She helped us work within our budget, and assured us that we would all have rooms on the same floor, including several suites with ocean views. We received all the confirmation numbers and a rooming list and I thought we were all set. However, when our guests began arriving the day before the wedding, your hotel had changed its tune. Not only were we scattered all over the hotel, we had only two ocean view rooms. My cousin Will and his family have never visited the ocean before and were looking forward to experiencing that view—not a

view of the parking lot. Angela's grandmother and grandfather, who were supposed to be in a no-smoking king room, ended up in a smoking room with two double beds. But that was still better than what my sister Elizabeth got. She was told that there were no more rooms available and was sent to a hotel two blocks away. Doesn't a confirmation number mean anything to you people?

3. When I met with your food and beverage manager (I believe his name is Edgar), his assistance was invaluable as we selected food, flowers, and entertainment for the dinner and reception. He assured us that the kitchen would have no problem accommodating our request for vegetarian entrees (we needed 22). I was also pleased when he told us there would be no charge for the banquet room because our liquor bill was so large.

Alec stopped reading as both Keisha and Stuart voiced their indignation over this bit of information. "May I go on?" he asked. They nodded sullenly, and he continued:

4. Most of the food for the reception was excellent—just what I had come to expect from the Purvis. The salads, however, must have sat on the tables for quite a long time; they were warm and wilted. And no vegetarian entrees had been prepared. It was quite distressing for our guests—including three of the bridesmaids—to have to sit and munch on a roll while they waited and waited for something they could eat. We had to delay the cutting of the wedding cake so they could eat their meals, after everyone else was practically done. That said, the rest of the reception went well: the band was terrific, the flowers beautiful, and the service satisfactory.

5. Finally, we had requested late checkouts on Sunday morning, and were told this was no problem. To our amazement, our request was not honored. The calls from the front desk asking us when we were checking out were more than a little annoying. I did not appreciate feeling that we were being shoved out of our rooms. If people were waiting for rooms, that is a problem of poor planning on your part, not mine.

When my husband and I were presented with the bill for the reception and the rooms for the wedding party, we refused to pay until we could speak to a manager. We were told that the manager would not be back on the property until Monday morning and that there was no one we could speak to. We expressed our dismay, but fully expected a phone call from you on Monday morning. Since we have not heard from anyone, we are putting our complaints in writing. I have no intention of paying this bill until we can discuss matters and receive an adjustment to the bill. I expect to hear from you within the week.

Sincerely,

Cecilia Worthington

Alec looked around the table at the assembled managers. "What happened here? Mrs. Worthington and her family certainly didn't have the experience they planned for and expected. But obviously she thought everything was going well.

During the planning stages everyone was—let's see what she says—'helpful, courteous, invaluable, friendly.' But the execution left something to be desired. Let's go around the table and find out where things went wrong. You first, Keisha."

"I thought everything was under control with the Worthington wedding," said Keisha. "I worked with her on the initial details and set up appointments for her with everyone she needed to see. Everyone got a function sheet relevant to their part in the wedding. I did my part. And I did check the system for availability of the Starglow Room. It was available. I wouldn't book a room that was already booked."

Edgar broke in. "But I had that room booked. You should have known."

"But you didn't tell me," said Keisha.

"I did so," replied Edgar. "I called and left a voicemail that I had booked that room. It's not my fault you didn't get it."

"Well, that's one mystery solved," said Alec. "Luis, what about the rooms situation?"

The rooms manager glared at Stuart, the revenue manager. "The Worthington's reservations were probably handled by Julie. She does a lot of our room blocks. I remember approving a group rate for them—they wanted a lot of rooms, so we gave them a good rate. They were thrilled."

"I bounced them out of those rooms," Stuart declared. "A hotel is a money-making operation and I saw the opportunity to substantially increase RevPAR for the month. We had some corporate clients who were going to pay full rates for those oceanside rooms. I have the power to override any room block I want. Besides, we only had to walk one person in their party, and she was still nearby. What's the big deal?"

"The Worthingtons are good customers," said Keisha.

"You only get married once," Stuart replied. "Corporate clients mean repeat business."

Keisha shook her head. "The Worthingtons have *three* daughters. Do you think the other two are going to want their wedding receptions here after what happened to their sister? Besides, Mrs. Worthington's sister—the one you walked—is CEO of a company that was considering this hotel for its next conference. And the emphasis is on the 'was.' I think we can kiss that business goodbye."

"I do my job as I see fit," said Stuart. "I had business in hand that was going to bring in more money than your wedding. Same goes for the late check-outs. We can't afford to let some guests linger on when we've got paying customers waiting for rooms."

Alec shook his head. "Edgar, how about the F&B problems? The salad? The vegetarian plates?"

"I remember talking about the vegetarian entrees with Mrs. Worthington, but I guess they never showed up on the function sheet that the chef got," said Edgar. "He didn't even believe her at first until she showed him the contract that definitely stated 22 vegetarian entrees. Even though he apologized and did his best to deliver, we didn't have enough ingredients on hand. The chef really had to improvise.

"As for the salads, we had several functions that evening and were short-staffed to boot," he recalled. "We had to set the salads early while we had the staff, or else they might not have gotten set at all."

Next at the table was Ray Dorsett, the engineering manager. "I guess I'm the only one who got off scot-free in this mess," he grinned. "At least nothing broke down during the reception."

"I came out pretty good, too," said Li Fong, the human resources manager.

"I wouldn't say that," Edgar said. "If we had enough people working in banquet services, we wouldn't have had to ruin those salads by setting them out so early. I can't be expected to make every function perfect when I don't have enough staff."

"Well, if you would keep me informed about your staffing needs, I might be able to bring in some temporary help—or help you with better scheduling," Li replied. "I can't take care of things you don't tell me about."

Alec held up his hand for silence.

"I get the picture," he said. "I think I may have been overly optimistic when I called this group the management team. You're not really a team at all."

"What do you mean?" asked Keisha. "We work together—kind of. We get our jobs done. That's what matters, right?"

"Why don't you ask Mrs. Worthington?" said Alec. "She seems to be the victim of a serious lack of teamwork at this property. We need to come to a decision about how to respond to her complaints, and then come up with a plan so that this doesn't happen again. I think we can do that, but it's going to take a lot of work to become a high-performing team that will bring operations up to the standards people expect at our hotel. Let's meet again in three days to lay the groundwork for creating a team that really is a team, and not just a working group."

## Discussion Questions

1. What breakdowns in teamwork affected the way the staff of the Purvis Hotel handled the Worthington wedding?

2. If you were the general manager, how would you use a problem-solving team to prevent this situation from occurring in the future?

3. What can supervisors do to foster teamwork, even when the management level doesn't model this behavior?

---

Case Number: 2509CA

The following industry expert helped generate and develop this case: Joseph "Mick" La Lopa, Associate Professor, Department of Hospitality and Tourism Management, Purdue University, West Lafayette, Indiana.

# Chapter 10 Outline

Power and Empowerment
    Enhancing Position Power
    Enhancing Personal Power
    Enhancing Power through Alliances
Get to Know Your Employees
Identifying Motivation Problems
Leadership Styles and Motivation
    Autocratic Leadership
    Bureaucratic Leadership
    Democratic Leadership
    Laissez-Faire Leadership
    Factors Affecting Leadership Styles
Increasing Employee Participation
    Employee Suggestion Programs
    Employee Task Groups
    Informal Participatory Techniques

# Competencies

1. Identify types and sources of power and describe how supervisors can enhance their personal and positional power. (pp. 283–286)

2. Explain why it is important for supervisors to get to know their employees and identify various motivational strategies. (pp. 286–291)

3. Identify problems that might be related to motivational challenges. (pp. 291–293)

4. Describe leadership styles and the factors affecting them. (pp. 293–297)

5. Explain how supervisors can increase employee participation in the workplace. (pp. 297–298)

# 10

# Motivation and Leadership

Supervisors cannot motivate employees; employees must motivate themselves. **Motivation** is an inner drive that moves a person to attain a personal goal. A supervisor's primary strategy should be to provide a work environment in which employees can fulfill their personal needs, interests, and goals while achieving the department's and the hospitality organization's objectives.

**Leadership** is the ability to attain objectives by working with and through people. A leader creates conditions that motivate employees; he or she does this by establishing goals and influencing employees to attain those goals. Your role as a supervisor is to create the conditions under which employees motivate themselves to succeed.

In the not-too-distant past, a supervisor might have simply told an employee what to do. If the work was done, employees and higher-level managers generally considered the supervisor a good leader. Today, however, changes in the workplace and in managers' and employees' perceptions of the supervisor's role have made this tactic less useful.

In today's world, leadership and supervision imply the need to guide, facilitate, and influence—rather than order—employees to undertake specific actions. The role of the supervisor is fast changing from yesterday's "dictatorial taskmaster" to that of a coach who assembles resources and provides guidance. The supervisor who is flexible and who can use a leadership style that is comfortable to work with and appropriate for the employee and the situation will best be able to foster a motivating environment.

## Power and Empowerment

Technology, rising costs, increased consumer demands for value, and changing employee attitudes toward work are among the trends that have affected the ways in which supervisors interact with employees. As a result, **empowerment** has become a significant leadership tactic.

Empowerment involves redistributing power within an organization so that managers, supervisors, and employees can perform their jobs more efficiently and effectively. The overall goal of empowerment is to enhance guest service and increase profits for the organization by delegating decision-making responsibility, authority, and accountability to the organization's lowest levels.

The empowerment process involves redefining the responsibilities of managers, supervisors, and employees, and creating a flatter organizational structure with a greater decentralization of power.

**Power** can be defined as the ability to influence the behavior of others. A manager's power is a function of authority and accountability. One important aspect of authority is the fact that power is vested in the position, not the individual. A supervisor exercises authority when making decisions, issuing orders, and using resources to achieve departmental and organizational goals.

**Accountability** relates to the consequences that supervisors must accept for their decisions. They must justify their actions to those above them in the chain of command. A supervisor's authority should relate to the responsibilities that accompany his or her position within the organization. When supervisors are given responsibility for achieving certain goals but do not have the authority to take the necessary steps toward achieving them, their jobs become difficult, if not impossible. To get the job done, they must rely on the authority of managers higher in the chain of command, and their work becomes a source of frustration.

Power may be either organizational or personal. Exhibit 1 reviews organizational and personal sources of power. Power based on organizational sources includes position power, reward power, and coercive power. **Position power,** also referred to as legitimate power, stems from the formal authority granted to a position within the hierarchy of an organization. Employees generally accept position power as legitimate and therefore comply with a manager's work-related directives. **Reward power** results from a manager's authority to provide rewards for employees. For example, managers can influence the behavior of others by providing formal rewards such as pay increases, promotions, bonuses, and days off. They can also influence behavior by providing informal rewards such as attention, praise, and recognition. **Coercive power** stems from a supervisor's authority to withhold rewards or dispense punishment. Managers exercise coercive power when they influence behavior by denying pay increases or reprimanding, demoting, or firing employees.

Personal sources of power include expert power and referent power. **Expert power** stems from an individual's special knowledge or skills in relation to tasks performed by members of his or her staff. For example, food production employees

**Exhibit 1   Sources of Power**

| Types of Organizational Power | Source |
|---|---|
| Position Power | Authority granted to a position within the hierarchy of an organization |
| Reward Power | Authority to provide rewards |
| Coercive Power | Authority to withhold rewards or administer punishment |
| **Types of Personal Power** | **Source** |
| Expert Power | Specialized knowledge, skill, or expertise |
| Referent Power | Personal characteristics admired and respected by others |

might follow many of the executive chef's recommendations simply because they trust his or her superior knowledge of cooking. In the hospitality industry, supervisors have often been promoted because they have mastered basic skills. Their expertise might become a source of expert power that influences staff members.

**Referent power** results from the admiration and respect that others have for an individual's personal characteristics and interpersonal skills. For example, the front desk staff of a hotel might admire the way their supervisor relates to them and to guests. Their admiration becomes a source of referent power for the supervisor; staff members wish to follow his or her example when they interact with guests and each other.

## Enhancing Position Power

Successful supervisors make the most of formal and informal opportunities to expand their spheres of influence by increasing their position power. Building upon the formal authority granted to their positions within the hierarchy, supervisors can enhance their position power by:

- Increasing the flexibility of their jobs

- Becoming an important part of the organization's information loop and thereby increasing their visibility

- Promoting the importance of their work

Position power can diminish when routine activities take up all of a supervisor's time. Supervisors need flexibility in their work schedules so that they are available to participate in task forces within the organization or to initiate projects on their own. These types of activities enhance a supervisor's position power.

With greater job flexibility, supervisors can become more aware of the important issues facing the hospitality organization and work toward gaining greater access to the flow of critical information through it. The more a supervisor is part of this "information loop," the more others see and acknowledge his or her position power. Working in isolation does not enhance power; being recognized for one's efforts does.

Supervisors who want to increase their activities and visibility within an organization must take care to maintain their performance of regularly assigned duties and responsibilities, which are the foundation of their position power. When supervisors become overly concerned with increasing their importance and position power, they might find that others in the organization perceive them as power-hungry. The best way for supervisors to be noticed is to promote the importance of their *fundamental* responsibilities and make sure that others in the organization know about the excellent performance of their staff members.

## Enhancing Personal Power

Supervisors can enhance their personal power by promoting their current achievements and abilities, refining their interpersonal skills, and obtaining more specialized knowledge. A supervisor's expert power increases as it makes him or her more useful and he or she becomes more visible to others in the organization.

Staff members, peers, and superiors recognize the abilities of a supervisor when they experience firsthand how those abilities help them achieve their own goals and objectives. Likewise, obtaining more specialized knowledge or skills increases a supervisor's expert power as long as the new knowledge or skills meet the needs of the organization.

## Enhancing Power through Alliances

Another important method through which supervisors can enhance their personal power and increase their influence within an organization is to tap the power of others by forming strategic alliances. Power alliances are effective when a plan of action requires that supervisors in several areas work together to influence the behavior of others.

Exhibit 2 presents a worksheet that can be used to assess an organization's power centers. The worksheet can help supervisors assess their own power and that of other supervisors. It does not provide an objective measurement of power; instead, the worksheet presents a method supervisors can use to think about an organization's sources of power and estimate the extent of a particular individual's influence. Such an analysis enables a supervisor to identify powerful allies he or she can recruit as needed.

Identifying powerful individuals can also help a supervisor identify a possible mentor. A mentor can increase a supervisor's influence because others in the organization will notice that the supervisor is interacting with a person who maintains a high level of organizational and personal power. A mentor can help a new supervisor get noticed, make the right decisions, and avoid unnecessary conflicts.

An alliance becomes disruptive when its intent is to fight turf wars with other departments, plan an end-run around another supervisor, or sabotage the efforts of peers. These power games are played at some level within almost every organization. However, these games usually have no winners, and many losers, because such actions rarely serve the organization's interests or support its goals.

## Get to Know Your Employees

Supervisors develop a motivated staff by creating a climate in which employees want to work *with* rather than *against* departmental and organizational goals. To help employees become motivated, you must understand their needs, interests, and goals. What motivates one employee might have little impact on another because each has different needs, interests, and goals. These motivational factors are a function of each individual's background, personality, intellect, attitudes, and other characteristics. Your challenge is to get to know employees under your supervision.

To be a successful motivator, a supervisor must know the factors that motivate his or her employees. This is not an easy task because some employees might not know, or at least cannot talk about, their needs and goals. Much motivation is subconscious. For example, some high-energy employees might be top performers because they fear rejection from coworkers if they do not produce above-average

**Exhibit 2   Assessing Organizational Power**

Person Being Rated: _____

| **Organizational Power** | **Power Scale** |
|---|---|

Position Power

      1   2   3   4   5   6   7   8   9   10

      No power              Great power

Instances of Use   _____

_____

_____

_____

_____

Reward Power

      1   2   3   4   5   6   7   8   9   10

      No power              Great power

Instances of Use   _____

_____

_____

_____

_____

Coercive Power

      1   2   3   4   5   6   7   8   9   10

      No power              Great power

Instances of Use   _____

_____

_____

_____

_____

| **Personal Power** | **Power Scale** |
|---|---|

Expert Power

      1   2   3   4   5   6   7   8   9   10

      No power              Great power

Instances of Use   _____

_____

_____

_____

*(continued)*

**Exhibit 2** *(continued)*

| Referent Power | 1 2 3 4 5 6 7 8 9 10 |
|---|---|
| | No power      Great power |
| Personal Characteristics | Respected by |

_____     _____

_____     _____

_____     _____

_____     _____

_____     _____

_____     _____

_____     _____

results. These employees might not even be aware that they are seeking approval from their peers.

Exhibit 3 summarizes a survey that was initially taken more than 50 years ago and that has been repeated more recently with similar results. The results show that significant differences exist between what supervisors *believe* employees want in the workplace and what employees *actually* want. The survey asked employees to rate the factors that most affected their morale and motivation levels. It also

**Exhibit 3**    **What Do Employees Want from Their Jobs?**

| Factors | Rank Given By | |
|---|---|---|
| | **Employees** | **Supervisors** |
| Full appreciation of work done | 1 | 8 |
| Feeling of being in on things | 2 | 10 |
| Help with personal problems | 3 | 9 |
| Job security | 4 | 2 |
| Higher wages | 5 | 1 |
| Interesting work | 6 | 5 |
| Promotion in the company | 7 | 3 |
| Personal loyalty of supervisor | 8 | 6 |
| Good working conditions | 9 | 4 |
| Tactful discipline | 10 | 7 |

Adapted with permission from John W. Newstrom and Edward E. Scannell, *Games Trainers Play: Experiential Learning Exercises* (New York: McGraw-Hill, 1980), p. 121.

asked supervisors to indicate the factors they believed were most important to their employees. Note that the employees' top three items (full appreciation of work done, feeling of being in on things, and help with personal problems) are the last three items as ranked by supervisors—a discrepancy that has existed for over half a century!

The first two items that employees deemed most important are fully within a supervisor's control. In fact, supervisors can do a number of things to improve their department's motivational climate at little or no cost to the organization. By acknowledging employees' performances and providing appropriate recognition, a supervisor tells employees that he or she appreciates their efforts. Also, a supervisor helps employees feel that they are "in on things" when the he or she effectively communicates the department's objectives, as well as significant events that affect the organization.

The third item that employees judged most important might not be fully within a supervisor's control. Personal problems are generally better addressed by trained professionals. However, a supervisor can communicate understanding and concern for employees experiencing personal problems outside the workplace. This attention might be all that many employees expect and would appreciate receiving.

Your understanding of employees' needs, interests, and goals forms the basis for developing motivational strategies. Exhibit 4 summarizes basic motivation principles. By incorporating these principles into the motivational strategies you develop, you will increase the likelihood that your efforts will succeed. The following paragraphs describe the ways in which motivational strategies can be developed in relation to the basic human resources functions carried out by supervisors.

Your interviews with job applicants offer an excellent opportunity to learn about the individual needs, interests, and goals of prospective employees. With practice and experience, you can sharpen your interviewing skills and identify candidates who seem motivated from the start to contribute to your department.

New employees are usually highly motivated to succeed. During orientation, your job is to keep that motivation level high and lay the foundation for future success.

Effective training programs create the conditions in which employees can become motivated. Training sends a strong message to employees. It tells them that the supervisor, the department, and the organization care enough to give

## What Is On-Boarding?

**On-boarding** is a term describing activities that introduce an applicant/new hire to the job and the culture of the organization. These activities can begin during employee recruitment and not end until several weeks or more after orientation. These activities help new employees recognize that the hospitality organization cares about them and wants them to be successful.

On-boarding activities that reinforce the employee's decision to join the organization lay the foundation for motivation and help the property become an employer of choice rather than an employer of last resort.

**Exhibit 4   Principles of Motivation**

1. *Compatibility with objectives.* People being motivated must (a) have clearly defined objectives, and (b) these objectives must be in concert with those of the organization.

2. *Motivational flexibility.* The type and degree of motivational efforts must be varied.

3. *Multi-directional force.* The manager must be the driving force behind the motivational efforts.

4. *Management maturity.* The type and direction of motivational efforts must change as the organization matures.

5. *Self-motivation.* Motivational efforts by the supervisor must be designed to yield self-motivation.

6. *Effective communications.* There must be an open and trustful atmosphere based upon respect in order for motivational efforts to be effective.

7. *Employee participation.* Employees must be able, to the extent possible, to be involved in matters which affect them.

8. *Credit and blame.* The supervisor must give credit to employees when due and accept responsibility to share blame when problems occur.

9. *Authority, responsibility, and accountability.* To motivate employees, a supervisor must give them the authority and responsibility necessary to perform their work and must, at the same time, hold them accountable for effective performance.

10. *Conscious self-motivation.* The most effective type of motivation comes from a serious and deliberate effort by the individual employee.

11. *Genuine respect.* A supervisor cannot be an effective motivator until he/she genuinely respects employees, recognizes their rights, and accepts their capacity for self-direction.

them the necessary instructions and directions to ensure their success. Tools such as organization charts, job descriptions, job lists, and job breakdowns tend to make work requirements rigid and uniform. This need for consistency is good from the organization's perspective. However, you should try to find ways within established limitations for employees to address personal goals on the job.

Cross-training can be a valuable motivational tool, removing many of the obstacles that block an employee's growth and advancement. From an employee's perspective, cross-training eliminates the feeling that he or she is locked into a particular job, and helps him or her acquire additional work skills.

One critical motivational strategy is to formally and informally let employees know how well they are performing. Coaching and performance evaluations are among the best tools a supervisor has to increase employee motivation and improve department morale. Such strategies are effective because they:

- Give the employee formal written feedback on job performance
- Identify performance strengths and offer a plan for improving weaknesses
- Give the supervisor and the employee the opportunity to mutually develop specific goals and due dates to accomplish desired results

Communication is key to any motivational program. Keeping employees informed about events and activities in the department and organization will yield positive results. Employees who know what's going on feel a greater sense of belonging and value.

To keep communication lines open, develop a departmental or organizational newsletter. Write-ups might be job-related or personal in nature, and include such topics as:

- Promotions
- Transfers
- New hires
- Resignations
- Quality tips
- Special recognition
- Employees-of-the-month
- Birthdays
- Engagements, marriages, births

A bulletin board provides a place to post schedules, memos, and other important information. Bulletin boards are most effective when they are in an area accessible to all employees and when employees are asked to view the boards daily.

Many departments also send out updates and recognition via e-mails, or post them on intranet pages.

## Identifying Motivation Problems

How can you determine when an employee has a motivation problem or when low morale levels are affecting your work area? Common-sense observations can help; sophisticated studies are not always necessary. You can begin by investigating a number of factors that indirectly relate to low motivation or morale levels. These factors include:

- High absenteeism rates
- High turnover rates
- Increases in the number of accidents
- Excessive breakage or waste
- Unusually high numbers of complaints or grievances from employees

Further observation might uncover a general lack of cooperation among employees, or increasing conflicts in the work environment.

You must also know how to determine when lack of motivation might be the cause of an employee's poor job performance. Poor performance occurs when an employee's behavior falls short of established standards. A motivation problem exists when the difference between expected and actual performance on the job is due to a lack of effort on the employee's part.

The sample performance analysis worksheet shown in Exhibit 5 can help you identify the possible causes of an employee's poor performance. Once you've identified the causes, you can generate appropriate strategies to address them. Use the worksheet to rate an employee along two dimensions: how well the employee performs on the job and the level of knowledge or skill the employee has in relation to the job. The job performance scale (low to high) is at the bottom of the worksheet; the job knowledge/skill scale (also low to high) is along the left side of the worksheet. The two ratings for an employee will intersect and, generally, fall into one of four areas:

• Box A—An employee rated high in the job knowledge/skill area but low in relation to job performance might have a motivation problem.

**Exhibit 5    Performance Analysis Worksheet**

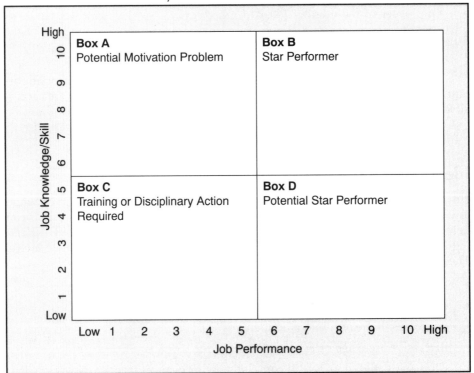

Source: Adapted with permission from John W. Newstrom and Edward E. Scannell, *Games Trainers Play: Experiential Learning Exercises* (New York: McGraw-Hill, 1980), p. 33.

- Box B—An employee rated high in the job knowledge/skill area and high in relation to job performance is probably a valued member of your staff.

- Box C—An employee rated low in the job knowledge/skill area and low in job performance might pose a serious problem, especially if the employee has persistently rejected your training and coaching efforts. Some type of disciplinary action might be required.

- Box D—An employee rated low in job knowledge/skill but high in job performance is apparently getting the job done in spite of a lack of training. Providing the necessary training and coaching might turn this employee into an exceptional performer.

## Leadership Styles and Motivation

The following sections examine four leadership styles: autocratic, bureaucratic, democratic, and laissez-faire. Each leadership style creates conditions that can affect employees' motivation levels. Rather than adopting any one of these styles, develop the flexibility to turn styles into strategies. For example, if you must give detailed instructions (such as when training a new room attendant), you should reflect this fact in the leadership style you use. Conversely, a food and beverage director who supervises a creative chef will likely employ a different approach.

Seen as strategies, leadership styles become tools to create the conditions in which employees become motivated to achieve department goals. Exhibit 6 summarizes some of the major points discussed in the sections that follow.

### Autocratic Leadership

The **autocratic leadership style** is a classical approach to management. Supervisors adopting this style make decisions without much input from their employees. They generally give orders without explanations, and expect those orders to be obeyed. Often, a structured set of rewards and punishments is used to ensure compliance by employees. While all supervisors must be results-oriented, the autocratic supervisor places results above concerns about employees' motivation levels. Autocratic supervisors assume that employees are already motivated, or at least motivated enough to follow orders.

Autocratic supervisors accept the authority and responsibility their bosses delegate, but they are generally unwilling to delegate to employees under their own supervision. As a result, employees often become extremely dependent on autocratic supervisors. Because they are given little, if any, discretion about how to perform their jobs, employees suppress their creativity and simply follow orders.

When practiced during the wrong situations or with the wrong type of employee, this leadership style can be disastrous. Low employee morale, high absenteeism and turnover, and even work stoppage could result. However, in some situations, this leadership style is both necessary and effective. Consider, for example, a situation in which lunch business unexpectedly doubles from the forecasted volume. The kitchen and dining room staff might need fast, specific instructions on how to modify normal procedures to properly serve all the guests. In this type of

**Exhibit 6   Overview of Leadership Styles**

| Name | Also Called | Basic Description of Leadership Style | Type of Employee with Whom It Might Be Used |
|---|---|---|---|
| Autocratic | Authoritarian or Dictatorial | Supervisor retains as much power and decision-making authority as possible. He/she is like a dictator, making decisions without consulting employees. Orders are given and must be obeyed without discussion. | New employees who must quickly learn work tasks, difficult-to-supervise employees who do not respond to other styles, and temporary employees. |
| Bureaucratic | | Supervisor "manages by the book." Emphasis is on doing things as specified by rules, policies, regulations, and standard operating procedures. Supervisor must rely on higher levels of management to resolve problems not addressed by the ground rules. | Employees who must follow set procedures (such as accountants concerned with tax matters or purchasing staff who must comply with bidding/ordering requirements) and employees working with dangerous equipment or under special conditions. |
| Democratic | Participative | Supervisor involves employees as much as possible in aspects of the job which affect them. Their input is solicited; they participate in the decision-making process and are delegated much authority. | Employees with high levels of skill and/or extensive experience, employees who will need to make significant changes in work assignments (if time permits), employees who want to voice complaints, and employee groups with common problems. |
| Laissez-Faire | Free-Rein | Supervisor maintains a "hands off" policy. He/she "delegates by default" much discretion and decision-making authority to the employees. The supervisor gives little direction and allows employees extensive levels of freedom. | Highly motivated employees such as staff technical specialists and in some instances, consultants. |

situation, employees might expect the supervisor to adopt an autocratic leadership style and tell them, "This is what must be done. Here is how to do it. Now let's get to work." Autocratic leadership techniques can also be successful when:

- The supervisor knows how to do the employees' work.

- New and untrained employees do not know which tasks to perform and/or which procedures to follow.

- Supervision is conducted through orders and detailed instructions.

- An employee does not respond positively to any other style of supervision.

- The supervisor's authority is challenged.

## Bureaucratic Leadership

The **bureaucratic leadership style** is one in which a supervisor focuses on rules, regulations, policies, and procedures. Bureaucratic supervisors manage by the rules and rely on higher levels of management to make decisions about issues not covered "by the book."

A bureaucratic supervisor is more of a police officer than a leader. Normally, a supervisor adopts this enforcement style only when other leadership styles are inappropriate or when employees can be permitted no discretion in the decisions to be made. For example, when an employee operates potentially dangerous equipment, he or she must follow rules and procedures to the letter. In addition, a bureaucratic leadership style might be appropriate for situations in which procedures exist for employees performing routine or repetitive tasks. For example, clerical staff must exactly follow the established procedures for filing documents and information.

## Democratic Leadership

The **democratic** (also called participative) **leadership style** is almost the reverse of the autocratic style. The democratic supervisor informs employees about all matters that directly affect their work, and shares decision-making and problem-solving responsibilities. This type of supervisor emphasizes the employees' roles in the organization, and provides opportunities for employees to develop a heightened sense of job satisfaction. The democratic supervisor seeks employees' opinions and seriously considers their recommendations. Typically, the democratic supervisor:

- Develops plans to help employees evaluate their own performance

- Allows employees to help establish goals

- Encourages employees to grow on the job and be promoted

- Recognizes and encourages achievement

In effect, the democratic supervisor is akin to a coach leading a team.

This leadership style might seem vastly more appealing than the autocratic or bureaucratic approaches, but it does present limitations and potential disadvantages. For example, the democratic leadership style might lead to longer decision-making periods because a number of employees are involved in the process—a fact that would prove detrimental in situations calling for prompt action. Also, the act of involving employees in matters that are straightforward and easily resolved by the supervisor might not be cost-effective.

The democratic leadership style might be most appropriate for use with highly skilled or experienced employees. This style can be effective when implementing operational changes or resolving individual or group problems.

## Laissez-Faire Leadership

The **laissez-faire** (also called free-rein) **leadership style** is a hands-off approach in which the supervisor does very little leading. He or she provides little or no direction and gives employees as much freedom as possible. In effect, the supervisor gives all authority to the employees, and relies on them to establish goals, make decisions, and resolve problems. The basic motto of this type of supervisor is "don't rock the boat."

There are relatively few times when this approach will prove effective, but it might be appropriate for highly skilled or experienced employees who have been trained in decision-making and problem-solving techniques.

## Factors Affecting Leadership Styles

Ideally, an effective supervisor adopts the leadership style most appropriate to the situation. For example, the supervisor would know the needs, interests, and goals of each employee and then use the most appropriate leadership style to provide an optimal atmosphere for motivation. In practice, however, this is seldom possible. You have developed attitudes, feelings, and a personality based on your unique background. These factors generally limit your ability to move easily among radically different leadership styles.

The following sections examine major factors that influence a supervisor's leadership style. These factors include:

- The supervisor's personal background
- Characteristics of employees
- Organizational climate

**The Supervisor's Personal Background.** Your personality, knowledge, values, and experiences shape your feelings about and reactions toward employees. Some supervisors feel comfortable freely delegating work and like to involve several employees in a team approach to defining and resolving problems. Other supervisors like to do everything themselves. Simply put, your feelings about appropriate leadership are important in determining the specific leadership style you will use. Also, the success you achieve with a particular style might affect your willingness to adopt a different style. If you experienced success with an autocratic style, chances are that you will use (and perhaps prefer) this leadership model in other situations. Conversely, if the democratic approach has proven successful, you will likely continue using it.

**Characteristics of Employees.** Employees are individuals with different personalities and backgrounds. Like their supervisors, they are influenced by specific factors. Employees who want independence or decision-making responsibility, who identify with the property's goals, and who are knowledgeable and experienced might work well under a democratic leader. Conversely, employees with differing expectations and experiences might require a more autocratic leader. The ability of employees to work effectively in groups also affects the usefulness of specific leadership styles.

**Organizational Climate.** The organizational climate, the composition of the work group, the type of work, and related factors also influence leadership style. The organization's traditions and values might influence your behavior. For example, some organizations stress human relations. Other organizations focus on the bottom line—at the sacrifice, if necessary, of extensive employee participation in the management process. To be effective in any organization, you must at least consider, and probably adopt, the prevailing organizational philosophy.

# Increasing Employee Participation

The democratic leadership style attempts to raise employees' motivation levels by increasing their participation in decision-making and problem-solving activities. The following sections examine three techniques that can increase employee participation and motivation: employee suggestion programs, departmental task groups, and informal, democratic leadership actions.

## Employee Suggestion Programs

Employee suggestion programs are examples of formal employee participation programs. The suggestion box and the company newsletter's "letters to the editor" often help boost communication among managers, supervisors, and employees.

Formal employee suggestion programs provide many useful ideas, but implementing and maintaining such programs requires effort. Employees should find participation easy. For example, if the program requires employees to submit written suggestions, some employees might believe doing so is not worth the effort. In addition, managers' or supervisors' responses to employee suggestions are critical to the success (or failure) of any formal employee suggestion program. If you react to employee suggestions as if they were criticisms directed at your ability to supervise, you might discourage employees from providing additional comments.

Another critical element in the success of suggestion programs is feedback. Supervisors and managers must respond to employees who offer suggestions. Such replies should inform employees about the ways in which management is responding to their suggestions. This feedback might increase employees' knowledge of important business issues and motivate more employees to participate in the suggestion program.

Informal employee suggestions are also very useful. Supervisors can encourage them while coaching employees, during performance appraisals, and during formal and informal meetings with groups of employees.

Management must exert a significant amount of effort to ensure the success of an employee suggestion program. These programs often fail because supervisors do not provide the necessary feedback and follow-through.

## Employee Task Groups

A common employee participation activity involves the formation of task groups or work committees. Upper management frequently uses this technique, but it is appropriate at other organizational levels as well. Some properties have committees with representatives from all organizational levels who provide input on matters of property-wide interest. You can apply this concept to generate participation in work decisions within a specific department or work section. For example, you could appoint a formal task group to develop job lists or job breakdowns, ideas for energy management techniques or new recipes, and so on. If you use this method, be sure that high costs or time commitments do not offset its benefits.

## Informal Participatory Techniques

In most operations, a concerned and interested supervisor can easily use informal methods to promote employee participation. Consider, for example, the situation that arises when a decision must be made about a recurring problem. You might begin by writing down all the ways you can think of to resolve the problem, then follow up with a request for other ideas from affected employees. In doing this, you could talk to:

- Every employee affected by the problem.
- Informal group leaders.
- Experienced employees only.
- Selected employees whom you think would have specific ideas or would have a special interest in solving the problem.

Talking with any or all of these employees will likely generate helpful alternatives. As you continue with the problem-solving task, you could involve participating employees to determine:

- Advantages and disadvantages of each alternative.
- Procedures for implementing the selected solution.
- Methods for evaluating the effectiveness of the solution.
- Ways in which the solution might affect other aspects of the department.

As you consider whether to involve employees in decision-making, be aware that disagreements can result and that if they do, you must manage them. You will need to address conflicting interests and might need additional time for decision-making. In addition, even the best-intentioned employees might at times lack objectivity and allow their personal biases and concerns to influence their participation.

When you decide to involve employees in problem-solving and decision-making activities, the task at hand must really involve employee participation and not just persuasion on your part. Effective supervisors must use persuasion to "sell" decisions and solutions to employees, but should not do so under the guise of employee participation. When you have a definite solution in mind, you will do better to defend, justify, and sell it to employees rather than pretend your employees have an active role in the process.

## 🔑 Key Terms

**accountability**—A supervisor's acceptance of the responsibility that accompanies authority and the need to justify his or her actions to higher-level managers in the organization.

**autocratic leadership style**—A leadership style in which the supervisor retains as much power and decision-making authority as possible.

**bureaucratic leadership style**—A leadership style in which the supervisor "manages by the book" and enforces rules, policies, regulations, and standard operating procedures.

**coercive power**—A form of organizational power stemming from the authority to withhold rewards or administer punishment.

**democratic leadership style**—A leadership style in which the supervisor involves employees as much as possible in aspects of the job that affect them.

**empowerment**—The redistribution of power within an organization that enables managers, supervisors, and employees to perform their jobs more efficiently and effectively. The overall goal of empowerment is to enhance service to guests and increase profits for the organization by releasing decision-making responsibility, authority, and accountability to every level within the organization.

**expert power**—A form of personal power stemming from an individual's special knowledge or skill in relation to tasks performed by members of his or her staff.

**laissez-faire leadership style**—A leadership style in which the supervisor maintains a hands-off policy and delegates to employees as much discretion and decision-making authority as possible.

**leadership**—The ability to attain objectives by working with and through people. A leader creates conditions that motivate employees by establishing goals and influencing employees to attain those goals.

**motivation**—An inner drive that moves an employee to attain a personal goal.

**on-boarding**—Activities that can begin at the time of employee recruitment and continue until several weeks after orientation; these activities introduce the company and culture and help new employees understand that the organization wants them to succeed.

**position power**—A form of organizational power stemming from the formal authority granted to a position within the hierarchy of an organization. Also referred to as legitimate power.

**power**—The ability to influence the behavior of others.

**referent power**—A form of personal power resulting from the admiration and respect that others have for an individual's personal characteristics.

**reward power**—A form of organizational power resulting from a supervisor's authority to provide rewards for staff members.

## Review Questions

1. What are the definitions of power and empowerment?
2. What does authority within an organization carry with it?
3. What are the sources of organizational and personal power?

4. How can supervisors enhance their power?

5. Why can't supervisors motivate employees?

6. How can supervisors learn about the needs, interests, and goals of employees?

7. How can supervisory functions such as training, coaching, and evaluating become strategies by which to motivate employees?

8. What factors should a supervisor investigate to determine if there is a motivational or morale problem in the department?

9. What distinguishes an autocratic leadership style from a democratic leadership style?

10. How does a bureaucratic leadership style differ from a laissez-faire leadership style?

11. What factors affect the leadership style adopted by a supervisor?

12. How can supervisors increase employee participation in department activities?

 **Internet Sites** ⸺⸺⸺⸺⸺⸺⸺⸺⸺⸺⸺⸺⸺⸺⸺⸺⸺⸺⸺⸺⸺⸺

For more information, visit the following Internet sites. Remember that Internet addresses can change without notice. If the site is no longer there, you can use a search engine to look for additional sites.

Leadership Style Survey
www.nwlink.com/~donclark/leader/
  survstyl.html

Motivation and Leadership Styles
www.motivation-tools.com/workplace/
  leadership_styles.htm

Motivation Strategies Magazine
www.motivationstrategies.com

Team Technology: Leadership Styles
www.teamtechnology.co.uk/
  leadership-styles.html

# Chapter 11 Outline

Benefits of Conflict
Sources of Conflict
    Limited Resources
    Different Goals
    Role Ambiguity
    Work Relationships
    Individual Differences
    Organizational Problems
    Communication Problems
Types of Conflict
Outcomes of Conflict
Conflict Management Strategies
    Avoidance
    Accommodation
    Competition
    Mutual Problem–Solving
    Compromise
    Turning Styles into Strategies
Tips for Negotiating Conflicts
    Mediating Conflict Between
        Employees
    Resolving Supervisor/Employee
        Conflict
    Accepting Criticism from Your Boss

# Competencies

1. Identify the benefits of conflict. (pp. 303–304)

2. Review organizational sources of conflict. (pp. 304–307)

3. Outline different types of conflict. (pp. 307–308)

4. Explain typical outcomes of conflict. (pp. 308–309)

5. Describe basic strategies that can be used to manage conflict. (pp. 309–311)

6. List tips managers can follow to negotiate conflicts. (pp. 312–320)

# 11

# Managing Conflict

CONFLICT CAN BE AS SIMPLE as a difference of opinion or as complex as a lengthy battle over matters of significant importance. A conflict can be caused by an event or a clash of personalities. Conflict may also occur when people hold opposing views about a situation and how to handle it. Multiple cultures are often present in hospitality organizations; conflict may emerge through differences between cultural and organizational norms. Value differences resulting from different generations (age groups) can also create conflict. Supervisors must try to ensure that every employee respects the different beliefs of their co-workers. In doing so, they can help to reduce conflict within their hospitality organizations.

Left alone, conflict may cause serious problems that prevent your department from achieving its goals. If properly managed, however, some types of conflict can be constructive. This chapter first looks at the possible benefits of conflict to hospitality operations. Next, common sources of conflict, types of conflict, and possible outcomes of conflict are examined Later sections examine strategies to manage conflict and negotiating techniques supervisors may use to resolve conflict between employees, between themselves and employees, and between themselves and their bosses.

## Benefits of Conflict

There is conflict within all hospitality operations. A traditional management view holds that it should be avoided because it disrupts an organization and prevents optimal performance; however, a more accurate view is that conflict isn't necessarily good or bad, but it is inevitable. Supervisors must be ready to manage the range of workplace conflicts in a manner that does not alienate employees or guests.

Subtle conflict may force a group to focus on its goals, but it must be carefully managed and resolved. For example, during budget planning sessions, department managers compete for the limited resources of the operation. Their conflicting views on how resources should be allocated can lead to an analysis of the organization's goals and strategies to attain them. At the end of a budget planning process, the conflict that occurred will likely have allowed participants to learn more about where the organization is going and how it plans to get there. This beneficial outcome would not happen without conflict. However, a key tactic in successful conflict management is awareness of the feelings of everyone involved in the conflict. At some point in resolving the conflict, these feelings must be understood and addressed.

Some conflict is necessary for good work performance. When there is a low level of conflict and performance levels are low, the organization stagnates; i.e., it does not improve (see Exhibit 1). On the other hand, when there are high levels of conflict and performance, chaos is a potential result. As Exhibit 1 suggests, there is an optimal relationship between conflict and performance. Unfortunately, there is no standard set of rules about how to manage conflict to achieve optimal results.

Supervisors must foster honest and objective opposition that will help the department while preventing the kind of conflict that leads to disorganization and unmotivated employees. You will be better able to carry out this task if you understand sources of conflict within hospitality operations. In many ways, your success will be determined by how you assess different perspectives, acknowledge them, and respond to them.

## Sources of Conflict

There are numerous sources of conflict within an organization. Many arise from situations or personalities unique to it. However, there are sources of conflict common to most hospitality operations, including:

- Limited resources
- Different goals
- Role ambiguity

**Exhibit 1    Conflict and Performance**

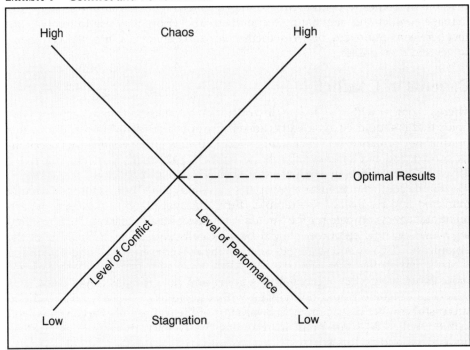

- Work relationships
- Individual differences
- Organizational problems
- Communication problems

Exhibit 2 lists these typical sources of conflict. It also suggests that a supervisor's ability to manage conflict often determines whether departmental goals are attained through cooperation, or if conflict blocks the department from reaching goals.

## Limited Resources

Resources are limited in every hospitality operation. No department has all of the people, time, money, equipment, and space it wants. Often, a department can obtain resources only at the expense of another department. For example, if two departments within an organization need an upgraded computer system and there is only enough money in the budget for one, one department will likely postpone its upgrade. This creates the possibility of conflict. However, as pointed out earlier, this type of conflict might prove beneficial. Limited resources force each department manager to justify the request for the system upgrade in relation to the organization's overall goals. The manager who persuades upper management that the organization's interests will be best served by upgrading the system in his or her department usually gets the resources.

Conflict over limited resources is not always easily resolved. For example, if two supervisors at a hotel apply for the same open manager's position, conflict may result. Both applicants are likely to view the open position as an opportunity for advancement; failure to land the job could be hard for either supervisor to handle. If the position is eventually filled by an external applicant, still more

**Exhibit 2    Supervisors and Conflict**

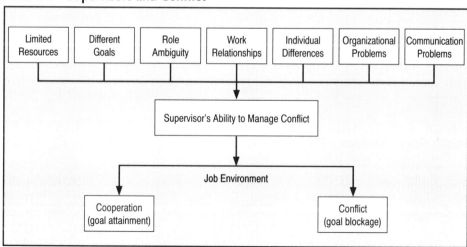

conflict could result if both supervisors feel that they are unable to advance within the organization.

## Different Goals

Departments and individuals in the same hospitality operation can have different goals. Conflict can result about who is right and what strategies to pursue. For example, a hotel's food and beverage director may want to minimize labor costs by scheduling fewer line cooks. However, this may conflict with the servers' ability to bring out food to the guests in a timely and satisfactory manner.

Supervisors are often caught in the middle of these conflicts. For example, if you are a supervisor in the kitchen operation described above, you will need to support both the kitchen and the servers as they attempt to do the best they can with a smaller staff while simultaneously adhering to the food and beverage director's decision. You can only follow your boss's direction and hope that an agreement about the extent to which each goal can be attained is reached.

## Role Ambiguity

Another source of conflict that can emerge through work relationships is role ambiguity. This occurs when actions seem to contradict each other. For example, one week an entry-level employee attends a staff meeting where the head chef talks about the importance of quality; however, the topic of the next weekly meeting is cutting costs. What actions should that employee take when he is setting up the salad bar after the second meeting and notices that the lettuce is starting to get a little brown around the edges? Should the employee think about the issue of quality addressed in the first meeting and, consequently, not use the lettuce? Or, alternatively, should he allow the lettuce to be used in light of the cost concerns discussed in the second meeting? These two requirements appear to be in conflict with each other. Determining how to meet both quality and cost objectives requires creativity, patience, and the ability to clearly and consistently communicate the requirements to the employees.

Another stress-producing variable related to role ambiguity is decision latitude. **Decision latitude** refers to the flexibility you have in determining a course of action when attempting to resolve difficult issues and situations. Low decision latitude means you are narrowly bound to a limited number of potential solutions. This limitation can increase stress and minimize the effectiveness of employees. In contrast, empowering well-trained and well-coached employees with high decision latitude is often a more effective approach.

## Work Relationships

The success of a hospitality operation depends on close cooperation from members of all departments. Often, employees can't do some or any of their work until others have completed theirs. For example, if front desk agents are to sell rooms to walk-in guests, they need up-to-the-minute room status information from housekeeping. Housekeeping room attendants depend on laundry to provide clean linens. Also, servers or buspersons can't set tables until clean tablecloths and napkins are available. Conflict can result when, for whatever reason, an employee, supervisor, or manager:

- Fails to complete an assigned task.

- Completes a task late.

- Fails to cooperate with staff members from other departments.

The most important factor in resolving conflict is trust among the individuals involved. Believing that your co-workers are competent and want to work together are important ingredients to moving forward in accomplishing the job to be done.

## Individual Differences

Differences among employees, supervisors, and managers due to personal attitudes and opinions, educational or cultural backgrounds, experience, age, or work-related duties and responsibilities can cause conflict. A diverse staff does not mean that employees will always be in conflict; however, it does mean that supervisors have an even greater responsibility to ensure that conflict does not become disruptive or counterproductive.

## Organizational Problems

Organizational problems can be sources of conflict. This occurs, for example, when one department believes its efforts are more important than those of other departments. Other potential sources of organizational conflict include change, overlapping job responsibilities, vague job descriptions, and other situations that cloud or obscure basic functions. Employees, supervisors, and managers can experience conflicts that create stress if their duties and responsibilities are not clearly defined. When the extent of a supervisor's authority is not clear, for example, conflicts can arise within the supervisor, between the supervisor and employees, and between the supervisor and his or her boss.

## Communication Problems

Communication problems are at the root of many conflicts. Effective communication about the organization's resources, goals, roles, work relationships, individual differences, and organizational problems can go a long way toward increasing cooperation within the organization and avoiding conflict that blocks goal achievement.

# Types of Conflict

While conflict can take many forms, the types of conflict supervisors are most often called on to manage are personal conflicts that occur within their department or work area. Anyone within an organization can experience mixed feelings about some of the organization's policies, about certain individuals, about job tasks and procedures, and about gaps between personal and organizational goals. Employees may deal with personal conflict by becoming quietly frustrated or physically expressing their concerns—slamming a door, for example. They may also withdraw from the conflict by daydreaming or pretending they are not angry or upset. These reactions can affect work performance. Other symptoms of unresolved conflict among employees include:

- Withdrawn employees who don't talk to each other or to you
- Inappropriate behavior such as name-calling or talking loudly
- Low group and/or individual morale
- Decreased productivity levels
- Distrust between groups and individuals
- Choosing sides, i.e., "It's us against them"
- Recurring operational problems that everyone seems to ignore

Conflict can also occur within a supervisor. For example, a new supervisor may feel internal conflict, especially if he or she has just been promoted from the ranks of the employees whom he or she must now supervise. The promotion places the supervisor in a new leadership role and with this role comes the need to enforce the property's policies and procedures. As the new supervisor manages employees who were formerly peers, an internal conflict about where friendships end and professional relationships begin is bound to arise. The success of a new supervisor may depend, at least in part, on how well he or she handles this unavoidable internal conflict.

Conflict also occurs between individuals at any organizational level. When two or more employees disagree over a situation, event, or "personality problem," their supervisor may have to serve as a mediator—an objective third party—to help the employees resolve their conflict.

Because the supervisor serves as a linking pin between higher and lower levels within the organization, conflict can occur between supervisors and employees. For example, supervisors will need to enforce unpopular rules and policies and may have to implement changes that the employees do not like. Conflict can also occur between a supervisor and his or her boss as the supervisor attempts to represent the best interests of his or her employees to upper management.

## Outcomes of Conflict

To effectively manage conflict, a supervisor should analyze each situation in terms of its possible outcomes. It is also important for a supervisor to understand how his or her management style can affect those outcomes and to be able to develop an appropriate strategy to reduce or resolve the conflict. Outcomes of resolving personal conflict can be described as lose-lose, win-lose, or win-win.

In a **lose-lose outcome**, no one involved in the conflict has all or even most of his or her needs satisfied. Typically, the basic reasons for the conflict remain and conflict may recur over the same issues until they are resolved.

In a **win-lose outcome**, one party's needs or concerns are satisfied while those of the other party or parties are not. Since this type of outcome typically fails to resolve all of the problems that created the conflict, future conflict may arise over the same or similar problems. Therefore, while a win-lose outcome may reduce the conflict temporarily for the "winning" party, it may not resolve the conflict. In addition, win-lose outcomes often cause resentment in the minds of the "losers."

In a **win-win outcome**, the needs of all parties are satisfied in some way and the conflict is resolved. To reach this outcome, those in conflict must understand each other's needs, confront the issues, and work together to objectively resolve the situation so everyone benefits. Only with a win-win outcome is a conflict truly resolved for the long term.

As a supervisor you can determine which outcome is best for each conflict and try to steer the parties toward that outcome. For example, if your goal is to temporarily reduce conflict, you may adopt a short-term strategy appropriate to a win-lose or lose-lose outcome. If your goal is to fully resolve the conflict, you must be prepared to spend the time and effort required to create a win-win outcome.

## Conflict Management Strategies

Many supervisors make the mistake of using the same strategy to manage all workplace conflicts. This is not a useful approach because the strategy used to address a conflict may itself determine the kind of outcome it produces. Therefore, supervisors who consistently manage conflict with the same approach often find themselves facing the same type of outcome—lose-lose, win-lose, or win-win—no matter what the conflict is or what outcome may be the most appropriate.

Conflict management strategies vary in relation to the supervisor's levels of assertiveness and cooperation. Five typical styles of managing conflict are:

- Avoidance

- Accommodation

- Competition

- Mutual Problem-Solving

- Compromise

The following sections examine each strategy and identify the conflict outcome that each style typically produces. Exhibit 3 diagrams each of these strategies in relation to the supervisor's degree of assertiveness and cooperation.

### Avoidance

A supervisor with low levels of assertiveness and cooperation probably wants to avoid conflict. **Avoidance** behaviors include withdrawing from conflict situations, remaining "neutral," sidestepping the real issues, or constantly postponing a confrontation. Instead of seeing the benefits of conflict, this type of supervisor focuses only on the negative aspects. However, supervisors who ignore problems in the hope that they will go away often find that the problems become worse and the intensity of the conflict increases. The avoidance style of managing conflict encourages lose-lose outcomes in which the needs of all parties in conflict go unaddressed.

**Exhibit 3   Approaches to Conflict**

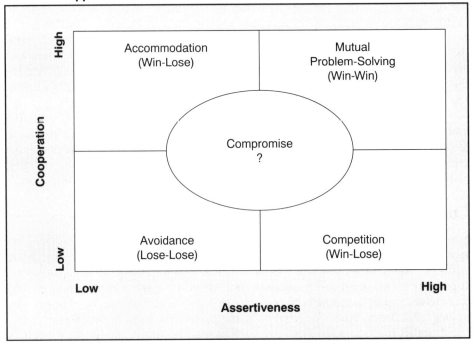

## Accommodation

A supervisor with a low level of assertiveness and a high level of cooperation will likely want to **accommodate** the needs of others, even if it means neglecting his or her own needs. Supervisors who sacrifice their interests inevitably end up on the losing side of win-lose outcomes. Accommodating supervisors often display avoidance behaviors. The difference as a conflict management style is that while both parties lose when conflict is avoided, when one party accommodates the other party wins by default; thus, the accommodating party loses by choice.

## Competition

A supervisor with a high level of assertiveness and a low level of cooperation will likely be competitive in conflict situations. A supervisor who uses **competition** often attempts to dominate others by using power or authority to ensure that his or her needs are satisfied. Obviously, competitive approaches to conflict usually force win-lose outcomes, with the supervisor determining the winner and the loser. When your employees lose all the time, resentment may build and job performance may suffer.

## Mutual Problem-Solving

A supervisor with high levels of assertiveness and cooperation will usually resolve conflict by collaborating with others to reach mutually agreed-upon solutions.

With the **mutual problem-solving** approach to conflict, both parties acknowledge that conflict exists and are willing to take the time to determine and understand each other's underlying needs and objectives. Both parties search for commonalities and don't dwell on their differences. Potential solutions to the conflict are developed together, and the solution selected is the one that best meets both of their needs. Honesty and hard negotiating generally lead to creative solutions that can meet the needs of everyone concerned. This approach encourages win-win outcomes.

## Compromise

A supervisor with moderate levels of both assertiveness and cooperation will likely respond to conflict by seeking a **compromise**. Generally, a compromise allows each party to partially satisfy some needs and concerns. Depending on how the parties in conflict view the partial solution, a compromise could create a number of different outcomes:

- Lose-lose outcome—if neither party is satisfied with the partial solution.

- Win-lose outcome—if one party feels it has won (or lost) at the other's expense.

- Win-win outcome—if, over time, the parties in conflict learn to accept the partial solution.

Regardless of your management style, there will be times when compromise is the most effective outcome.

## Turning Styles into Strategies

Rather than adopting one of these styles for responding to every conflict, an effective supervisor develops enough flexibility to use all of these styles, depending on the conflict in question. When seen in this way, styles become strategies: tools with which you can try to direct the parties involved toward the best outcome.

For example, accommodation may be a poor style, but it's not necessarily a poor strategy; it depends on the situation. If you are in conflict with your boss, you may wish to accommodate him or her to avoid a win-lose outcome in which you will most likely be the loser. While mutual problem-solving may appear to be the most appealing style, you may not have the expertise, time, or desire to manage win-win outcomes for every conflict.

You can use Exhibit 3 to analyze the conflict management style of others involved in the conflict and identify the type of outcome toward which their styles seem to be leading. This analysis alerts you to behavioral changes that may be necessary for those involved in the conflict if the conflict is to have a desirable outcome. For example, a conflict may involve two employees, one of whom is very assertive, while the other is unassertive. If, in this specific conflict situation, the assertive employee is (to simplify the example) "wrong" and the unassertive employee is "right," you should encourage the unassertive employee to speak up and defend his or her viewpoint in order to move the conflict toward the desired outcome.

---

### Individual Meetings

Some supervisors prefer to meet with the contending employees individually before meeting with all of them. This strategy is appropriate when the conflict is complicated or serious in nature. On rare occasions two or more employees can't talk about the conflict in the same room without arguing or getting upset. If this is the case, it's best to talk to each employee alone. Minor conflicts usually can be resolved when all parties meet together.

---

## Tips for Negotiating Conflicts

A large part of how well you manage personal conflict depends on how well you can negotiate. Diplomats have the fates of their countries, even their lives, hinge on the words they use, how they say them, the approach to their audience—in short, on how well they negotiate. Whether you lead the hospitality business or a department or team of employees within it, you must be good at negotiating. As a leader in your department, you must perfect your negotiating skills in order to become the best supervisor you can be.

Most negotiation takes place during a meeting. The meeting can be very informal—in a hallway, for example—or very formal—a closed-door meeting in your boss's office. As a supervisor, you should carefully choose where you meet your employees. The location affects the meeting's tone and how your employees respond to you.

The best place to meet depends on the nature of the conflict. Deal with a serious conflict between you and your employees in your office with the door closed. If you do not have an office, choose a private area with a formal feel to it—a small conference room, for example, as opposed to a location like the employee break room. Some supervisors borrow their boss's office for serious meetings. If the conflict is less serious, or if the employees involved will be too intimidated in a formal setting, choose an appropriate informal location. With minor conflicts, sometimes a five-minute hallway meeting wherever the employee or employees happen to be is appropriate.

### Mediating Conflict Between Employees

Conflict between employees occurs more often than most supervisors would like. While dealing with personalities and emotions can be difficult, it has to be done. Dealing with employee conflict is one of a supervisor's most important contributions to the efficiency of his or her department.

Once you have decided on the site and have chosen a time for the meeting, there are several things you should do before, during, and after your meeting with the employees who are in conflict.

The most important thing to avoid before the meeting is jumping to conclusions. Despite what you may feel about the participants or the conflict, you must try to keep an open mind. For some conflicts, you may want to get a version of the situation from third parties. Ask other department employees who have remained neutral for their perspective on the conflict and how it is affecting their work. If the conflict is serious, be ready to hear negative, unpleasant, critical and even confused feedback from your employees. They may be emotional, and there are likely to be different versions of the events or situations that led to the conflict.

A meeting to discuss a conflict can become disorderly and lead almost anywhere if you let it. Tips for maintaining control during this kind of meeting include:

- Do not take phone calls during the meeting.

- Prevent interruptions unless they are absolutely necessary.

- Keep focused during the meeting. Don't keep looking at your watch, at papers, or at the computer screen.

- Maintain eye contact.

- Avoid taking notes, especially if employees don't know why you're taking them.

- Investigate the issues thoroughly.

Additionally, the following six steps can help you keep the discussion organized and under control:

1. Set the tone.

2. Get the feelings.

3. Get the facts.

4. Ask for help.

5. Get a commitment.

6. Follow up.

**Set the Tone.** First, greet the employees cordially and try to establish an open and non-threatening tone for the meeting. This can be done by the words you choose and the way you say them as you open the floor for discussion. You can begin by saying something like: "Over the last few days I've noticed that there seems to be a problem with you two, and I think it is affecting your work. Is there anything that you want to talk about?" This or a similar approach is better than a more abrupt statement such as "You guys have got a problem, and we're going to get to the bottom of it right now." Such statements put employees on guard and make it difficult to facilitate a productive meeting.

**Get the Feelings.** After setting the tone, focus on discovering the employees' feelings. Your objective in emotional conflict situations is to give the employees opportunities to release their emotions and clear the way for effective solutions. Often what you'll get from the employees at first is a rush of words as they release emotions that have been held in check, perhaps for a long time. Don't interrupt or seek clarification at this time; it's very important to allow the employees to express their frustrations. By allowing the employees to "talk out" their feelings, you are helping to defuse the conflict and enabling them to gain control of their emotions. Once the person has talked it out, you should summarize the feelings expressed and re-state them for clarification.

As employees express their feelings, avoid giving any indication that you approve or disapprove. If employees think you are judging them, they may become silent and withdrawn. Don't question, criticize, interpret, sympathize with, or try to convince the employee. At this point, you should just encourage the employees to clearly express what they feel.

Some supervisors do not want to ask employees to state their feelings about a conflict. Others think about how they themselves would feel in the same situation and then project their feelings onto the employees. Rather than assuming you know what your employees feel, ask and encourage them to clearly express their feelings.

Sometimes, employees will remain silent even after you have asked them how they feel about the situation. This is not surprising since many people have difficulty talking about their feelings. Try to make it easier for these employees to express themselves. If you know something about the conflict, try paraphrasing what you think each employee is feeling. This sometimes encourages the employees to start talking. You must be careful with this technique, however; you are trying to discover their feelings, not show agreement with their feelings. The objective is to move from emotion and feelings to reason and solutions. However, you must deal with the emotions first.

It's also important that you don't become emotional yourself. Only when *you* remain under control can you move toward rational thinking and help your employees work things out effectively.

**Get the Facts.** Once employees have talked their feelings through, you can move on to investigating the facts. Listen patiently to what the employees have to say, even if you think their input may be inaccurate or irrelevant. You can keep employees talking without agreeing with them by nodding or occasionally saying "I see" or "Yes." Listen for the feelings the employees are expressing as well as the content of their message.

Keep your questions to a minimum during the fact-finding stage. You can review and clarify the facts after each employee has said his or her piece. Don't respond to the employees with "That's not right," "I can't believe that's true," and similar statements because they tend to make employees stop talking.

Listen for what isn't said—the absence of important information, for example—or quick agreements that seem evasive. These can be clues about something the employee wishes to hide. Watch for nonverbal communication as well. Are the employees sending you mixed messages? Do their postures, gestures, and facial expressions agree with the words being said?

If the fact-finding discussion gets bogged down in an argument, there are several strategies you can use to move the discussion to a more productive level:

- Try to depersonalize the conflict. Talk about it as if it could have happened to anyone in order to reduce tension.

- Ask the employees to put aside their feelings for the moment and pretend they are third parties trying to discover the factors that contributed to the conflict.

- Ask each employee to think about how the other employee may have seen the situation that led to the conflict. This may reveal information gaps or incorrect assumptions about where the other employee was coming from. Often, personal conflicts are partly or entirely based on these misunderstandings.

Save most of your comments until you have all the facts. Make sure you can accurately describe the situation as each employee sees it before you make any personal evaluations. Choose your words and tone of voice with care. When speaking to the employees, ask yourself if you would talk to your boss or to a peer in the same way. Treat employees like responsible adults, and most will respond in kind.

**Ask for Help.** At this point, many supervisors tell employees what they should do to solve the conflict. It's better, however, to encourage them to work out their own solution. Employees must manage their conflicts, and they must work harder than you to resolve them.

When you "tell" employees what they should do to solve the conflict, you invite them to play the "Yes, but ..." game. Here, you suggest a good solution and the employees respond with, "Yes, but ..." and they give two or three reasons why your solution won't work. When you offer another solution, again they respond with, "Yes, but ..." This game can go on until you run out of ideas.

Asking the employees for help invites participation and commitment. It also helps build the employees' self-esteem. The employees will be more willing to resolve the conflict, especially if you use the ideas they suggest. Your role is to help them explore their ideas by asking questions like, "If you do that, what might happen?" or, "What do you see as the likely consequences of doing exactly as you suggested?"

Ask open-ended questions that invite the employees to identify causes and offer solutions. Don't accept solutions such as, "We'll try harder to get along." Ask additional questions to help the employees specify what they will actually do to "try harder." Help the employees be as specific as possible about the future actions they will take to resolve the conflict. Remember, it is the employees' responsibility to resolve the conflict. Your job is to facilitate the discussion, adding your own suggestions as appropriate and securing commitment from both parties.

You may have a desired outcome in mind for some conflicts. If so, it's best to steer employees toward that outcome rather than to impose it on them. If the employees come up with a different but effective solution to the conflict, it's often best to go with it. They are more likely to follow their own plan because they have more ownership of the solution and, therefore, more to lose if the solution doesn't work.

**Get a Commitment.** After you have agreed on what to do, ask the employees to commit themselves to performing their part of the solution. You may want to help the employees put their plan in writing. The plan should indicate what is to be done, who will do what, how it's to be done, when it will be done, and with what help (if any). If it's a serious conflict, it may be useful to have the employees sign the plan they've created.

**Follow Up.** Schedule a follow-up meeting to check whether the employees' solution is being implemented and is working. Let the employees know that they must

---

### Negotiation and Conflict

**Negotiation** involves a discussion in which both parties determine what is really important to the other and agree to solutions that address each other's needs. To achieve a long-term commitment to resolve the conflict, you and the employee must believe that the agreement reached during the meeting considers both of your needs.

Negotiating is not a series of "hints" or "demands." Don't hint; ask directly for what you want to reduce misunderstandings and later disappointments. Be sure to ask; don't demand. Since your position as a supervisor carries formal authority, a demand will be viewed as an order. Ordering an employee to meet your needs is not negotiating. Exercising your authority may force compliance, but it does not necessarily yield agreement.

---

follow through with what they have agreed to do. Tell employees that if their plan doesn't work, you have your own plan ready. Let the employees know about your plan and under what conditions you will implement it.

After the meeting, take some time—immediately afterward, if possible—to analyze what happened by asking yourself questions such as:

- What did I do that worked?

- What did I do that didn't work?

- What strategy or tactic was most successful?

- What concessions did each employee make and when?

- Did I make any concessions and when?

- What happened as a result of these concessions?

- What information came from the meeting that will be of long-term benefit?

- What would I do differently next time?

## Resolving Supervisor/Employee Conflict

Resolving a conflict between you and an employee is difficult because you must step back from your own feelings and try to see yourself objectively. Many of the techniques you apply to conflicts between two or more employees apply to a conflict between yourself and an employee or group of employees. You must think of yourself as just another party to the conflict, while retaining your roles as supervisor and mediator. The first step in this process is to thoroughly review the employee's "side" of the conflict.

To achieve a win-win outcome in a conflict with an employee, the supervisor must make it clear to the employee that both the supervisor and the employee must win to have a satisfactory agreement. "Winning" does not mean the other person must lose. A supervisor should not attempt to achieve the department's or organization's objectives at the expense of the employee. Also, a supervisor's role is not to "sell" the employee on what the supervisor wants to achieve. Employees who are "sold" often don't stay sold. What may have sounded good because of a supervisor's persuasive skill later may not look good at all. Instead, resolving the conflict becomes an act of negotiating.

**Before the Meeting.** Never attempt to resolve a conflict when you are angry or upset. Put some distance between your reaction to the situation and the meeting you eventually schedule. However, don't delay too long because, in many cases, a long delay can build the conflict.

Analyze the situation without emotion. Focus on the facts, not your reaction to them. Look for ways in which you may have exaggerated aspects of the situation.

**During the Meeting.** Greet the employee cordially and begin the discussion in a non-threatening way. Try to establish a relaxed and open tone with your introductory remarks. Then ask the employee how he or she feels about the situation. Just letting employees know that their feelings are important to you can reduce some of their anger or tension. Don't interrupt or ask too many questions—just let them relate their feelings about the situation.

After you have acknowledged the employee's feelings, ask the employee to explain the conflict as he or she sees it. Experienced supervisors recognize the truth in the old saying that "There are two sides to every story." Even if you were present when the conflict occurred, the employee's version of the situation may be very different and may cause you to reassess your own interpretation of what happened.

This is the time to ask questions and listen to the responses. Asking questions can help clarify the conflict for the employee as well. Respect the employee's need to think about your questions. When responding to your questions, the employee may discover his or her real needs and wants and be open to an agreement that works for both of you.

After you have listened to the employee, tell your side of the story. Aim for reconciliation. If appropriate, identify how you may have contributed to the problem. Don't overreact if you are interrupted or misunderstood. Having someone interrupt or say "I don't understand your point" tends to make people irritated or defensive even in non-stressful situations.

If the employee does not understand what you've said, re-state your position differently. Talk slowly and take pauses to ask if the employee understands you.

If the employee interrupts you, stay calm. Rather than saying, "Can't you let me finish?" try to be diplomatic. Say something like "This may be difficult for you, but I don't think you'll understand my side of the situation unless I can finish my train of thought."

Sometimes the conflict is resolved after both of you have given your interpretation of the situation. One or both of you may have lacked a vital piece of information or misunderstood something. If the conflict is not resolved so easily, you must work it out with the employee. Ask the employee for his or her ideas and brainstorm a list of alternatives together. When brainstorming, don't evaluate the ideas—simply record them. Your task is not to judge the ideas, but to get as many ideas from the employee as you can. After you have a list of ideas, compare them and select the best from among them.

---

## What if an Employee Refuses to Follow Through?

If the employee does not follow through on the plan, some sort of disciplinary action may be necessary. Or, if the conflict is serious, you may want to ask a third party to act as mediator at another meeting between you and the employee. The mediator may be another supervisor, your boss, or some other manager. A mediator not involved with the conflict brings a fresh, objective viewpoint to the situation and may be helpful in sorting out what happened and what actions should be taken.

---

Before ending the meeting, summarize the discussion, highlight major areas of agreement, and spell out the next steps. Put in writing what each of you agrees to do. Get a commitment from the employee to follow the plan and promise to do your part as well. Mark calendar dates for completion and establish a date for a follow-up meeting to monitor your progress. Plan a specific time when you and the employee will meet again to deal with problems that might arise.

**After the Meeting.** Just as you would after a meeting concerning conflict between employees, take some time to analyze what happened. Are you happy with the outcome? Were you competitive, forcing the employee to be on the losing side of a win-lose outcome? Did you accommodate too much, because you don't like conflict or wanted the employee to like you? Did you compromise—settle for part of what you wanted? If so, do you feel good about that? Or did you achieve a win-win outcome? Analyzing the outcome you achieved and how you reached that outcome will help you with future negotiations.

## Accepting Criticism from Your Boss

There are many possibilities for personal conflict with your boss. Sometimes your boss's deadlines might seem unreasonable, for example. Or some of his or her rules may seem unnecessary. But, because of your organizational relationship with your boss, most situations that hold a possibility for personal conflict are "resolved" because you accommodate your boss rather than try to negotiate with him or her. This avoids personal conflict, although sometimes it can cause you internal conflict.

Many supervisors see criticism from their bosses as a form of personal conflict. Most bosses do not wish their comments to be perceived in this way, but criticism from your boss can lead to internal or personal conflict if you are not careful. Everything depends on how you perceive your boss's criticism.

Never take criticism from your boss as a personal attack. If you do, you will become anxious, defensive, and too emotionally involved to see the real points behind the criticism. Everyone makes mistakes. Criticism from your boss generally identifies a mistake you have made. This type of criticism usually tries to get you to adopt new behaviors or strategies that will prevent you from making the mistake again. As a supervisor, you will always have opportunities to learn more about your role. Feedback from your boss should be viewed as a chance to learn behaviors that will help you become a more effective leader.

You don't have control over where your boss will meet with you to comment on your performance—your boss does. Where he or she chooses to hold the meeting conveys a message, just as you convey a message to your employees through where you meet with them. The meeting site provides you with a clue as to how serious the criticism of your performance will be.

**Before the Meeting.** Avoid jumping to conclusions before you meet with your boss. The criticism may not be as serious as you fear. If you are nervous, ask yourself, "Realistically, what's the worst that can happen? How likely is it? How can I deal with that outcome?"

If your boss has given you an idea of what the meeting will be about, think about the problem or behavior that will be discussed. How has it affected your productivity? What steps can you take to rectify the situation?

Above all, tell yourself that you are not going to get upset or angry. Take the view that the purpose of the criticism is to help you solve problems and grow professionally. A confrontation will only move you or your boss into rigid positions that make communication difficult.

**During the Meeting.** Make sure your boss knows you are actively listening to the criticism. Remain calm and concentrate on the discussion.

Tell your boss that you appreciate the effort to help you improve your performance. Maintain a comfortable amount of eye contact. Ask questions to clarify issues and paraphrase some of your boss's points. This indicates to your boss that you are receiving the message.

Don't change the subject because it is a defensive or evasive tactic. Never joke about issues raised in the discussion because this also indicates defensiveness or a lack of sincerity, which may lead your boss to think you don't care about resolving the situation.

After listening to your boss, take responsibility for the problem. Concentrate on the present and offer positive solutions. At this point your boss may tell you his or her plan for correcting the situation. If you think the plan will work, agree to it. Diplomatically raise any serious objections you have and give reasons for each one. If your boss does not outline a plan, offer one of your own. This demonstrates that you took the criticism seriously and can correct matters on your own.

With some problems, it's obvious that you can take certain immediate steps to quickly solve them. Other more serious or complicated problems may take time. In these cases, it's usually a good idea to ask your boss for a timetable. Find out how much time is appropriate for resolving the problem, and strive to meet or beat the deadline.

**After the Meeting.** Take a moment to analyze what happened. Do you feel good about the discussion? Why or why not? Did your boss seem to be steering the situation toward a specific outcome—lose-lose, win-lose, or win-win? Did you learn something new about your boss's management style that will help you in the future?

Most important, do everything you can to make the solution to the problem work. If necessary, request a follow-up meeting with your boss to make sure the problem is corrected.

## Key Terms

**accommodation**—A conflict management style usually practiced by supervisors with a low level of assertiveness and a high level of cooperation. This style typically leads to win-lose outcomes.

**avoidance**—A conflict management style usually practiced by supervisors with low levels of assertiveness and cooperation. This style typically leads to lose-lose outcomes.

**competition**—A conflict management style usually practiced by supervisors with a high level of assertiveness and a low level of cooperation. This style typically leads to win-lose outcomes.

**compromise**—A conflict management style usually practiced by supervisors with moderate levels of both assertiveness and cooperation. This style can lead to win-win, win-lose, or lose-lose outcomes, depending on how the parties in conflict view the compromise.

**decision latitude**—The flexibility you have in determining a course of action when attempting to resolve difficult issues and situations. Low decision latitude means you are narrowly bound to a limited number of potential solutions. High decision latitude means you are empowered to develop and implement potential solutions.

**lose-lose outcome**—An outcome of conflict in which no one involved satisfies all or even most of his or her needs. With a lose-lose outcome, the basic reasons for the conflict remain and conflict may recur.

**mutual problem-solving**—A conflict management style usually practiced by supervisors with high levels of assertiveness and cooperation. This style typically leads to win-win outcomes. Supervisors with this style resolve conflict by accepting the needs of others and negotiating solutions that meet all or most of the needs of those involved in the conflict.

**negotiation**—A probing discussion in which both parties determine what is really important to the other and agree to solutions that protect each other's needs.

**win-lose outcome**—An outcome of conflict in which one party's needs are satisfied while those of the other party are not. A win-lose outcome typically fails to address all of the problems that created the conflict, so future conflict may arise over the same or similar problems.

**win-win outcome**—An outcome of conflict in which the needs of all parties are satisfied and the conflict is resolved. To reach a win-win outcome, those in conflict must acknowledge each other's needs and work together to resolve the situation so that everyone benefits.

 **Review Questions**

1. What are some benefits of conflict?

2. What are some sources of conflict within a hospitality organization?

3. What is a win-lose outcome?

4. What are some behaviors common to the avoidance style of managing conflict?

5. What should a supervisor do before holding a meeting with employees who are in conflict?

6. What are the advantages and disadvantages of managing conflict through mutual problem-solving?

7. What steps should be taken during a meeting with employees in conflict?

8. Why is it not a good strategy to tell employees how to solve their conflict?

9. What are some special issues supervisors have to deal with in resolving supervisor/employee conflict?

10. How can supervisors cope positively with criticism from their boss?

 **Internet Sites**

For more information, visit the following Internet sites. Remember that Internet addresses can change without notice. If the site is no longer there, you can use a search engine to look for additional sites.

Free Management Library: Conflict Management in Groups
www.managementhelp.org/grp_skll/grp_cnfl/grp_cnfl.htm

Conflict Management Skills
www.cnr.berkeley.edu/ucce50/ag-labor/7labor/13.htm

The Institute of Conflict Management
www.conflictmanagement.org/

The International Association for Conflict Management
http://iacm-conflict.org/

The Foundation Coalition: Understanding Conflict and Conflict Management
www.foundationcoalition.org/publications/brochures/conflict.pdf

## Chapter 12 Outline

Myths Concerning Time Management
Time Analysis
    Procedures
    Time Robbers
Time Management Tools
    Daily To-Do Lists
    Weekly Planning Guides
    Calendars
    Software Applications
Delegation
    Barriers to Delegation
    Steps in Effective Delegation

## Competencies

1. Identify common myths of time management. (pp. 323–324)

2. Explain how to analyze time use to create more efficient procedures and reduce time robbers. (pp. 324–327)

3. Describe how to use such time management tools as daily to-do lists, weekly planning guides, calendars, and software applications. (pp. 327–333)

4. Explain how delegation can be an effective time management tool when supervisors use it correctly. (pp. 333–339)

# 12

# Time Management

TIME IS ALWAYS A SCARCE and precious resource for a supervisor. Few supervisors have all the time they would like to get their work done. There are only 24 hours in a day, and no sophisticated management procedures or technological innovations can change that. That limitation makes it critical for supervisors to effectively manage the time they do have available.

While the work you do is important, you must also have adequate time for your family and personal life, professional growth, and, of course, leisure activities and rest. Supervisors who manage their time wisely lead well-rounded lives. Those who cannot may become workaholics, working during time they should spend on other activities. If you can learn to manage your time well, you'll accomplish more personally as well as professionally, and, at the same time, experience less stress and feel better about yourself.

## Myths Concerning Time Management

Some supervisors think that, while the concept of time management is good, they can't manage their time because of the nature of their job. Let's look at some of the excuses supervisors often give for not managing their time:

- *"My job is to deal with people, problems, and emergencies that don't lend themselves to specific schedules."* This is true some of the time. There are days when supervisors are confronted with "a million things to do at the same time" — many of which cannot be planned. However, there are also slower, less-demanding days or times during a busy day when time can be planned. Furthermore, some time-consuming problems and emergencies can be avoided if supervisors use principles of time management.

- *"I can't delegate because no one else can do the work."* Unfortunately, this observation is often true. A primary reason is that the supervisor has not taken the time to train and develop employees so they can take on additional responsibilities. Supervisors who believe this time management myth are actually saying that they have not given priority to helping their employees grow on the job.

- *"Time management doesn't work for big projects."* It takes months to plan a budget or to make arrangements for significant events. However, most time-consuming projects can be broken down into small, manageable parts that can be worked on over a period of days. Some supervisors allocate a specific time period each day to work on long-term projects.

- *"I don't need a formal schedule to manage my time."* This may be true for a few supervisors. But most supervisors with many things to do are not able to do and remember everything without some type of schedule or, at least, notes.

- *"Frequent interruptions make time management impossible."* If you have tried to practice time management principles before and have been thrown off schedule by unplanned interruptions, you may believe this myth. There are many practical ways to manage interruptions.

- *"I don't have time to plan a schedule."* It should be obvious that the supervisor who believes this myth really needs to learn how to plan and use a time schedule.

## Time Analysis

### Procedures

The first step in learning how to manage time is analyzing how you spend it now. **Time analysis** is the process of determining how one currently spends time and then reviewing the results of the analysis to discuss patterns. The first step is to use a **daily time log**. Choose a day and record your activities at half hour intervals. Be honest—no one but you will see the log. If an employee or visitor stopped by and the two of you chatted about non-work-related subjects, write that down. Make explanatory notes on each activity. For example, if a task took longer than usual, write down the reason(s). Begin your activity log at the start of your work day. If you begin at 5 A.M. (or P.M.) find the time on the Daily Time Log in Exhibit 1 and begin recording your activities. Your activities will "wrap" from the bottom of the log to the top of the record. Conversely, if you begin your shift at 7:30 P.M. (or A.M.) the list will be a sequential one.

At the end of the shift, note whether it was typical, busier than usual, or less busy. Think about the time you spent on each major activity and make any important comments at the bottom of the daily log. Use the back of the sheet if necessary.

For best results, you should record your activities each day during a typical week. At the end of the week, analyze the information you gathered. Did any patterns or tendencies emerge? Were there times when you were not productive? Are you delegating enough? Who, or what, accounted for your interruptions, and how can you control or eliminate these interruptions?

Other questions you may ask include:

- Which part of each day was most productive? Least productive? Why?

- What percentage of your time was spent on productive activities? Are you surprised?

- Did you work on tasks you enjoy at the expense of higher-priority tasks? How often?

- Did you expect to be working on this task at this time during the shift?

**Exhibit 1  Sample Daily Time Log**

**Daily Time Log**

Day of Week: ___ M ___ T ___ W ___ T ___ F ___ S ___ S        Date: _____

**Activity (Check √)**

| Time | Planning | Supervisory | Physical Work Tasks | Interacting with Guests | Completing Projects | Other | Comments |
|------|----------|-------------|---------------------|--------------------------|---------------------|-------|----------|
| 7:00 | | | | | | | |
| 7:30 | | | | | | | |
| 8:00 | | | | | | | |
| 8:30 | | | | | | | |
| 9:00 | | | | | | | |
| 9:30 | | | | | | | |
| 10:00 | | | | | | | |
| 10:30 | | | | | | | |
| 11:00 | | | | | | | |
| 11:30 | | | | | | | |
| 12:00 | | | | | | | |
| 12:30 | | | | | | | |
| 1:00 | | | | | | | |
| 1:30 | | | | | | | |
| 2:00 | | | | | | | |
| 2:30 | | | | | | | |
| 3:00 | | | | | | | |
| 3:30 | | | | | | | |
| 4:00 | | | | | | | |
| 4:30 | | | | | | | |
| 5:00 | | | | | | | |
| 5:30 | | | | | | | |
| 6:00 | | | | | | | |
| 6:30 | | | | | | | |
| 7:00 | | | | | | | |

Was this shift: _____ Typical?
_____ More busy than usual?
_____ Less busy than usual?

Additional comments: _____
_____
_____

- Are there any tasks you consistently avoided?

- How many of your activities were inappropriate or otherwise did not contribute to achieving one of your objectives?

- Where are your best opportunities for increasing your efficiency?

- Did you basically keep "on schedule" during the shift? If not, what happened? What, if anything, could be done to reduce the possibility that this problem could reoccur?

Again, be honest when you analyze your daily time logs. Only you will know the results. You can't solve your time problems until you identify them.

## Time Robbers

Chances are that you may have discovered several **time robbers** as you created and analyzed your daily time log. A time robber is something that requires time but does not contribute to reaching your objectives. Time robbers can be divided into two categories: those you create, and those that others create. Obviously, you have the most control over the time robbers you create yourself. Most supervisors have a long list of self-created time robbers, including:

- Procrastination ("putting things off")

- Attempting too much

- Never saying "No"

- Disorganized work station areas (including office and computer files)

- Lack of planning

- Personal errors that require re-work

- No objectives or those that are not clearly defined

- No priorities

- Spending personal time on the job

- Unrealistic time estimates

- Spending too much time on enjoyable tasks

- Making telephone calls and sending text messages. Note that many hospitality operations have policies about employee cell phone use on the job.

Time robbers that others create include interruptions, meetings, requests for help, crises, mistakes by others, unclear directions, lack of information, waiting for others (employees, your boss, and meeting attendees, for example), and unimportant e-mails. Supervisors have a harder time controlling or eliminating these time robbers, but there are strategies that can help. Supervisors often cite interruptions as the time robber over which they have the least control.

Interruptions include telephone calls, unexpected visitors, unscheduled meetings, emergencies, and even self-imposed unplanned activities. When you analyzed your daily time logs and thought about your daily activities, you probably were not surprised to learn that much of your time is spent on interruptions, many of which appear to be unavoidable. In fact, some interruptions are very important. Wise supervisors do not try to avoid interruptions, but, rather, try to more effectively manage them.

Before you can start managing interruptions you must first categorize them as high-priority or low-priority interruptions. An example of a high-priority interruption is an unscheduled meeting with your boss or needing to interact with a guest. With a high-priority interruption, you should usually stop what you're doing and attend to it.

Many interruptions such as phone calls, questions from employees, and other supervisors stopping to chat can be considered low priority. Another common interruption occurs when supervisors think all e-mails must be answered immediately. A better approach would be to, when possible, set aside two or three hours each shift to take care of important e-mails. One way to manage low-priority interruptions is to set aside a block of time each day that is most convenient for you to deal with them and postpone them until then. If your employees tend to drop by many times a day, perhaps one short meeting can be an acceptable substitute. Conversely, if they ask a question while you are in their work area, a quick to-the-point coaching interaction will likely be sufficient. You can let other drop-in visitors know that you have set aside a time of day for them to stop by—1:00 P.M. to 1:30 P.M., for example. Other times, you can say things like, "I'm sorry, I have a deadline I'm trying to meet. Can I e-mail or call you?" or "Can we talk about this some other time?"

Shifting all or at least most low-priority interruptions to a specific time that's convenient can often free a lot of your time and lower your frustration level.

## Time Management Tools

Time management tools include **daily to-do lists**, **weekly planning guides**, and calendars. Using them may seem awkward at first. With practice, however, it gets easier and you'll find shortcuts that work for you. You'll discover that planning your time can help you avoid crises. You'll be able to get the most important things done first and still have time for other activities that are important to you and your organization.

### Daily To-Do Lists

Many supervisors find to-do lists valuable for keeping track of jobs and details that they might otherwise forget. You can use pocket-size notebooks, legal pads, pre-printed forms, or computer-based files. There is no set way to keep a to-do list; you should use the format with which you're most comfortable. The sample to-do list shown in Exhibit 2 can be duplicated for use in a notebook, replicated in another size, or reproduced as a computerized version.

A to-do list allows you to note tasks to be done each day, their priority, and who can assist. You can also indicate (with a check mark) whether each activity has been completed. The sample format in Exhibit 2 includes an area to record future

**Exhibit 2   Sample Daily To-Do-List**

| Date: _____ | | | | |
|---|---|---|---|---|
| **Business Tasks** | **Priority #** | **Help From (Name)** | **Completed** | |
| | | | Yes | No |
| | | | | |
| | | | | |
| | | | | |
| | | | | |
| | | | | |
| | | | | |
| | | | | |
| Notes:  Future Tasks | | | | |
| Other notes: | | | | |

tasks that may be entered on the next (or another) day's to-do list, and other information to best help keep you organized.

Some supervisors develop to-do lists at the beginning of the day, while others do so at the end of the day (for the next day). Some do this planning on their own time. You'll regain the time it takes to develop a to-do list (probably 5 to 10 minutes) and then some, as you make efficient use of time throughout the day because you're better organized.

When you develop your to-do list each day, put down all the tasks you can think of. Don't worry about which tasks are most important. When the list is complete, look it over and decide what to do first, second, third, etc. Consider deadlines, work flow, number of employees, special projects, and other variables. Cross off items that do not have to be done that day.

Avoid the mistake of writing a list so long that you get discouraged before you begin. It takes practice to write a realistic list that includes only those items that truly must be done that day. Another mistake is to be too general. Instead of a vague statement like "Get organized," write "Properly file all the papers on my desk."

After you have written a to-do list and have assigned priorities, ask yourself, "What do I have to do myself, and what can I delegate?" Write the names of the people who will do the jobs tasks that can be delegated.

If you haven't used a to-do list in the past, it may take a while to get comfortable with making one out and scheduling your day. Don't give up! Supervisors have many demands on their time. Your boss and other people often assign new tasks, which might cause you to rearrange your priorities. Don't fight it—rearranging priorities is part of your job. Your to-do list helps you stay flexible so you can rearrange your priorities without forgetting about your own plans. Once you've completed the newly assigned tasks, you can return to your list and pick up where you left off. You'll be better organized, you'll get more done, and you'll feel more in control.

**Sticking with Priorities.** It's one thing to develop a to-do list; it's another to follow it. When it's time to do the work, do the high-priority items first. What if your most important task will likely take all day? Then you must make a decision: Can I afford to let everything else go today to complete this task, or can I divide this big project into smaller pieces that can be done over several days? If you are able to separate the project into smaller parts, establish each part's priority and include only the most important parts in your to-do list.

It may be simple to say that you'll do the most important jobs first, but sometimes it can be hard to actually do. You can come up with lots of excuses for not sticking with your priorities. Supervisors can feel overwhelmed by all the activities, tasks, and deadlines they face. Yet it's precisely at the point that you feel overwhelmed that you must set and follow priorities to stay in control and effectively supervise.

You must determine priorities for your employees as well as yourself. One important responsibility is to create a smooth work flow for your staff. If you continually pull your employees from one project to the next to meet last-minute deadlines, you may meet the deadlines—for a while, anyway—but you may also create frustration and resentment that will be counterproductive over the long run.

Chances are greater that you can avoid reshuffling your priorities and pulling employees from project to project if you meet with your boss occasionally to outline the work priorities as you see them and explain what you've done so far. Point out significant obstacles or problems. Then ask questions. "Do you have any advice on how to solve this problem?" or "Given this situation, which project should be done first?" are questions that can save you lots of time. If you have fully explained the situation and all the steps you've taken so far, your boss will be able to help you with problems and share ideas with you. As this occurs, it is more likely that you and your boss will agree about your priorities and your to-do list will be more effective.

If you consistently have trouble setting priorities or getting things done, ask your boss to review your responsibilities. An informal discussion may be all that's necessary. However, sometimes it pays to go over your job description with your boss, especially if your organization's job descriptions are out-of-date. You may find that your boss's ideas about your job responsibilities are different from your ideas. Resolving any such differences or misunderstandings can eliminate a lot of problems and inefficiencies.

Some supervisors save time by doing similar tasks in batches. For example, they might try to complete all reports, or return all telephone calls and/or e-mails received during a specific time period, at the same time. If a supervisor plans to have a talk with someone, he or she might make notes of discussion topics ahead of time (especially in the case of a discussion with someone who is not at the job site) so all the points can be covered in a single conversation.

## Weekly Planning Guides

In addition to daily to-do lists, weekly planning guides can help you manage your time. You can use these guides to help you allocate time for the most important activities, projects, and people you must attend to during the week. An example of a weekly planning guide is shown in Exhibit 3. Modify this form to meet your specific needs, or create your own guide.

Set up a specific time each week to fill out your weekly planning guide. It should take only a few minutes. As the week progresses, you'll probably have to update the guide. You may need to shift priorities, add new tasks, and reschedule activities. Still, using the guide will help you keep on track.

**Exhibit 3   Sample Weekly Planning Guide**

| WEEKLY PLANNING GUIDE | | | | Week of: _____ | | |
|---|---|---|---|---|---|---|
| **Priorities** | | | | **Schedule** | | |
| Day/Date | Activities | Projects | People | Morning | Afternoon | Evening |
| Monday_____ | Inspect Kitchen | Work on Special Function | Meet with F&B Director | 6:00 | 12:00 | 6:00 Plan Special Function |
| | | | | 7:00 | 1:00 | 7:00 |
| | | | Meet with Ron—employee review | 8:00 To-do list | 2:00 Meeting—F&B Director | 8:00 |
| | | | | 9:00 Inspect kitchen | 3:00 | 9:00 |
| | | | | 10:00 Meeting with Ron | 4:00 | 10:00 |
| | | | | 11:00 | 5:00 | 11:00 |
| Tuesday_____ | Safety Committee Meeting | Complete work on Special Function | George—Sales Rep. | 6:00 | 12:00 | 6:00 |
| | | | | 7:00 | 1:00 | 7:00 |
| | | | | 8:00 To-do list | 2:00 George | 8:00 |
| | | | | 9:00 | 3:00 | 9:00 |
| | | | | 10:00 | 4:00 | 10:00 |

## Calendars

Many supervisors use a calendar to mark important dates, meeting times, and activities throughout the current month and year. Calendars can help remind you about long-term commitments. You should look at the calendar each day before you make out your to-do list. Inform your employees of upcoming deadlines affecting them as soon as possible.

## Software Applications

Many off-the-shelf and commonly used software programs have basic time management tools built into them. Increasingly, hospitality supervisors are using computerized time management software systems that have the same basic objectives as the manual systems previously discussed; that is, to help users increase productivity and use time more effectively. Exhibit 4 presents a sample screen used to enter a new task into a supervisor's electronic time management system. When entering a task, you input basic information such as:

- Subject
- Due date
- Status
- Priority

**Exhibit 4    Electronic Tools—Recording a Task**

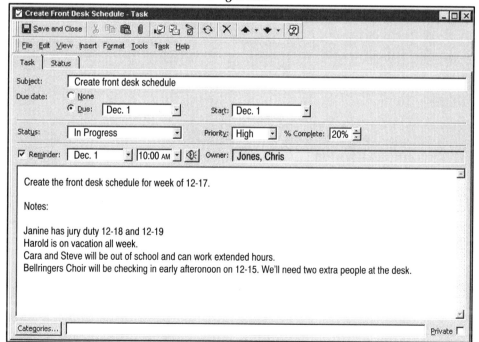

You can also post the status of the task in terms of categories such as:

- Not started
- In progress
- Completed
- Waiting on someone else
- Deferred

The priority of a task can be set as (or changed to) high, low, or normal. A useful feature enables you to set (in minutes, hours, or days) an automatic display to prompt a "reminder" screen in relation to some aspect of the task's completion. As the supervisor completes the task, the percentage of completion can be input as well. Identifying the "owner" of the task is a helpful feature for supervisors as they delegate work to members of their staff. Applications generally provide convenient ways for users to track their own tasks as well as those tasks that are assigned to others.

Time management software programs generally offer calendar systems for scheduling tasks, appointments, meetings, and events. Exhibit 5 presents a sample screen used to enter a new appointment into a supervisor's electronic time management system. When entering an appointment, you input basic information:

**Exhibit 5    Electronic Tools—Recording an Appointment**

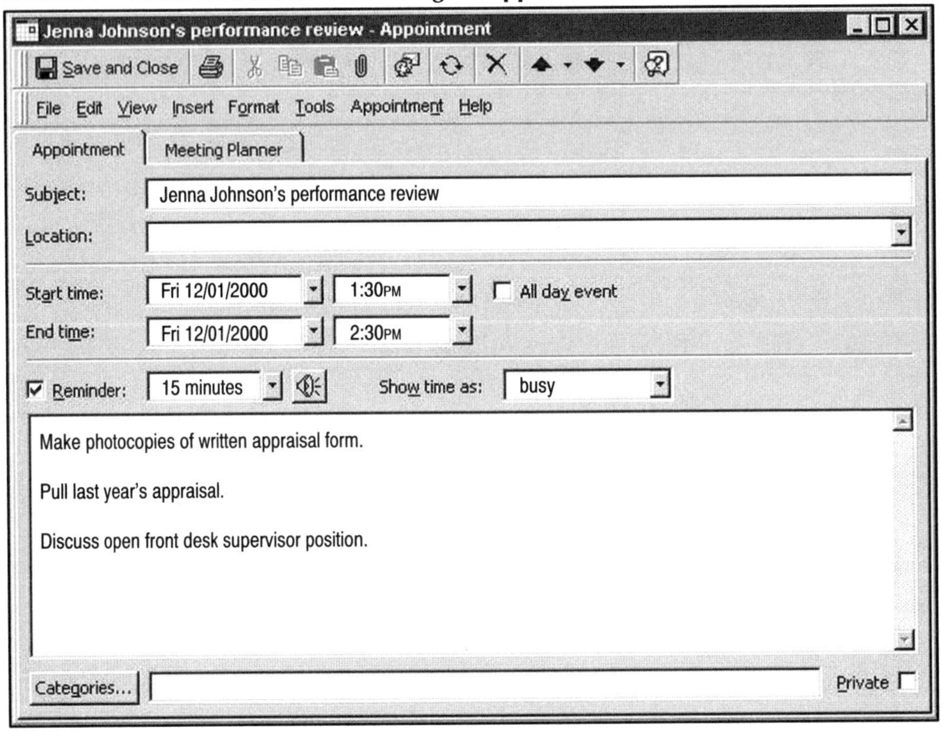

---

## Time Management Software Resources

Want to learn more about computerized time management software? Each of the following websites has some type of tutorial that can provide a simple overview of how you can team up with technology to manage your time.

- Effexis Software
  www.effexis.com

- Taskline: Task Scheduler for Microsoft Outlook
  www.taskline.com

- RescueTime
  www.rescuetime.com

---

- Subject
- Location
- Start time
- End time

A useful feature enables you to set (in minutes, hours, or days before the appointment) an automatic display to prompt a "reminder" screen indicating the appointment's approaching time. Also, short or extensive notes can be input in the box provided, enabling you to truly "remind" yourself of the purpose and function of the appointment. Appointments that regularly occur can be blocked into the calendar on the appropriate days for several weeks, months, or even years into the future.

Once data are entered into the application, you can display or print daily, weekly, or monthly calendar plans showing tasks as well as appointments. Exhibit 6 presents a sample weekly calendar plan that breaks out the tasks and appointments for a particular day.

# Delegation

**Delegation** involves assigning tasks to your employees for which you are still accountable. The concept is very much in line with a basic definition of management: "Getting work done through other people." However, it is fundamentally different from simply assigning work. Assigning work is asking an employee to do a specific task that is part of the employee's job. Delegation means first looking at what tasks you perform that can be delegated to an employee, and then seeing how you can help that employee successfully complete the delegated task. While you can delegate the **authority** (power) to complete the task, you cannot delegate **accountability** for accomplishing the task. You are still obligated to see that whatever you delegate is accomplished. This is why successful delegation depends so much on your willingness and ability to follow up and to help the employee succeed.

Exhibit 6   Sample Weekly Calendar Plan

**12/1/20XX — Friday**

|  |  |
|---|---|
| 7 AM | |
| 8 00 | Daily occupancy meeting |
| 9 00 | |
| 10 00 | Shift meeting |
| 11 00 | |
| 12 PM | |
| 1 00 | Jenna Johnson performance review |
| 2 00 | |
| 3 00 | |
| 4 00 | |
| 5 00 | |
| 6 00 | |

**TaskPad**

- ☐ Create front desk schedule
- ☐ Conduct Jenna Johnson's performance review
- ☐ Review front office activity report
- ☐ Write weekly revenue management goal
- ☐ Respond to complaint letter from Mr. Clark
- ☐ Train Cindy in lost and found procedures
- ☐ Talk to staff members about effectiveness of current registration cards

**11/27 - 12/3**

| 11/27 | 11/30 |
|---|---|
| Daily occupancy meeting | Daily occupancy meeting |
| Front desk attendant interviews | Quality team problem-solving session |

| 11/28 | 12/1 |
|---|---|
| Daily occupancy meeting | Daily occupancy meeting |
| Revenue management meeting | Shift meeting |
| Firefighter's convention checks in | Jenna Johnson performance review |

| 11/29 | 12/2 |
|---|---|
| Daily occupancy meeting | Firefighter's convention checks out. |
| Group sales meeting | |
| Lunch banquet for sales staff | |

| 11/29 | 12/3 |
|---|---|
| | |

Why is delegation important? First, it's one of the best ways you can save time for yourself and your organization. Second, it's important because you can't do everything. This seems obvious, but many supervisors try to do just that, because "these jobs are too important to assign to someone else," "it has to be done right," "I'm the only one who can get this done right and on time," or other reasons. You must remember that a major part of your job is to manage the work of others, not to do the work of others.

Delegation is also important to your staff. If you're willing to delegate, it shows that you trust and respect them. They can take greater pride in their work, because they've been given a decision-making role. This increases their participation, involvement, and commitment. When you delegate, you give your employees the opportunity to develop both personally and professionally.

Are you a good delegator? The quiz shown in Exhibit 7 can help you find out. The more times you answer "yes" to the questions in Exhibit 7, the more you need to learn to delegate.

## Barriers to Delegation

Some supervisors are reluctant to delegate because they do not trust their employees or have confidence in their abilities. Other supervisors shy away from the risk involved. They believe an employee's failure reflects badly on the supervisor and shows that he or she is unable to delegate authority effectively. Still others know that an employee can do a good job, but are reluctant to share the credit with an employee for a job well done. Other reasons that supervisors may be uncomfortable with delegating include:

**Exhibit 7   Are You a Good Delegator?**

1. Do you take work home regularly?
2. Do you work longer hours than your employees or other supervisors?
3. Are you unable to keep on top of priorities?
4. Do you rush to meet deadlines?
5. Are you still handling activities and problems you had before your last promotion?
6. Do you spend time on routine details that others could handle?
7. Do you spend time doing for others what they could be doing themselves?
8. Are you constantly interrupted with questions or requests about ongoing projects or assignments?
9. Do you like to be personally involved with every project?
10. When you return after a vacation or some other absence from the office, is your in-basket too full?
11. Do you want to help some of your subordinates be promoted?

The more times you answer "yes", the more you need to learn to delegate.

- Lack of experience

- Lack of organizational skills

- Insecurity

- Fear of being disliked by employees

- Perfectionism

- Reluctance to spend the time it takes to train employees to perform delegated tasks

- Failure to establish effective control or follow-up procedures

Your staff themselves can present other barriers to delegation. Employees may not want the freedom and authority involved in delegation. They may fear criticism or failure or lack self-confidence. Some might have a concern that they are doing work you should be doing. Others may feel they won't be rewarded for a job well done, and that they will be punished if the job is not done right. Or, in the past, they may have been rewarded for asking their supervisor how to do everything and for strictly following orders.

The reluctance of many employees to be placed in what they perceive to be an uncertain situation is an often-overlooked barrier to delegation. Generally speaking, there are three levels of delegation, and, unless you make it clear on which level an employee is operating, the employee may resist your efforts to delegate. The three levels are:

- *Level 1:* Full authority is given to the employee to take whatever actions are necessary to carry out the assignment, without consulting or reporting to you.

- *Level 2:* Full authority is given to the employee to take whatever actions are necessary to carry out the assignment, but you must be informed of the actions taken.

- *Level 3:* Authority is limited. The employee must present his or her recommendations to you and cannot take action until you make a decision.

If your own boss is sometimes unclear about what level of authority you have when he or she delegates a task to you, you'll have an idea of how uncomfortable your employees may be when you're unclear with them. The best way to delegate is to tell employees up front exactly how much authority they have to carry out the task.

Lastly, many supervisors believe "I can do it better myself," which is perhaps the greatest obstacle to delegation. Most new supervisors have the determination, sense of responsibility, and ability to "get the job done," and that is often why they were promoted to the position. As a new supervisor, you may feel that no one else can do a task like you can, and this leads you to want to do everything yourself. The problem is that every time you complete a task rather than assigning it to an employee and providing any necessary coaching, you're ensuring that you'll have to do the task every time because you haven't taught anyone else how to do it.

Even if you can do a better job, is the quality of your work so much better than your employees' that it's better for the organization that you do the work rather than spend the time planning, delegating, supervising, coaching, and training? These are tasks your employees can't do, and that you must do. Supervisors who trust their employees and take the time to train and build a good staff typically outperform and outlast those supervisors who burn themselves out trying to do it all.

## Steps in Effective Delegation

There are many ways to delegate effectively. Exhibit 8 presents questions for supervisors to answer before delegating tasks to employees. Each supervisor develops his or her own particular style. However, there are general steps that supervisors should take when delegating work to others.

**Think the Project Through.** Carefully think about the project before you assign it to an employee. What materials or other resources are needed? What are the

**Exhibit 8  Questions to Answer Before Delegating Tasks**

- Which tasks can be done better at a lower level? What is the lowest level that can handle the task?
- Which tasks are supervisory tasks that cannot be delegated? (For example, taking disciplinary action and handling confidential issues.)
- Are there any problems that stand in the way of delegating this task?
- Is there time to delegate this task?
- Will my boss have a problem if I delegate this task?
- What is the risk if the employee fails in the delegated task? Is the risk acceptable?
- What is the complexity of the task? Can the task be taught in a reasonable amount of time?
- Who is best suited to take on the task?
- Is there someone who can do it better than I can?
- Will the individual be overloaded if he or she takes on this additional responsibility? If so, are there parts of his or her work that could be delegated to others?
- Does the individual want this additional responsibility?
- Will performing this task help the individual grow and develop?
- Is it better to split the task up into several sub-tasks, and assign each part to a different employee (reducing the load and giving each a chance to show what he or she can do)?
- What should be the employee's authority level for the delegated task?
- What is a successful performance of the task? How will I, and the employee, know that the delegated task has been done well?
- What will a specific training plan look like for this employee on this task?
- Who should I inform that this task is going to be delegated?

results you want? What options can you give the employee? The more alternatives you provide, the more the employee acquires a sense of responsibility and ownership of the task and its solution.

**Set a Deadline.** If it's up to you to set a deadline for the project, be realistic. Don't set a target date that can't possibly be met just to impress your boss. (The boss won't be impressed when you miss it.) Develop a reputation for getting things done on time, but don't pad your schedules with extra time so that you always meet your deadlines. You'll be building wasted time into the schedules and, sooner or later, your boss will catch on. If you consistently establish realistic deadlines and then meet most of them, your boss will probably be willing to negotiate when a job takes more time than you allotted for it.

Many supervisors ask the employee who is performing the work to help set the deadline for its completion. Including the employee in this decision-making process is recommended whenever possible.

If your boss sets the deadline, you must do everything you can to meet it. If possible, negotiate with your boss if you feel you haven't been given reasonable time or other resources to do the project. Keep in mind, however, that your boss may have had the deadline handed down from higher-level managers.

**Choose an Employee.** Consider your employees' abilities and workloads, jobs that are coming up in the near future, the importance of the project, and other variables before choosing an employee. Make sure the employee you have in mind has the time and skills to get the job done.

**Meet with the Employee.** Fully explain the project and its importance to the employee. This meeting should address:

- What needs to be done
- Why it needs to be done
- How the delegated task fits into the overall objectives of the department
- Suggestions as to how the task can be completed
- Whom the employee should contact to complete the task
- Expected results
- Priority of this task relative to other tasks in the employee's job
- When to start on the task, and by what date it should be finished
- What intermediate steps and follow-up (check-up) dates are important
- Any other needed information—especially things that you know that are not in writing

Occasionally you may need to adjust the deadline because of your discussion with the employee. As mentioned previously, you might not even establish a deadline until you ask the employee to help set it. Tell the employee what level of authority he or she has to get the job done. Point out any possible obstacles you foresee, and suggest possible ways to overcome them. Encourage the employee to ask questions and listen to his or her ideas on how to approach the task. End the meeting only when both of you agree on how the project should be tackled. Last but not least, express your confidence that the employee can do the job. Also, remind the employee that you are available if questions or problems arise.

**Monitor Progress.** Don't constantly ask about project progress. On the other hand, don't wait until just before the deadline to check progress. Despite your best efforts, sometimes employees misunderstand what is expected of them. See how things are going soon after you've delegated the task to the employee and help him or her correct any start-up problems. Be friendly and helpful, not judgmental. Check on the employee from time to time as the project moves forward.

**Provide Assistance if Necessary.** If an employee gets stuck or goes off in a wrong direction, give him or her just enough help to get going again. Only on the most unusual or difficult task should you provide more help. Don't be condescending or sarcastic, and don't take over the project.

**Praise the Employee.** Throughout the project, be generous with your praise. This will help build the employee's self-confidence. When the project is finished, thank the employee and make sure he or she receives recognition for the work. Nothing is more discouraging to an employee than having a supervisor take all the credit for an accomplishment.

 **Key Terms**

**accountability**—An obligation to complete a task or duty assigned by one's boss; same as responsibility.

**authority**—The power that a manager or employee has to complete a task or assignment.

**daily time log**—A standard form used for keeping track of a supervisor's activities during the day.

**daily to-do lists**—Lists that supervisors can create to help them determine and set priorities for tasks that must be done each day.

**delegation**—The supervisory task of assigning authority to employees to perform tasks or make decisions for which the supervisor is still accountable.

**time analysis**—The process of determining how one currently spends time and then reviewing the results of the analysis to discover patterns that may suggest ways to save time.

**time robbers**—People or activities that require time but do not contribute to reaching your objectives. Time robbers can be divided into two categories: those the supervisor creates and those that others create.

**weekly planning guides**—Guides supervisors use to help them allocate time for the most important activities, projects, and persons they must attend to during the week.

## ? Review Questions

1. What are some myths of time management?
2. What is the first step in learning how to manage your time?
3. Into which two categories do time robbers fall?
4. How can you control interruptions?
5. How can you use to-do lists?
6. Why should you discuss your job description with your boss?
7. How can you use weekly planning guides and calendars?
8. What are advantages to using computerized time management systems?
9. Why is delegation important?
10. What are some barriers to delegation?
11. What are steps in effective delegation?

# Chapter 13 Outline

# Competencies

1. Define change and distinguish external forces of change from internal forces of change. (pp. 343–346)

2. Explain how a model for change can guide supervisors in planning and implementing change. (pp. 346–349)

3. Describe actions that supervisors can take to minimize employee resistance to change. (pp. 350–354)

4. Describe steps supervisors can use when communicating change to employees. (pp. 354–359)

5. Explain why indicators of effective change are essential to the evaluation of the change process. (pp. 359–360)

# 13

# Managing Change

YESTERDAY'S SOLUTIONS may not solve today's problems. In the fast-paced world of hospitality, the needs, wants, and expectations of our guests seem to change almost constantly. Managers develop new procedures to more cost-effectively attain standards. Effective supervisors are challenged by opportunities to address these changes, and, in the process, help the organization to better attain its goals.

Today's solutions may not solve tomorrow's problems. Applying existing procedures to new situations cannot replace the need to be innovative and to think carefully about the future and how it may be quite different from the present. Supervisors who respond positively to the need for change will be recognized as valuable contributors within their organizations and may be considered first when promotional opportunities arise. Conversely, those who resist purposeful change might be viewed as unable to contribute to the continuing growth and success of the company. This may lead management to overlook them when filling positions that require increased responsibility.

**Change** occurs when there is a variation, alteration, or revision in the way things are done. When change occurs, it usually affects an initial area in the organization and a specific group of employees. For example, the addition of a new equipment item, such as a tilting skillet in the kitchen, may have little effect on other areas of the organization. Yet, within the kitchen, cooks may need to change their methods for preparing some menu items, and staff will need to learn how to clean and maintain the new equipment.

Change that, on the surface, seems to affect only one aspect of a single department may in fact affect other departments or the entire organization. For example, a change in laundry processing in the housekeeping department can affect the availability of table linens in the hotel's restaurant. Normally, the greater the amount of change that is planned, the greater the likelihood that other aspects of the organization will be affected. Consider the implications of change when a new marketing strategy is implemented at a hotel. Top-level executives may decide to attract a new market segment, or to increase business from a particular market segment, such as from corporate travelers. In this instance, it is very likely that the change in marketing strategy will create the need for change in virtually every department within the hotel. Appropriate managers and supervisors may need to adjust performance and productivity standards, upgrade amenities, provide express check-in and check-out service, consider how to manage small meetings, and address many other concerns.

This chapter begins by identifying the types of forces that create change within the hospitality work environment. Next, a model for analyzing the process of change is examined. Later sections of the chapter focus on how you, as a supervisor, can be a successful **change agent** and effectively plan, implement, and evaluate changes within the work place.

# The Forces of Stability and Change

In hospitality operations the forces of stability and change operate at the same time. Exhibit 1 reviews some of the pressures that are at work simultaneously to emphasize the need for stability (no change) and to push for change. Every operation needs some form of continuity. To plan effectively, you must be able to assume that some conditions affecting how work is done today will persist in time and affect the way work is done tomorrow. Let's review what Exhibit 1 suggests.

There are many elements of stability within the work environment, such as the physical facility, the available equipment, and the basic needs of the guests. These elements generally do not change quickly. In addition, the relationships established among departments and among employees within departments serve as **stabilizing forces** providing consistency in day-to-day activities. Also, the tendency of staff members at all organizational levels to resist change can serve as a stabilizing force—working to keep things as they are. In opposition to these stabilizing forces are external and internal forces that drive change within an organization.

## External Forces of Change

**External forces of change** arise from changing social, economic, political, legal, and technological conditions. The changing wants and needs of guests form the most important external force affecting hospitality operations. Many of the

**Exhibit 1   Forces of Stability and Change**

changes in guest behavior reflect wider societal changes. For example, a health-conscious public may demand more nutritious meals in restaurants or fitness facilities in hotels. Also, a public concern about drunken drivers and the number of alcohol-related highway deaths may motivate guests to purchase non-alcoholic beverages and to hold those properties that serve alcoholic beverages accountable when accidents occur. Business travelers will usually select hotels with in-room computer services such as high-speed Internet access and wireless connectivity in public and meeting areas.

The shrinking labor market serves as another example of how external social change may drive changes within a hospitality organization. As it becomes more difficult to find new employees, managers and supervisors will need to implement changes to reduce turnover. Political and economical changes, such as an increase in minimum wage, may require managers and supervisors to find more innovative ways to increase productivity to control rising labor costs. Changes in the political and legal climate may also drive change within an operation. For example, an increased focus on workers' rights and an increase in the number of lawsuits brought against employers for wrongful dismissal may require an organization to improve the processes for selecting, hiring, and evaluating employees.

## Internal Forces of Change

**Internal forces of change** are also at work within an organization. These forces are closer to the day-to-day operation of the business and are usually more in the realm of management's control than are external forces. Generally, they cover anything "new" such as a new task, new equipment, a new employee in the department, a new boss, and new policies and procedures. All of these create change that affects your employees and you.

The following sections briefly examine change as it relates to three aspects of hospitality businesses: employees, technology, and organizational structure. They are closely related and a change in one aspect may affect the others.

**Employees and Change.** One of your most important responsibilities as a supervisor is to constantly seek ways to improve employee performance. This often means changing the behavior or **attitudes** of employees. Improving employees' job performance by focusing your efforts on changing their behavior is frequently easier, quicker, and more effective than trying to change their attitudes. Attitudes are difficult to assess; behavior, on the other hand, is observable and measurable.

Supervisors train, coach, and evaluate performance in efforts to change the behavior of individual employees. Team-building activities and group training programs are techniques that supervisors can use to try to change employees' behavior when working with groups. Supervisors can use these same techniques to try to change employee attitudes. However, the process of changing employee attitudes will be difficult at best, even when experienced supervisors apply these techniques.

**Technology and Change.** New technology often creates the need for change within an organization. At times, change is forced upon an organization. Hotels need modern, computerized reservations systems to be competitive. On occasion, the organization itself may desire technological change. For example, a food and beverage department may choose to implement a computerized beverage system for added control in bar areas. Introducing new technology will require changes in the skills employees need to function effectively and, in some cases, may create a need to restructure part of the organization.

**Organizational Structure and Change.** There are many ways by which change can affect the structure of an organization. For example, the owners or top executives of a hospitality business may wish to decentralize operations. Decentralizing would mean establishing smaller, self-contained organizational units with increased decision-making power. As a supervisor, you might welcome such a change because it may offer increased opportunities to motivate employees in smaller work units and enable you to more carefully structure both the work unit and the employees' tasks. Changes in organizational structure also occur when top-level managers revise the chain of command, to increase (or decrease) areas of responsibility for departments or positions. For example, a hotel may move the responsibility for reservations out of the rooms division and into the sales department. Organizational changes such as this may result in revised job descriptions for the affected positions. Also, as new employees enter the organization and assume leadership positions, they are likely to use their influence to initiate changes.

Another structural approach to change focuses on improving the work flow within the organization. This is usually done to increase employee productivity. Think about how changes in the work flow between stewarding, the kitchen, and banquets (service and setup) could improve the management of banquet activities. Given a limited amount of cross-training, tasks could be reassigned based on the volume of business and the number of employees at hand on any given day. For example, tasks currently performed by banquet setup or service employees, such as requisitioning china and silver or preparing table setups (placing water, butter, and other items), could be reassigned to stewards. Tasks usually assigned to kitchen staff, such as transporting meals, could also be reassigned to stewards. Or, tasks currently assigned to stewards, such as setting up and organizing breakdown tables in banquet corridors, could be reassigned to banquet setup crews. Under certain conditions, any of these changes could potentially improve overall productivity by enabling staff already available to assist in the completion of necessary tasks.

# A Model for Change

The model for change that was developed many years ago is still useful today.[1] According to this model, three procedures are necessary for change to occur: first, the existing situation must be *unfrozen;* next, the change agent (the supervisor) must work toward the desired change; then, the revised situation must be *refrozen.* Exhibit 2 diagrams this model for change as it operates under the pressures exerted by the external and internal forces of change just discussed.

While it simplifies the discussion of change to suggest that the process is composed of three distinct, sequential parts, you should remember that change is a continuous process without an obvious beginning or end. Change occurs at more

**Exhibit 2   A Model for Change**

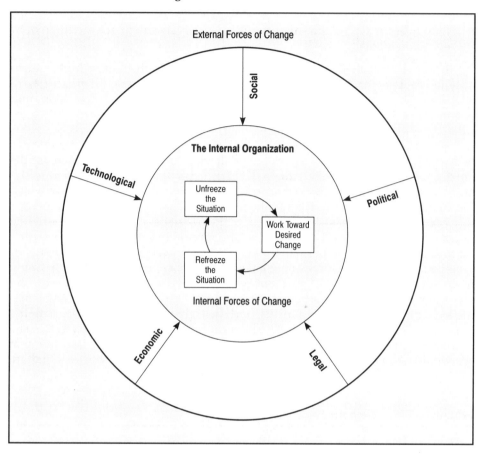

than one point in the organization at the same time. The following sections examine each of the steps within the model for change.

## Unfreeze the Existing Situation

Unfreezing the existing situation applies to those planning change (change agents, such as the supervisor) as well as to those who will ultimately be affected by it. To develop strategies to unfreeze the situation, change planners must analyze the driving and restraining forces at work in the existing situation. For example, consider high turnover within a department. There may be a variety of forces driving the high turnover, such as:

- Employees may not feel comfortable about their jobs because the provided training has been inadequate.

- Wages may not be competitive within the area, motivating employees to seek jobs at other properties.

- Employees may feel that opportunities for advancement are too limited, or even nonexistent.

If left uncontrolled, these driving forces could result in even higher turnover. On the other hand, restraining forces that could be keeping the existing turnover from becoming even higher might include pleasant working conditions and environment, fair management practices, reliable equipment, and recognition for work done well.

By unfreezing the existing situation, the supervisor can develop strategies that will decrease the impact of any single driving force, or that will increase the impact of any single stabilizing force. The key in planning for change is to recognize that any existing situation is the result of a variety of forces, any one of which can be modified to unfreeze the situation.

**Force field analysis** can be used to identify the driving forces and the restraining forces in any situation. The situation may involve change affecting the entire organization, a particular department, or even a single individual. For a simple example of how force field analysis works, suppose that Chris, a dining room supervisor, wants to figure out why she is reluctant to speak up during management team meetings. She draws a large "T" on a sheet of paper, and labels the left side "plus," or driving forces, and the right side "minus," or restraining forces (See Exhibit 3). Above the "T" she writes the situation or problem that she is analyzing, and above this she writes the ideal or solution to the problem that she would like to achieve. Under "driving forces," she lists those forces that are

**Exhibit 3   Force Field Analysis**

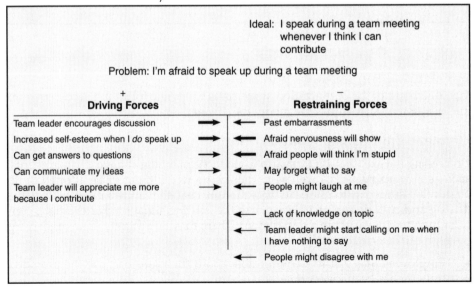

holding her back from reaching the ideal or solution. The thickness of the arrows indicates the strength of the forces she lists; a thick arrow indicates a strong force, while a thin arrow indicates a weaker force. As you can see from Exhibit 3, at present the restraining forces are stronger than the driving forces. Therefore, Chris is not likely to voluntarily contribute ideas or comments during management team meetings until she can strengthen the driving forces and/or weaken the restraining forces.

Change agents must consider ways to unfreeze the situation for those who will ultimately be affected by the change. The first step in this process should be to generate a need for change in the minds of affected staff members. As the change agent, you must show employees why *they* should be dissatisfied with the current situation. A need for change might be developed by explaining reasons for the change, by increasing pressure for change (with rewards or punishments), or by taking action to reduce employee resistance to change. A later section in this chapter examines how supervisors can prepare themselves as change agents by analyzing change from the perspective of employees affected by a proposed change. By anticipating the advantages and disadvantages of change, a supervisor can develop strategies to unfreeze the situation for employees and lead them toward the desired change in behavior.

## Work Toward Desired Change

The process of working toward the desired change generally requires that you attempt to modify employee behavior, analyze affected policies, and train staff in improved job methods and operating techniques. These tasks are easier when you have the respect of your employees. Also, it is better to work first with those employees who are highly respected by their peers or who are informal group leaders in the department.

If employees are placed in job situations in which they confront new problems (or old problems that must be resolved with new methods), the process of change might, by necessity, be easier. For example, an employee who does not want to use a new piece of equipment will likely have to use it when the older equipment is no longer available. In this instance, the employee has only two options—continue to "fight" the equipment or adapt by learning how, and in what way, to use it.

## Refreeze the Situation

After the desired change is implemented, stabilizing forces tend to create a new status quo. This is called the refreezing process. New relationships are established, and the new behavior, procedures, and policies become part of the day-to-day activities. However, over time the new job situation (which continues to be influenced by the organizational structure, existing work procedures, and currently employed staff members) will be affected by external and internal forces that may initiate further changes in the job situation. The change process will evolve once again. This process will yield a revised job situation, which will itself, over time, be influenced by external and internal forces stimulating change. In this respect, then, the process of change is cyclical and ongoing.

# Overcoming Resistance to Change

Change is often difficult to implement because people who feel comfortable with what they are doing typically want to maintain established routines. Employees are no exception; most have a natural tendency to resist changes required by revised work procedures. As a supervisor, you must understand why employees might resist specific changes so that you can develop strategies to overcome their resistance. Exhibit 4 reviews factors and implications that help supervisors to determine how employees may respond to change.

## Why Employees Resist Change

Some employees may resist change simply because it is inconvenient to learn new procedures and assume extra duties. They might fear that they are unable to learn "the new ways" to do the work. An effective strategy in this case is to conduct appropriate training sessions. At the very least, you should explain new procedures and other work requirements to employees. In addition, if the training is conducted with informational and persuasive techniques designed to reduce **resistance to change**, the training sessions can be even more valuable.

Other employees respond to change with feelings of uncertainty and anxiety. They may feel threatened. These fears can create an emotional resistance to change. Some employees may even feel anxious about "good news," such as promotions or transfers. An effective strategy for these situations is to communicate with employees and explain the "who, what, where, when, and why" behind the proposed change. Employees may just be resisting change because they fear the unknown. You can reduce or eliminate this fear simply by providing appropriate information to those both directly and indirectly involved with the change.

Change can disrupt professional and personal relationships. Employees relate with other staff members and work groups on the job; they know about

## Exhibit 4   Employee Responses to Change

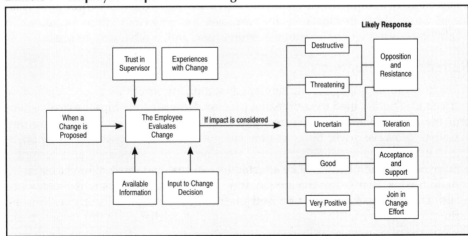

status, leaders and followers, task specialists, and other aspects of their current work groups. As changes occur on the job, patterns of personal and professional relationships may be disrupted. These and related social dimensions of change will influence the employees' ability to accept change. In this type of situation, persuasive leadership techniques may be helpful. During an individual counseling session you may discover the reasons for an employee's resistance. Then, you can identify the problems with the employee's reasoning, supply the proper information, and explain how the change will be beneficial to him or her. Using this approach with informal group leaders might make them "salespersons" for the proposed change.

Before discussing other strategies you can use to overcome resistance to change, it is important to stress some positive aspects of the employee tendency to resist change. As a supervisor, you should look for ways in which employees' resistance to change can work for you, not against you.

Earlier, this chapter identified resistance to change as a stabilizing force within an organization. Almost everyone within an organization will resist change when reasons for the change are not clearly explained. Without an accompanying explanation, a proposed change often seems pointless, as merely "change for the sake of change." Because employee resistance to change creates the need for an explanation, you can identify poorly thought-out changes early and thus avoid trouble. Also, impulsive decisions made by those in higher positions of authority can be evaluated and revised.

Your role as a supervisor is to anticipate the types of resistance employees may have and prepare reasonable explanations for the proposed change. By anticipating employee resistance, you may be able to identify specific areas in which change could create problems, and then you can take corrective action before serious problems arise. This will help employee resistance to change work for, not against, you, because as you justify a proposed change you refine any issues that you may have overlooked.

## The Employees' View

Anticipating resistance to change begins with knowing your employees and using this knowledge to modify your leadership styles to meet the needs of the situation. Try to look at the situation from the employees' perspective. How would you feel if you were an employee? What could make you feel differently about the need for change?

For example, in some instances, change can have an economic impact on employees. Employees may be greatly concerned about their job security regardless of whether this is a real threat. You must anticipate the economic implications of proposed changes and inform employees about them. If employees realize there are no economic disadvantages to the change and, in fact, there are advantages, they will be more receptive to it. You should practice thinking about change—and how to discuss it—from the employees' perspective. This will help identify major issues to discuss and resolve with employees. The need to explain, defend, and justify reasons for changes—from the employees' perspective when possible—is critical to the process of successfully planning and implementing change.

There are often major differences between how employees might benefit from a change and how a department or organization benefits from that same change. Exhibit 5 suggests some of these differences. If employees see positive effects for themselves in job-related changes, their reactions are more likely to be supportive. Trouble occurs when employees perceive potentially negative consequences for themselves, even if the department or organization benefits. Changes that affect job security (like downsizing and major reorganization) have the most serious effects in terms of affecting morale and stress.

Just as a salesperson translates features of the property into benefits for guests, you may need to "sell" change by translating aspects of the change into concrete benefits for employees. And, just as a salesperson overcomes objections that clients

**Exhibit 5    Perspectives on Change**

---

Type of Change: Change in Leadership

    Departmental/Organizational Benefits—Increased effectiveness

        Employee Benefits—Relief

        Employee Concerns—Fear of the unknown

Type of Change: Merger

    Departmental/Organizational Benefits—Increased financial strength

        Employee Benefits—Better job security

        Employee Concerns—More competition for promotions

Type of Change: Major Reorganization

    Departmental/Organizational Benefits—Less duplication of tasks

        Employee Benefits—Job will be easier to do

        Employee Concerns—Loss of control; loss of job

Type of Change: Employee Empowerment

    Departmental/Organizational Benefits—Higher quality service

        Employee Benefits—More authority and responsibility

        Employee Concerns—Fear of making a mistake

Type of Change: Downsizing

    Departmental/Organizational Benefits—Increased profit

        Employee Benefits—Better communication

        Employee Concerns—Fear of job loss

Type of Change: Technology Enhancements

    Departmental/Organizational Benefits—Greater cost efficiency

        Employee Benefits—Challenge of new skills

        Employee Concerns—Fear of learning new skills

Type of Change: Job Rotation

    Departmental/Organizational Benefits—More flexible work force

        Employee Benefits—Opportunity for growth

        Employee Concerns—"I do my work, then I do yours?"

---

may raise, you need to be able to overcome employee resistance to change by acknowledging and addressing fears or concerns they have about the change.

Employees often have emotional responses to change. Fear, anxiety, or worry can arise from apprehension about the unknown. Employees are not certain about what will happen, or whether they will be able to handle it. A known situation in the present generally feels more comfortable than an uncertain future. Impending change may cause employees to feel less in control; this feeling can often be a major source of resistance. An organizational change resulting from an altered value system can cause conflict within employees who have difficulty identifying with the new values. For example, a person who has worked for a small, independent hotel or restaurant may feel that fundamental values are at risk if the operation becomes affiliated with a major chain.

To help minimize employee resistance to change, you can:

- Stress how the change is in line with the organization's values, vision, and mission.

- Maintain open communication relating to the change.

- Time the introduction of the change appropriately.

- Involve the employees in the change process.

- Build and maintain a high level of trust with your employees.

- Help employees with issues that arise during the change process.

When communication about the change is inadequate, the grapevine or rumor mill takes over and can quickly confuse and distort what is really happening. Your credibility as a supervisor can be undermined and/or diminished if your employees feel they're the last to know what's going on. In contrast, employees will usually support a change that they help to plan.

A change can be introduced too quickly, resulting in chaos, or too slowly, resulting in a buildup of anxiety. For example, if plans for consolidating departments or functions are announced without specifics and implementation is weeks away, employees may become apprehensive. When people know that change is coming, the tension and uncertainty of waiting can be paralyzing. Therefore, if sweeping change is planned, it is usually better to make the changes all at once rather than piecemeal.

It is important for individual employees to become involved in the change process. Involvement can begin when changes are first considered because employees may have ideas about alternatives. It continues to the actual decision-making process (employee input is important) and concludes with the employee's involvement in the trial, implementation, modification, and evaluation processes. Their level of involvement is often determined by the kind of change being implemented. However, it's up to you to involve your employees whenever possible.

Make employees aware of a situation or problem and give them an opportunity to generate ideas for change. To the extent that you can use employee input to develop and select alternatives, your work in the implementation phase will be easier since resistance to change is likely to be lower. Employees who are involved in the decision-making process leading to change will more likely accept change than those who are "kept in the dark." Some employees (probably not all) will want to become involved in the process. To the extent possible, these employees should become partners with you as you implement changes.

Employees who do not trust or respect their supervisors are likely to resist change. Past experiences influence reactions to present or future expectations. Perhaps changes have not been effective in the past: "Here comes another change; I wonder how long it will last" may be a common thought. If there have been problems with changes before—ideas did not work out, unexpected results occurred, or employees were hurt by changes in unexpected ways—it will be difficult to convince employees that new changes will be beneficial. Clearly, the supervisor who emphasizes one thing today and another thing tomorrow is likely to be confronted with employees who will resist change.

Perhaps the most important factor in implementing change successfully is for you to develop and maintain an atmosphere of trust and respect in all of your interactions with employees. Employees are more likely to respond favorably to changes when they trust you; that is, when they agree with your stated reasons for the change and when they concur with your assessment of the benefits they will gain from the change. You cannot, however, develop an atmosphere of trust simply to implement change. A history of honesty, fairness, and concern for employees influences the development of a positive attitude toward you; as this occurs, the relationship will carry over in the acceptance of change.

## The Supervisor as Change Agent

Supervisors serve as change agents when they assume responsibility for helping to create changes in an employee's behavior or within the organization itself. Serving as a change agent is an integral part of a supervisor's job. You must constantly be alert to situations and problems, remain open to new ideas, and support change efforts spearheaded by higher management levels within the organization. Exhibit 6 reviews helpful procedures for supervisors to follow when implementing change.

In most situations, there are three options for communicating change to employees:

- Tell the work group as a whole.

- Meet with each employee individually.

- Meet with informal leaders first.

A supervisor's choice often depends on the particular circumstances of the change situation—including the timing of the change, who will be affected by it, and the level of trust that has been established with the employees affected by the change. In most cases, it is better to hold the initial discussion about a change at a meeting with the entire work group. This prevents information from leaking out before you've had a chance to talk with each employee individually. If specific employees will be affected differently, you may follow the group meeting with individual discussions. If only a few employees will be significantly affected by a change, a meeting with the entire group would be inappropriate. It may also be easier to deal with individual reactions in one-on-one discussions.

**Exhibit 6   Steps in the Change Process**

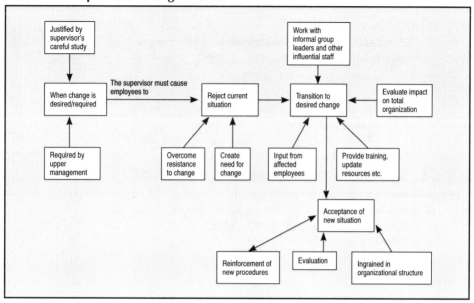

If you anticipate considerable resistance to a particular change, it might be helpful to meet with informal leaders of the work group before making a general announcement to the group. However, if you do this, it is important that you respond to the questions and concerns these informal leaders may have before asking for their help in dealing with the rest of the work group.

The following sections review some of the principles previously discussed and focus on basic steps in communicating change to employees as outlined in Exhibit 7.

## Step 1—Explain the Details

To avoid suspicion, anxiety, and unnecessary rumors, give your staff as much information as possible about the "who, what, where, when, and why" behind the proposed change. You can strengthen trust if you communicate as completely as possible, even when you have to say, "I don't know," in response to some employee concerns. Suppose, for example, you must implement a new computerized system for banquet and catering sales operations. You might say to your employees: "Our department is slated for a technology upgrade. The decision was made to improve our current efficiency in anticipation of the increased business we expect as we carry out our plan to attract new market segments. Training on the new system is scheduled to begin on the first of the month. The goal for converting to the new software program is 30 days."

Explain how the employees will benefit from the change. The fundamental question in many employees' minds will be: "How will I be affected by this change?" Give the benefits as well as the drawbacks. The benefits you highlight

**Exhibit 7   Steps in Communicating Change to Employees**

---

Step 1—Explain the details.

    Emphasize how employees benefit from the change.

    Identify what will *not* change.

Step 2—Ask for opinions/listen for feelings.

    Respond to employee's negative feelings without becoming defensive.

    Demonstrate acceptance of each employee's feelings:

        Listen and observe.

        Reflect the employee's feelings and opinions.

        Check for understanding.

Step 3—Solicit ideas on how to accomplish the change.

Step 4—Request commitment and support.

    Ask for help.

    Emphasize positive past performance.

    Offer help and support yourself.

    Express confidence in the employee's ability to adapt.

Step 5—Follow up.

---

should be the ones that are important to the particular employees involved. When possible, ask the employees themselves to state how they might benefit from the change.

After you've addressed effects and benefits from the employee's perspective, it can be useful to relate those benefits to larger departmental or organizational goals. For example, you might explain how the new banquet and catering software will reduce communication problems across departments. However, be sure that you've addressed the benefits for the employees before you bring up departmental or organizational benefits.

Be sure to stress what will *not* be affected by the change. Reactions to change are often irrational. You can help allay fears by stressing what is stable in the situation.

## Step 2—Ask for Opinions/Listen for Feelings

It is important for employees to understand the effects and benefits of a change; however, employee responses to proposed changes may be more emotional than rational. Supervisors must be prepared to deal with emotional reactions. Providing employees opportunities to express their feelings will help defuse their resistance to change. When asking employees for their opinions and feelings, you may encounter negative feedback that can sound judgmental and trigger defensiveness on your part. It is important that you respond to an employee's negative feelings without becoming defensive.

You might explain how you felt in the past in a similar situation; or, if appropriate, how you feel about the current change. This self-disclosure reinforces the message that it's okay for employees to express their feelings. Be careful, however, that you don't downplay the current change situation or the feelings expressed by the employees. It would be entirely inappropriate to respond with: "You think you've got it bad. Let me tell you what this change is going to do to me!" It will also be important to support the change if it has been mandated by those at higher organizational levels.

When asking for opinions and listening for feelings your goal should be to bring the emotions into the open where you and the employee can address them. You don't want to ignore these feelings or have the employee keep them bottled up inside. This creates the possibility of those bottled-up emotions pouring out in unproductive ways in the work place. You can encourage your employees to be open with their emotions by demonstrating your acceptance of their feelings.

Acceptance demonstrates understanding—not necessarily agreement. By demonstrating your acceptance of an employee's feelings about a particular change, you are not trying to reinforce or encourage resistance. You are simply acknowledging that feelings and emotions exist and you are demonstrating that you are sincerely trying to understand the employee's reaction. What you're accepting is the reality of the employee's reaction. You may find it necessary to make it clear that, while you accept their feelings, you have certain expectations about your employees' behavior.

After asking employees for their opinions and feelings associated with a proposed change, you should:

- Listen and observe.

- Reflect the employee's feelings and opinions.

- Check for understanding.

Listening for tone of voice and watching facial expressions and other non-verbal signals is important. Observing will give you clues as to whether the employee is saying one thing yet possibly feeling something else. Listening is hard work. It takes concentration and energy to actively listen and focus on the feelings that may or may not be expressed. If your employees seem reluctant to express their feelings and are silent and withdrawn, you will need to draw them out.

One way to invite additional feedback and encourage your employees to talk more about their concerns is by showing that you are actively listening to them. One of the best ways to do this is by stating, in your own words, what you hear them saying, and the feelings they may be expressing or implying. For example, an employee might say: "I can't see how this is going to make anything better!" As the supervisor, you might respond with: "You seem pretty angry about this new system. It sounds like you aren't convinced it will work."

Perhaps the most difficult part of demonstrating acceptance of an employee's feelings is identifying and accurately labeling the employee's emotional reaction. We sometimes lack the descriptive words needed. Exhibit 8 presents lists of descriptive words for feelings and emotions. The more these words enter your working vocabulary, the more skilled you may become in clarifying the feelings and emotions expressed by your employees.

Employees may not even hear you explain a change the first time if their fears and emotions are dominant. Supervisors must be sure to check for understanding.

**Exhibit 8    Words for Feelings**

| SCARED | MAD | Pleased |
|---|---|---|
| Panicky | Jealous | Hopeful |
| Insecure | Agitated | Excited |
| Uncertain | Bitter | Grateful |
| Vulnerable | Angry | Enthusiastic |
| Frightened | Envious | Important |
| Anxious | Frustrated | |
| Unsure | Upset | **CHEATED** |
| Confused | Furious | Neglected |
| Nervous | Hostile | Unappreciated |
| Doubtful | Irritated | Burdened |
| Intimidated | Disgusted | Rejected |
| | Offended | Used |
| **SAD** | Humiliated | Abused |
| Depressed | Resentful | Left Out |
| Helpless | Exasperated | Slighted |
| Drained | | Overwhelmed |
| Bored | **GLAD** | Ignored |
| Down | Happy | Hurt |
| Embarrassed | Surprised | Guilty |
| Lost | Elated | |
| Disappointed | Confident | |
| Crushed | Proud | |
| Ashamed | Secure | |
| Discouraged | Delighted | |
| Torn | Relieved | |
| Trapped | Fulfilled | |
| | Needed | |

You might take responsibility for any miscommunication by saying, "I'm not certain if I made everything clear. Just to make sure, could you tell me in your own words what you understood?" This makes the request to repeat back what you said seem less like a test or quiz.

## Step 3—Solicit Ideas

You can involve your employees in a change by asking for ideas on negotiable items. However, it is important to clearly identify the aspects of a particular change over which employees have no control. This helps focus the discussion, keeps you from constantly having to defend the change, and alerts employees that resistance is not productive in these areas. Whenever possible, invite employees to offer suggestions regarding a change. If you do, they are more likely to support and help implement the change.

To obtain input from employees, you can use questionnaires, suggestion boxes, brainstorming, and open meetings, as well as direct requests for input. Supervisors must sometimes use creative measures to generate employee input, especially if the trust level is low.

## Step 4—Request Commitment and Support

A direct request for commitment and support can be extremely powerful: "From what we've discussed, you can see this will take a real team effort to make a smooth transition. Can I count on your help?"

Also, one of the best ways to get support is to give it. When your employees feel they can come to you with problems that arise and you will make their needs, ideas, and concerns known to those higher up in the organization when necessary, their resistance can be reduced and their motivation to try to make change work increases. Remember, high expectations often lead to high performance. When you express confidence in your employees' ability to adapt to a change, you exert a powerful influence on their behavior.

If informal leaders exist and were not involved earlier, this is another opportunity to enlist their help. They can be a powerful asset in managing change or a powerful force in resisting it. Take time to communicate with them so they, in turn, can communicate with others in a positive way.

## Step 5—Follow Up

A supervisor's job in managing change is not complete when he or she has communicated the change to employees, no matter how effective the communication might have been. Too often a change is implemented and then assumed to be working satisfactorily. Actually, the time following a change can be stressful for employees as they adjust to its "newness." Positive reinforcement is particularly important as employees begin coping with new situations. Reinforcing even small improvements with positive feedback increases employee motivation and self-confidence in the current situation, and also helps to create a receptive climate for future change.

When implementing a major change, remember that things may often get worse before they get better. Even when there is minimal resistance to the change, it takes time for positive results to show. Employees must unlearn old ways of doing things as well as learn new techniques.

# Evaluating Change

Supervisors often find it difficult to evaluate changes that have been implemented because necessary information is either unavailable or inaccurate. In many cases, these difficulties arise because the expected results of the change were never stated in measurable terms.

For example, if changes are implemented to "increase productivity," the supervisor must determine how much productivity must increase for the change to be effective. In situations where objective measurement is not possible, you can be alert to the possibility that further change may become necessary. If differences between what is observed and what is expected are significant, it is possible that the change has not been successful because it did not accomplish what was expected.

The importance of stating objectives, or **indicators of effective change**, cannot be overemphasized. Without such indicators, you have no target or benchmark by which to measure the effectiveness of change. Other aspects of evaluating change include:

- Determining whether any additional changes are necessary
- Assessing whether the change has created any spin-off problems
- Analyzing the procedures by which changes have been made

By evaluating all of these aspects of change, supervisors may be able to refine and simplify tasks when change is again necessary. Exhibit 9 reviews many of the factors that must be incorporated into the process by which change is effectively managed.

## Endnote

1. Kurt Lewin, *Frontiers in Group Dynamics: Human Relations Concept, Method, and Reality in Social Science*, vol. 1, no. 1, 1947, pp. 5–41.

## Key Terms

**attitude**—A person's predisposition toward or feelings about a person or thing.

**change**—A reaction to a variation, alteration, or revision in the way things are done.

**change agent**—A person responsible for planning, implementing, and evaluating changes within the work environment.

**external forces of change**—Social, economic, political, and legal conditions that drive change within an organization.

**force field analysis**—A planning technique that helps you identify and visualize the relationships of significant forces that influence a situation, problem, or goal.

**grapevine**—An informal communication network within an organization that circulates unofficial information and rumors.

**indicators of effective change**—Measurable, expected results that are used to evaluate the effectiveness of implemented changes in the work environment.

**internal forces of change**—Conditions within a hospitality operation that drive change within the organization.

**resistance to change**—The tendency of individuals to maintain established routines.

**stabilizing forces**—Conditions that create continuity within an organization and work in opposition to external and internal forces of change.

## Review Questions

1. What are examples of ways that an entire organization can be affected by changes implemented by a single department?
2. What role do stabilizing forces play in the operation of hospitality businesses?

**Exhibit 9    Supervisor's Checklist for Implementing Change**

|  | Yes | No |
|---|---|---|
| 1. Is change necessary? | ☐ | ☐ |
| 2. Do you completely understand—from your perspective as a supervisor—why the change is necessary and what exactly it is supposed to do? | ☐ | ☐ |
| 3. Do you think about possible reasons why employees might resist the change and develop effective counterarguments for these reasons? | ☐ | ☐ |
| 4. Do you use individual counseling techniques to discuss the change and its implications with each affected employee? | ☐ | ☐ |
| 5. Do you use a persuasive technique to discover employee perceptions of disadvantages and then counter these with information that will help employees see advantages to the change? | ☐ | ☐ |
| 6. Do you involve both formal and informal group leaders and request their help in gaining acceptance to change? | ☐ | ☐ |
| 7. Do you use a trial approach (test the proposed change and then modify it as necessary) rather than implement the change on an "all-or-nothing" basis? | ☐ | ☐ |
| 8. Do you make sure that affected employees know what must be done differently before changes are implemented? | ☐ | ☐ |
| 9. Do you provide carefully designed training experiences before changes are implemented? | ☐ | ☐ |
| 10. Do you carefully supervise employees during the transitional period when changes are being implemented? | ☐ | ☐ |
| 11. Do you develop indicators of effective change that measurably describe what the situation should be after the changes are made? | ☐ | ☐ |
| 12. Do you evaluate the results of the change based upon the extent to which indicators of effective change are seen in the new situation? | ☐ | ☐ |
| 13. Do you try to recognize any benefits that may result from employee resistance to change? | ☐ | ☐ |
| 14. Do you know how to generate a need for change? | ☐ | ☐ |
| 15. Do you have the respect of the employees who must change? | ☐ | ☐ |
| 16. Do you have a good track record for implementing change with few surprises for employees? | ☐ | ☐ |

*(continued)*

**Exhibit 9** *(continued)*

|  | Yes | No |
|---|---|---|
| 17. Do you know what other changes are occurring in the organization at this time? | ☐ | ☐ |
| 18. Do you know the impact of the proposed change on other departments? | ☐ | ☐ |
| 19. Do you have necessary training programs already planned and in place? | ☐ | ☐ |
| 20. Do you know if existing work flows will be improved as a result of the change? | ☐ | ☐ |
| 21. Do you know whether the situation requiring change is of continuing importance to the organization? | ☐ | ☐ |
| 22. Are all employees permitted, to the extent possible, to participate in all activities relating to change? | ☐ | ☐ |
| 23. Do you know what you can and should do to increase pressure for change? | ☐ | ☐ |
| 24. Do you have all the information you need to make the change? | ☐ | ☐ |

3. How do external forces of change differ from internal forces of change?

4. How can change affect the structure of an organization?

5. How can supervisors use the model for change discussed in this chapter to guide their efforts as change agents?

6. How can supervisors develop strategies for implementing change by analyzing driving and restraining forces?

7. In what ways do supervisors benefit from employees' resistance to change?

8. Why should supervisors analyze change from the employees' perspective?

9. Why should supervisors involve employees in the change process?

10. How can informal group leaders be involved in the change process?

11. Why are indicators of effective change essential to the evaluation of changes which have been implemented?

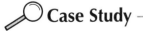 **Case Study**

### Turning Around the Turnaround

Ashcroft Hotels, a mid-size chain with an outstanding track record of turning around underperforming properties, recently acquired the Lincoln Hotel. The

Lincoln posed a considerable challenge—even for the Ashcroft chain. The transition began with corporate executives deciding to replace the Lincoln's general manager with Martin Wood, the most experienced and successful manager of the chain's turnaround team. Martin would be responsible for assessing the current staff at the Lincoln Hotel and making the necessary changes to improve the property's performance.

The only restriction was that Martin had to replace the current food and beverage director with Theo Waters, a rising star at the corporate flagship hotel. Joanne Landis, Ashcroft's vice president of food and beverage, insisted that now was the time for Theo's big test.

Martin expressed some concern. He felt that turning around the Lincoln Hotel posed enough of a challenge. He didn't need the additional burden of mentoring some hotshot who never faced serious problems and always had the resources available to help him succeed.

Joanne understood Martin's concerns and took full responsibility for Theo's placement. "You'll see," Joanne said, "Just turn him loose and he'll turn it around." Unconvinced, Martin gave in to the demand, but insisted that Theo had to be part of the management team at Lincoln. Joanne readily agreed that Theo, like the other managers, would be accountable to Martin. Her last comment was, "I don't want to interfere with your responsibilities, Martin. I only want to give Theo a chance to shine at another property. I'll have HR send you a copy of his file this afternoon."

Theo Waters was indeed a rising star at Ashcroft. He had bused tables and worked as a food server in college while he earned his hospitality degree. After graduation, he entered Ashcroft as a management trainee at the flagship hotel. He was soon promoted to assistant restaurant manager. His first department head position was as the room service manager. Most recently, he was the fine dining restaurant manager. He learned the chain's standards and procedures at the finest and best-run hotel in the chain. Even in this environment, he helped fine-tune an already profitable, smoothly running operation into an even more profitable one. In addition, he was instrumental in launching the company's new award-winning fine dining concept, which the company planned to roll out to other properties, like the Lincoln.

The next week, Theo arrived at the Lincoln Hotel. At an hour-long meeting, Martin welcomed Theo as the first new member of the high-performance team that would turn the hotel around.

"Theo," Martin began," it's important that we start things off right. Change is always difficult, but at underperforming hotels, like the Lincoln, change is often resisted, especially if managers and employees perceive changes as personal attacks."

"I understand," responded Theo, "changing procedures at the flagship wasn't easy, you know. But once we let the staff know how serious we were, people straightened up and we moved ahead."

Martin paused and momentarily regretted giving in to Joanne. "Yes Theo. You did a fine job there. But we're not just changing procedures here—we're challenging and changing a whole culture of work."

"Sure. It's a bigger job. What are some of the immediate problems?" asked Theo.

Martin handed Theo a short list of several areas that needed immediate improvement:

- First off, the restaurant is operating at a loss. Profitability must be restored as soon as possible.

- The inventory levels are too high, as are costs, but the staff also complains of frequent stockouts of critical items.

- Food production is often of inconsistent quality and portion size and food items are late coming out of the kitchen for waiting guests.

- Sanitation levels are often unacceptable both in the kitchen and in the dining areas.

- Table linens sometimes come back from the in-house laundry with stains still on them, and employee uniforms are dated and poorly maintained.

- A couple of ovens in the kitchen are not working properly and most of the appliances are old and need some sort of maintenance, but complaints to engineering just seem to pile up.

- Guests often complain about poor service. The hotel's director of sales is reluctant to bring potential clients to the hotel's own restaurant because of the service, which has embarrassed her too often before.

- There are scheduling problems, especially (but not only) during high occupancy periods, when the restaurant is often understaffed to meet the demand.

Martin continued, "As you can see, there are problems with the management team as well as with the line staff. I suspect that the director of sales and the rooms director are understating forecasts so they can always exceed them. This puts staffing in the restaurant at risk—you're always short-handed. I don't know what the deal is with engineering, but I'll find out."

"I'm sure I can tackle my area's problems right away," Theo offered.

"Theo, for the next thirty days I'm going to be focused on several critical areas of the hotel. But don't be the Lone Ranger. I'm here for support and advice, so don't hesitate to meet with me. This has to be a team effort."

Theo began by calling a restaurant department meeting, during which he made it very clear that the level of performance that had been acceptable in the past would no longer be tolerated. "I intend to make this restaurant's service rival that of our flagship property," he announced.

He distributed a new procedures manual that he recently helped revise in his previous position and insisted that everyone read it thoroughly and begin following its contents. Theo pointed out, "There will be no more eating in production or service areas of this restaurant—that's why we have a break area."

Theo continued, "I'm bringing in a leading customer service training program that guarantees to increase the restaurant's average check and total revenue. This training program will also address the top ten guest complaints and give the servers responses and tools that will help them satisfy unhappy guests." He banned the servers' current practice of pooling tips, "I don't believe that pooling tips encourages the kind of superior service we want at this restaurant," he declared.

A few days later, Theo unveiled a new work schedule with major changes in a deliberate attempt to upset underperformers. When some staff members complained, he responded, "There are a lot of restaurants in this town. If you don't like it here, a person has to do what a person has to do."

Over the next couple of weeks, Theo was kept busy putting out one fire after another. He disciplined the chef for allowing cooks to give servers food prepared by mistake. He found a group of servers still pooling tips and threatened to fire them. It seemed like every time he turned around, the staff was doing all it could to ignore his directives and undermine his authority.

One day, near the end of the month, things just blew up. The restaurant was very busy because of high occupancy at the hotel. As Theo walked through the dining room, he heard a guest complain angrily that his food was taking forever to arrive. Theo went to the kitchen and asked the chef what was causing the delay. The chef explained that he was not prepared for this business volume. "My cook was swamped and burned the first plate, which had to be redone."

Theo returned to the waiting guest and as he comped the meal, another guest at the next table complained that she had been sitting for several minutes and no one had even brought her water to drink. Theo rushed to the kitchen and accused Beth, that table's server, of failing to take a guest's order within the time frame set out in the procedures manual. Beth lost her composure and let Theo have it, "I'm working a double station. How am I supposed to keep up according to your standards? Why don't you get off people's backs. We're working awfully hard to cover up for your stupid new schedule. What do you expect when we're always understaffed?"

Theo pitched in and began helping servers get the food out. In the dining room he noticed the director of sales leaving with a client. She called him over and privately said, "This is exactly the kind of service that always embarrasses me when I'm with clients." Theo snapped back, "If you didn't sandbag your occupancy projections, we could schedule staff appropriately and this wouldn't happen!" As Theo walked away, another server rushed up to him and said he couldn't get the cappuccino machine to work properly. After comping another meal, Theo struggled to control his emotions, "Engineering has known about the cappuccino problem for days. Why doesn't anything ever get done right?"

By the end of his first month, despite increased customer counts, the restaurant's revenue performance had not noticeably improved. However, Theo had managed to alienate not only the restaurant staff, but also most of the hotel's management team. Even the controller, who had cautiously supported Theo initially, started to doubt his "superstardom" because she saw a lot of comped checks and no increase in net revenue. Her willingness to cooperate with Theo was beginning to ebb.

Martin called Theo into his office for an end-of-month progress report.

## Discussion Questions

1. Do you agree with corporate's decision that Theo is an excellent candidate for this new position? What about his background and experience would help prepare him to succeed at the Lincoln Hotel? Why did Martin Wood have

misgivings about Theo's abilities? What about Theo's background and experience would hinder his ability to succeed at the Lincoln Hotel?

2. What did Theo do well in approaching his new assignment? Why did Theo's efforts to create change fail? What could Martin Wood have done to avoid the end-of-month situation?

3. At the end-of-month meeting, what is Martin likely to say to Theo? How might Theo respond? What are the next steps that Theo should take in his effort to turn his department around?

---

Case Number: 3564CA

The following industry experts helped generate and develop this case: Philip J. Bresson, Director of Human Resources, Renaissance New York Hotel, New York, New York; and Jerry Fay, Human Resources Director, Aramark Corporation, Atlanta, Georgia.

This case also appears in *Managing Hospitality Human Resources*, Fifth Edition (Lansing, Mich.: American Hotel & Lodging Educational Institute, 2012), ISBN 978-0-86612-396-9.

# Chapter 14 Outline

Owning Your Development
    Managers Stumble in Development
    Reach Out to Others
Planning for Your Development
    Gathering Feedback
    Write Goals and Set Priorities
Create the Plan
    Setting Objectives
    Motivation
    Learning Activities
    Timetables and Measurements
    Resources
    Barrier Identification
Execute the Plan
    Daily Investments
    Opportunities Before You
    Gathering Feedback
    Eliminating Defensiveness
    Overcoming Barriers
    Monitoring
Next Steps

# Competencies

1. Explain why it is important for managers to take control of their personal development. (pp.369–371)

2. Outline ways to plan for personal career development. (pp. 371–373)

3. List the steps in creating a career development plan. (pp. 373–380)

4. Describe how to execute a career development plan. (pp. 380–385)

# 14

# Professional Development

**F**ROM THE MOMENT WE ARE BORN, our brains begin processing information. Every day becomes a learning experience. Childhood development experts break experiences into several categories, including physical development, mental development, and verbal development. However, development doesn't end with childhood. Throughout the rest of our lives, we develop in many ways, including as a partner, a parent, and an employee.

This chapter focuses on a single aspect of your development: your professional development as a hospitality supervisor. In this chapter, you'll learn why you must take responsibility for your own professional development, how to plan what you will learn, and how to follow through with that plan.

Your career is a journey that ends only when you retire. Opportunities are plentiful for the hospitality professional who takes charge of his or her career.

## Owning Your Development

When it comes to **professional development**, you must "own your own." The success or failure of your professional development lies primarily in your hands. No one else knows your skills, interests, and values as well as you do. Nor can anyone else as accurately gauge the development activities you will find most profitable and effective.

Professional development is the process by which an employee becomes proficient at the job he or she is doing and, if desired, prepares for responsibilities in future positions. When you identify your skills, interests, and values, you can also identify those areas in which you can become even better. Professional development ensures that you continue gaining the knowledge and skills necessary for success.

Professional development is a never-ending process. You will never encounter a point at which you will be able to say that you have learned all there is to learn and are as skilled as it is possible to be. Taking control of your career requires taking control of your professional development.

Professional development lets you accomplish several objectives:

- *Maintain your current position.* In a changing world, you have an obligation to constantly update your skill set. Even if you simply want to do what you are doing for the rest of your career, what you are doing will evolve and change. Hospitality professionals create work through other people, and their skill sets have to shift.

- *Provide mobility.* If you desire mobility, doing well in your current position improves your ability to do so. Even if you are not formally promoted, professional development enriches you and gives you a higher degree of professionalism. It can also help you retain interest in your job.

- *Make promotion a possibility.* If you want to be promoted, you must start developing the skill set you will need for the position you want. Employees who are high performers in one job sometimes find themselves promoted to jobs for which they do not have the proper skills.

## Managers Stumble in Development

Why not simply rely on your manager to provide you with opportunities and training? Certainly most managers want their employees to succeed. They definitely want their employees to be high performers capable of taking on challenging tasks and providing superior guest service. It is not a lack of interest that prevents managers from taking ownership of their employees' professional development. Rather it is a lack of time and, often, a lack of knowledge or skill.

Many managers and supervisors in many organizations would probably say that they are not very good at planning and implementing professional development programs for those whom they supervise. They might also admit that they are not very good at planning their own personal learning activities. It's not that they don't want to; in many cases, they simply have too many other priorities and, sometimes, a feeling that good fortune will reduce their need to plan formally.

## Reach Out to Others

While your professional development is wholly your responsibility, you don't have to do it alone. Indeed, you will be much more effective if you systematically involve other people, including your manager, your peers, your subordinates, hospitality professionals at other properties, and educators.

Nearly every person with whom you come into professional contact has something he or she can teach you. Try to find something to learn from every person, even if it is how *not* to do something. You can learn through observation, conversations, experience, training, attendance at professional meetings, etc.

Some people can become more formally involved in your professional development planning and activities. When you start forming your professional development plan, talk to your manager. He or she might have advice about important skills you should acquire. In addition, he or she might be aware of resources you can access. Determine the types of formal opportunities available from your property or corporate offices.

Fostering a **mentor** relationship with a skilled manager can also greatly accelerate your professional development. A mentor is someone who acts as a coach, advisor, teacher, and role model. A mentor can give you feedback on your performance and encourage you in your development. He or she can help you excel at what you do. What sorts of things might a mentor do? Here are some ways that mentors might assist you:

- Serve as a role model.

- Share knowledge and experiences.

- Encourage you and help build your self-confidence.

- Coach you about what to do and what not to do.

- Provide information about the hospitality industry so that you have a context for decision making.

- Make suggestions regarding career planning.

- Encourage you to change and grow.

- Provide opportunities, set performance expectations, and help you learn about and develop your talents, interests, ideas, and competencies.

# Planning for Your Development

Dwight Eisenhower once said, "Plans are nothing; planning is everything."

There is no such thing as a perfect **professional development plan.** However, perfection is not really the goal. Excellence and movement toward excellence are what really matter.

To set professional development goals, you must determine what you want to be good at and how good you are at it now. You must also determine how good you want to get and how good your manager needs you to get.

Before creating a professional development plan, you need to assess your strengths and determine what areas you want and/or need to develop. To determine what you are good at, start with a **self-assessment**. Ask yourself very frankly about your current skill and competency levels. You will be able to answer these important questions better than anyone else because you have a personal perspective on your interests and abilities.

There are many ways to conduct a self-assessment that determines your development needs. Some of the tools include:

- Past performance reviews

- Conversations with your peers, managers, and subordinates

- Lists of strengths, weaknesses, values, and interests

Using a model or tool can help you conduct a more structured assessment of your strengths and weaknesses. It can also prevent you from overlooking critical skills. Exhibit 1 shows a sample tool you can use to assess your strengths and needs in core supervisory competencies. (To view other tools, enter "competency self-assessment form" into your favorite search engine.) Remember that while you must develop yourself in areas you classify as "weaknesses," you must also develop your strengths. You are successful because of your strengths, so you can benefit from capitalizing on them.

## Gathering Feedback

Once you have conducted a self-assessment, you should gather **feedback** from people around you. Feedback will help you verify your skills and needs, as well as identify your organization's needs now and in the foreseeable future. People who can provide feedback on your skills include your manager, peers, and employees.

**Exhibit 1   Competency Assessment Form**

Circle the number that best represents your mastery of the following supervisory competencies.

1=Weakness                    2=Below standards                    3=Competent
     4=Better than average                    5=Strength

| 1 | 2 | 3 | 4 | 5 | Understanding the role of the supervisor |
|---|---|---|---|---|---|
| 1 | 2 | 3 | 4 | 5 | Providing leadership |
| 1 | 2 | 3 | 4 | 5 | Improving communications |
| 1 | 2 | 3 | 4 | 5 | Conducting orientation and training |
| 1 | 2 | 3 | 4 | 5 | Handling problems and conflict |
| 1 | 2 | 3 | 4 | 5 | Motivation and team building |
| 1 | 2 | 3 | 4 | 5 | Scheduling |
| 1 | 2 | 3 | 4 | 5 | Evaluating employees |
| 1 | 2 | 3 | 4 | 5 | Coaching employees |
| 1 | 2 | 3 | 4 | 5 | Managing time |
| 1 | 2 | 3 | 4 | 5 | Recruiting and selecting |
| 1 | 2 | 3 | 4 | 5 | Controlling labor costs |
| 1 | 2 | 3 | 4 | 5 | Conducting discipline |
| 1 | 2 | 3 | 4 | 5 | Managing change |
| 1 | 2 | 3 | 4 | 5 | Planning career development |

The practice of soliciting feedback from your manager, peers, and employees is called **360-degree feedback**. You can use several methods to collect this feedback. Some hospitality organizations have feedback systems in place; if yours does, you must simply tap into it and ensure that you carefully evaluate the information. If your organization does not have a formal feedback system, you will have to gather information from other sources. Information about how others see your strengths and development needs can be found: in past performance appraisals; during discussions with your manager; during conversations with trusted peers, a mentor, and/or your employees; and on guest comment cards and letters.

## Write Goals and Set Priorities

The next step is to determine the direction in which you want your professional development to proceed. This involves writing **goals** for each of your strengths and weaknesses, then setting priorities for those goals.

For each of the competencies on which you rated yourself, write a goal that describes where you would like to be. A professional development goal might be "provide employee feedback" or "make contacts."

Focus on two or three of these goals and create a plan for developing them. While your self-assessment and 360-degree feedback tools might identify several areas you wish to develop, you will find that making real progress on two or three of your most important goals is more rewarding than making only a few steps toward all your goals without reaching any of them.

Several methods exist for setting priorities:

- *Determine which skills and competencies your organization needs now and in the foreseeable future.* We have defined professional development, in part, as the process of becoming skilled at your current job. Therefore, when setting your priorities, consider your work environment. What does your organization need from you? What skills would most help your organization meet its goals?

- *Work on your weakest areas first.* Many professionals focus their development efforts on their biggest weaknesses. This strategy can be an effective way of setting priorities if the weaknesses you identify are so essential to your job that you will not be able to perform to standards unless you improve those skills.

- *Build up your strengths and highest interest areas first.* It is much easier to become motivated to learn about a skill in which you already have a great deal of confidence or interest. An enthusiastic start to your professional development activities can create a momentum that will carry over when you begin working on other areas.

- *Combine the three methods above.* It is also helpful to determine both your short- and long-term visions. Think about where you are and where you want to be in one year, five years, and ten years. Think about which skills you will need if you want to achieve your goals within those timeframes.

Keep in mind that the difficulty of achieving developmental goals will be different depending on the type of skill you are developing or the type of knowledge you are attaining. Some skills are easy to develop, others are not. Likewise, you will have an easier time assessing, monitoring, and attaining feedback for some skills than you will for others. See Exhibit 2 for examples.

## Create the Plan

Once you have laid the groundwork and know the areas in which what you need to improve (as well as your goals and priorities), you will create the plan that gets you there. This detailed development plan will include goals, action steps, identifications of people involved, time frames for completion, and methods through which you will measure success. Exactly how you format the plan depends on which techniques you find most useful and appropriate. Exhibit 3 shows one format you could use or adapt.

This section explores the steps you should follow to create a development plan, including:

- Setting objectives.
- Getting motivated.

**Exhibit 2   Managerial Skills by Developmental Difficulty**

|  | Easiest to develop | Average to develop | Hardest to develop |
|---|---|---|---|
| **Easiest to assess and provide feedback** | Guest service<br>Timely decision-making<br>Technical skills | Interpersonal communication<br>Listening<br>Negotiating | Creativity<br>Trust and integrity<br>Composure |
| **Average to assess and provide feedback** | Delegation<br>Recruiting and staffing<br>Time management<br>Problem solving | Conflict management<br>Peer relationships<br>Perseverance | Upper management relationships<br>Building team spirit<br>Confronting employees |
| **Hardest to assess and provide feedback** | Process management<br>Self-knowledge | Compassion<br>Developing subordinates<br>Managing diversity<br>Self-development<br>Personal learning | Ethics and values<br>Motivating others<br>Organizing<br>Balancing life and work |

- Determining learning activities.
- Establishing a timetable.
- Identifying resources.
- Anticipating barriers and constraints.

## Setting Objectives

As you set the **objectives** that will help you meet each goal, you should determine a clear reason why the goal is important to you and your organization. To achieve your goals, you must commit to them; the only way you will maintain commitment is if you pursue goals you actually want to reach.

One suggestion to achieve this end is to develop action plans that identify what you should:

- Begin doing that you don't like to do, have never done, or are unaware of.
- Quit doing because it isn't helping you.
- Continue doing because it is helping you.

Use the "begin," "quit," and "continue" tactics as you develop your professional development objectives. Objectives should be highly specific, focused, and definite so that you know when you have achieved them. Other characteristics of good objectives are that they are verifiable, measurable, challenging, relevant, and cost-effective. They must also balance needs, as well as have time limits and controllable outcomes.

**Exhibit 3   Sample Development Plan**

| Strength or Need Targeted | | Action Plan | Resources Needed | Target Dates |
|---|---|---|---|---|
| Provide corrective feedback.<br><br>Objectives: | 1. | Communicate my expectations to employees. | Staff | 2/21 |
| • Correct employees in a timely manner when they make mistakes. | 2. | Concentrate on a single performance issue. | None | ongoing |
| | 3. | Explain the consequences in meaningful terms to employee. | Staff | ongoing |
| | 4. | Criticize only the performance, not the performer. | Staff | ongoing |
| | 5. | Give employees a chance to respond. | Staff | ongoing |
| | 6. | Ask employees how they can correct the problem. | Staff | ongoing |
| | 7. | Create action plans with employees. | Staff | 3/15 |
| Coach employees<br><br>Objectives: | 1. | Develop checklists for group check-in procedures. | Policy manual | 4/20 |
| • Improve my skill in identifying my employees' strengths. | 2. | Analyze effectiveness of training manual. | Training manual, staff | 5/1 |
| | 3. | Volunteer to be trained as an in-house trainer. | Personnel manager | 3/15 |
| • Improve my skill in identifying my employees' development needs. | 4. | Attend the corporate two-day coaching and motivation seminar. | Boss | 5/1 |
| • Provide feedback to employees that will help them develop their strengths and improve their weaknesses. | 5. | Assess areas where each of my employees could benefit from coaching. | Staff | 5/10 |
| | 6. | Plan ways to approach employees to provide them with coaching. | None | 5/15 |

The best objectives:

- Are difficult to attain; they often lead to heightened performance so long as they are attainable.
- Are specific rather than vague.
- Provide feedback about performance; people will be motivated to work harder if they know about the progress they are making toward their objectives.
- Are attainable; you must have the abilities and skills required to reach the objectives.

For example, if your goal is to provide meaningful feedback to employees, your objective might read: *"Conduct performance reviews with specific feedback within two weeks of employee's anniversary date."*

Because professional development plans must be focused, you should typically develop only two or three areas at a time. You can then revise the plan to address additional improvement objectives.

## Motivation

Many factors can motivate your professional development. One example is the development of a short-term challenge at your workplace. Assume your operation is experiencing a budget crisis and needs your leadership to address financial challenges. In such a situation, you might need to concentrate your development efforts on financial management.

Make sure you divide your plan into reasonable steps. If you break your plan into small steps, you will likely experience a greater sense of accomplishment as you make progress. If you expect too much at once, you might get discouraged.

Enlist others to be part of your plan. Ask them to provide feedback and to support your progress. Involve as many people as you can, because no one person will meet all your development and feedback needs. Who might you involve?

- Colleagues
- Direct reports
- Managers
- Team leaders
- Human resources staff
- Role models and mentors
- Family and friends

Ask these people to test your assumptions and identify areas within the organization that should be priorities. Try to find people who will be open and candid while still encouraging and challenging you.

## Learning Activities

Once you have determined your priorities, you must determine *how* you are going to learn what you need to learn. People learn in different ways. Some people learn best by reading, others by doing, and others by hearing. You should determine how you best learn. Consider things you have learned outside of work. What are you good at? How did you learn that skill or talent? Did you gain knowledge through reading? Through doing it with others? Through watching someone else do it?

**Learning styles** break down into several categories. Three basic categories are visual, auditory, and kinesthetic. Which learning style is best for you?

**Visual learners:**

- Use highlighters when reading.

- Memorize chapters and notes.

- Recopy notes in colors.

- Visually organize or reorganize notes using columns, categories, outline forms, etc.

- Remember where information was located in a visual field.

- Create timelines, models, charts, grids, etc.

- Write or rewrite facts, formulas, and notes on wall hangings, posters, or cards for visual review.

- Put facts, formulas, and notes in index cards arranged on a wall, bulletin board, floor, or bed.

- Use color-coded markers or cards.

**Auditory learners:**

- Prefer to listen without taking notes.

- Like group discussions and/or study groups.

- Must discuss concepts with someone immediately after learning something.

- Frequently do homework with a friend by telephone or computer.

- Tape record lessons or notes so that they can listen to them again later.

- Set information to rhyme, rhythm, or music to aid retention.

- Remember information in auditory fields (frequently tag "who said that?" to information).

- Use different voices to study.

- Use television, video, or radio supplements.

- Study with background music.

- Prefer a quiet study environment.

**Kinesthetic learners:**

- Copy notes over and over.

- Must use white-out or start a new page after several mistakes.

- Prefer to take notes during a lesson to help concentration.
- Must take notes even when a detailed outline is provided.
- Doodle while studying.
- Must move about when studying.
- Alternate sitting still and moving during studying.
- Move hands or feet for rhythm emphasis while studying.
- Make charts, grids, timelines, and diagrams (usually several times).
- Trace key words with finger, marker, or hand.
- Re-enact situations while studying.
- Prefer learning by doing.
- Frequently take things apart or tinker with them for understanding.
- Like to make on-site visits.

Several websites offer surveys or short evaluations that can help you determine your learning style. (To find them, enter "surveys to discover learning style" in your favorite search engine.)

Traditionally, many people have emphasized distance learning or on-site courses as primary tools for professional development plans. Secondary learning sources include other people (such as contacts made during networking or from mentoring relationships) and on-the-job activities. Increasingly, however, many observers emphasize on-the-job activities, followed by personal contacts and course enrollment.

Specific activities associated with each type of learning follow.

**On-the-job learning activities include:**

- Improving a process or procedure.
- Starting something new.
- Representing your manager at meetings or functions.
- Coaching someone who is weak in an area in which you excel.
- Managing new projects.
- Making presentations.
- Taking on special assignments that challenge you.
- Offering to follow up on agenda items from meetings.
- Volunteering to lead a task force or committee.
- Transferring to a different job, function, or business to gain experience.
- Interviewing counterparts in other organizations about their "best practices" and summarizing what you've learned at a staff meeting.
- Practicing a skill or behavior in the actual work situation.
- Seeking assignments that use and stretch your strengths.

**Learn from other people by:**

- Joining or leading community groups.

- Volunteering with a community organization to practice a new skill.

- Making presentations to civic organizations.

- Modeling others who are competent in a skill and asking them how to handle certain situations.

**Off-the-job learning experiences include:**

- Attending workshops and training courses.

- Attending seminars.

- Taking adult education or distance education classes.

- Reading books, articles, and manuals.

- Taking certification review courses and exams.

Include a mixture of activities to add depth and perspective to your education, and to give yourself the greatest chance of success. Even activities outside of your personal learning style can complement your development by stretching your abilities.

After you have selected learning activities that will help you achieve each objective, incorporate those activities into your plan as action plan statements. For example, if your objective is "Conduct performance reviews with specific feedback within two weeks of employee's anniversary date," your action plans might read:

1. Talk to the front desk manager about how she collects data for performance reviews.

2. Form a committee to review the effectiveness of the current performance review form.

3. Attend a seminar about improving employee performance.

4. Read about performance evaluations in hospitality human resources textbooks.

## Timetables and Measurements

Your professional development plan is very much like any other strategic or business plan. For it to be most effective, it must have deadlines and methods through which you can measure success. The former will provide motivation and the latter will suggest the learning activities' effectiveness.

Schedule a completion or target date for each goal and checkpoints along the way for each objective. Give yourself enough time to accomplish the objectives, but not so much time that the deadline is meaningless.

The timetable you create should include steps you want to accomplish at various intervals. For example, you might have objectives you want to meet within three months, within one year, and within three years.

Timetables and deadlines help measure goals and objectives over time. You should measure your development according to an overall change over an extended period of time, not simply on a single performance date.

Determine the objective's outcome. State exactly what will happen when you accomplish your objective. Be specific about whether you will measure productivity, observations of changed behavior, or other measures. Then determine how you will measure these outcomes. Will you have reports to which you can point? Guest comment cards? Feedback from your manager? Lower expenses? Higher sales?

## Resources

Everything we do requires resources of some sort. These resources might be money, equipment, other people's support, or time. Once you have identified what and who you will need to accomplish your objectives, you can plan how you will obtain your resources.

## Barrier Identification

Planning is important, but some occurrences cannot be predicted. Plans stumble when the planner fails to anticipate barriers and constraints.

When planning your professional development, identify items that might keep you from accomplishing your objectives. By doing this, you can plan ways around them or methods of addressing them.

Barriers to your development can be either external or internal. External barriers are those over which you might have little or no control. They include barriers in the economic environment, within your organization, and from other people. Internal barriers are those over which you have the most control. They consist of a personal resistance to development, such as a lack of discipline, fear of the unknown, or a lack of education or skill.

Once you have identified barriers, you must identify strategies for overcoming them. Suggestions include:

- Show your plan to other people. By doing so, you increase your commitment and involve others in your support network.

- Focus on a simple process. If a process gets too complex, you might find it intimidating rather than motivating.

- Be patient. Real change takes time.

- Record what happens when your progress begins to slip. Look for the patterns and trends that gave you problems.

- Create reminders for yourself.

# Execute the Plan

When you created your plan, you drew the roadmap for your development. Once the plan is in place, you must begin moving toward your destination. It's time to execute your plan.

Throughout your development efforts, you will find the following activities helpful:

- Making daily investments
- Finding opportunities where you are
- Seeking honest feedback
- Minimizing defensiveness
- Overcoming barriers
- Monitoring progress

Exhibit 4 contains additional activities that can help you execute your professional development plan.

## Daily Investments

You should actively schedule professional development activities as opposed to simply completing them when you have time. Pick a regular time to which you can generally commit on a daily basis. This time might be right before work, at lunch, or at the end of the day. Determine which time works best for you. Evaluate your energy level and determine when you will be fresh and most amenable to learning. Consider your other time constraints so that you don't consistently sacrifice your development activities in favor of other demands.

Leave reminders for yourself so that your development activities don't get crowded out on a busy day. You might leave notes for yourself in a day planner,

**Exhibit 4   Daily Steps in a Professional Development Plan**

- Spend a few minutes every day thinking about how you will feel about yourself after you attain your goals.
- Remember that you can learn something every day.
- Do something every day to move forward, even just a little bit, toward your goals.
- Ensure you set and move toward goals that you—not others—want.
- Use negative feedback as an opportunity to learn more about things you don't know.
- Keep your list of short-term goals short and remember them.
- Develop a clear long-range professional goal and take daily "baby steps" toward it.
- Remember that a little progress toward several important goals is much better than a lot of progress toward less-important goals.
- Tell others about your goals so that you have further incentives to attain them.
- Learn from your mistakes.
- Remember what you have learned and use that input to learn more.

make marks on a calendar, or use an electronic reminder that pops up on your screen like an alarm clock.

## Opportunities Before You

Each day, look for development opportunities that might be right under your nose. Take a careful look at your routine. Can you do something standard or "old" in a new way?

For example, say your goal is to provide more specific employee feedback. In the past, you have coached only when your employees needed correction. You looked for opportunities to correct your employees. Determine instead that you are going to try to "catch someone doing right" every day this week, and praise him or her with specific observations.

Learn to take calculated risks. Experiment with the tasks you complete and the ways in which you interact with your employees and peers. Try to forecast what will happen if you do something differently. What is the worst-case scenario? Can you live with that? Often, risk-taking pays off with greater opportunities and rewards.

Also, look for opportunities to volunteer in your workplace. Frequently more work exists than there are people to complete it. You likely also have a very busy schedule, but if you make time to complete tasks outside your normal job description, you can enhance your career and build on your skills and knowledge. Some of the activities you might volunteer for are:

- An ad hoc assignment. Something must always be started or fixed. Research new information; find a way to fit these assignments into your tight schedule.

- An activity that will stretch you.

- Training others; some say teaching is learning twice.

- Working with others outside your unit. Such work helps you make contacts, learn new skills, improve teamwork, and learn more about the overall operation.

## Gathering Feedback

While you retain responsibility for your development, you do not have to work on it alone. By involving others in your development, you quicken your success and expand your knowledge. You also get essential feedback and support from people who can objectively observe your skills and abilities.

Here are some ways to involve others:

- Realize that no single person will fill all your development and feedback needs. Keep a diverse list of people who can support your development. Colleagues, direct reports, managers, team leaders, human resources staff, role models, mentors, family, and friends can all support your development in various ways.

- To ensure that you are on the right track, involve others in the act of testing your assumptions and conclusions. Choose people who will give you candid feedback and encourage you to take risks.

- Ask others about significant events in their careers to get a better view of the experiences and challenges you will likely face as you assume greater responsibility.

- Observe others who are skilled or knowledgeable about the areas you are attempting to develop. When observing their behavior, note what they do well and what they don't do well. Integrate the positive aspects into your own behavior.

- Learn from people outside of work. Leaders from other professions or organizations, as well as community leaders, can serve as effective coaches and role models. They might expose you to skills, styles, and techniques you have not encountered in your current situation.

- Ask for support when you get frustrated or feel discouraged. Other people can serve as sounding boards when you face barriers or sluggish progress toward your development goals.

Seeking honest feedback can be a difficult endeavor because many people feel uncomfortable giving negative opinions; at times, you will likely encounter this hesitance. When soliciting feedback, keep other people's reluctance in mind and use a strategy to gain useful information. First, know what you want. The type of feedback you need will be different at different times. For example, when you start working on a task or goal, you need broad feedback that helps you head in the right direction. As you get closer to your goal, you need more detailed, specific feedback to ensure you aren't learning anything that is inaccurate. Ask questions to get the type of feedback you need and let your sources know the type of information for which you are looking.

Ensure that your direct supervisor is one of the people you ask for feedback. By asking your supervisor for specific comments and suggestions, you obtain the most relevant information and keep your manager interested in your development.

Also consider soliciting feedback from your employees and peers. Ask them for information about ways you can be more effective, what they think you should change, and how your skills and abilities affect them.

Feedback is important, but not all feedback will be helpful or useful. Some respondents might be vague; in such cases, you must ask for specifics about what you did well or what you did poorly. Once you feel certain that you understand their opinion, ask yourself the following questions:

- Does it make sense?

- How do I want to change?

- Is the feedback truthful and accurate?

- Is the feedback important?

Always thank the people who provide feedback. Thank them verbally, then demonstrate your appreciation by making your changes and improvements—especially the ones they suggested—obvious. If you will not be changing, explain to your feedback sources why you are not changing in the ways they suggested. By doing this, you make them more willing to provide feedback in the future.

## Eliminating Defensiveness

Defensiveness is normal when someone criticizes you or points out ways that you could improve. Your first impulse is likely to explain why you do things the way you do. Don't do this because it prevents the person from giving you honest and useful feedback. When someone is giving you feedback, stop yourself from arguing, debating, or explaining. Don't interrupt, and be aware of the nonverbal messages you might be sending. Nonverbal messages that might tell a speaker you are resisting their feedback include furrowing your brow, fidgeting, drumming your fingers, crossing your arms over your chest, and biting your lip.

Summarize the feedback you received. Be careful that you don't sound condescending or programmed. Offer your perspective only if the person asks you for it. You might also ask the person providing the feedback if he or she thought you were receptive or if you said or did anything that made him or her feel uncomfortable.

## Overcoming Barriers

When creating your plan, you identified barriers you might face. You also developed strategies for overcoming them. As you execute your plan, you must ensure those strategies are effective and change them as necessary.

You should anticipate feelings of uncertainty or ambiguity about your goals. You might question whether the effort to attain them is worthwhile. Such feelings are only temporary, as real change takes time. You might experience less uncertainty if you separate "learning" from "performance." Learning is what you know now that you didn't before, while performance relates to how well you do something. For example, assume you have learned the steps to resolving a guest complaint. When you next handle a complaint, you do not perform the "follow-up" step as well as you should have. However, you can identify what you should have done and what you will try to do differently in the future. You have *learned* even if you are not yet *performing* all that you have learned.

Create reminders for yourself that recognize the progress you are making, and always remember the goals you are working to attain. Place your goals in places you can see them, whether that be in your desk drawer, on a mirror, or in your wallet or purse.

## Monitoring

You should continually monitor your progress and reflect on what you have learned or accomplished. When you set goals, you made them measurable; now you should actually measure how close you have come to your goals, or by how much you have exceeded them.

Reflection is an important part of the learning process. While much of your development plan will focus on activities (i.e., doing, reading, talking, watching), for the plan to become a useful, long-term teaching experience, you must take time to think about what you have done.

You can build progress checks into your overall development plan using several tactics:

• Schedule time to compare your actual accomplishments to your plan's goals.

- Discuss your development plan and the extent to which you are meeting its goals with your manager and others.

- Track your progress toward goal attainment.

- "Celebrate success" as you reach a significant milestone or attain a goal.

- Maintain a journal or diary and make notes about what you learn, how you do things differently, and how you will apply what you have learned.

## Next Steps

Professional development is a process that will continue for the rest of your career. Throughout the professional development process, you will encounter stages during which you strive for your goals, reach them, and become ready for new ones. When you have accomplished a goal, acknowledge your progress and share your success with others. Reward yourself!

People who are most successful at attaining professional development goals like to learn new things and keep up to date on the skills and knowledge required for their chosen fields. They know that professional development is an ongoing process.

If you were not successful in reaching a goal, develop new strategies and action plans. Analyze the reasons your activities were not successful, and focus on factors that will make a difference.

Finally, take the time to set new goals or rewrite current goals to focus on additional achievement. Then go back to step one and, having already reaped the rewards of the process, continue to execute your plan for the rest of your career.

## Key Terms

**360-degree feedback**—Feedback is solicited from many different people such as managers, peers, and employees.

**feedback**—Information about performance, skills, and learning given to an individual.

**goals**—Specific, measurable statements that describe what a person would like to accomplish or learn.

**learning style**—The way in which a person learns. Common learning styles are auditory, visual, and kinesthetic.

**mentor**—A person who assists in the professional development of another person by offering advice, feedback, guidance, and contacts.

**objectives**—Highly specific, tightly focused, and concrete statements for reaching each goal.

**professional development**—The process of improving skills and abilities needed for success on the job.

**professional development plan**—A written and structured road map of professional development goals, strategies, and timelines.

**self-assessment**—The process of determining one's strengths, weaknesses, interests, and values.

 **Review Questions** ─────────────────────────────

1. Why is it important to engage in professional development?

2. What role can a mentor play in your professional development?

3. What are the steps to planning your professional development?

4. What are the characteristics of an effective professional development goal?

5. How does your personal learning style affect your professional development?

6. What are some strategies for overcoming barriers to your professional development plan?

7. How can you execute a professional development plan?

 **Case Study** ──────────────────────────────────────

### Earth to Marlene! Anybody Home?

"Earth to Marlene! Anybody home?" Dining Room Supervisor Marlene Robbins looked up from her teacup and smiled tiredly at Donovan Marsh, a front desk supervisor at the hotel where they both worked.

"You were lost in thought. Were you trying to read the future in your tea leaves?" Donovan joked.

"Kind of," sighed Marlene. "I'm trying to decide what I want to do with my career."

Donovan pulled up a chair and sat down next to Marlene. The employee break room was nearly deserted.

"So, are you planning to apply for Alan's job now that he's moved on to greener pastures?" he asked. Alan Jacomet had been the hotel's dining room manager and Marlene's boss. Although he'd left three weeks ago, his position remained vacant in spite of widespread recruitment efforts.

"Yeah, right," said Marlene. "I can't even handle the job I'm in now. How could I take over his job? Actually, I was thinking about quitting." She turned her attention back to her tea so that Donovan wouldn't see the frustration in her eyes.

The front desk supervisor was stunned. "Quit? But I thought you loved it here! Why would you want to leave? You're a terrific supervisor!"

"Am I?" Marlene asked. "Sometimes I wonder. My employees like me, but they're always taking advantage of me—trading shifts, calling off at the last minute, expecting favors. I try to make sure the dining room runs smoothly during the day and that everything is prepped and stocked for the dinner shift, but the evening supervisor doesn't return the courtesy. My shift always has extra work in the morning to finish the work his crew left undone the night before. They complain to me, but what can I do? I feel like I don't have any control."

She paused, embarrassed about venting to her co-worker. Donovan looked sympathetic and thoughtful.

"Did Alan have anything to say about how you were doing?" he asked.

Marlene explained that while Alan had recruited her for the daytime supervisor's position nearly two years ago, he hadn't really given her much guidance or insight into how to do her job. He seemed satisfied that she was making the numbers—just barely—and always gave her positive performance evaluations.

"Take my last evaluation, for instance," she told Donovan. "Overall, it was fine, but he told me I needed to work on scheduling, communicating with others (I think he meant with Ron, the evening supervisor), and leadership. But he didn't give me any ideas about how to get better at these things. Now he's gone, and I don't have a clue what I'm supposed to do."

Donovan considered Marlene's words as he sipped his soft drink. "Have you considered taking a class at the community college? I hear that the hotel has a tuition reimbursement plan for employees who …"

"I couldn't do that," Marlene cut him off. "I've got three kids at home. Once I leave here, I'm busy with them. I don't have time to take a class somewhere. Besides, it's been years since I've been in a classroom. There's no way …"

"Yeah, you're probably right," said Donovan. "I wouldn't want to sit in a classroom after working all day either. Is there anyone you know who could help you with the things you want to learn? You know, someone who could be a mentor for you?"

"Do you have a mentor?" Marlene asked. When he nodded, she seemed surprised. "I didn't even know we had a mentoring program here," she said.

"We don't," he told her, explaining that he had met his mentor during a seminar he'd attended several months earlier. "I liked the things she was saying during the session, so I introduced myself during a break. We hit it off, and now we get together every few weeks to talk about what's happening at work and how I can move ahead with my career."

Marlene shook her head. "You're a lot more outgoing than I am."

Donovan looked at his watch. "Look, I've got to go in just a minute. The team that's been working on strategies to replace transient sales with more room blocks is holding a wrap-up meeting in the director of sales' office. You know," he mused, "I learned more about teamwork from working on this project than I did from the workshop on team building I went to last year. And I know that the sales director is trying to put together a team to work out the problems that the catering manager is having getting banquet and dining room service staff to work together more effectively. Why don't you volunteer for that?"

Marlene looked intrigued, but said reluctantly, "I don't know. Nobody asked me to participate. It does sound interesting, though. But where will I find the time? Then again, if I don't, they'll probably just come up with some new processes that I'll have to implement without having any say in the matter. Maybe …"

Donovan laughed at her indecision. "I've got to run. Think about that team, though. It could be just the thing you're looking for to get your career moving in the right direction."

Marlene gazed into her now-empty teacup. Was Donovan right? What could being on a team to get the banquet and dining room service staff to work together better teach her about scheduling, communication, and leadership? Well, there was only one way to find out, she thought, and got up to find the sign-up sheet for people interested in joining the team.

## Discussion Questions

1. How could participating in a team project help Marlene with her professional development goals of learning more about scheduling, communication, and leadership?

2. Create a professional development plan for Marlene. Be sure to include development needs to be targeted, action steps, involvement of others, target dates, and resources needed.

3. If you were the human resources manager at this property, what kinds of activities would you put in place to help employees meet their professional development goals?

4. What kind of barriers might Marlene face as she pursues her professional development goals?

---

Case Number: 25014CA

This case was created with the help of Michael Sciarini, Associate Professor, Department of Hospitality and Tourism Management, Grand Valley State University, Allendale, Michigan.

# Index